Advance Praise for
THE IMPOSSIBLE DREAM

"Thomas C. Hunt has succeeded admiral[...] [Am]erican education from its early stages in the [...] [t]o and including school-to-work programs. The [...] [...]p, his book treats such crucial topics as: the c[...] [...] [ni]neteenth century over religion and education; the growth of industrial schools for African Americans in the post Civil War era; and the varieties of educational ideologies that emerged as a response to industrialization and other social forces. Students and readers generally will appreciate Dr. Hunt's clear and balanced expositions of the main currents in the history of American education."

Herbert M. Kliebard,
Professor Emeritus, University of Wisconsin-Madison

"Dr. Hunt's book chronicles how politicians and education entrepreneurs vending panaceas to a gullible public repeatedly victimize an ahistorical nation bent on instant progress. I highly recommend it."

Jim Garrison,
Professor, Virginia Tech

"Educators find themselves in a precarious position. They expect new ideas but they fail to fully understand past answers. The void of historical knowledge is filled quite nicely by this book. His goal is to inform and by informing Hunt provides the knowledge readers need to contextualize their 'innovative' ideas."

Thomas J. Lasley II,
Dean, School of Education and Allied Professions, University of Dayton

The Impossible Dream

History of Schools and Schooling

Alan R. Sadovnik and Susan F. Semel
General Editors

Vol. 4

PETER LANG
New York • Washington, D.C./Baltimore • Bern
Frankfurt am Main • Berlin • Brussels • Vienna • Oxford

Thomas C. Hunt

The Impossible Dream

Education and the Search for Panaceas

PETER LANG
New York • Washington, D.C./Baltimore • Bern
Frankfurt am Main • Berlin • Brussels • Vienna • Oxford

LIBRARY OF CONGRESS CATALOGING-IN-PUBLICATION DATA

Hunt, Thomas C.
The impossible dream : education and the search for panaceas / Thomas C. Hunt.
p. cm. — (History of schools and schooling; vol. 4)
Includes bibliographical references and index.
1. Education—United States—History—19th century.
2. Education—United States—History—20th century. I. Title.
LA217.2 .H86   370'.973'09034   99-045892
ISBN 0-8204-3747-6
ISSN 1089-0678

DIE DEUTSCHE BIBLIOTHEK-CIP-EINHEITSAUFNAHME

Hunt, Thomas C.:
The impossible dream : education and the search for panaceas / Thomas C. Hunt.
—New York; Washington, D.C./Baltimore; Bern; Frankfurt am Main; Berlin;
Brussels; Vienna; Oxford: Lang.
(History of schools and schooling; Vol. 4)
ISBN 0-8204-3747-6

Cover design by Joni Holst

The paper in this book meets the guidelines for permanence and durability
of the Committee on Production Guidelines for Book Longevity
of the Council of Library Resources.

Printed in the United States of America

I affectionately dedicate this book to three people: my father and mother, Caspar F. "Cap" Hunt and Marion Kinney Hunt, and to my wife of some 33 years, Karen Koehler Hunt. I recall many good things about my dad and mother, chiefly their ability to live out what "family values" really mean. They modeled living moral principles, based on their strong Catholic faith, rather than merely seeking transient popularity. They taught us kids to hold fast to moral principle and to do the best we could in whatever we attempted, and they counseled perseverance in all of those endeavors.

My wife has helped me in many ways. As the mother of our two fine daughters, Staci and Eryn, she kept the household together as I taught in the evenings and in many places in Virginia Tech's far-flung land-grant mission and participated in conferences at various sites. She also supported my writing and backed my participation in the numerous community activities that took me out of our home on many an evening. Never did she have any difficulty accepting the risks that came with some of my actions that were based on moral principle; indeed, without flinching or wavering, she affirmed them.

She has encouraged me to continue to write and in particular has urged me to complete this book, despite the many delays that ill health has caused. Possessing much more knowledge about computers than I have, she has also provided much-needed technical assistance to me on several occasions.

I look forward to sharing with her the time that we still have.

Thomas C. Hunt
Dayton, Ohio

Contents

List of Illustrations

Foreword

I arrived on the campus of Virginia Tech in the summer of 1971 to participate in the creation of a new College of Education at that institution. Fresh from the midwestern plains where I had served with some recognition as superintendent of schools in a progressive school district, I was prepared to bring a wide range of "innovative" concepts tested and judged successful in the K-12 environment to this new setting. Surely our success in implementing a continuous progress learning system that employed differentiated staffing in open-space learning environments and used modular-flexible scheduling and an extended school year would not only be applicable but widely accepted by my new colleagues in the Academy. Armed with copies of the 10,000 learning packages we had developed—all with clearly stated learning objectives (appropriately categorized according to Bloom's taxonomy), pre- and post-tests, alternative learning activities supported by the most up-to-date technology (tape recorders, 8mm videocassettes, language laboratories, and reel-to-reel video tape players), we seemed well positioned to implement a model program in competency-based teacher education. Or so I thought.

Within a short period of time, no more than a semester, two insights occurred. The first was that the time required for change in the higher education environment was much longer than I had been used to in the K-12 public school environment; the second, which was related to the first, was that the decision-making process in higher education was dramatically different from what I had been accustomed to. Though I had viewed myself as a "democratic" leader in my earlier life, I was hardly prepared for the collaboration and shared decision-making expected in the university setting—much less the challenges of colleagues (though I didn't think of them as colleagues in those early days) to my proposals and ideas.

It was a young professor, Tom Hunt, and his band of freshly minted assistant professors in the Curriculum and Instruction Division that I headed, who taught me how a university worked and how colleagues behaved. It was Professor Hunt, too, who supplemented my inadequate knowledge of and appreciation for the historical roots undergirding much of what I believed to be "new and innovative." Early on, Tom and I became close friends. We were both midwesterners, we were both experienced building principals, and we were both passionate in our commitment to improving schools. During those early years we spent many hours reflecting on the recycled ideas, programs, and initiatives held up as the "silver bullets" that would somehow magically transform schools into institutions that could meet all of the disparate expectations of the public. It was early in our conversations that our dialogue began to focus on the litany of failed efforts to transform schools—the panaceas that weren't. Now, some thirty years after those initial conversations, this work has emerged.

Professor Hunt has selected an interesting array of panaceas for presentation. Included are chapters that describe initiatives reflecting the dynamic tension with regard to the purpose of public education in this country. Horace Mann, Thomas Jefferson, George Counts, Admiral Rickover, Charles Silberman, and David Kearns are among those whose interests have been reflected in the varied roles proposed for our nation's schools. Beginning with the chapter on "The Common School Movement" and concluding with a trio focusing on school-to-work, Hunt provides a reasonable and reasoned selection of panaceas reflecting those diverse panaceas. Other chapters explore a range of administrative practices intended to promote school quality, among them: use of time (school calendar), organizational structure (open education, the junior high school), and arrangements to promote efficiency (performance contracting, and behavioral objectives). All are well written and balanced with respect to the views of advocates and detractors.

The lessons to be taken from these selected portraits of education in America are many and varied. Among those most obvious are: 1) building consensus about the mission, purposes and goals of the nation's schools remains an elusive challenge; 2) without a clearly defined and agreed-upon purpose, our nation's educational institutions will be subject to an unachievable range of demands and unreasonable expectations; 3) blurred goals and changing priorities will stimulate an endless supply of recommended practices to achieve that which has not been defined or agreed upon—creating a continuing menu of panaceas. Hunt's final lesson is that in spite of the incredible challenges facing the American schools and the complex political and social systems within which those schools operate, they have and will continue to serve us well.

Professor Hunt, in the tradition of his mentors, Professors Kliebard and Krug, has produced a work that is well researched, easy to read, and a valuable contribution to those of us who search for Camelot. I am hopeful that he will begin a second volume soon. With block scheduling, continuous improvement, high stakes testing, value-added leadership, and "new" programs, concepts and initiatives emerging daily, there will be no shortage of panaceas to be explored.

Wayne M. Worner
Blacksburg, Virginia

Preface

It was while I was a doctoral student at the University of Wisconsin over thirty years ago that I first noted the oft-recurring presence of panaceas in the annals of American education. There, under the most able tutelage of Herbert Kliebard and the late Edward Krug, I became curious about the reasons for this phenomenon. I recall reading with interest the opening lines of the "Preface" to the first edition of Henry Perkinson's excellent book, *The Imperfect Panacea: American Faith in Education 1865–1990:*

> One day while she was typing the manuscript for this book, my secretary looked up and asked me, "If the schools can't solve these problems, then who can?" This question rests on what I consider to be two basic assumptions of most Americans: first, that all social problems are solvable; second, that the schools are the panacea for all social problems.[1]

In the early 1970s, as a new assistant professor in the College of Education at Virginia Tech, I observed with interest the positions of several of my colleagues that would have mandated one, and only one, way of doing certain things. For instance, several believed that the faculty should be required to use behavioral objectives in their instruction. A few others, equally well meaning, wanted to mandate the five-chapters format advocated by "leading" schools of education and to forbid historical and other "divergent" kinds of dissertations. Still others tried to dogmatize the use of the APA citation style. When I asked one of them why, his paraphrased response was that then if someone looked at our dissertations on the shelf they would all be uniform! Form, obviously, was more important than substance. Thankfully, none of these attempts prevailed, and we went about our business as a professional school should.

It was David Tyack's outstanding book, *The One Best System: A History of American Urban Education,* that next whetted my inquisitiveness. Tyack wrote in his "Prologue" that in his judgment, "The search for the one best system has

ill-served the pluralistic character of American society."[2] He provided several instances in this justly-famed work that illustrate the propensity of educators to look
for the "one and only way." For example, he quotes Portland, Oregon's first superintendent, Samuel King, as to why a uniform curriculum was necessary:

> System, order, dispatch and promptness have characterized the examinations and exerted
> a helpful influence over the pupils by stimulating them to be thoroughly prepared to meet
> their appointments and engagements. Next to a New England climate, these examina-
> tions necessitate industry, foster promptness, and encourage pupils to do the right thing
> at the right time.[3]

Classrooms were not exempt from this kind of thinking. Joseph Rice, who visited
hundreds of urban classrooms in the 1890s related what it was like in one of these
schools: "During recitation periods, when students were to demonstrate that they
had memorized the text," children were expected to "stand on the line, perfectly
motionless, their bodies erect, their knees and feet together, the tips of their shoes
touching the edge of a board in the floor."[4] "How can you learn anything," one
woman asked, "with your knees and toes out of order?"[5]

One last illustration will have to suffice. This one is taken from my experience
in my early days at Tech. A young undergraduate, just returned from observing a
nearby school that had adopted modular scheduling, confidently announced to
his classmates and to me that "Modular scheduling will solve all of the schools'
problems." Within a few years, "gain time" became widely known as "lost time,"
and modular scheduling disappeared from the educational scene.

Armed, if that is the correct verb to use, with incidents and books and journal
articles such as the above, one afternoon I developed a list of educational panaceas, divided them up into institutions, movements, curricular models, and pedagogical techniques, and resolved to one day write a book on the subject.

Over the years my thinking expanded as I noted the repetitive tendency to
seek the panacea in American schooling. Taking the shape of "reforms," these endeavors have dotted the educational landscape since the time of Horace Mann's
common school reform in the 1830s. Indeed, it was Mann himself who proclaimed that the common school was the "greatest invention ever made by man."[6]

These reforms, well intentioned and worthwhile in themselves, have been
plagued by several factors. Among these are the "bandwagon" tendency, so prevalent in American schooling; the attraction presented by the "novel," which often
turns out to be a "fad"; and the compulsion that Americans have to get everything
done in a hurry (at the latest by tomorrow morning). The crusading behavior of
the reformers is another contributing factor. They feel driven to depict present
practices as worthless, inane, and ineffective (and I am using charitable words for
their accusations); they seem to believe that their salvific action alone will rescue

the world of education from the forces of darkness, superstition, selfishness, and traditionalism. So, it would seem, is the innovators' tendency to reduce complex interactions to a one-shot, sure-fire remedy, constituting reductionism at its worst.

Several underlying causes for these phenomena seem to exist. Among these are John Goodlad's observations that the question of formulating goals for American schooling is a "conceptual swamp" and that the "schools suffer from a lack of a clearly articulated mandate and so are peculiarly susceptible to fads and fashions."[7] Another is the ahistorical nature of our nation. Consequently, as Seymour Sarason says in his *The Case for Change,* reforms are doomed to failure because we underestimate the complexity of what we are up against and are unable or unwilling to use the cumulative experience we have acquired over the years.[8] David Tyack and Larry Cuban, in their award-winning work, *Tinkering Toward Utopia,* state bluntly, "To judge from the ahistorical character of most current policy talk about reform, innovators may consider amnesia a virtue."[9] And when they do involve history, they "often portray the past in politicized, stylized ways as a golden age to be restored or a dismal legacy to be repudiated." They advise their readers that:

> Anyone who would improve schooling is a captive of history in two ways. All people and institutions are the product of history (defined as past events). And whether they are aware of it or not, all people use history (defined as an interpretation of past events) when they make choices about the present and future.[10]

In their "Epilogue" to this excellent book, Tyack and Cuban point to the dangers of ignoring history in attempts to reform schooling:

> The concepts of progress and decline that have dominated discourse about educational reform distort the actual development of the educational enterprise over time. The ahistorical nature of most current reform arguments results in both a magnification of present defects in relation to the past and an understatement of the difficulty of changing the system.[11]

Overlooking history has its consequences in other fields as well. Consider just one example from recent American policy decisions. Robert S. McNamara, Secretary of Defense during the Vietnam conflict, admitted a few years ago that it was the ignorance of Vietnam's history and culture that led to the tragic policy decisions of the Johnson administration relative to Vietnam.[12]

Perhaps it is natural for people involved in an activity such as schooling to attribute more power to that institution than it actually has. Schools, as Perkinson cautioned years ago, are limited institutions. In an era where other institutions seem to have lost some of their clout, perhaps it is inevitable that the social institution of schooling be given responsibilities for outcomes larger than their "domain extends."[13] We have no right, Robert Evans tells us, to expect schools to "solve societal problems they didn't create and can't control." Accepting this limitation does not "trivialize work of dedicated teachers or let bad ones off the hook. It doesn't mean that school doesn't matter; school matters hugely."[14] But school "reformers of all stripes must begin to reconcile the intensity of their commitments with the modesty of the school's clout. . . . Surely, we must challenge teachers and administrators to do their utmost, but not to work miracles. And not by themselves."[15] Hayes Mizell warns us that too often "policyholders, whether state legislators, state boards of education, or local school boards" assume that school personnel have a much greater capacity to implement reforms than is actually the case.[16]

Change, innovation, and especially reform have long had a magnet-like attraction in education. Thomas Sergiovanni reminds us that few "topics are of greater interest to policymakers, to policy scientists, and to educational consultants than is educational change," who believe that finding the "right change strategy promises victory in the national and even the international brain race."[17] He calls attention to the standards issue as an illustration:

> Increasingly, schools are considered successful if they adopt state-mandated standards, invent clever strategies for aligning the curriculum with these standards, figure out how to teach this curriculum, and get good scores on state-provided standards assessments. The better schools are at implementing this chain of events, the more successful they are thought to be at improving.[18]

When it comes to educational reform, he maintains, "Instead of worrying about substantive issues, policy scientists interested in change find themselves absorbed in struggling to find out the best methods to get teachers and schools to change," and as a consequence, place "process over substance."[19]

The pace has accelerated since the publication of *A Nation at Risk* in the mid 1980s, it would appear. Denise Gelberg argues that in the last fifteen or so years reform has been concerned to "produce graduates ready to be employed by our nation's business and factories." Efforts to accomplish this have been "modeled on corporate efforts to root out waste and improve performance in industry."[20] Reform proposals should concentrate on how well they will allow each child to be educated, she wrote, "not only for the world of work, but also for the arts, serious inquiry, exploration of the world about us, and democratic living with other complicated human beings."[21]

In a brief piece that appeared in *Education Week* in the summer of 1999, noted historian David Tyack called for more of what he termed "Educational Conservationists." He pointed out the vast disparity in meaning between a "conservationist" in society and one in education. His words bear repeating:

The word "conservationist" has an honorable ring when citizens struggle to preserve wild nature or fine old buildings. When people work to preserve what is good in education, however, they are often dismissed as traditionalists or stand-patters. When real estate developers propose paving over wetlands, environmental activists protest. But when educational innovators want to transform educational practice few ask what might be lost in the process. Government requires environmental-impact statements for construction projects, but not student- and teacher- impact reports for educational reforms. Who will be there to defend endangered species of good schools, or good educational programs, from the relentless, if zig-zag, march of educational progress?[22]

He then addressed the workings of "progress":

Believers in progress through educational reform often want to reinvent schooling. . . . Inspired by the progress syndrome, innovators often exaggerate defects to motivate by alarm, try to wipe the educational slate clean, and then propose a short time frame for their favorite projects, hoping to see results before the next election or job opportunity or grant proposal.[23]

Human beings, not devices that guarantee progress, Tyack observed, are what make education both memorable and effective. He tells the story of the many people with whom he has spoken with about their schooling. He has asked: "What was their most positive experience in school?"

They may have forgotten whatever fad was sweeping education or the teenage culture, but they remembered key relationships, especially with teachers. They spoke, often with great warmth, about teachers who challenged them to use their minds to the full, who kindled enthusiasm for a subject, who honed their skills on the playing field with relentless goodwill, who were there to support them in times of stress or sadness, and who knew and cared for them as individuals.[24]

Teachers were of like mind. Nine out of ten said that "helping students to learn and grow as social beings" constituted their "greatest satisfactions." Tyack did not treat the task lightly:

The conservationist cannot look only backward, for preservation involves planning for the future as well. The work of the educational conservationist, like the defender of wild animals, is a challenging one. It takes resources and smarts and political savvy to preserve Mongolian Gazelles or good schools.[25]

Lynn Burlbaw reports that "Ten years ago Robert Slavin wrote: 'Educational innovation is famous for its cycle of early enthusiasm, widespread dissemination, subsequent disappointment, and eventual decline—the classic swing of the curriculum.'"[26] One reason for educators' "lack of historical understanding is that the history of ideas and programs seldom appears in the documents read by decision makers." She based that conclusion on a careful study of two journals that are mainstays for educators: *Educational Leadership* and *Phi Delta Kappan,* which have a combined membership of over 250,000.[27] Addressing the issue of "pendulum swings" in curriculum, renowned curriculum historian Herbert Kliebard offered four hypotheses that in his view could account for the "occurrence of cyclical change in curriculum affairs as it is commonly observed."[28] The first dealt with the "boundless expansion of the scope of the curriculum in conjunction with direct and immediate utility as the supreme criterion of success." Thus, there were no boundaries for what could be included, and so "any contender for admission is legitimate." Second, he held that "because the rhetoric of reform" is usually "more powerful" than that of its opposition, a "reform is inaugurated without the accompanying structural changes in the system that are needed to make it succeed." When this happens, the "life span of the reform is almost bound to be short."[29] The changes are really a "resurfacing of a temporarily submerged position," rather than a new ideology replacing another, and they are brought about by "favorable social and political conditions." Finally, "rapid changes in curriculum fashion" are connected with the "rise of a professional class of school administrators whose professional status and perhaps even their survival depend simply on being at least up-to-date as the school system down the road." Change, then, is itself "perceived as desirable rather than change in a particular direction, and therefore, change tends to be more for the purposes of public display than the result of firmly held pedagogical beliefs."[30]

This book is not an attempt to present a comprehensive history of American schooling. Rather, it presents a number of innovations, the expectations advanced for each, the reasons for which they were advanced, what conflicts arose over the proposed changes, and what resulted from the implementation of the innovation.

The importance of *time* and *place* are emphasized to help in the understanding of the whys and wherefores of the various claims. Thus, the "magic elixirs" are considered in their appropriate context.

Before addressing each of the chapters in order, I give one last sample in this "Preface." A scant few years ago, policymakers in education were swamped by claims made on behalf of Total Quality Management (TQM), the creation of W. E. Deming. Hailing from the corporate world, the fourteen points of TQM were presented on a broad scale to educators as a surefire way to reform schooling. (One wonders what the costs were in terms of professional time alone devoted to meetings held at participating institutions.) A few years later, TQM has faded into oblivion, replaced by Continuous Process Improvement (CPI). And the band plays on. . . .

The topics addressed in the various chapters range in terms of importance and benefit. For instance, millions of youngsters and the nation itself have benefited from the idea of Horace Mann of a common school open to all, rich or poor, boy or girl, with a common curriculum, which is the subject of Chapter One. On the other hand, "The Hampton Model," treated in Chapter Four, has no such kind of pedigree. The result of an unholy alliance between northern industrialist and southern aristocrat, the "Hampton Model," as James Anderson has so clearly documented in his *The Education of Blacks in the South, 1865–1930,* existed to maintain a social class structure that would keep the freedmen in a state of dependency and on the lower rung of southern society.[31]

The chapters are arranged chronologically. As stated above, they vary in terms of importance, but they were chosen to give the reader a "flavor" of the various kinds of panaceas that have been presented in the annals of American schooling.

Chapter One deals with "The Common School Movement." Its purposes were, in the view of Mann and his supporters, to eradicate ignorance, crime and poverty, and to establish a nonsectarian Christian blessedness in the nation. Chapter Two treats the role of the Bible in the schools, a role advanced by its Protestant advocates. Considered the heart of education, the Bible (King James version) and its devotional reading should occupy a central place in the school. If it did, all would be well because the nation would remain a Christian commonwealth, committed to the Protestant version of Christianity.

Chapter Three tells of a change that took place in American society and its schools in the wake of the Civil War. The "American" public school was to play a fundamental role in the development of a new American character, one still related to Protestant Christianity, but in certain parts of the nation perhaps as akin to Deism as to traditional Christian religion.

"The Hampton Model" is the subject of Chapter Four. It was developed by an alliance of northern industrialists and southern aristocrats as the "solution" to the kind of schooling "appropriate" for southern African Americans to assume their subordinate position to whites in southern society. Headed at first by Samuel Chapman Armstrong, Hampton Institute was connected with Booker T. Washington, who began his educational career in the night school there. Chapter Five is the first of three chapters grouped together under the title of "The Era of Social Efficiency." Social efficiency was the response of the schools to the effects of immigration, urbanization, industrialization, and the consequent growth of American cities and their manufacturing industries at the turn of the twentieth century. The task of the schools was made difficult by the arrival of the immigrants, who were described by that eminent stalwart of public education, Ellwood P. Cubberley, as:

> Largely illiterate, docile, lacking in initiative and almost wholly without the Anglo-Saxon conceptions of righteousness, liberty, law, order, public decency, and government, . . . their coming has served to dilute tremendously our national stock and to weaken and corrupt our political life.[32]

The resulting task of the school to "Americanize" these "undesirables" was clear. It was to be accomplished with the aid of prominent businessmen and the "scientific" aid of testing with as little waste as possible.

The founding and growth of "vocational education" comprises Chapter Six. Abandoning the "common school, common curriculum" ideas of Horace Mann et al., American education now emphasized curriculum differentiation, basing a student's educational program on the school's prediction of his or her future economic station in life. It was accompanied by an increased dependency on testing and the advent of vocational guidance.

The last chapter of the trilogy on Social Efficiency is "Secondary Education." It features two sections: the first, the junior high school, and second, the comprehensive high school. The junior high school, alleged by its backers to be "humanistic," advocated early curriculum differentiation (by the seventh grade) and fit neatly into the social efficiency package. It represented the "newest and fondest hope for the future" in the early twentieth century.[33] One definition of this new institution, which was to truly reform American education, was:

> The Junior High School is the living presence of a visioned idea which had been so dearly cherished that it had been relegated to the rare rendezvous with school folk only in the quiet hour of "Best Moments."[34]

Who could argue with an institution that was so defined? The comprehensive high school was established as a peculiarly "American" institution, to provide secondary education within the context of American democracy. Brought into being because of the alleged declining influence of home and church, the institution was to provide unity in an increasingly heterogeneous population. It has gone down in history as the document of the "Seven Cardinal Principles," which are not principles but aims. All subjects were to be "practical," the criterion of importance.[35] It is also remembered for the emphasis it placed on assemblies, student activities, and extra-curricular affairs.

The functional curriculum of "Life Adjustment and Its Critics" occupies Chapter Eight. The life adjustment movement and the controversies it generated are further illustrations of the tensions that surround American secondary education. Downplaying the academic side of high school, this movement enjoyed a brief period of ascendancy, was challenged first by the academicians as "anti–intellectual," and then was ingloriously routed by reactions to the Soviet Union's launching of Sputnik in the fall of 1957.

What could be more worthwhile than a "War" to end poverty, especially in the most affluent nation on earth? Chapter Nine deals with that "War," a most laudable activity but one that the schools, which were called on to play the leading role in eradicating the ravages of that debilitating condition, were ill-equipped to fight and incapable by their very nature of winning.

Hard upon the heels of the "War" came open education. Due in large part to the "romantic critics" of education, led by Paul Goodman, the open movement called for a "naturalistic" education, one less formal and certainly more humane. It ascended the heights rapidly in an age of "crises," as Charles Silberman put it,[36] peaked, and then fell to the onslaught of accountability.

Titled "The Age of Accountability," Chapter Eleven tells the story of the shift of responsibility for results in schooling from the student to the schools and their personnel. Spearheaded by Leon Lessinger, and framed in business terminology, accountability was yet one more evidence of the growing influence of corporate America on the schools.

"Performance Contracting," the subject of Chapter Twelve, is one manifestation of how accountability was applied in education. Patterned on business practices, performance contracting called for the schools to enter into contracts with private firms that would guarantee specific learning results based on performance tests by students, for a pre-set cost. It had a meteoric rise and an equally swift descent.

Under the mantle of Robert Mager first, and then of "Dr. . . . Objectives,"[37] James W. Popham, behavioral objectives "ruled the roost" in educational instruction in the 1970s. Relying on the tenets of Skinnerian behaviorism, educational behaviorists called for a prior statement of changes in learner behavior that were to occur as a result of instruction, changes that could be precisely measured.

If anyone in educational circles thought that business interests and vocational concerns were to have a long hiatus from the educational scene in the United States, he or she was to have a rude awakening. Under the aegis of "Career Education," these interests made a comeback of monstrous proportions in the 1970s. Employing slogans such as "All Students—All Occupations—All Subjects" career education enjoyed as rapid a rise to popularity as can be found in the history of American schooling. It is the subject of Chapter Fourteen.

The school calendar is the focal point of Chapter Fifteen. "Year-Round Education," or the "Extended School Year," terms by which it was known, had a long, if unknown, history in the annals of American schooling. Advanced both on pedagogical and economic grounds in the 1970s, it underwent a decline, but still exists in a number of communities in the nation today.

Chapters Sixteen through Eighteen comprise the second set of three chapters in this book. This set is devoted to the extant educational movement known as "school-to-work." It is a powerful movement, fueled by economic and social interests, on the international, national, state, and local levels, the outcome of which is undecided as of this writing. (It should be noted that another important movement – the standards movement – which merits the status of a panacea, existed and still exists parallel to the "school-to-work" movement, but was not considered in this book.)

Chapter Sixteen deals with the social and economic forces following *A Nation at Risk* which led to the passage of the School-to-Work law in May of 1994 and its educational consequences. Chapter Seventeen examines the many claims made on behalf of the law in the first few years after its enactment. Its feverish supporters, which included governmental agencies, vocational educators, and segments of the private sector, saw school-to-work programs as cure-alls that would control the curriculum, its purposes, and its goals. The chapter also looks at the rationale put forth by those who were opposed to school-to-work programs, sometimes with equal emotion to its advocates.

Finally, the concluding chapter of this book, Eighteen, assesses the progress of school-to work curricula as the curtain came down on the twentieth century. The conflict which the Law had generated was at least as intense between 1997 and 1999 as it was between 1995 and 1997. One is left to wonder if education's purpose in the United States should be to prepare productive workers for the successful operation of American business on the international, national, state, and local levels, with the overriding goal of maintaining world leadership.

These last three chapters raise vital questions about the status of American education. First, if the goals of schools really include developing critical thinkers, would not these critical thinkers evaluate the conditions of work as well as preparation for a job in a modern high-tech company? As Ellen Goodman pointed out, in 1998 the "CEOs at major companies earned 419 times the pay of the average blue-collar worker."[38] Would not such disparity lead critical thinkers to ask Why? Economic productivity, for the nation, the individual, and the business firm, certainly merits the standing of an important goal of education. But at the expense of all others? How about understanding the four freedoms guaranteed in the First Amendment? Or the entire Bill of Rights itself? Or the "equal protection" clause of the Fourteenth Amendment? Or the Declaration of Independence? Are these not among the goals of the first order in a democracy? Should they be submerged by the tide of economic productivity in education? Should not students delve into the history of the institution of slavery to learn how it became entrenched in a "Christian" society and why it held sway in the United States for all too long? Should they not be made aware of people like Sojourner Truth and her heroic efforts in the Underground Railroad? How about contemplating the relative rights of the citizen and her or his government? Perhaps consider the essay on "Civil Disobedience" by Henry David Thoreau (Martin Luther King did), written in the mid-nineteenth century. How about investigating the reasons why so many people are homeless in the most affluent nation in the history of the world? Is their plight due entirely to their indolence, as some would have us believe, or might the very economic system of which students are urged to become a part be at least a partial

contributor to their extreme poverty? Why did McCarthyism all but paralyze the
nation in the mid-twentieth century? How much control or influence should the
government have over basic social matters? Is government control always benign?
Should we ask the Native Americans? How about the Cherokees and the Trail of
Tears? Was Manifest Destiny really manifest? By whose order? Should we "Remember the Maine" the way our government, following the lead of the Hearst
chain, would have us do? Why was the struggle of the suffragettes so difficult? If
government held a monopoly, even de facto, in basic social matters such as education, might it not control the flow of information its youthful citizens received?
What consequences could result? What about the aesthetic realm? Where do appreciation of art and music and literature fit in? Only when they contribute to students being prepared for the "world of work"? These, and other legitimate educational questions receive scant, if any mention in the platform of school-to-work
zealots. And these questions comprise but a minuscule part of the potential number of queries that should be asked in education, a list that is almost endless.

Let's look at that overworked word, "relevance," and the misused phrase, the
"real world." So much of today's rhetoric defines relevance in terms of preparation
for work, able to be "measured" as of practical, immediate value. Is not truly powerful critical writing creative, in the sense of creating alternative possibilities? Tell-
ing the history that does not get told is part of freedom in education. It is where
aesthetics and ethics meet. A person cannot "know" his or her moral imperative,
cannot know what ought to be, unless he or she sees alternative possibilities.
Without possibilities, there is no real choice. Reducing all choice to market
choice, hence to market values, creates false choices, hence the oppression of the
mind. The "real" world is a world of infinite possibilities, some good, some
mixed, some downright evil. The actual world is simply one of an infinite number
of possible worlds. To equate the actual world with the real world is to make a serious mistake. When some people say, "You need to learn about the 'real world,'"
there is a good chance they are oppressing moral and aesthetic imagination.[39]

Schools are important agencies in the United States; they have many worthwhile and laudable goals. They are, however, neither omnipotent nor omniscient.
The search for the panacea is no more beneficial than the search for the "one best
system." There is no cure-all, no absolute remedy that schools can use to solve all
of the nation's ills or to bring, by themselves, unlimited and unbounded prosperity and virtue to the land. It is time to recognize those realities. In that vein, perhaps the best way to conclude this "Preface" is with the words of Justice Robert
Jackson of the United States Supreme Court in the *Barnette* flag-salute case in
West Virginia in 1943:

Struggles to coerce uniformity of sentiment in support of some end thought essential to
their time and country have been waged by many good as well as evil men. Nationalism is

a relatively recent phenomenon but at other times and places the ends have been racial or territorial security, support of a dynasty or regime, and particular plans for saving souls. As first and moderate methods to attain unity have failed, those bent on its accomplishment must resort to an ever-increasing severity. As governmental pressure toward unity becomes greater, so strife becomes more bitter as to whose unity it shall be. Probably no deeper division of our people could proceed from any provocation than from finding it necessary to choose what doctrine and whose program public education officials shall compel youth to unite in advancing.[40]

Notes

1. Henry J. Perkinson, " Preface to the First Edition," *The Imperfect Panacea: American Faith in Education 1865–1990.* Third Edition. New York: McGraw-Hill, 1991.
2. David B. Tyack, *The One Best System: A History of American Urban Education.* Cambridge, MA: Harvard University Press, 1974, p. 11.
3. Quoted in ibid., p. 47.
4. Quoted in ibid., p. 55.
5. Quoted in ibid., pp. 55–56.
6. Jonathan A. Messerli, *Horace Mann: A Biography.* New York: Alfred A. Knopf, 1972, p. xii.
7. John Goodlad, *A Place Called School: Prospectus for the Future.* New York: McGraw-Hill, 1984, p. 48.
8. Seymour B. Sarason, *The Case for Change: Rethinking the Preparation of Educators.* San Francisco: Jossey-Bass, 1993, p. 43.
9. David Tyack and Larry Cuban, *Tinkering Toward Utopia: A Century of Public School Reform.* Cambridge, MA: Harvard University Press, 1995, p. 6.
10. Ibid.
11. Ibid., p. 134.
12. "Ex-defense chief: 'We were wrong' about Vietnam," *Roanoke Times and World News,* April 9, 1995, pp. A1-A2.
13. James J. Gallagher, "Education, Alone, Is a Weak Treatment," *Education Week,* 17, 42, July 8, 1998, p. 60.
14. Robert Evans, "The Great Accountability Fallacy," *Education Week,* 18, 21, February 3, 1999, p. 35.
15. Ibid.
16. Hayes Mizell, "Educators: Reform Thyselves," *Education Week,* 19, 30, April 5, 2000, p. 56.
17. Thomas J. Sergiovanni, "Changing Educational Change," *Education Week,* 19, 23, February 16, 2000, p. 27.
18. Ibid.
19. Ibid., pp. 27, 31.
20. Denise Gelberg, "The 'Business' of Reforming American Schools," *Education Week,* 18, 4, September 30, 1998, p. 30.
21. Ibid., p. 33.
22. David B. Tyack, "Needed: More Educational Conservationists," *Education Week,* 18, 41, June 23, 1999, p. 68.
23. Ibid.
24. Ibid.
25. Ibid.

26. Lynn M. Burlbaw, "Journal-Induced Historical Myopia," *Journal of Curriculum and Supervision* 15, 3 (Spring 2000): 267.

27. Ibid., p. 268.

28. Herbert M. Kliebard, "Fads, Fashions, and Rituals: The Instability of Curriculum Change," in Laurel N. Tanner, ed., *Critical Issues in Curriculum: 87th Yearbook of the National Society for the Study of Education*. Chicago: National Society for the Study of Education, 1988, p. 16.

29. Ibid.

30. Ibid., pp. 16–17.

31. James D. Anderson, *The Education of Blacks in the South, 1865–1930*. Chapel Hill: The University of North Carolina Press, 1988, especially pp. 33–78.

32. Ellwood P. Cubberley, *Public Education in the United States*. Boston: Houghton Mifflin Company, 1919, p. 338.

33. Edward A. Krug, *The Shaping of the American High School 1880–1920*. Madison: The University of Wisconsin Press, 1964, p. 327.

34. S. O. Rorem, quoted in Krug, ibid., p. 335.

35. National Education Association, *Cardinal Principles of Secondary Education*. Washington, DC: Government Printing Office, 1918, p. 9.

36. Charles E. Silberman, *Crisis in the Classroom: The Remaking of American Education*. New York: Random House, 1970, p.vii.

37. James W. Popham, *Educational Evaluation*. Second Edition. Englewood Cliffs, NJ: Prentice-Hall, 1988, p. 63.

38. Ellen Goodman, "Society Starts to Rethink CEO Pay," *Dayton Daily News,* April 19, 1999, p. 7A.

39. Jim Garrison, personal communication, December 27, 2000.

40. *West Virginia State Board of Education v. Barnette*. 319 U.S. at 640–641 (1943).

Acknowledgments

There are many people who deserve to be acknowledged who directly and indirectly influenced the course of events that led to the production of this book. Let me begin with identifying some former colleagues in the College of Education at Virginia Tech.

First and foremost, I am indebted to Wayne Worner, a very good friend, who not only wrote the "Foreword" to the book, but whose interest in and support of my career was and is appreciated. Dr. Worner is the epitome of what is good about public education, and there is much. Next is Jim Garrison, another good friend and former colleague at Tech, who helped shape the direction of the book in the many conversations we had "going up and down the road" to teach at Telestar in Falls Church. Many more could be named, most notably David Alexander, Charles Atwell, John Burton, Don Creamer, Margaret Eisenhart, Dan Fleming, Patricia Kelly, Rosary Lalik, Mike Moore, Jerry Niles, David Parks, Bob Richards, Judith Shrum, Bob Small, and Ken Underwood. I appreciate all of them immensely.

I want to thank those of my former colleagues at Tech who met with me in 1995–1996 to provide leads on what works should be consulted in their curricular areas. Though the book ultimately did not follow that plan, their generosity is acknowledged. They, and many others in the College of Education (and some in the University at large and others in the Blacksburg community), who are too numerous to name in a section like this, contributed in a major way to an overall rewarding quarter century, either at Blacksburg or one of its off-campus sites. I am indebted to them.

In the fall of 1996, I returned to Catholic education. I would be remiss if I did not identify a number of people who have contributed in a major way to this book or to my transition. First, there is Dean Tom Lasley, a scholar himself, who has been most supportive of my efforts in several areas. This book would not be published at this time—perhaps never—without the support he provided. His Associate Dean, Dan Raisch, has seen to it that the guarantees given by Dean Lasley were carried out. Graduate assistants Chad Raisch, Brian Luke, and Jose Cortez helped identify and gather potential material. Tina Strasburger, Julie Slife, and Anita Middleton provided excellent clerical support. Dianne Hoops and her coworkers in the Roesch Library furnished willing and helpful assistance. Josh Schrank contributed technical expertise.

There are many others, both at Dayton and in the Catholic education community at large, who made this return both pleasant and fulfilling. Dean Emeritus Ellis Joseph merits special mention in this group, as does Bill Losito. I thank all of them.

I want to express my gratitude to Peter Lang for publishing this book. In particular, I appreciate the cooperation of Managing Director Christopher Myers and Series Editor Alan Sadovnik. The book will be six years from contract to seeing the light of day. Chris and Alan have understood the health problems the writer has encountered in this period; their patience and support have been exemplary!

Finally, let me acknowledge once again "Dempsey" Worner for his "Foreword"; and Herb Kliebard, Jim Garrison, and Tom Lasley for consenting to write blurbs for the cover. I regard their contributions most highly.

CHAPTER ONE

The Common School Movement

Primary schooling in the early nineteenth century United States, including Massachusetts, took many forms. There were pauper schools for the poor, private schools for the affluent, schools run by churches, and district schools. In some instances, village schools reflected the influence of the particular church to which the majority of villagers belonged. In these cases, the distinction between public and private to which we are so accustomed today did not exist.

Well-known American patriots, men such as George Washington, Thomas Jefferson, and Benjamin Rush, maintained that Americans should be educated in America, not on the European continent. In the first quarter of the nineteenth century, there was a call for a kind of primary education that would fit the republic. In 1820, for instance, Daniel Webster spoke of the expected benefits of the "Free Schools" that had taken root in New England:

> For the purpose of public instruction, we hold every man subject to taxation in proportion to his property. . . . We regard it as a wise and liberal system of police, by which property, and life, and the peace of society are secured. We seek to prevent in some measure the extension of the penal code, by inspiring a salutary and conservative principle of virtue and of knowledge at an early age. We strive to excite a feeling of respectability, and a sense of character. . . . By general instruction, we seek, as far as possible, to purify the whole moral atmosphere. . . . We hope for a security beyond the law and above the law. . . . We hope to continue and prolong the time . . . there may be undisturbed sleep within unbarred doors. And knowing that our government rests directly on the public will . . . we confidently trust, and our expectation of the duration of our system of government rests on that trust, that, by the diffusion of general knowledge and good and virtuous sentiments, the political fabric may be secure, as well against open violence and overthrow, as against the slow, but sure, undermining of licentiousness.[1]

Horace Mann

Horace Mann, known as the "Father of the Common School," accepted the invitation of Governor Dwight of Massachusetts and assumed the position of Secretary of the State Board of Education, taking office in 1837. Mann, a Whig, gave up a promising career in politics to assume this post. Mann's work was described by Gabriel Compayre, a leading figure of the radical educational program of the Third Republic in France, as follows:

> Mann was well aware that his real mission was first of all to conquer souls, to stir up good will, to create a movement of opinion . . . a militant, a tribune, a missionary who went from city to city, from village to village, peddling his ideas and his faith, a Peter the Hermit preaching a crusade against ignorance.[2]

While Mann was undoubtedly the leader of the common school crusade, others, such as Henry Barnard, Horace Bushnell, and James G. Carter, were also prominent advocates of this form of schooling, and of its primacy, indeed indispensability, among institutions in providing unbounded benefits to American society.

The Nature of the Common School

The existence of the common school, Mann averred, was ordained by Providence, which proved the "*absolute right* of every human being . . . to an education; and which, of course proves the correlative duty of every government to see that the means of that education are provided for all," a right that was "incapable of being abrogated by any ordinance of man."[3] This right of the child to an education that "will enable him to perform all domestic, social, civic and moral duties," was founded on the natural law as was his or her right to breathe.[4]

The Need for the Common School

Writing in his *First Annual Report,* Mann, basing his remarks on a recent visit to England, claimed that the "one remedy and one preventive" to sectarian strife was the "elevation of the common schools."[5] The need for the common school, according to Horace Bushnell, was especially crucial in Massachusetts, due to the immigrants who had entered the state. If there were no common schools run by the state for these children to attend, then the children of these immigrants "will be shut up in schools that do not teach them what, as Americans, they most of all need to know. . . . They will be instructed into the foreign prejudices and superstitions of their fathers, and the state, which purposes to be clear of all sectarian affinities in religion, will pay the bills!"[6] It was critical, the Rev. W. S. Dutton intoned, that "their children should be neither uneducated, nor educated by themselves . . . that they be *educated together* . . . not as Roman Catholics or Protestants . . . but as Americans, as made of one blood and citizens of the same free country . . . educated to be one harmonious people."[7]

Universal education had, in the view of Mann, the power to redeem the state from every manner of vice and crime. As such, it became the "centre and circumference" of the "wheel of Progress."[8] The "primary schools," Michigan state superintendent John Pierce contended in 1837, were the "chief support of all our free institutions."[9] Support of them was a necessity, Thaddeus Stevens of Pennsylvania held, "if an elective republic is to endure for any great length of time."[10]

In his final annual *Report* in 1848, Mann extended the indispensable role of the common school in society. Under the heading of "Physical Education," he argued that the "Common school is the only agency" to thoroughly diffuse "sanitary intelligence" in society.[11] He concluded this *Report* with one last eloquent claim of the social necessity of the common school system:

> . . . it is a *Free* school system. . . . It knows no distinction of rich and poor, bond and free. . . . Without money and without price, it throws open its doors, and spreads the table of its bounty, for all the children of the State. Like the sun, it shines, not only upon the good, but upon the evil, that they may become good; and, like the rain, its blessings descend, not only upon the just, but upon the unjust, that their injustice may depart from them and be known no more.[12]

The Proclaimed Benefits of the Common School

The benefits proclaimed for society if only the common school were instituted were as impressive as they were manifold. The common school would make good citizens, achieving unity in an increasingly diverse society. Horace Bushnell wrote:

> This great institution, too, of common schools . . . is imperiously wanted as such, for the common training of so many classes and conditions of people. Without common schools . . . the disadvantage that accrues to the state, in the loss of so much character, and so many cross ties of mutual respect and generous appreciation, the embittering so fatally of all outward distinctions, and the propagation of so many misunderstandings . . . weakens immensely, the security of the state, and even of its liberties.[13]

Pennsylvania legislators added their voice of support in 1834 when they recommended:

> Let them all fare alike in the primary schools; receive the same elementary instruction;
> imbibe the same republican spirit; and be animated by a feeling of perfect equality. . . . It
> is the duty of the State to promote and foster such establishments.[14]

Mann, justifying taxation for the support of common schools in his final *Report* in 1848, contended:

> . . . they [the schools] are the most effective means of developing and training those pow-
> ers and facilities of a child, by which, when he becomes a man, he may understand what
> his highest interests and his highest duties are.[15]

Order in society would result from the common school. For instance, Horace Bushnell wrote:

> . . . the common school is, in fact, an integral part of the civil order . . . is itself a part of
> the public law, as truly so as the legislatures and judicial courts . . . the teachers are as truly
> functionaries of the law as the constables, prison-keepers, inspectors and coroners . . . an
> application against common schools, is so far an application of the dismemberment and
> reorganization of the civil order of the state . . . the civil order may as well be disbanded,
> and the people given over to their ecclesiastics, to be ruled by them in as many clans of re-
> ligion as they see fit to make.[16]

Thaddeus Stevens, the leader of the fight for common schools in Pennsylvania, responding to those who objected to a tax on their property for the support of common schools, wrote:

> Many complain of this tax, not so much on account of its amount, as because it is for the
> benefit of others and not themselves. This is a mistake. It is for *their own* benefit, inas-
> much as it perpetuates the government, and ensures the due administration of the laws
> under which they live, and by which their lives and property are protected. Why do they
> not urge the same objection against all other taxes?[17]

Stevens went on to point out how the "industrious, thrifty, rich farmer" paid taxes for law enforcement officials and jails, and never protested, but "loudly complains of that which goes to prevent his fellow being from becoming criminal, and to obviate the necessity of those humiliating institutions."[18]

Crime prevention, intimately related to order in society as just witnessed, was another explicitly proposed benefit of the common school. If it were allowed to function as it ought, "nine tenths of crimes in the penal code would become obsolete," promised Mann.[19] Writing a few years later in his *Eleventh Annual Report* in 1847, Mann declared he would prove, by "unexceptionable and consuming" proofs, that the "great body of vices and crimes which now sadden and torment the community, may be dislodged and driven out from amongst us, by such improvements in our present Common School system, as we are abundantly able immediately to make."[20] Not only would crime "decline sharply," Lawrence Cremin observed, but so would "intemperance, cupidity, licentiousness, violence and fraud."[21]

Crime would not be the sole casualty of the advent of the common school. Poverty would also "most assuredly disappear as a broadening popular intelligence tapped new treasures of natural and material wealth."[22]

The advocates of the common school claimed that it would bring a reign of morality and virtue into the commonwealth; it would elevate the character of its citizens. Bushnell argued that without it, the "loss of so much character . . . weakens immensely, the security of the state, and even its liberties."[23] Henry Barnard, Mann's counterpart in Connecticut, contended that his state would become "more elevated by intelligence, morality and religion" with the advent of the common school.[24] Mann echoed similar sentiments a year later when he said that the education provided by common schools was not "a mere capacity to read, write and cipher; but . . . some generous unfolding of the whole spiritual being."[25]

But there was more. As the Superintendent of Schools of the State of Michigan proclaimed in 1837, the establishment of free schools would erase the aristocracy of wealth, because the schools would not permit the "rich a monopoly of learning," upon which the monopoly of wealth rested.[26] Writing in his last Report, Mann reinforced these sentiments. Only:

> Universal Education can counter-work this tendency to the domination of capital and the servility of labor. . . . But if education be equably diffused, it will draw property after it . . . for such a thing never did happen, and never can happen, as that an intelligent and practical body of men should be permanently poor. . . . Education, then, beyond all other devices of human origin, is the great equalizer of the conditions of men—the balance-wheel of the social machinery.[27]

The Role of Teachers

The common school, with all of its potential, needed one more ingredient—the right kind of teachers. Mann and his fellow reformers were convinced that neither itinerant teachers nor graduates of academies or liberal arts colleges, be they lay or clerical, could properly teach in the common schools. A special institution, under the control of the state, was called for: the normal school. Mann, spoke of this at the dedication of a building for the normal school in Bridgewater:

> I believe Normal schools to be a new instrumentality in the advancement of the race . . . without them, Free schools . . . would be shorn of their strength and their healing power, and would at length become mere charity schools. . . . Neither the art of printing, nor

the trial by jury, nor a free press, nor free suffrage, can long exist, to any beneficial and salutary purpose, without schools for the training of teachers.[28]

These schools, upon which the "universal diffusion and ultimate triumph of all-glorious Christianity"[29] depends, where teachers were to be "properly trained," with a "popular disposition towards schools as a wise legislation might affect," could eradicate "95% of the immoralities which afflict society."[30]

Mann was neither the first nor the last to believe in the omnipotence of normal schools. James Carter, one of his predecessors in common school reform pinned the entire free school enterprise on the proper training of teachers. He wrote, "The character of the schools, and of course their political, moral and religious influence depend, almost solely, upon the character of the teachers."[31] He was joined by Charles Brooks, a Unitarian minister in Massachusetts, who maintained that "school instructors should be as fully prepared for their duties as is the clergyman for his. Teachers, teachers, yes I say teachers, have an inconceivable and paramount agency in shaping the destinies of the world."[32]

Brooks insisted that "teachers thoroughly prepared, would put a new face on elementary education, and produce through our State an era of light and of love."[33]

For the common schools, conducted by proper teachers, to have this salutary effect, it was necessary that its subjects be young, hence pliable. As Mann put it, not only is the school "universal" in its operation, the "materials upon which it operates are so pliant and ductile as to be susceptible of assuming a greater variety of forms than any other earthly work of the Creator." The adult resembled the "ruggedness of the oak"; the "lithe sapling or the tender germ, are but feeble emblems to typify the docility of childhood, when contrasted with the obduracy and intractableness of man."[34]

Schools should not be conducted under the authority of churches, which would lead to sectarian strife. Nor should they be the province of parents, who would look first to their private gain. The republic, the state, was the legitimate and necessary authority in schooling. The common school must be the place where "those articles in the creed of republicanism, which are accepted by all, believed in by all, and which form the common basis of our political faith, shall be taught to all."[35]

Conclusion

As is well known, Mann and his allies had a number of opponents. Conservatives, advocates of local control, the Boston schoolmasters, and Roman Catholics were generally in the ranks of those who resisted his programs. Writing in the early twentieth century, that eminent stalwart of public education, Ellwood P. Cubberley, described the conflict as follows:

I. *For public schools.*

   Men considered as:

      1. "Citizens of the Republic."
      2. Philanthropists and humanitarians.
      3. Public men of large vision.
      4. City residents.
      5. The intelligent workingmen in the cities.
      6. Non-taxpayers.
      7. Calvinists.
      8. "New-England men."

II. *Lukewarm, or against public schools.*

   Men considered as:

      1. Belonging to the old aristocratic class.
      2. The conservatives of society.
      3. Politicians of small vision.
      4. Residents of rural districts.
      5. The ignorant, narrow-minded and penurious.
      6. Taxpayers.
      7. Lutherans, Reformed-Church, Mennonites, and Quakers.
      8. Proprietors of private schools.
      9. The non-English speaking classes.[36]

In Cubberley's view, the common school ultimately "took its place as the most important institution in our national life working for the perpetuation of our free democracy and the advancement of the public welfare."[37] He wrote about Mann that:

> No one did more than he to establish in the minds of the American people the conception that education should be universal, non-sectarian and free, and that its aim should be social efficiency, civic virtue, and character, rather than mere learning or the advancement of sectarian ends.[38]

Horace Mann wrote of the common school "experiment" that "Education has never yet been brought to bear with one hundredth part of its potential force, upon the natures of children, and, through them, upon the character of men and of the race."[39] Mann argued that "The property of this commonwealth is pledged for the education of all its youth, up to such a point as will save them from poverty and vice, and prepare them for the adequate performance of their social and civil duties."[40] Given all that he and his co-workers claimed on behalf of the common schools, it is no surprise that he could exclaim that they were "the greatest invention ever made by man."[41] The common school indeed qualifies as an educational panacea.

Notes

1. Daniel Webster, "First Settlement of New England," in Robert H. Bremner, ed., *Children and Youth in America: A Documentary History*. Vol.1. 1600–1865. Cambridge, MA: Harvard University Press, 1970, p. 4351.
2. Charles L. Glenn, *The Myth of the Common School*. Amherst, MA: The University of Massachusetts Press, 1988, p. 116.
3. Horace Mann, *Tenth Annual Report* (1846), in Lawrence A. Cremin, ed., *The Republic and the School: Horace Mann on the Education of Free Men*. New York: Teachers College Press, 1957, p. 63.
4. Ibid, pp. 63–64.
5. Mann, *First Annual Report* (1846), ibid., p. 33.
6. Horace Bushnell, "Common Schools," (1853) in Rush Welter, ed., *American Writings on Popular Education: the Nineteenth Century*. Indianapolis: The Bobbs-Merrill Co., 1971, p. 186.
7. Rev. W. S. Dutton, quoted in Glenn, *The Myth of the Common School*, p. 223.
8. Mann, *Eleventh Annual Report* (1847), in Cremin, ed., *The Republic and the School*, p. 78; Cremin, "Horace Mann's Legacy," in Cremin, ed., *The Republic and the School.*, p. 9.
9. John Pierce, *Report of the Superintendent of Public Instruction of the State of Michigan* (1837), in Sol Cohen, ed., *Education in the United States: A Documentary History*. Vol. 2. New York: Random House, 1974, p. 1025.
10. "General Education-Remarks of Mr. Stevens," in Cohen, ed., ibid., p. 1065.
11. Mann, *Twelfth Annual Report* (1848), in Cremin, ed., *The Republic and the School*, p. 83.
12. Mann, ibid., in Cremin, ibid., p. 112.
13. Bushnell, "Common Schools," (1853), in *Life and Letters of Horace Bushnell*. New York: Charles Scribner's Sons, 1903, p. 300.
14. "Report of the Joint Committee of the Two Houses of the Pennsylvania Legislature, on the Subject of a System of General Education." In Bremner, ed., *Children and Youth in America*, 1, p. 460.
15. Mann, *Twelfth Annual Report* (1848), in Cremin, ed., *The Republic and the School*, p. 104.
16. Bushnell, "Common Schools," (1853), in Welter, ed., *American Writings on Popular Education*, pp. 181–182.
17. Stevens, in Cohen, ed., *Education in the United States,* 2, p. 1066.
18. Ibid.
19. Mann, quoted in Glenn, *The Myth of the Common School*, p. 80.
20. Mann, *Eleventh Annual Report*, in Cremin, ed., *The Republic and the School*, p. 78.
21. Cremin, "Horace Mann's Legacy," in Cremin, ed., ibid., p. 9.
22. Ibid., p. 8.
23. Bushnell, "Common Schools," (1853), in Welter, ed., *American Writings on Popular Education*, pp. 182–183.
24. Henry Barnard, "What Connecticut Would Be With Good Schools," (1839), in Welter, ed., ibid., p. 72.
25. Mann, "An Appeal to The Citizens of Massachusetts In Behalf of Their Public Schools," (1844), in Welter, ed., ibid., p. 79.
26. Pierce, *Report of the Superintendent of Public Instruction of the State of Michigan* (1837), in Cohen, ed., *Education in the United States,* 2, p. 1025.
27. Mann, *Twelfth Annual Report* (1848), in Cremin, ed., *The Republic and the School*, pp. 86–87.
28. Mann, quoted in Glenn, *The Myth of the Common School*, p. 138.
29. Ibid.

30. Ibid., p. 167.
31. Carter, quoted in Glenn, ibid., p. 135.
32. Brooks, quoted in Glenn, ibid., p. 137.
33. Ibid.
34. Mann, *TwelfthAnnual Report* (1848), in Cremin, ed., *The Republic and the School,* p. 80.
35. Mann, *Twelfth Annual Report* (1848), in Cremin, ed., ibid., p. 97.
36. Ellwood P. Cubberley, *Public Education in the United States.* Boston: Houghton Mifflin Company. 1919, p. 120.
37. Ibid., p. 123.
38. Ibid., p. 167.
39. Mann, *Twelfth Annual Report,* in Cremin, ed., *The Republic and the School,* p. 101.
40. Mann, *Twelfth Annual Report,* in Cohen, ed., *Education in the United States,* 2, p. 1099.
41. Mann, quoted in Jonathan A. Messerli, *Horace Mann: A Biography.* New York: Alfred A. Knopf, 1972 p. xii.

CHAPTER TWO

The Bible and Its Reading

Perhaps no more fitting place to begin a chapter on the Bible and its reading as a panacea is with the famous *Twelfth Annual Report* of the Unitarian founder of the Common School movement, Horace Mann. Writing in 1848, Mann declared that it was easy to "prove that the Massachusetts school system is not anti-Christian nor un-Christian. The Bible is the acknowledged expositor of Christianity . . . Christianity has no other authoritative expounder. This Bible is in our Common Schools, by common consent."[1] In his twelve years as Secretary of the State Board of Education in Massachusetts, Mann contended that he had "never heard an objection made to the use of the Bible in school, except in one or two instances."

> If the Bible, then, is the exponent of Christianity; if the Bible contains the communications, precepts, and doctrines, which make up the religious system, called and known as Christianity; if the Bible makes known those truths, which, according to the faith of Christians, are able to make men wise unto salvation; and if this Bible is in the schools, how can it be said that Christianity is excluded from the schools; or how can it be said that the school system, which adopts and uses the Bible, is an anti-Christian, or an un-Christian system?. . . wherever the Bible might go, there the system of Christianity must be.[2]

Mann's words reflected the belief of nineteenth century America, Protestant America, Bible America.

At its inception in 1848, the state of Wisconsin was no exception to the place of the Bible in its society and in its public schools. It will serve as a "case study" of sorts for this chapter. Fifty-one of the sixty-nine delegates to the state's constitutional convention hailed from either New England or New York. Historian Milo Quaife portrayed their role as follows:

Men of the old American stock, from the northeastern section of the Union, reinforced by English speaking aliens from the British isles, were chiefly instrumental in laying the foundation of the commonwealth of Wisconsin.[3]

The Bible's place in society was paramount. For instance, Chapter 51, Section 8 of *The Revised Statutes of Wisconsin of 1849* held the master responsible "for teaching the apprentice to read and write . . . and that the master will give to such apprentices, at the expiration of his or her service, a new Bible."[4] Chapter 153, Section 9 held the "keeper of each prison shall provide . . . a copy of the Bible" for each prisoner who desired it.[5] Section 5 of Chapter 102 listed articles of personal property that were exempt from seizure on the occasion of a prisoner's execution; the first named was "the family Bible."[6] The *Statutes* also held the state superintendent of public instruction responsible for discouraging "the use of sectarian books and sectarian instruction in the schools"[7]; the Bible was not included, as is clear from the response of Superintendent Eleazar Root in 1850 that "under our laws the Bible is not regarded as a sectarian book."[8] He reiterated this view a year later:

> Our Constitution prohibits all sectarian instruction in the common schools, whether political or religious, but it does not prohibit simply the reading of the Bible in School,—for the Bible under our law is not regarded as a sectarian book.[9]

Root, an Episcopal clergyman,[10] was succeeded by Azel P. Ladd, a New Hampshire native.[11] Ladd declared that "there can be no doubt, under our laws, of the Bible being a lawful book to be read in common schools"; yet he ruled that sectarian books could not be placed in school libraries.[12]

The Benefits of the Bible's Use in Schools

It is clear that the Bible and its reading permeated early Wisconsin society. The reason its use was held in such high esteem was the benefits its reading would bring to society. Superintendent Lyman C. Draper attested to this reality in 1858 when he wrote that the people of Wisconsin would not consent to the banishment of the Bible from the schools because such an action would "virtually repudiate its unequalled teachings of virtue and morality as unfit for the instruction and guidance of . . . children." Draper worried about the consequences if such an action were to occur, pointing out that the schoolchildren of today would become "the rulers and law-givers of the State, and custodian of all that we now hold dear and sacred, our homes, our country, Christianity and the Bible."[13]

In the case of conflict, Draper said that at all costs, "Let the Bible be read, whatever be the version, reverently and impressively, and the blessing of the God of the Bible will never fail to attend it."[14] The preeminent place of the Bible in the development of the student's character and the well-being of society was uppermost in his mind:

> . . . and I should ever feel bound to regard with special favor the use of the Bible in public schools, as pre-eminently first in importance among textbooks for teaching the noblest principles of virtue, morality, patriotism and good order—love and reverence for God— charity and good will to man.[15]

The source of the conflict over the use of the Bible in the public schools was, for the most part, the increasing presence of Roman Catholics in the state. The Protestant clergy continued to support the Bible in the state's public life. In 1856 the Rev. Charles Brooks wrote that "God is our teacher and the Bible our class book."[16] Three years later, speaking at the Wisconsin Teachers Convention, the Rev. M. P. Kinney claimed that "The Bible is pre-eminently the book of God, and as such it belongs, by divine grant, to every human being. It has an equal right to the school-room with the air which the same God has made."[17]

State educational officials did not cease their advocacy of the "nonsectarian" Bible in schools. Assistant Superintendent Craig ruled in 1860 that the Bible could not be considered sectarian instruction.[18] The Bible held a place in the "recommended textbook" section of the Superintendents' *Reports* in the 1860s, under textbooks to be used in "Moral Instruction."[19] The state's journal for professional educators, the *Wisconsin Journal of Education,* reflected similar sentiments. An editorialist opined in 1864 that:

> There is enough—thank God there is enough—of common Christian ground in the Bible, for all sects to meet on and cultivate the Christian truth, love and brotherhood, without impaling themselves on sectarian points of irrevocably diverging into sectarian by-paths.[20]

State educational authorities recommended Francis Wayland's, *The Elements of Moral Science,* as a textbook. This work quoted Chillingworth's "The Bible, The Bible, The Religion of Protestants," and then stated that "what is contained here alone is binding upon conscience."[21] Wayland's views on the New Testament were that it was "intended for the whole human race," and was a "final revelation of the will of God," containing "all the moral precepts both of natural religion and the Old Testament," along with "whatever else it was important to our salvation that we should know."[22] Finally, Superintendent John McMynn in 1866 looked to the common schools to contribute to the cause of religion and morality "without usurping the office of preacher . . . by imparting the leading truths of the Bible, and thus laying the foundation for parent and minister of the gospel to build upon.[23]

The Bible Under Attack

As Robert Michaelsen has observed, "Most American religious groups have regarded the Bible as the special source of divine disclosure, and most have affirmed Biblical roots for their faith."[24] He also recorded the words of Justice Hagans of the Cincinnati Superior Court in a case *(Minor* v. *Board of Education of Cincinnati)* that challenged its use in public schools in 1870, which contended that the Holy Bible impressed:

> . . . on the children of the common schools, the principles and duties of morality and justice, and a sacred regard to truth, love of country, humanity, universal benevolence, sobriety, industry, chastity, moderation, temperance and all other virtues which are the ornaments of modern society.[25]

That same year Samuel Fallows, a Methodist minister and former secretary of the Wisconsin Methodist Conference was appointed superintendent of schools in Wisconsin.[26] Noting the changing complexion of the state's population, the Methodists that year issued a forceful statement on the relation of the Church and the Bible to the common schools. They declared that the common school system was the offspring of the Bible; and that popular education existed only among evangelical Protestants because that version of Christianity alone was capable of furnishing the inspirational base for the system's existence.[27] The Roman Catholics were the assailants; they wished to evict the Bible, replace the Bible-centered common schools with their own rigidly sectarian system, and put the rest of the country under "atheistic influence."[28] The Methodists sprang to the defense of the Bible and its virtues in the common schools:

> The pretense of excluding the Bible we regard as a very shallow one, and the people ought not to be deluded by it. It is argued that much of the teaching of the Bible is disbelieved by a portion of the community. So is much of Homer . . . but nobody proposed to discard them on this account. Evidently it is not so much the reading of the Bible that is objected to, as all positive religious instruction. . . . It is the voice of the nation; are the cherished convictions of a great people to be sacrificed to the abnormal prejudices and caprices of exceptional individuals?[29]

The Methodists called upon their members to "cherish and maintain the system," to insist that no part of it should be neglected:

> . . . least of all that which is the highest and most important. As the religious principles of the Bible have been the basis and inspiration of the system from the beginning, so they should continue to inform and animate it, and that . . . in the interest of culture, embracing especially those moral and religious elements which humanity is known to crave and profit by . . . in all places of public trust there may be found men and women of sound learning, of incorruptible integrity and of genuine piety.[30]

The Edgerton Bible Case

The issue of the place of the Bible in the common schools in Wisconsin came to a head in the 1880s when a group of Catholics in Edgerton brought suit against its use in their common schools.[31] In its response, the Edgerton School Board maintained, among other points, that the Bible was an important text, unable to be replaced by any other book, and was an important part of the students' instruction.[32]

Judge John R. Bennett, presiding judge over the 12th Circuit Court, Rock County, Janesville, ruled in favor of the Board.[33] The Bible was a unique book, he averred, and was a "good, true and ever faithful friend and counselor."[34] A. A. Jackson, attorney for the Board, pressed the case for the Bible further. It was, he said, the foundation of the Christian religion, which in turn was the common witness of the founders of the nation and of its school system. It was, he claimed, "THE BOOK" to be used in teaching morals and the fundamentals of the Christian religion, and it could not be lawfully excluded from the common schools by any authority.[35] Jackson concluded his defense of the Bible with these stirring words:

> Shall then this wonderful book that has commanded the admiration of men wherever it is known, whose teaching is the rule of action of people of this great nation, that has molded the form, and aided in a most remarkable degree the wonderful growth and development of this nation, and that has been, and is a guide in life, a consolation in death, be excluded from the schools where our children are taught?[36]

Despite this impassioned plea, the Supreme Court of Wisconsin ruled in favor of the petitioners, adjudging that the use of the Bible in common schools was unconstitutional. The response of some Protestant Christians to this decision demonstrates that to them the Bible and its reading in the schools was indeed a panacea.

The Congregationalist Position

Meeting in 1890, Wisconsin Congregationalists assessed the decision as weakening the moral fiber of the nation. They adopted the resolution of Professor J. J. Blaisdell of Beloit College to illustrate its indispensable role:

> 4. That, as in the conception of our fathers, in which the Common School had its origin, the primary truths of religion were a fundamental element, so we hold the maintaining of that to be indispensable. Without it what the pupil learns ceases to have for him its true significance and relation to his life as a citizen and as a man, and morality has neither ground of authority nor directive principle. Without it the school will not preserve

society from disregard of government and from falling sooner or later into fatal confusion. Inasmuch, then, as the principle for which we contend is recognized in the Constitution of the Commonwealth, we require that the common and higher public schools, where the youth of the State are instructed, be not hindered from teaching them, in connection with the use of the Bible and otherwise, that they are beholden to a Divine Ruler of the universe in the terms of duty and ought to practice the spirit, as exemplified and taught by Jesus Christ, of obedience toward Him and of brotherhood toward all men.[37]

Blaisdell expanded on his views in a paper read at a meeting of the Beloit Congregational Convention at Palmyra, Wisconsin on May 23, 1890. He pleaded that the Bible be returned to the schools for the safety of the republic:

But religion—the religion of the Bible—is provided for in the Constitution of our commonwealth as our birthright in the school-room, our birthright everywhere. The Constitution recognizes it as the common atmosphere of our civic life. To that birthright we make our claim.[38]

The Presbyterian Reaction

The reaction among Presbyterians was closely akin to that of the Congregationalist. The Presbyterian General Assembly of the United States declared its loyalty to the Bible as the "Magna Carta of our best moral and religious influences" and stated that it would regard its expulsion from the public schools as a "deplorable and suicidal act."[39] The Assembly urged all Presbyterians to "cooperate with all Christian people in maintaining the place of this Book of God as an educating force among the youth of our land."[40]

The Synod of Wisconsin unanimously adopted a resolution protesting the decision. Its members predicted that dire calamities of immense proportions of social, moral, and intellectual nature would soon befall society unless the decision were reversed:

WHEREAS, This decision tends to weaken the schools as instruments of both intellectual and moral education, as well as to impair confidence in them and so to prepare the way for their supersedure by the system of denominational schools promotive of class feeling and social alienation; and

WHEREAS, This decision tends to weaken moral conviction at a time when the public conscience needs all the quickening and invigoration it can get from every quarter, and so is fraught with most baleful consequences to society and the commonwealth; and

RESOLVED, 3d, That ministers, Sunday School teachers, and heads of families be urged to take advantage of the public interest in this question to make more widely known, through sermons, books, and otherwise, the inestimable service rendered to the cause of liberty, of civilization, of progress and of human welfare in general by the Christian Scriptures.[41]

A year later the Synod expressed its chagrin that "no practical remedy" to the decision seemed available, but awaited the "return of a better mind both to the bench and to the enemies of the book which made our commonwealth free and great."[42] Vowing their loyalty to the Bible-less schools, the Presbyterians acknowledged that the system would be "defective" if moral training, "based upon fundamental religious convictions" was excluded, and asked their fellow citizens to "aid us in deriving means for its revival." They concluded their protest with a request that Presbyterians do all in their power, within the confines of the law, to restore the Bible to its deserved exalted position in American society.[43]

The Madison Presbytery added its voice to the chorus of dissent. Expressing "profound astonishment and grief" at the decision "forbidding the use of Christian scripture in the common schools of this state," the Madisonians forecasted disastrous consequences in education if the Bible were to be removed from the schools. These "far reaching consequences . . . are certain to be of such a nature as to give the Christian patriot cause for the gravest concern."[44] The "lamentable and disastrous" decision was "out of keeping with our institutions, which are fundamentally Christian; puts an unseemly stigma upon the book to which we owe our liberties." It was "especially unbecoming" because it forbade the very Book from the schools which that "Book alone made free."[45] Declaring the decision would weaken the entire fiber of the schools and society, they lamented:

> We cannot but regard the decision as greatly weakening our whole system of common schools. It impairs their efficiency as instruments of intellectual awakening and instruction by removing from them the greatest educational force and the most important body of literature known to mankind. It tends to a relaxation of discipline by silencing in the schools the only authoritative voice of moral obligation recognized in Christendom. And it sows broadcast the seeds of distrust in our common schools, in regard to their moral influence.
>
> We regard the decision as having a dangerous tendency in the community at large as well as in the schools. The vast and grave social and political problems that are about and before us can only be successfully met by a people whose moral convictions are perpetually quickened and reinvigorated. This great work the Bible is alone equal to, and therefore, as citizens and patriots profoundly interested in our country's welfare, we deplore every action of our authorities that tends to lessen its influence.[46]

The Fond du Lac Presbytery joined in the protest. Noting that the Bible was the "source of our liberties and the true standard of moral authority," they maintained that the reading of the Bible in the public schools was an "essential and necessary factor to the full, complete and healthy moral and educational development of the youth of our state and country."[47]

The Methodist View

The Methodists matched the travail and anguish exhibited by the Presbyterians over the ouster of the Bible from the schools and the deleterious consequences that would befall the nation as a result. The Wisconsin Conference, meeting in 1890, called for the creation of a "commission of five to be appointed to co-operate with other denominations in such action as may be thought necessary" to address the situation.[48] Methodists feared that the decision would head the state toward the dreaded "union of Church and State."[49] Reflecting a common Methodist theme, the Rev. Mr. Creighton of the Summerfield Methodist Church in Milwaukee accused the Catholic hierarchy of conniving to oust the Bible with the goal of "the downfall of public schools and the establishment of sectarian schools on their ruins."[50] Creighton protested:

> Shall Bible America, at the beck of a foreign autocrat who has commanded that the system which lies at the basis of our nation's prosperity and moral elevation shall be separated and broken up, permit an intolerant priesthood to put the heel of oppression upon her neck? God forbid.[51]

Creighton had company. The Rev. D. C. John of Racine lashed the Court for its decision, claiming that nations that had exhibited disrespect for the word of God had come to ignominious ends.[52] John was joined by the Rev. F. S. Stein of the Washington Avenue Methodist Episcopal Church in Milwaukee, who also blamed the Roman Catholics for the decision. Stein maintained that the object of public schools was to make good American citizens. The nation's Christian origins, based upon the Bible, had produced the Christian character of the nation. The Bible was as much a part of the curriculum as the "three R's":

> Our youth must be taught in public schools that the Ten Commandments are as important as the ten digits; that a lie is to be avoided as much as bad grammar; that dishonesty is to be guarded against as much as a wrong answer in arithmetic; that honesty and purity are as essential as history and physics. The Bible should therefore be the standard text book on morality in every school room.[53]

Stein concluded his remarks with a blast at the Roman Catholics, who he said were intent on destroying American institutions:

> With the aid of Atheists and time-serving politicians the Catholic Church has succeeded, here and there, in driving the Bible from the school room and disparaging the teaching of Christian morality. Now on the plea that the public schools are godless, for which condition, if it exists, they are responsible, they aim at the abolition of our school system. That they will ultimately succeed there is great danger. . . . Let us, therefore,

faithfully guard this citadel of the republic. For with the destruction of our school system our American institutions will be jeopardized.[54]

The Protestant Press

The mainstream Protestant press was also distressed with the decision and its future consequences. One writer argued that "morality without religion is impossible," and he foresaw legions of young Americans graduating from the public schools morally bankrupt because they had been deprived of the character-building influence of the Bible.[55] Another predicted that "Wisconsin is well on the way toward the religion and morality of the Hottentots and of the French revolutionists"; the decision was "certainly a covenant with death and an agreement with hell."[56] The decision was described as one that was "at war with the good of our system of public schools" and would result in "two things to be tabooed and banished and forever kept out of the public schools . . . the idea of God and any holy sense of honor and reverence to Almighty God."[57] Unless reversed, one minister predicted, the decision would "bring the wrath of Almighty God on the whole nation."[58] Another contended that the "Secularized mind is not educated, and woe to the community when that form of ignorance becomes general," because while history has had its moral infidels, "there never has been, and there never will be, a 'moral infidel community'."[59]

The Catholics came in for their share of guilt here as well. The Protestant publication, *The Advance,* blamed the protest on the Catholics, "prompted by their priests," and asked, "Is it because Roman Catholics thrust the Bible from the home, as they do from the school, that such a large percentage of saloon owners were Catholic?"[60]

Conclusion

Perhaps the headlines in *Our Church Work* best capsulized the general Protestant reaction with its headline "Our Public School, in the Future, as in the Past, must be American, Non-Sectarian, Christian." It editorialized in that same issue that it had "no apologies" for printing the entire talk of Congregationalist Professor Blaisdell of Beloit College in its 19 June issue because, in its words, "It had to do with the foundations and life of our nation."[61] Much to the chagrin of Protestants, the decision stood and was effective. The Bible, the very foundation of morality and the republic and its institutions, was no longer welcome in Wisconsin schools. Bereft of their unique and unequaled moral panacea in the public schools, they awaited the Armageddon.

Notes

1. Horace Mann, *Twelfth Annual Report,* in Lawrence A. Cremin, ed., *The Republic and the School: Horace Mann on the Education of Free Men.* New York: Teachers College Press, 1957, p. 105

2. Ibid., pp. 105–106.

3. Milo M. Quaife, *Wisconsin: Its History and Its People.* Vol. I. Chicago: The S.J. Clarke Co., 1924. p. 447.

4. *The Revised Statutes of the State of Wisconsin, 1849.* Southport: C. Latham Sholes. 1849, pp. 404–405.

5. Ibid., p. 736.

6. Ibid., p. 541.

7. Ibid., p. 89.

8. *Decisions in Appeals, Wisconsin Superintendents of Public Instruction.* Vol. I. December 3, 1850. p. 94.

9. Ibid., August 28, 1851, p. 240.

10. Dwight L. Agnew, et al, eds., *Dictionary of Wisconsin Biography.* Madison: The State Historical Society of Wisconsin, 1960, p. 306.

11. Ibid., p. 217.

12. *Decisions in Appeals,* I, February 21, 1852, pp. 287–288; *Decisions in Appeals,* I, November 15, 1853, p. 399.

13. Lyman C. Draper, "Moral and Religious Insruction in Public Schools," in the *Tenth Annual Report on the Condition and Improvement of the Common Schools and Educational Interests of the State of Wisconsin for the Year 1858.* Madison: Atwood and Rublee, 1858. pp. 242–243.

14. Ibid., p. 243.

15. Ibid., p. 244.

16. Rev. Charles Brooks, "The Best Method of Teaching Morals in Common Schools," *Wisconsin Journal of Education* I, 6 (August 1856): 161.

17. Rev. M. P. Kenney, "Religious Instruction in Common Schools—Methods of Imparting it," *Wisconsin Journal of Education* IV, 3 (September 1859): 2.

18. *Decisions in Appeals,* II, February 18, 1860, p. 2.

19. *Tenth Annual Report on the Condition and Improvement of the Common Schools and Educational Interests of the State of Wisconsin, for the year 1858.* Madison: Atwood and Rublee, 1858, p. 246: *Twelfth Annual Report on the Condition and Improvement of the Common Schools and Educational Interests of the State of Wisconsin, for the year 1860.* Madison: James Ross, 1860, p. 80; Fifteenth *Annual Report of the Superintendent of Public Instruction of the State of Wisconsin for the Year Ending August 31, 1863.* Madison: William J. Park, p. 102.

20. "Religion in Schools," *Wisconsin Journal of Education* (NS), I, 3 (September 1864): 80.

21. Francis Wayland, The Elements of Moral Science, edited by Joseph L. Blau, Cambridge, MA: Harvard University Press, 1963, p. 129.

22. Ibid., p. 132.

23. *Annual Report of the Superintendent of Public Instruction of the State of Wisconsin for the Year Ending August 31, 1866.* Madison: Atwood and Rublee, 1867, p. 53.

24. Robert S. Michaelsen, *Piety in the Public School.* New York: The Macmillan Company, 1970. p. 32.

25. Ibid

26. Agnew, et al. eds., *Dictionary of Wisconsin Biography,* p. 126.

27. The Relation of the Church to the Common School," in *the Minutes of the Twenty-Fourth Ses-*

sion of the Wisconsin Annual Conference of the Methodist Episcopal Church 1870. Milwaukee: Index Printing Office, 1870, p. 29.

28. Ibid.

29. Ibid., p. 30.

30. Ibid., p. 31.

31. "Petition of Relaters, State ex rel. Weiss and others, Appellants, vs. The District Board of School District No. Eight of the City of Edgerton, Respondent." *Wisconsin Reports. 76 Wis. 177*. Chicago: Callaghan and Co., 1886.

32. "Return of the District Board," ibid., pp. 181–186.

33. John R. Berryman, *History of the Bench and Bar of Wisconsin*. Vol. II. Chicago: H.C. Cooper., Jr., and Company, 1898, pp. 56–57.

34. Judge John R. Bennett, *Opinion in the case of Weiss, et al., vs. the School Board of Edgerton*. Edgerton: F. W. Coon, 1889, pp. 483–484.

35. "Brief of A. A. Jackson," *State of Wisconsin. In Supreme Court. The State of Wisconsin ex rel., Frederick Weiss, et al., Appellant vs. The District Board of School District No. Eight of the City of Edgerton, Respondent*. Edgerton: F. W. Coon, 1890, p. 171.

36. Ibid., p. 198.

37. *Minutes of the Fiftieth Annual Meeting of the Congregational Convention of Wisconsin 1890*. Madison: Tracy, Gibbs and Co., 1890, p. 45.

38. J. J. Blaisdell, "The Edgerton Bible Case—The Decision of the Supreme Court of Wisconsin." A paper read before the Beloit Congregational Convention at Palmyra, Wis., May 23, 1890. Madison: State Historical Society of Wisconsin, 1890, p. 36.

39. *Minutes of the General Assembly of the Presbyterian Church in the United States of America 1890*. New Series, XIII, Philadelphia: Mac Calla and Co., 1890, p. 104.

40. Ibid., pp. 104–105.

41. *Minutes of the Synod of Wisconsin of the Presbyterian Church 1890*. Madison: Tracy, Gibbs and Co., 1891, p. 15.

42. Rev. W. A. McAtee, "The Bible in the Public Schools," in the *Minutes of the Synod of Wisconsin of the Presbyterian Church 1891*. Madison: Tracy, Gibbs and Co., 1891, p. 15.

43. Ibid., p. 16.

44. Madison Presbytery, "An Official Deliverance in Regard To the Late Decision of the Supreme Court of Wisconsin, Concerning the Bible and Our Public Schools." Janesville: Wm. F. Brown, Stated Clerk, 1890, p. 1.

45. Ibid., p. 2.

46. Ibid.

47. *Milwaukee Sentinel,* April 11, 1890, p. 10.

48. *Minutes of the Wisconsin Annual Conference of the Methodist Episcopal Church, Forty-Fourth Session 1890*. John Schneider, Editor and Publisher, 1890, p. 62.

49. *Minutes of the Thirty-Sixth Annual Session of the West Wisconsin Conference of the Methodist Episcopal Church 1890*. Evansville: R. M. Antes, 1890, p. 47.

50. *Milwaukee Sentinel,* April 14, 1890, p. 12.

51. Ibid.

52. *Milwaukee Sentinel,* April 21, 1890, p. 21.

53. *The Bennett Law, Newspaper Clippings*. March 3, 1890. A Scrapbook in the Library of the State Historical Society of Wisconsin, Madison.

54. Ibid.

55. E. H. Merrell, "The Bible Outlawed from the Public Schools," *Our Church Work,* IX, 7, April 20, 1890, p. 2.

56. Rev. John A. Dodds, *Milwaukee Sentinel,* May 21, 1890, p. 4.
57. "A Monstrous Judicial Decision: The Bible Unconstitutional," *The Advance,* March 27 1890, p. 238.
58. Dodds, *Milwaukee Sentinel,* May 21,1890, p. 4.
59. Merrell, "The Bible Outlawed from the Public Schools," p. 2.
60. "A Monstrous Judicial Decision." *The Advance,* March 27, 1890, p. 238: *The Advance,* April 10, 1890, p. 277.
61. "Editorial," *Our Church Work.* IX, 9, June 19, 1890, pp. 1, 6.

CHAPTER THREE

The "American" Public School

The overriding theme of the nineteenth century was "a common religion for the common school." As the century progressed, however, the trend toward "Americanizing" the pan-Protestant common school grew, especially in areas that were affected by immigration; in particular, in urbanized, industrialized America, where huge numbers of impoverished Irish settled, having fled their homeland due to the ravages of hunger. In these areas, and in the rural Midwest that was "home" to German immigrants, the consensus that had undergirded Mann's compromise no longer held. Abetted by the national sentiment created in the North by the Civil War, some American educators began, in the latter decades of the nineteenth century, to speak of a distinction between religion and morality, in which the former was the province of home and church, the latter of the "American" public school.

Nationalistic sentiment focused on the use of the English language in schools, which led to conflict with many Catholic- and Lutheran-sponsored schools in the Midwest, which used German as the medium of instruction. These schools were increasingly seen as unpatriotic because of their failure to use English, a threat to the "American way of life." One state passed compulsory attendance legislation in which a school was defined as one in which the subjects were taught in the English language. Schools in urban areas were bureaucratized, compulsory attendance laws were passed, and staffs were differentiated in a way that put administrators, white males, at the top. These schools were, as Joel Spring has observed, expected to bring forth "the good society by improving economic conditions, providing equality of opportunity, eliminating crime, and maintaining political and social order."[1] Ellwood P. Cubberley has described in positive terms the process of secularization of American life, which included state-controlled public schools, as "an unavoidable incident connected with the coming to self-consciousness and self-government of a great people."[2] This process of secularization was to result in a challenge to the "parallel institutions strategy," a phrase coined by the Protestant historian William B. Kennedy, which looked first to the pan-Protestant common school and then to the denominational Sunday school to accomplish the mission of moral education.[3] Indeed, Cubberley's secularized "American" public school was to become, in the eyes of some American educators, the new panacea.

The 1850s: The Trend toward Secularization Begins

Once again the state of Wisconsin was the scene of conflict over education, this time with regard to the right of the state to compel attendance and to define what constituted a school. Although it was not an urban state, Wisconsin became a battleground in the war between those who believed that the secular state should administer education and those who argued that parents (many of whom were German-Americans) and churches should educate children. Accordingly, events in Wisconsin will be mixed with national happenings in this chapter.

As early as 1849–50 State Superintendent Eleazar Root, taking note of the presence of the 94 private schools and their 2,359 pupils that in the state, penned that the existence of such schools was "contrary to the genius of our republican institutions."[4] Root's successor, Azel P. Ladd, bemoaned the fact that only 4,648 of Milwaukee's 12,679 eligible children were attending that city's public schools; the private schools were siphoning off the offspring of the wealthy.[5]

That wealth was not the only reason for choosing private schools is evident from the response of Superintendent H. A. Wright to an appeal in 1854. Wright declared that "A district school taught in the German or any other than the English language is not such school as will entitle the district to receive any portion of the public fund, and is not a district school within the meaning of the law."[6] Wright reminded the appellant that English was the "language of our country," and he expressed the hope that "our German fellow citizens will feel the necessity and the importance of having their children well and thoroughly instructed in the English language."[7]

The need for a law requiring private schools to report their attendance to the state was evident, State Superintendent James McMynn wrote in 1865, because those schools were not doing that of their own volition; thus, it was impossible to ascertain if Wisconsin's youth were in school.[8] Compulsory attendance legislation was necessary, McMynn averred, because education "protects property by preventing crime."[9] That public schools were clearly superior to private ones in his eyes is clear from his statement that "true educational progress is usually measured by the degree of public interest manifested in supporting the public schools. . . . The true friends of education . . . will labor to make the public schools so good, that private schools cannot successfully compete with them."[10] McMynn believed that "under

God," the country owed its existence "as a nation, to our public schools" and that "inestimable as are the blessings" the system had "already conferred, they are few and small compared with those we shall enjoy in years to come."[11]

The 1870s: The Growing National Struggle

The speech of President Ulysses S. Grant to the "Army of the Tennessee" in Des Moines, Iowa on September 29, 1875, both reflected the growing national sentiment on behalf of the common school and gave sustenance to the movement. In his address, Grant urged the Civil War veterans to work to strengthen the Union they had fought to preserve. A key means of doing that, he maintained, was to "Encourage free schools," and "Resolve that neither the State nor nation, nor both combined, shall support institutions of learning other than . . . a good common school education, unmixed with sectarian, pagan or atheistic dogmas."[12] But a few months later, Senator James G. Blaine proposed a federal constitutional amendment that would have forbidden any public financial support of schools other than public. Blaine's amendment passed the House by a whopping majority of 180 to 7, but it failed to obtain the necessary two-thirds majority in the Senate where its margin was 28 to 16.[13]

The task of the public schools to save the nation was compounded in the cities by the presence of large numbers of immigrants, often Irish-Americans. As David Tyack has noted, the nation's cities had experienced exceptional growth in the years between 1820 and 1860, tripling the rate of the overall population. Immigrants accounted for a large proportion of this growth. Boston added 37,000 Irish to its population of 114,000 in the single year 1847.[14] As early as 1850, 41 percent of the inmates of the Massachusetts reform school were Catholic (most of whom were Irish immigrants or their children); the foreign-born population of Massachusetts as a whole that year was 18.93 percent.[15] In 1858, the Boston School Committee envisioned its task as:

> . . . taking children at random from a great city, undisciplined, uninstructed, often with inveterate forwardness and obstinacy, and with the inherited stupidity of centuries of ignorant ancestors; forming them from animals into intellectual beings; giving to many their first appreciation of what is wise, what is lovely, and what is pure—and not merely their first impressions, but what may possibly be their only impressions. . . .[16]

The School Committee's words reinforced those of an editorial on the "Irish Immigrant" in *The Massachusetts Teacher* in 1851, which clearly identified the Irish as the "problem" and "EDUCATION" the "great remedy."[17]

That the problem with immigrant children did not evaporate is clear from

Andrew Peabody's description of his work as a teacher in Massachusetts's public schools in 1876: "I at one time had under my supervision a school in which 95 per cent of the children were of foreign parentage and hardly one of the whole from a home level with the lowest stratum of native-born intelligence."[18]

Though there was considerable sentiment that these youngsters did not belong in the schools, that they would impede the work of the schools with the "regular" children, nonetheless the prevailing sentiment was that expressed in 1885 by John Philbrick that "Public instruction cannot be considered as having fulfilled its mission until it secures the rudiments of education to every child. To accomplish this object coercion is necessary."[19] Nationally, then, compulsory attendance laws, featuring the use of the English language, passed especially for the immigrants and their children, in public schools if at all possible, became the goal in urban areas.

The Wisconsin Story Continues

The most vexing "problem" facing the public schools' civilizing task in cities was the immigrants, often the Irish; in the midwestern states, for example, Wisconsin, Germans posed the biggest challenge. At a state teachers' meeting in Sparta in 1873, the superintendent of schools in Eau Claire County, the Rev. A. Kidder, presented a resolution calling for the state and nation to enact legislation that called for the "compulsory education . . . of all children of our country in the English language" in order that "the progress of virtue and morality, as well as the safety of the nation" be secured.[20] Several years later, state superintendent William C. Whitford, formerly the pastor of the Seventh Day Baptist Church in Milton and president of Milton College,[21] called on citizens to overcome any feeling of repugnance toward coercive measures in education because "our whole public school system is based upon compulsory provisions." He noted that of 117 boys sent to the State Reformatory in Waukesha in 1877, 68 could not write, which in his view showed both the causal connection between illiteracy and crime and the state's responsibility to eradicate, or at least lessen, crime through compulsory schooling.[22]

Some private schools, including those in Milwaukee and La Crosse (each of which had a sizeable proportion of private schools), made no report of their attendance to the state superintendent's office in 1882, leading Superintendent Robert Graham to complain that these entities were impeding the lawful work of the state on behalf of the common good.[23] In some sectors of the state, German Americans contributed to this difficulty. For instance, Mr. A. Marschner, superintendent of schools in Sheboygan, argued that the Germans' commitment to founding schools that were conducted in German blocked the efforts of the public school system, which was the "very cornerstone of our liberty," to instill good citizenship in the students.[24] Similar sentiments were expressed the following year by W. H. Rohr, superintendent in Watertown, who felt that the sectarian German schools would "always be an impediment" to public education.[25] Taking note of the language question in schools, and its relation to patriotism, the Wisconsin legislature passed a law in 1869 that gave district school boards the power to permit instruction "in any of the foreign languages, not to exceed one hour each day."[26] State Superintendent Craig spoke to the purpose of the legislation when he said its intention was to "limit the introduction of other languages than the English language," thereby making it state policy to have all state residents learn their country's common language.[27]

The 1880s: A Decade of Promise and Conflict

Nationally, the rising tide of immigrants evoked considerable concern. This concern was most evident in the nation's teeming cities. In 1881 Senator Morrill of Vermont characterized the threat posed by the immigrants:

> The paramount question must be asked, whether or not there is visible cause for alarm, lest among the miscellaneous multitude of foreign immigrants annually landed on our shores, trained to widely diffused institutions, with a babel confusion of tongues, including paupers, lunatics, idiots and criminals, there may not be introduced many vicious and incontrovertible elements, more dangerous to the individuality and deep-seated stamina of the American people, and more worthy of rigid quarantine, than even the most leprous disease. I refer to those whose inherent deficiencies and iniquities are thoroughbred, and who are as incapable of evolution, whether in this generation or next, as is the leopard to change spots.[28]

Some contended that it was time to "call a halt, and stop this stream of pauperism that pours its filthy contents on our shores."[29] Termed "sickening garbage" by some,[30] remedies had to be found to cure the source of evil. Some looked to stricter immigration laws; others turned to the public schools:

> We dare not to be diversive as a people; to stand we must be united; and how shall this union be secured? Put every solitary child of all the diverse nationalities who comes to us into the hopper of our public schools and grind them out, and when the grist comes through they will be like Edward McGlynn, American citizens. If they refuse, then return them whence they came; and the quicker the better for all concerned.[31]

Expectations of what the "American" public school could achieve, even in the face of such dreadful challenges, were manifold and growing as the century progressed. Perhaps the words of Senator Henry Blair in 1882 best epitomize these expectations: "Educate the rising generation mentally, morally, physically, just as it should be done, and this nation and this world would reach the millennium within one hundred years."[32] The comprehensive secular school was up to the task, as the Rev. David H. Greer, an Episcopal clergyman who would later be bishop of New York, declared in 1889:

> My point is just this: that the public schools of this country being the creations of the state, which is itself secular, must be of a secular character, and that this secular character must not be tampered with or encroached upon by any religious body, Catholic or Protestant, on any ground or pretext whatsoever. They are for all creed and for no creed, for Catholic, Protestant and Agnostic. They are for all nationalities, native-born and foreign, for the Irish, German, and Italian, as well as for the American child, and the impartial, secular, and comprehensive character of the public schools is the only one which can be in this country consistently and safely maintained.[33]

Complementary statements abounded. William Torrey Harris declared that the "Will of Providence" accounted for the separation of religion and education.[34] The secular public schools, which "reflect the object of the founders of the nation," wrote Griffin, have proved to be the "strongest bulwark" against "bigot, skeptic and anarchist."[35] It was only under our "godless constitution" that these schools, "without reliance upon Church or Bible," could teach morals sufficient to produce good citizens.[36] The public schools, as agents of the state, which has the right of educational custody over the child (which the church does not have), were portrayed by another writer as the agency competent enough to teach the morals of good citizenship.[37]

These sentiments were to be played out in Wisconsin. Their key advocate was William Dempster Hoard, governor of the state in the late 1880s. Responding to a request from State Superintendent Jesse B. Thayer for legislation that would require non-public schools to report their attendance to his office, Hoard asked the solons for such legislation, based on the rights of future citizenship for the child, that would require "reading and writing" to be taught daily in English.[38] A lay Methodist minister, Hoard had become convinced while on duty with the Union Army in Virginia during the Civil War that it was the absence of popular education in the South that had caused the southerners' immoral attitude toward slavery.[39] Religiously committed to a broad, tolerant Christianity, he had little use for the "narrow creeds and the dogmas of man-made religion."[40] Hoard felt strongly that the use of the English language in schools was the indispensable vehicle by which the country's traditions and heritage could be maintained and a true American nationality, a loyal citizenship with general religious underpinnings, could be forged.[41]

In his view, the chief obstacles to obtaining such a patriotic citizenry were the private schools that used the German language. Hoard was to orchestrate this theme, which had previously been identified by others. For instance, in 1887 John Nagle, the Catholic superintendent of Manitowoc County public schools, had called the denominational schools a "perpetual menace" to the public schools, the state, and the English language.[42] Nagle's comments followed a memorial to the Vatican in 1886, which was supported by Archbishop Heiss of Milwaukee that included a request that "the German language should be taught in German parochial schools."[43]

The result of the agitation was the controversial Bennett Law, which among other features defined a school as one in which "there shall be taught herein, as part of the elementary education of children, reading, writing, arithmetic and United States history, in the English language."[44] Confronted by vocal protests mostly from Catholic and Lutheran sources, that viewed the law as a threat to their schools' existence and as an insult to their nationality, Hoard held firm, contending that the "parent is subject to the state in all matters pertaining to the necessities of the state," of which a schooling in the English language was one such necessity.[45]

Hoard had his allies; chief among them was Horace Rublee, the editor of the *Milwaukee Sentinel*. Protestant clergymen also supported him. One, Dean Babbitt of St. John's Episcopal Church in Milwaukee, was an early ally. Babbitt saw the contest as one that pitted the Catholic Church against the "common school system, reared at such expense, loved with so much ardor, so useful, so needful, so benevolent."[46] The *Sentinel* argued vehemently for the right of the state to "enforce instruction in English," if it considered that "essential." Under Hoard's leadership it was indeed considered "essential."[47] He argued that the "right of the state" in education was at stake, and that the "whole common school question" was involved.[48] It was the foreign element in the Catholic Church that opposed the "true behests of the state in matters of education."[49] Hoard's position on the influence of "foreignism" in the Catholic Church was supported by the *Chicago Tribune,* which claimed that "It is impossible for men educated in Munich or Maynooth, Innsbruck or All Hallows to share American ideas and feelings to the same extent . . . [as those born in America]."[50]

A German Catholic convention in Milwaukee provided the setting for some who opposed the program of the "American" public school. Father Buechler, of St. Francis Seminary in Milwaukee, delivered the opening sermon, declaring that:

> An edict has gone forth to deaden the Catholic Church by means of killing the parochial schools. Who can completely await the planned murder of children for whom Jesus Christ shed his blood? Whoever refuses [to work together] will be cursed with the curse and disgrace of apostates.[51]

Bishop Katzer of Green Bay, who had earlier called the Bennett Law a "step by which Antichrist is trying to promote its attacks on the Church and accomplish its oppression by the state,"[52] gave the keynote address at the convention.

Katzer stressed that the basic rights in education belonged to the family, and could not be usurped by the state under the pretense of the necessity for English education. Katzer concluded with the statement that the "next thing we shall hear is that the state appoints a commission to prescribe what your wives must cook for dinner."[53]

Wisconsin's embattled superintendent, Jesse B. Thayer, presented the state's case at the meeting of the National Education Association (NEA) in 1890. He argued that the "education which relates primarily to the rights, duties and needs of sovereign citizens must be entrusted to the state for its welfare." The Bennett Law strife was not over compulsory attendance, he averred, but dealt with the very existence of one of the nation's free institutions, and he accused the Catholic and Lutheran clergy in particular of not being "in harmony with the principles laid down by the fathers of this republic."[54]

Protestant Reaction

Baptists

At their state meeting in 1890 the Wisconsin Baptists took note of the growing struggle over schooling in the state. They took a "stand by our public schools and demand for them a permanent place in our land." Without specifically mentioning the Bennett Law conflict, they did take note of the vast number of immigrants in the state, who had created a "perilous heterogeneity out of which is to come the future civilization of the state."[55] One local group, the Janesville Baptists, testified to their loyalty to the public schools with a resolution that held that the "common school system" was "one of the great bulwarks of American liberty and citizenship" and they heartily endorsed "compulsory education in the English language" as necessary for the future safety of the country.[56]

Congregationalists

Congregationalists, although they were more directly embroiled with the Bible-reading controversy entered the fray as well. The congregation of the Grand Avenue Congregational Church in Milwaukee burst into applause when the Rev. W. G. Gardner of Michigan cloaked the Bennett Law in the American flag in his sermon:

> The youth of this country should be taught that the country's flag was the same flag that Washington unfurled at Cambridge. They must be taught that the language of the country was the language in which Abraham Lincoln wrote the proclamation emancipating a race of people.[57]

Methodists

The Rev. Mr. Theodore Clifton of the Hanover Congregationalist Church in Milwaukee was that denomination's leading spokesman in this struggle. Clifton argued, among other points, that the Catholic Church was out to destroy the public schools and other free institutions in this nation, with the ultimate hope of controlling the country. Their position on the Bennett Law was but their first step in this direction.[58] The position of the Congregationalists on the relationship of the public schools to American life was laid out most clearly in an editorial in their publication, *Our Church Work:*

> We want our schools to be American rather than foreign. We ask that every child have an adequate English education such as shall fit for citizenship. . . . Now along with this, let the idea of a Christian manhood, as the highest and best embodiment of all that is truly American, rise above all things else. This it seems to me we have a right to ask, not in the interest of any particular church but in the interest of our children and our American life.[59]

The Methodists, as was the case with their mainstream Protestant brethren, were mainly involved in the Bible-reading issue. But they, too, addressed the issue of "American" public schools in the Bennett Law controversy. They supported the preeminent right of the state in education at their 1890 state gathering:

> In educational affairs the state must deal with its citizens as such, knowing neither birthplace, creed, nor party, but affording its privileges and protection to all, without invidious preference for any. . . . It is a question of American schools for American children.[60]

Methodist sentiment also contained references to what the Rev. J. R. Creighton referred to as "the increasing power of numbers of the lower masses," who had once constituted some of Europe's "undesirable population" and who had now entered the state and country. In his view, "unless these millions can be assimilated and influenced by the principles of Christianity," their presence in the United States constituted an "imminent peril to the Republic."[61] The schools played an indispensable role in establishing and upholding these "American" virtues:

> Compulsory education in the language of the land, the language in which the Declaration of Independence was written, Christian morality and the instruction of our children as absolutely necessary to a responsible and loyal citizenship, common schools and not parochial schools for the elementary training of our future citizens. . . . Let us stand invincibly by these principles—by our common school system as the noblest product of American civilization.[62]

Creighton asserted he did not want the schools to "teach our children the catechism" but to be the "training place for American democracy, the preparation place for the busy active life and citizenship of this free country, and the nursery where the first lessons of republican liberty and American loyalty are learned." If this type of education, which could be achieved through the common schools and the English language were neglected, he alleged, the country would face "ruin and disaster." He concluded his sermon with a reference to the assimilation of the immigrants:

> There is one other item. Let every foreign importation and custom be absorbed in Americanism. We talk about Irish, German, Scotch, English, Americans. There should be no such qualifying terms, and these foreigners coming to our shores should leave their differences, their prejudice, their customs and their nationality behind.[63]

Official Methodism saw the struggle as a "question of domestic or foreign domination." For them the question was:

> Shall there be one or many nationalities on our soil? Shall Roman Catholicism and Lutheranism maintain foreign ideas, customs and languages to the exclusion of what is distinctively American? We can conceive of nothing more dangerous to the traditions and spirit and institutions of our country.[64]

Only by requiring "every citizen of the state to attain an education in English" could the foreigners be assimilated into the country and "know and love the government of their adoption." To that end, the Methodists pledged loyalty to the common schools and an education in English, and promised to work for their preservation.[65] The government had the God-given right, the Milwaukee Ministerial Association, a Methodist group, claimed, "to demand that every child be taught the American language."[66]

Presbyterians

The state's Presbyterians took note of the growing presence of foreigners in the state with alacrity. Under the heading of "Christian Citizenship," the Synod urged Presbyterians, lay and clerical, to do all they could to preserve the "integrity and power of our free institutions" in the face of the onslaught of foreign influence, as evidenced in the opposition to the English-language Bennett Law.[67]

The Unitarian Position

Horace Mann's Unitarian descendants went beyond that of the position of mainstream Protestants. Their stance on the absolute necessity of the English language and the secular "American" public schools for the survival and progress of American republican institutions was made perfectly clear by their leader in this struggle, the Rev. Joseph H. Crooker of Madison. Crooker argued that there was "no question" but that the Catholic hierarchy meant to use "every political means to win America to the papal throne," and that the bishops claim *"to speak in the name of the Almighty with an authority higher than that of the state"* in their attempt to "strike down the Public School, or any other distinctly American institution."[68] The basic issue was *"Whether we shall maintain the modern state as a secular institution and its necessary function of secular education, or whether we shall surrender to the papacy and turn human progress back four centuries."* The Bennett Law strife was but an indication of the high stakes involved:

> We must recognize that the perpetuity of civil liberty and modern civilization depends on the maintenance of the district school with its free and secular instruction; and we must also recognize that the opposition to our system of secular education is deep-seated and far-reaching. Surrender to it means the extinction of American liberty, *and any compromise that shall impair the efficiency and sovereignty of American citizenship means an eclipse of humanity.*[69]

The public school, like American citizenship, was a "purely secular function." It was the duty of the state to provide its citizens, including those "in embryo," with a secular education. Any attack on this system of education must perforce be viewed as an assault on the American system of government, since education was an "imperative duty and an essential part of the State itself."[70] Thus, the state had the prior claim in education and the right to tax all its citizens to ensure intelligent citizenship in accord with republican principles.[71]

Conclusion

Social and educational challenges connected with immigration were about to intensify, and with that intensification more demanding tasks would confront the nation's public schools. The years from the late 1840s to 1890, however, filled as they were by urbanization and immigration, led American advocates of republicanism to see the "American" public school, which featured the use of the English language, aided by compulsory attendance laws, as the indispensable means to make the young into loyal citizens, who would be committed to the "American way of life." Those who did not agree were depicted as unpatriotic, foreign, and "un-American." These schools thus became, in the eyes of many American leaders and public educators, the new panacea.

Notes

1. Joel Spring, *The American School 1642–1985*. New York: Longman, 1986, p. 109
2. Ellwood P. Cubberley, *Public Education in the United States*. Boston: Houghton-Mifflin, 1919, p. 173.

3. William B. Kennedy, *The Shaping of Protestant Education*. New York: The Macmillian Company, 1966, p. 27.

4. *First Annual Report of the State Superintendent of Public Instruction for the Year Ending December 31, 1849*. No publication data given, p. 7; *Second Annual Report of the State Superintendent of Public Instruction for the Year Ending December 31, 1850*. Madison: Robert B. Wentworth, 1851, p. 27.

5. *Annual Report of the State Superintendent of Public Instruction for the State of Wisconsin 1853*. Madison: David Atwood, 1854, pp. 60–62.

6. *Decisions in Appeals, Wisconsin Superintendents of Public Instruction*. Vol. I. February 17, 1854. Madison: State Historical Society of Wisconsin, p. 9.

7. Ibid.

8. *Seventeenth Annual Report of the Superintendent of Public Instruction of the State of Wisconsin, for the Year Ending August 31, 1865*. Madison: Atwood and Rublee, 1865, p. 12.

9. *Annual Report of the Superintendent of Public Instruction of the State of Wisconsin, for the Year Ending August 31, 1866*. Madison: Atwood and Rublee, 1866, p. 11.

10. *Annual Report of the Superintendent of Public Instruction of the State of Wisconsin, for the Year Ending August 31, 1867*. Madison: Atwood and Rublee, 1867, p. 19.

11. Ibid., p. 56.

12. "The President's Speech at Des Moines," *Catholic World*, XXII, 130, January, 1876, pp. 433–434.

13. Alvin W. Johnson, *The Legal Status of Church-State Relationships in the United States*. Minneapolis: The University of Minnesota Press, 1934, p. 21.

14. David B. Tyack, *The One Best System: A History of American Urban Education*. Cambridge, MA: Harvard University Press, 1947, p. 30.

15. Michael B. Katz, *The Irony of Early School Reform: Educational Innovation in Mid-Nineteenth Century Massachusetts*. Boston: Beacon Press, 1968, p. 176.

16. Quoted in Michael B. Katz, ed., *School Reform: Past and Present*. Boston: Little, Brown and Company, 1971, p. 171.

17. Quoted in Sol Cohen, ed., *Education in the United States: A Documentary History*. Vol. II. New York: Random House, 1974, pp. 995–997.

18. Quoted in Katz, ed., *School Reform*, p. 173.

19. Quoted in Tyack, *The One Best System, p. 71*.

20. *Annual Report of the Superintendent of Public Instruction of the State of Wisconsin. for the School Year Ending August 31, 1873*. Madison: Atwood and Culver, 1873, p. 170.

21. Dwight L. Agnew, et al., eds., *Dictionary of Wisconsin Biography*. Madison: The State Historical Society of Wisconsin, 1960, p. 374.

22. *Annual Report of the State Superintendent of the State of Wisconsin, for the School Year Ending May 31, 1879*. Madison: David Atwood, 1880, p. 56.

23. *Annual Report of the State Superintendent of the State of Wisconsin, for the School Year Ending May 31, 1882*. Madison: David Atwood, 1882, p. 11.

24. *Annual Report of the Superintendent of Public Instruction, for the Year Ending August 31, 1868*. Madison: Atwood and Rublee, 1868, p. 152.

25. *Annual Report of the Superintendent of Public Instruction of the State of Wisconsin, for the School Year Ending August 31, 1869*. Madison: Atwood and Rublee, 1869, p. 112.

26. *The Laws of Wisconsin 1869*, Chapter 50 Section 1, in *Laws of Wisconsin Relating to Common Schools, Normal Schools and the State University*. Madison: Atwood and Culver, Book and Job Printer, 1870, p. 85.

27. Ibid.

28. Quoted in William M. F. Round, "Immigration and Crime," *Forum* VIII (December 1889): 428.

29. Amos B. Kendig, "The Public or Parochial School, Which?" Sermon delivered at the Methodist Episcopal Church, Brooklyn, New York, Thanksgiving Day, November 29, 1888. In the form of a pamphlet at Madison: State Historical Society of Wisconsin, p. 12.

30. "Shall the Common Schools Teach Christian Morals?," *Our Day,* III, 17, May, 1889, p. 464.

31. Kendig, "The Public or Parochial School, Which?," p. 26.

32. David B. Tyack and Elisabeth Hansot, *Managers of Virtue: Public School Leadership in America 1820–1980.* New York: Basic Books, 1982, p. 15.

33. Quoted in Anson Phelps Stokes, *Church and State in the United States.* Vol. II. New York: Harper Brothers, 1950, p. 687.

34. William T. Harris, "Religious Instruction in the Public School," *The Andover Review* XI (June 1889): 502.

35. William Elliot Griffin, "The Public Schools and Religion," *The Andover Review* XI (April 1889): 365.

36. Ibid.

37. J. R. Kendrick, "Romanizing the Public Schools," *Forum* VIII (September 1889): 74.

38. William Dempster Hoard, "Governor's Message," in *Governor's Message and Accompanying Documents of the State of Wisconsin 1889.* Vol. I. Madison: Democrat Printing Company, 1889, p. 18.

39. Agnew, et al., eds., *Dictionary of Wisconsin Biography,* p. 172; George W. Rankin, *William Dempster Hoard.* Fort Atkinson, WI: W. D. Hoard and Sons, 1925, p. 124.

40. Rankin, ibid., p. 210.

41. Ibid., p. 123.

42. *Biennial Report of the State Superintendent of the State of Wisconsin, for the Two Years Ending June 30, 1888.* Madison: Democrat Printing Company, 1888, p. 164.

43. Sister M. Justille McDonald, *History of the Irish in Wisconsin in the Nineteenth Century.* Washington, DC: The Catholic University of America Press, 1954, p. 214.

44. *The Laws of Wisconsin, Except City Charters and Their Amendments. Passed at the Biennial Session of the Legislature of 1889.* Vol. I. Madison: Democrat Printing Company, 1889, pp. 729–733.

45. *Milwaukee Sentinel,* March 19, 1890, p. 4.

46. Ibid., March 27, 1890, p. 2.

47. Ibid, March 28, 1890, p. 4.

48. Ibid, April 6, 1890, p. 11.

49. Ibid.

50. *Chicago Tribune,* April 10, 1890, p. 7.

51. *Milwaukee Sentinel,* May 28, 1890, p. 1.

52. Benjamin J. Blied, *Three Archbishops of Milwaukee.* Milwaukee: 1955, pp. 52–54.

53. *Milwaukee Sentinel,* May 28, 1890, p. 1.

54. Jesse B. Thayer, "Discussion," *National Education Association Journal of Proceedings and Addresses.* Topeka: Kansas Publishing House, Clifford C. Baker, 1890, p. 12.

55. *Minutes of the Wisconsin Baptist Anniversaries 1890.* Evansville: R. M. Antes, 1890, p. 30.

56. *Minutes of the Twenty-Ninth Anniversary of the Janesville Baptist Association 1890.* Brodhead: Independent Print, 1890, p. 12.

57. *Milwaukee Sentinel,* June 9, 1890, p. 3.

58. Ibid., May 12, 1890, p. 3.

59. "Our Schools," *Our Church Work,* IX, 5, February 20, 1890, p. 1.

60. *The Bennett Law.* Newspaper Clippings, dated April 1, 1890. A scrapbook in the Library of the State Historical Society of Wisconsin, Madison.

61. *Milwaukee Sentinel,* July 7, 1890, p. 7.
62. Ibid.
63. Ibid.
64. *Minutes of the Wisconsin Annual Conference of the Methodist Episcopal Church, Forty-Fourth Session 1890.* John Schneider, Editor and Publisher, 1890, p. 56.
65. Ibid., p. 57.
66. *Milwaukee Sentinel,* September 9, 1890, p. 3.
67. *Minutes of the Synod of Wisconsin of the Presbyterian Church 1890.* Madison: Tracy, Gibbs and Co., 1890, pp. 8–14.
68. Rev. Joseph H. Crooker, *The Public Schools and the Catholics.* Madison: H. A. Taylor, Printer and Stereotyper, 1890, pp. 3–5.
69. Ibid., p. 6.
70. Ibid., p. 7.
71. Ibid., pp. 9–10.

CHAPTER FOUR

The Hampton Model

~

After the post-Civil War Reconstruction, there was considerable ferment over the kind and amount of schooling that would be available to the freedmen. The ante-bellum ruling caste of whites and their successors returned to dominance in the former Confederacy; with their return came vastly diminishing opportunities for the former slaves, indeed, for all African Americans in the area. The "Hampton Model," as it has been called, served as a panacea for these whites in the kind of educational offerings available to African Americans, a curriculum with specific, limited, social goals for the freedmen.

Hampton Normal and Agricultural Institute opened its doors in Virginia in 1868 with an enrollment of twenty students.[1]* Initially, it was supported by funds from the Freedmen's Bureau and "northern friends" of its founder and first Principal, Samuel Chapman Armstrong.[2] The American Missionary Association (AMA), an abolitionist wing of the Congregationalist Church, had donated the land.[3]

The Institute was staffed by its Principal, Armstrong, a Treasurer, General F. B. Marshall (who had been with Armstrong's parents when they were missionaries in Hawaii),[4] a male farm manager, and five single women teachers who were "Christian ladies from the North."[5] The membership of the Board of Trustees also reflected AMA and northern influence. For instance, General O. O. Howard was a member, and the Reverend George Whipple of the New York-based AMA was its chairman.[6]

Hampton, according to its act of incorporation, was "to prepare youth of the south, without distinction of color, for the work of organizing and instructing schools in the southern States."[7] The institution was charged with diffusing throughout the South the "best advantages of education,"[8] by filling the void of agricultural and normal schools in that region. Originally established for all youth

---

* The overwhelming majority of the citations in this chapter were made possible through the "Courtesy of Hampton University Archives."

without "distinction of color," it soon was apparent that only African American students were attending.

Samuel Chapman Armstrong

The son of missionaries to Hawaii, Samuel Chapman Armstrong graduated from Williams College, where he had been taught by the famous Mark Hopkins, had served in the Union Army where he had risen to the rank of General and been placed in command of African American troops.[9] During Reconstruction he was assigned command over ten counties, including Hampton. It was then that he determined to found an industrial, normal and agricultural school for the freedmen. The Hampton Plan, as he reported, was based on his and General Marshall's twenty years of observation of the "educational system of the Sandwich Islands," which was introduced by American missionaries and "built up chiefly by the labors of the Rev. Richard Armstrong," his father, who was minister of public instruction there.[10] In his Founder's Day Address in 1902 Franklin Carter said that "love of the degraded natives of the Hawaiian Islands . . . was the original force that produced the heroic man, for which we thank God today."[11]

Hampton's Philosophy

Hampton's initial philosophy may most accurately be described as a blend of manual labor, which would instill discipline, which in turn would lead to self-control, to result in a moral person. This combination was founded on a pan-Protestant version of the Christian religion and was accompanied by some specific social and racial views.

Labor was first required of all students for the "purpose of discipline and instruction."[12] Hampton was to prepare its students for a life of usefulness, which was necessary because they came from families bereft of "right home influences."[13] Consequently, boarders were much preferred over day students. Hampton, Armstrong contended, was to fill a role in the South parallel to that of Harvard and Yale in the North.[14]

The benefits of student labor would be many. Needy students could pay their bills through work, and the high standards of discipline generated from the labor would weed out the unworthy through a "perfectly fair and firm administration" that would result in the "production of skilled, persevering teachers, of wise leaders, of peacemakers rather than noisy and dangerous demagogues."[15] Hampton's administration required white leaders, Armstrong maintained, because African Americans were unreliable. There were already too many "superficially educated leaders" who had the "most unlimited influence among the colored people." This phenomenon resulted in the classic case of the "blind leading the blind" and the "spread of the belief that political rights are obtained by political warfare than by advancement in knowledge and in ability to take care of themselves."[16] In 1875, subsequent to the development of some difficulties encountered with the labor system, e.g., "cost and day pupils,"[17] Armstrong still argued for the benefits of the alliance of labor and study, which if properly employed, would correct the "false standards of ordinary schools" and assert the superiority of character achieved by this alliance over scholarship.[18] So fortified, Hampton's graduates would be in a position to teach others the habits of living and labor, of general deportment, and the "right ideas of life and duty," which were indeed the "important lessons of life." Hampton's work, according to Armstrong, was "to civilize; class instruction is not all of it."[19]

Hampton's Racial Views

Hampton's educational philosophy was intrinsically connected with Armstrong's biased social and racial views during the 1870s. Repeatedly, he portrayed African Americans as existing in a depraved state, in absolute need of direction and guidance from whites, and of an education in keeping with their low status. The system he developed was to "be at once constructive of mental and moral worth, and destructive of the vices characteristic of the slave. What are those vices? They are improvidence, low ideas of honor and morality, and a general lack of directive energy, judgment and foresight."[20] The former slaves' "deficiencies of character are, I believe, worse for him and for the world than his ignorance." To send out teachers with "moral strength as well as of mental culture" was his aim. To do that, the system had a threefold aspect: "industrial, moral and intellectual, and disciplinary or administrative."[21]

Hampton was to educate "in the original and broadest sense of the word—to draw out a complete manhood." A course of study was designed that made "allies" of the "needle, the broom, and the wash-tub, the awl, the plane and the plow," of the "globe, the black-board and the text-book."[22] The "moral and intellectual" aspects were to be combined. Freedwomen were likewise in desperate need of this combination, both for themselves and for their men. The "freed woman is where slavery left her. Her average state is one of pitiable destitution of whatever should adorn and elevate her sex."[23]

Armstrong took special pride in the "disciplinary features" of the institution. To become a "strong and worthy man," the freedman was in need of "much external force, mental and moral, especially upon the plastic natures with whom we deal." The work "upon the heart is the most important of our work," which called for the teaching of the "vital precepts of the Christian faith, and of striving to awaken a genuine enthusiasm for the higher life."[24]

A year later Armstrong spoke to the training of African American teachers at Hampton, teachers who would labor in the racially separated schools that were extant in Virginia at that time. The normal school that would prepare them, he averred:

> . . . should strive quite as much to be a center of moral as of intellectual light, for defi-
> ciency of moral force and of self-respect are the chief misfortunes of the race. The tone of
> their society is low; the law of marriage and chastity is scarcely understood. It is vitally
> necessary that their course of Instruction should aim to enlighten their consciences and
> elevate their religious sentiments.[25]

Unless such a program was implemented, Armstrong warned, the teacher-graduates might participate in the "dangerous social and political combinations" that were being pushed by the race's "superficially educated leaders." The race's "plastic character" puts them completely under the control of their leaders, he argued, unable to take care of themselves.[26]

That Armstrong's views had widespread and influential support is evident from the "Report of the Committee of Visitors" to Hampton following their visit in 1873. They wrote:

> The colored race are not overrated, either morally or intellectually. On the contrary, their
> characteristic infirmities are distinctly recognized, and diligently combated. Conse-
> quently the immediate neighbors of the institution, and the white people of Virginia gen-
> erally, as they come to understand the matter, are more friendly from year to year. . . . and
> the negroes admit they will have themselves only to blame, if they go to the wall.[27]

Armstrong did not deviate in his opinion of African Americans. Writing in 1876, he described them as being in a period of "pupilage and docility," which required having their meals presided over, bathing mandated, personal attire inspected, and rooms visited daily.[28] The type of education fitting for the freedmen was possible only in boarding schools under the supervision of whites,[29] which ran counter to the ideas of some African American youth, who thought the "advantage of the more-favored classes" was in "book-knowledge."[30] These youths had suffered from faulty leadership of their own race, Armstrong contended, the "class of preachers, politicians, and editors."[31] Hampton's students in 1877 needed agricultural education, which provided a combination of labor, study, and discipline, because the students often hailed from cities, not from plantations, and as often had not experienced slavery.[32] The opponents to Hampton's charge of preparing "not only teachers but civilizers"[33] refused to recognize the mental capacity of the African Americans that Armstrong held to be "considerably below that of the average white youth."[34] The opposition to Hampton's programs for its students by African American leaders and newspaper editors, was countered, according to him, by the "commendation of intelligent southern men of every class," which was inevitable because Hampton had recognized the "deficiency of character" that was the major problem of the ex-slave.[35] He claimed that as a result of substituting the union of experiences and work for "pure schooling," there has been a "progress in southern sentiment in respect to the negro, readily apparent only to those who can look behind the front presented by politicians and periodicals."[36] Robert Church and Michael Sedlak point out that Armstrong believed that no African American could "claim equal status with the white until the entire black race as a whole had reached a higher level of moral culture"; Hampton was designed to train them to be able to "elevate their fellow freedmen's moral character. Classical education was irrelevant to that goal."[37] Further, these authors observed, Armstrong never said how long African Americans were to "remain inferior" and require a different education. Thus, he opened the door to those who opted for industrial training as a permanent feature for the education of African Americans.[38]

Armstrong reiterated these basic beliefs in the early 1880s. In his 1880 "Report," he commented that while lower-class African Americans were "passionately responsive to certain doctrines of Christianity," they did "not take kindly to its morality." The only antidote for this deficiency was "moral" work, not political remedies.[39] Overall, African American students had a weak "mental digestion," and it would take "generations" before they could reach the level of the whites. The most formidable obstacle to their progress remained a deficiency in "moral strength," because this stemmed from "inherited tendencies . . . like mill stones about their necks dragging them down."[40]

The Curriculum

Hampton's curriculum was geared to its purpose: to prepare students to teach schools for African Americans in the South, mostly in Virginia. Its focus on the value of work has been considered above, as has its aversion to college preparatory studies. The very name of the institution, Hampton Normal and Agricultural Institute, provides a strong indication of what the curriculum looked like. The three-year course of study in 1871–1872 was divided into the Normal Course, which included Language, Mathematics, History, Natural Science and "Miscellaneous," which incorporated instruction on Moral Science and Bible Lessons, to name but two. The other course of study embraced the Agricultural Course, the Commercial Course, and the Mechanical Course.[41] By 1882 the curriculum, while remaining basically the same as a decade earlier, had branched out to include the following departments: "Academic and Normal" (which now listed a pastor, a treasurer, instructors in military tactics, a resident physician, and sixteen instructors in "academic" subjects); a "Night School for Work Students," which encompassed "Preparatory Studies" and accounted for eight faculty; an "Indian Department," which counted twelve faculty; a "Women's Industrial Department," that was subdivided into three units: "Sewing and Tailoring," "Cooking," and "Household Work," with a total of eight personnel; and a "Men's Industrial Department," where seven males were employed in the "Huntington Industrial Works," "Agriculture," "Engineering, Machine Shop and Gas Works," "Painting Office," "Shoe Factory," and the "Indian Workshop."[42]

Enrollment

Twenty students greeted the opening of Hampton Institute when it opened its doors in 1868[43]; within a year enrollment had reached sixty-six, fifty-eight of whom were boarders.[44] Several years later there were 133 pupils enrolled in the year course, ranging in age from fourteen to twenty-five.[45] Candidates for admission were "expected to be able to read and write, and to pass a satisfactory examination in Arithmetic through Long Division." They were to provide testimonials of good character, to be of sound health, and to declare their intention to complete the three-year course of study. The *Catalogue* advised that "Preference will always be given to those who expect to become teachers."[46]

Armstrong reported in 1876 that attendance had reached 250, with forty-three being "day scholars." Attendance was irregular, however, due to "poverty," which made attendance average slightly over two hundred. Enrollment was "open," as reflected in Armstrong's remark that "Students are not all in before Christmas, and enter occasionally until March."[47]

The *Report* of 1879 pointed out a change in the demographics of enrollment. The total had reached 316, but not as many were from "schools maintained by Northern charity" (the Freedmen's Bureau Schools), which "prepared students well." Armstrong lamented that:

> The State schools which have taken their place have, except in the cities, but three or six months sessions, poor apparatus and usually inferior teaching. . . . Hampton attracts chiefly country youth who don't mind hard work and have had very few opportunities.[48]

The decline in quality of enrolling students accentuated the "weeding-out" process, which accounted for about twenty percent of the enrollees, "principally for weakness of character or for dumbness of intellect."[49]

Two years later Armstrong returned to this theme of incompetence, referring to the "deplorable illiteracy and dangerous ignorance" of the African American students who came to Hampton. He argued that the students from the mountains were superior to those from the tidewater area, though, because they displayed "more individuality," and a "finer temperament"; were "more energetic," supposedly due to "climate" and a "less repressive and more domestic form of slavery."[50]

By 1883 enrollment had climbed to 528, with thirty-five "teachers and officers," and a "plant" worth $350,000.[51] The student population now included 109 Native American students; Armstrong said that the "Indian question" was "one of honor and justice"; the "negro question" addressed the "salvation of the country."[52]

The Education and Work of Teachers

The overarching aim of Hampton Institute was to prepare "a body of colored teachers . . . thoroughly trained, not only in the requisite knowledge and best methods of teaching, but also in all that pertained to right living, including habits of intelligent labor."[53] Three years later, in 1872, Armstrong attested to the importance of teacher education to society in general and as part of Hampton's mission in particular:

> The teacher is a great power in society; always, indeed, in the background, but at sources of influence. Hence, a nobly endowed institution for training teachers becomes a strong pillar to the state; and, if properly surveyed, it will command respect for itself and its course among men of all opinions.[54]

In his appeal for funds the following year, Armstrong described Hampton"s work as follows:

> Can you make better use of seventy dollars a year, than by giving education to a colored student here who shall become a teacher? Can you, in any better way, fulfill your duty to the ignorant and unfortunate?[55]

The Work of Hampton's Graduates

In his 1872 "Report," Armstrong noted that twenty graduates of Hampton had already taught more than a year in either Virginia or North Carolina and that twenty-three more would soon join them. He argued that their work proved that Hampton's mission was a success.[56] Almost a decade later he contended that

Hampton's graduates had instructed about 30,000 students.[57] His annual "Reports" gave glowing accounts of their accomplishments. In 1873, he uttered a warning about the formidable challenges they would face:

> The work of our graduates as teachers has commended itself to many of the best men of the South, and promoted a better public opinion upon negro education. The ability of colored youth to acquire any degree of knowledge can no longer be doubted. The question now is whether they will hold out against the sensuality and corruption in the midst of which they will labor. The moral tone of negro society is appallingly low. The race needs enlightened consciences and pure religious sentiments. It is the aim of this institution to send out educators of high moral purpose, who will stand for principle rather than personal advancement and oppose the rising tide of corruption, created by bad living and political combinations, the radical idea of which is to get a living by something else than hard work.[58]

Armstrong often cited superintendents of schools as proof of the worth of Hampton graduates and of the magnitude of the challenges they faced. In 1872, for instance, Major W. W. Ballard of Roanoke County, one of a number of former Confederate officers who served as superintendent of schools at the time, wrote glowingly of two Hampton graduates who were employed as teachers in that division:

> I am gratified that . . . those from your institute realize the low state of morals existing among the colored people, and look upon the position they hold as so many levers to elevate from their deplorable state, those who are placed under their instruction.[59]

Hampton's growing reputation as a producer of good teachers contributed to the demand for their services, Armstrong maintained, especially since so "much of the work now done in colored schools is worthless" because of the lack of properly trained teachers.[60] The role of the teacher was broader than mere instruction. Armstrong penned that they were "not only routine teachers, but civilizers," that they would not be "mere pedagogues"[61]; that Virginia needed 1,000 more like them[62]; that "nearly every graduate conducts a Sunday-school and many of them are useful as evangelists"[63]; and that the "little army of Hampton's graduates is becoming a power."[64]

Armstrong looked to the Institute's graduates as yet another source of the proof of the value of their work. Their letters, which he called "encouraging," told of their work, their gratitude to their alma mater, the challenges that temperance posed to their people, the ignorance of their people, their low wages, and the incompetence of the African American ministers.[65] It was, one graduate wrote, "the principles instilled in me while at Hampton" that he would never forget and would keep him steadfast in his work.[66]

Impediments to the Graduates' Work

There was an occasional reference in Hampton's official documents to opposition to the Hampton rationale. As noted above, Armstrong had referred to the necessity of "weeding out" students with a bad attitude. In 1877, he complained of prejudice against the Hampton work ethic by African Americans from the "large cities," lamenting that "Eight years ago over one-half of our boys were good plowmen; now a good plowman is an exception." He also addressed African American opposition to the curriculum: "The absence of classical instruction, which is better appreciated than good reading and spelling, is a cause of complaint against Hampton in some colored circles."[67] He recognized that this viewpoint existed among some Hampton students, who thought that the "advantage of the more-favored classes is in book-knowledge, and it is hard to impress him with the value of ordinary good sense and the moderate worth of mere mental acquirement in the struggle of life."[68]

African American teachers were also singled out for criticism in this regard; they were influenced, he averred, by "preachers, politicians and editors of their own race." These people, he wrote:

> . . . resent the introduction of intelligent ideas into religion and the regulations of life. They could easily be conciliated by instituting Latin for labor. The colored people at large and their leading men, as a whole, are, however, most appreciative and give the school and its graduates the heartiest support. But negro opposition is no novelty.[69]

Armstrong praised the Hampton model he had forged for its effectiveness, maintaining that it held the solitary hope for African Americans, not only in the South, but also in the nation. His students, he said:

> . . . seek education less universally, but with a better idea of what it is. It is not the "Open Sesame" they once deemed it was. Freedom is disillusioned. "Salvation by hard work," is an understood thing. . . . The freedmen are working into more settled and pleasant relations with their neighbors. Although rum, demagogues and other evil influences within and without are pushing them down, yet I believe with long-continued and wise effort, and by infinite patience and care, that "the fate of the negro, the romance of American history" may become a bright record.[70]

The Night School

James Anderson wrote that the heart of Hampton's manual labor programs was put in place in 1879 when Armstrong established the night school with Booker T. Washington as its principal.[71] Students were required to work ten hours per day, six days per week, eleven months per year for two years.[72] Two years of night school work were equal to one year of the normal school course; in their final two years of normal school the students had to study four days and work two days each week. The night school embodied Hampton's social philosophy because it gave the staff ample opportunity to observe the students' character, work habits and political attitudes, which presented an opportunity to "weed out" students with undesirable attitudes before admitting them to the regular normal school.[73] It became more critical in Hampton's operation as the nineteenth century progressed. During the 1880s day-school enrollment declined significantly; by 1893, 305 of Hampton's 541 total enrollment was in the night school. Night-school students were "chiefly farm laborers, domestic servants, and mill hands."[74]

It is crucial to note that the students' industrial training was not technical, it involved a low level of trade training, and it was extremely limited.[75] In 1887, the students protested the kind and amount of work training they were receiving to no avail. Armstrong, meanwhile, wrote that at Hampton there "was no begging except for more work."[76] Anderson points out that black educators and writers attacked the Hampton version of industrial training in the 1880s and 1890s; it was not directed at all to vocational and technical training.[77]

Illustrations of the Hampton Model

The disagreements between Booker T. Washington and William E. B. DuBois over the kind of education the freedmen and their successors should receive are well-known. Two illustrations document the Hampton Model's influence. The first is the "kitchen garden," developed by Emily Huntington in New York in the late 1870s, which was incorporated into the Hampton Model.[78] A visit to Hampton in 1907 revealed that on Monday morning children dusted the room of "invisible dust" and then washed clothes with real water and soap. That afternoon they hoed and raked in the garden. The girls ironed, did paper-cutting and folding, and took care of their baby dolls on Tuesday morning; on Wednesday they made doll furniture. The class visited an orchard to watch a farmer planting on Thursday and then made farm tools. They cleaned house on Friday. Children were being trained for careers in domestic and agricultural occupations, as "much as, or more than, being educated in a Froebelian fashion."[79]

The second example is taken from the Phelps-Stokes African Education commissions, headed by Thomas Jesse Jones, a former member of the staff at Hampton. The commissions applied the theories of General Armstrong in the colonies of East Africa in the 1920s. William F. Russell, dean of Teachers College of Columbia University, commented that the reports showed that the South provided "examples of the best that is found in American education," and showed that the

South could teach not only the United States about education but also the rest of the world.[80]

Conclusion

In his highly praised book, *The Education of Blacks in the South, 1860–1935,* James Anderson is critical of the Hampton Model. He argues that "Armstrong represented a social class, ideology and world outlook that was fundamentally different from and opposed to the interests of the freedmen." He refers to what transpired at Hampton in 1868 as "a conjuncture of educational pedagogy and social ideology of different origins and character," than what the ex-slaves sought.[81] Hampton's importance in teacher education, the fact that it was the leader of its kind, has been obscured by the "traditional emphasis on its trade and technical aspects; its primary mission, though, was to prepare teachers for the segregated primary schools of the South."[82]

This task was to be accomplished through the combination of work and Christianity, mixed with specific racial views that were permeated with a specific socio-political view. Leading northerners took an active role in this program. In 1883, for instance, eleven of the sixteen Trustees hailed from New York, New Jersey, Connecticut, Pennsylvania, or Massachusetts.[83]

It is clear that in its early years Hampton Institute reflected and influenced the prevailing view of African Americans on the part of the ruling white class, i.e, that they were of an inferior class in dire need of "civilizing" action by whites. The curriculum of Hampton was forged by the view that wedded labor and practical study, with the expected results of self-discipline, self-control, moral growth and, to a controlled extent, economic self-sufficiency for its graduates. It would then be the solemn duty of these graduates to communicate this message to the offspring of the freedmen in schools and to see that its philosophy was accepted by their fellows, who would accept their "place" in the post-Reconstruction South. Hampton's teacher graduates were to do their utmost to have African Americans be an economic asset to the South and to teach students to accept their political and economic subordination to whites in a white-dominated southern society of that and subsequent eras.[84] For this kind of society, the Hampton Model indeed constituted a panacea.

Notes

1. *Report upon the Hampton Normal and Agricultural Institute.* Hampton, VA: July 1869, p. 4; *Catalogue of the Hampton Normal and Agriculture Institute, for the Academic Year 1871–72.* Hampton, VA: Printed at the Normal School Press, 1872, p. 3.

2. *Catalogue, 1871–72*, p. 3.
3. Ibid., p. 4.
4. "Report of the Principal," *Reports of the Officers of the Hampton Normal and Agricultural Institute, Hampton, Virginia, for the Academical and Fiscal Year ending June 30, 1878*. Hampton, VA: Normal School Steam Press, 1878, p. 14.
5. *Catalogue, 1871–1872*, p. 5.
6. Ibid.
7. *Report, 1869*, p. 3.
8. Ibid.
9. Franklin Carter, "General Armstrong's Life and Work," Founder's Day Address, 1902. Hampton Institute, January 26, 1902, pp. 5–7.
10. *Report, 1878*, p. 14.
11. Carter, "General Armstrong's Life and Work," p. 7.
12. *Catalogue, 1871–72, p. 16*.
13. "Report of the Principal," ibid., p. 20.
14. Ibid., p. 21.
15. Ibid., p. 22.
16. Ibid., p. 28.
17. "Report of the Principal," *Reports of the Hampton Normal and Agricultural Institute, for the Fiscal Year, ending June 30, 1875*. Hampton, VA: Normal School Steam Press, 1875, pp. 6–7.
18. "Report of the Principal," *Reports of the Hampton Normal and Agricultural Institute, for the Fiscal Year, ending June 30, 1876*. Hampton, VA: Normal School Steam Press, 1876, p. 7.
19. "Report of the Principal," *Reports, 1875*, p. 7.
20. Armstrong, "Report of the Principal," *Catalogue, 1870–1871*, quoted in Robert H. Bremner, ed., *Children and Youth in America: A Documentary History*. Vol. 2. Cambridge, MA: Harvard University Press, 1971, p. 1193.
21. Ibid., pp. 1193–1194.
22. Ibid., p. 1194.
23. Ibid., p. 1195.
24. Ibid., p. 1196.
25. Armstrong, "The Training of Negro Teachers at Hampton, 1871–1872," *Catalogue, 1871–1872*, quoted in Bremner, ed., ibid., p. 1197.
26. Ibid.
27. "Report of the Committee of Visitors to Hampton Institute (1873)," quoted in Sol Cohen, ed., *Education in the United States: A Documentary History*. Vol. 3. New York: Random House, 1974, p. 1654.
28. "Report of the Principal," *Reports, 1876*, p. 9; "Report of the Principal," *Reports, 1875*, p. 8.
29. "Report of the Principal," *Reports, 1878*, p. 11.
30. "Report of the Principal," *Reports of the Hampton Normal and Agricultural Institute, for the Fiscal Year, ending June 30, 1877*. Hampton, VA: Normal School Steam Press, 1877, p. 6.
31. "Report of the Principal," *Reports, 1878*, p. 9.
32. "Report of the Principal," *Reports, 1877, p. 7*.
33. "Report of the Principal," *Reports, 1878*, p. 11.
34. "Report of the Principal," *Reports, 1877*, p. 6.
35. "Report of the Principal," *Reports, 1878*, p. 11.
36. Ibid., p. 14.
37. Robert L. Church and Michael W. Sedlak, *Education in the United States: An Interpretive History*. New York: The Free Press, 1976, p. 205.

38. Ibid., p. 206.

39. "Report of the Principal," *Reports of the Hampton Normal and Agricultural Institute, for the Fiscal Year, ending June 30, 1880.* Hampton, VA: Normal School Steam Press, 1880, p. 10.

40. Ibid.

41. *Catalogue of the Hampton Normal and Agricultural Institute, for the Academic Year 1871–72.* Hampton, VA: Normal School Steam Press, 1872, p. 6.

42. *Catalogue of the Hampton Normal and Agricultural Institute, for the Academic Year 1882–83.* Hampton, VA: Institute Steam Press, 1883, pp. 5–8.

43. *Catalogue 1871–72*, p. 3.

44. *Report 1869, p.* 4.

45. *Catalogue 1871–72*, pp. 7–13.

46. Ibid., p. 13.

47. "Report of the Principal," *Reports, 1876*, p. 3.

48. "Report of the Principal," *Reports, 1879*, p. 5.

49. Ibid., p. 6.

50. Ibid.

51. "Report of the Principal," *Annual Reports of the Hampton Normal and Agricultural Institute for the Academical and Fiscal Year ending June 30, 1883.* Hampton, VA: Normal School Steam Press, 1883, p. 5.

52. Ibid.

53. *Report upon the Hampton Normal and Agricultural Institute, 1869*, p. 3.

54. *Catalogue of the Hampton Normal and Agricultural Institute, for the Academic Year 1871–72*, p. 20.

55. Ibid., p. 24.

56. Ibid., p. 22.

57. "Report of the Principal," *Reports, 1879, pp.* 9–10

58. "Report of the Principal," *Reports, 1872*, p. 27.

59. "Report of the Principal," *Catalogue, 1873*, pp. 27–28. The practice of hiring former Confederate officers to serve as supervisors of the African American teachers was common. They were also often highly commended. For instance, Armstrong praised them for their "excellent supervision" in Norfolk ("Report of the Principal," *Reports, 1879*, p. 10).

60. "Report of the Principal," *Reports, 1877*, p. 5.

61. "Report of the Principal," *Reports, 1878*, pp. 10–11.

62. "Report of the Principal," *Reports,1875*, p. 9.

63. "Report of the Principal," *Report of the Hampton Normal and Agricultural Institute, for the Year ending June 30, 1874.* Hampton, VA: Normal School Steam Press, 1874, p. 6.

64. "Report of the Principal," *Reports, 1878*, p. 9.

65. Eunice C. Dixon, "Report on Graduates," *Annual Reports of the Hampton Normal and Agricultural Institute, for the Year ending June 30, 1882.* Hampton, VA: Normal School Steam Press Print, 1882, p. 10.

66. Miss A. E. Cleveland, "Report on Graduates," *Reports, 1882*, p. 6.

67. "Report of the Principal," *Reports, 1877*, p. 5.

68. Ibid., p. 6.

69. "Report of the Principal," *Reports, 1878*, p. 9.

70. Ibid., p. 14.

71. James D. Anderson, *The Education of Blacks in the South, 1860–1935.* Chapel Hill: The University of North Carolina Press, 1988, p. 54.

72. Ibid., pp. 54–55.

73. Ibid., p. 55.
74. Ibid.
75. Ibid., p. 59.
76. Ibid., pp. 60–61.
77. Ibid., pp. 64–65.
78. Barbara Beatty, "Child Gardening: The Teaching of Young Children in American Schools," in Donald R. Warren, ed., *American Teachers: Histories of a Profession at Work*. New York: Macmillan, 1989, p. 80.
79. Ibid.
80. Lawrence A. Cremin, *American Education: The Metropolitan Experience 1876–1980*. New York: Harper and Row, 1988, pp. 222–223.
81. Anderson, *The Education of Blacks in the South*, p. 33.
82. Ibid.
83. "Trustees," *Report, 1883*, p. 2.
84. See Anderson, *The Education of Blacks in the South*, pp. 33–78, for his overall interpretation of the Hampton Model.

CHAPTER FIVE

The Era of Social Efficiency

Part I. Immigration, Urbanization, and Industrialization

William C. Bagley described social efficiency as "the standard by which the forces of education must select the experiences that are impressed upon the individual."[1] Basically, the term meant subordinating the individual to society with as little waste as possible. Social efficiency was to become the dominant movement in American education in the early years of the twentieth century. Heavily influenced by urbanization, industrialization, and immigration, social efficiency was to make its mark in all aspects of American urban schools. For some educators, business leaders, and assorted others it was the panacea of their times.

Immigration

Slightly more than three-quarters (7,880,630 of 10,373,628) of the immigrants who came to this nation's shores between 1861 and 1890 hailed from northern and western Europe; approximately eleven percent (1,182,930) came from southern and eastern Europe. Those figures changed drastically in the next thirty years, beginning with 1891, when about twenty-five percent (3,643,752 of 18,218,761) came from the north and west of Europe and just over sixty-three percent (11,520,593) arrived from the south and east of Europe.[2] Many of these later arrivals settled in the northeastern part of the United States. They were a source of cheap labor for the many factories in that section of the country. As a result, the population of the northeastern states and their metropolitan centers increased notably. For example, over one-half of the population of Connecticut, Massachusetts, New Jersey, New York, and Rhode Island in 1910 was either foreign-born or had at least one parent born in a foreign country.[3] New York City had a population of four million in

1914, compared with 850,000 in 1860; Philadelphia grew from 563,000 to more than 1,500,000 in that same period.[4]

About ten million Bohemians, Greeks, Hungarians, Poles, Rumanians, Russians, and Slovaks entered the United States between 1890 and 1914.[5] They were greeted, in some instances, with public expressions of hostility and were regarded as "undesirable" by some native white Americans. Senator Morrill of Vermont represents an example of political hostility. He argued that the nation had no responsibility to become a "universal almsgiver," offering hospitality to "all classes of alien irreclaimable maniacs, mendicants and miscreants." The country had no compulsion, in his opinion, to support the "weak, vile and hungry outcasts" from Europe who had come here "not only to stay themselves but to transmit hereditary taints to the third and fourth generation."[6]

The recent arrivals spurred the growth and expression of social concerns as well. The American Protective Association was formed in 1887. The Immigration Restriction League was created to oppose unrestricted immigration. Its literature asserted that southern and eastern Europe were dumping large numbers of "illiterates, paupers, criminals, and madmen" into the United States, which was endangering the nation and its way of life.[7] The League spoke of four European races that should not be mixed. They were the "Teuton," the "Nordic," the "Alpine," and the "Mediterranean." It claimed that the first two of these four were far superior to the latter two and should avoid social interaction with them.[8]

"Scholarly" persons lent support to this view of the immigrants. For instance, Madison Grant, a New York aristocrat and President of the Museum of Natural History, wrote that the western Europeans were "always and everywhere a race of soldiers, sailors, adventurers, and explorers, but above all of rulers, organizers and aristocrats in sharp contrast to the essentially peasant character of the Alpines."[9] Edward A. Ross, a prominent sociologist, expanded on this idea. He argued that the new immigration, flowing from "different sources" tapped "lower human levels" than did the earlier. These "beaten members of beaten breeds, often the more aboriginal men that have been elbowed aside or left behind in the swayings of the mightier European races," could not but adversely affect the nation. They were, Ross wrote, "As undersized in spirit, no doubt as they are in body," and would necessarily "impede our progress." It could not be otherwise, he stated, because "The cheap stucco manikins do not really take the place of the unbegotten sons of the granite men who fell at Gettysburg and Cold Harbor."[10]

Educational leaders, faced with a huge influx of immigrant children into the schools of the nation's eastern cities, reacted with similar alarm. The following statistics show how immigration affected the schools. In 1909, 57.8 percent of the students in the schools of thirty-seven of the nation's largest cities were either immigrants themselves or the children of foreign-born fathers.[11] Over one-half of the students who were children of foreign-born fathers from non-English speaking countries came from homes where English was not spoken.[12] In one New York City classroom there were children from twenty-five different nationalities.[13]

Educators voiced their concerns at meetings, in journals, and in books. As early as 1890, one speaker at the National Education Association (NEA) convention praised the high school for the benign influence it had on the children of workers. He claimed that high school education lifted the curtain from the minds of these children that their social class had imposed on them.[14] Seven years later the state superintendent of New York's schools declared at the NEA that the children of the "plain people" were filling the schools, with the result that in a short time the "children of the masses and not of the classes will rule us."[15] One writer editorialized that immigration had placed the industries of the urban northeast "in a state of perpetual siege by an army of semi-savages."[16]

Ellwood P. Cubberley, one of the leaders in the developing field of educational administration, described the pernicious effect he said the immigrants had, and would continue to have, on American society:

> Largely illiterate, docile, lacking in initiative and almost wholly without the Anglo-Saxon conceptions of righteousness, liberty, law, order, public decency, and government, . . . their coming has served to dilute tremendously our national stock and to weaken and corrupt our political life.

They had caused "popular education" to become "everywhere . . . more difficult by their presence," Cubberley maintained.[17]

Others made similar arguments. Granville Stanley Hall, a leading child psychologist, was one of these. He spoke of the "great army of incapables" who were descending in droves on the public schools.[18] Two decades later, Lewis M. Terman, a leader in the field of intelligence testing who was well-known for his work with gifted children, remarked that "The racial stocks most prolific of gifted children are those from northern and western Europe, and the Jewish. The least prolific are the Mediterranean races, the Mexicans and the Negroes."[19]

As it regularly does in times of crisis, the nation looked to its schools for assistance. This time the schools were called upon to "civilize" or "Americanize" this horde of inferior foreigners, who were necessary to provide an ample supply of cheap labor for the country's burgeoning industries. One editorial looked to the schools as the "hope of salvation" for the "undisciplined and uncouth hordes of foreigners."[20] The director of Americanization in the United States Bureau of Education maintained that the schools ought to be "the hub upon which all the other forces of the state and community" revolved when working with immigrants.[21] Edward A. Ross described the formative role of the school in this social context as follows:

> To collect little plastic lumps of human dough from private households and shape them on the social kneedingboard, exhibits a faith in the power of suggestion which few people

ever attain to. And so it happens that the role of the schoolmaster in the social economy is just beginning.[22]

According to Ross, the school should promote order, serve as an economic system of police, and replace religion as "the method of indirect social restraint."[23]

Cubberley was of similar mind. To him the vast numbers of "foreigners" in the nation called for herculean efforts on the part of school people. Their task, as he saw it, was:

. . . to implant in their children, so far as can be done, the Anglo-Saxon conception of righteousness, law and order, and popular government, and to awaken in them a reverence for our democratic institutions and for those things in our national life which we as a people hold to be of abiding worth.[24]

Schooling became, as Richard Pratte says, the major if not the only educative force in society in the eyes of some public educators.[25] Some educators of the time, such as social efficiency advocate David Snedden, felt that the school was in a unique position to influence society, since it alone of all institutions was completely under state control.[26] Indeed, with so many immigrants as their students, the schools became, as Lawrence Cremin has observed, foster parents to immigrant children.[27]

This role cast the school in a powerful position. Sometimes, as with school baths in New York City, it operated as a humane force. At other times, imbued with some of the feelings toward immigrants described above, it was not so humane. In fact, in some instances the school became a divisive wedge between immigrant parents and their children. For example, one immigrant mother protested that the public schools had taught her children to despise their parents. A son, brought to trial for physically resisting his father's attempt to discipline him, argued that an American (himself) should not "get licked" by a foreigner (his father).[28] Instances such as these prompted Jane Addams to complain to the NEA in 1909 that the public school had often divided immigrant parents and their children. She urged that the schools welcome the immigrants into the mainstream of American society "upon the basis of the resources which they represent and the contributions which they bring."[29] Six years later she expressed a similar concern, asking "Why should that chasm between fathers and sons, yawning at the feet of each generation, be made so unnecessarily cruel and impassable to these bewildered immigrants?"[30]

The schools were not always able, even if willing, to follow Miss Addams' entreaties. There were a number of reasons for this. In addition to those identified above, there was the concern about the impending global conflict. The nation wanted to be sure of the loyalty of its recent arrivals; consequently, Civics and American History courses were extended and intensified in the schools. American heroes were extolled, and "American" virtues were praised in texts and in the lessons of teachers. Citizenship education took on the highest priority in the aims of schools, culminating in the Cardinal Principles Report of 1918 (more will be said of this report in the next chapter).

The Corporate Influence

American industry grew phenomenally in the last decade of the nineteenth century. It continued to expand at a rapid rate in the first few decades of the twentieth century. Some thought this industrial growth, brought about by corporate activity, was a sign of unmitigated progress. Through it the nation, by harnessing and controlling its resources, had become a world power.[31] The nation, a partner with other industrial nations of the western world, was ready to participate, according to Ross, in the "superior" form of culture the white man, who "spreads his economic gospel, one hand on a Gatling, the other on a locomotive," possessed through technology.[32]

American corporate enterprise, its principles, organization, and practices, became worthy, in the eyes of some, of almost unadulterated adulation. Other American institutions, including the schools, looked to (or were advised to look to) industry for a model to emulate. In 1894, for instance, the NEA officially praised President Grover Cleveland for his "wisdom and firmness" with which he broke up the Pullman strike.[33] A year later the U.S. commissioner of education advised the nation's school superintendents that they would obtain their best support from conservative business leaders.[34] Oscar T. Corson, president of the NEA, addressed the convention in 1900 and stressed how important it was for educators to rely on business people for advice and support and gain a business mentality themselves:

> Our real educational experts are not the visionary theorists whose opinions change so often as to make them practically worthless, but the thoughtful, conservative men and women whose business sense leads them carefully to consider the conditions which actually do exist. . . . The real educational leaders of this age whose influence will be permanent are those who have the business capacity to appreciate and comprehend the business problems which are always a part of the educational problem.[35]

Corson urged school leaders to maintain their ties with business, advocating that care should be taken lest "business and educational management of our schools" be separated, which would result in the development of "the false idea that business and education have nothing in common."[36]

The schools, by means of the business techniques they would adopt, could then prepare the young for a wasteless, "efficient," service as adults. Almost unlimited benefits would accrue to society if business procedures were followed. As

Callahan noted, evidence of business influence was seen again at the NEA convention in 1905, when the first topic of a symposium on the "Most Promising Subjects" for the NEA to pursue was entitled "Comparison of Modern Business Methods with Educational Methods." The speaker, George Martin, told the audience that by comparison, "educational processes seem unscientific, crude, and wasteful."[37] Indications that educators had accepted the business ideology appeared a few years later when William C. Bagley wrote in his book *Classroom Management* that problems of classroom management were fundamentally a "problem of economy: it seeks to determine in what manner the working unit of the school plant may be made to return the largest dividend upon the material investment of time, energy, and money."[38] Bagley wrote in the book, which went through thirty printings between 1907 and 1927, and which was written for training teachers, that "unquestioned obedience" was the "first rule of efficient service" for the teacher, whose situation was "entirely analogous to that in any other organization or system—the army, navy, governmental, great business enterprises (or small business enterprises, for that matter)."[39]

Enter Leonard P. Ayres and his study of retardation and elimination in schools, titled *Laggards in Our Schools.* Ayres contended that American urban schools were filled with retarded children (by retarded he meant overage for their grade regardless of how well they were doing in school). He also claimed that a majority of students dropped out prior to completing elementary school. Though he took no notice of social or economic factors, he found the schools responsible for the below-standard academic performance of the children.[40]

The schools were guilty of wasting the taxpayers' dollars, he argued, because they were not educating their pupils efficiently. Ayres developed an "Index of Efficiency," which he applied to the schools. In so doing, he was one of the first to picture the school as a factory and apply business and industrial values and practices to the schools. He wrote of the "money cost" of the repeater, and said that the process of repeating grades cost the taxpayers annually "about twenty-seven million dollars in our cities alone."[41]

Other critics, journalists and others, joined in the chorus of censure of the schools. In 1914, Dr. J. M. Rice wrote that:

> I have discovered not only the fundamental cause of the unsatisfactory results that are found in so many of the elementary schools of our country, but also a remedy that is capable of eliminating it. Moreover, the remedy does not partake of the nature of a fad . . . because it means no less than the introduction of scientific management into the conduct of our schools.[42]

It was an engineer, however, who took up the cause of "Scientific Management" and popularized it. Frederick W. Taylor held that attention must be focused on the worker in order to bring him up to his highest potential of productivity. This was the goal of the plant manager, because it meant the most efficient operation (the most profit at least cost) of the industry. Taylor's ideas were applied to the administration of public schools.

The wide-ranging criticism of public schools during the period 1911–1913, which focused on their alleged inefficiency, set the stage for Taylorism to enter the practices and goals of school administrators and planners.[43] In the wake of Ayres' criticism, Simon N. Patten of the University of Pennsylvania wrote in *The Educational Review* that the public school system was inefficient. He demanded that schools produce evidence of their usefulness to society or suffer budget cuts. The schools were to deliver "an education that increases efficiency and augments income. Educators must drop their platitudes and put the schools in a position to aid industrial progress." Patten argued that unless they could "stand objective tests such as other social reforms offer," schools deserved to lose their fiscal support. Failure to enact efficiency reforms would prevent the nation from having an "education worthy of the name."[44]

Callahan reported that criticisms such as Patten's, an "intemperate, anti–intellectual attack in which he both misunderstood and grossly oversimplified the educational process,"[45] were having their effect on the public. One evidence of this was an editorial "What Is the Matter?," which appeared in the *Ladies' Home Journal* in the fall of 1911. It reported an increase in dissatisfaction with schools by their readers.[46]

Educators were jolted further at the meeting of the Department of Superintendence of the NEA in the fall of 1912. They were reminded of the "new processes, new labor-saving devices, new methods of planning, more detailed instructions, more exacting records" that were being used in industry. The speaker, the secretary of the Permanent Census Board in New York City, urged educators to follow suit. How else, he asked, could the educator justify himself "when the businessman complains of his product?"[47]

Two popular periodicals, *The Saturday Evening Post* and the *Ladies' Home Journal,* joined in the attack upon the schools. The latter's approach is especially interesting. Its "crusade" began in the August 1912 issue with an editorial entitled "The Case of 17 Million Children: Is Our Public-School System Proving an Utter Failure?"[48] The returns did not justify the investment, the editor concluded. The *Journal* followed up with an article by Ella Frances Lynch, a former teacher, "Is the Public School a Failure? It Is: The Most Momentous Failure in Our American Life Today." Lynch maintained that the public school system, "as at present conducted, is an absolute and total failure." Schools spent "over four-hundred-and-three million dollars each year" to turn out "every year ninety-three out of every one hundred children . . . absolutely unfitted for even the simplest tasks."[49]

Several other articles continued the indictment. One quoted the dean of Teachers College, James E. Russell, to the effect that "our educational system is wasteful and inefficient."[50] The *Journal's* final assault came with a stirring critique by H. Martyn Hart, dean of St. John's Cathedral in Denver. Hart blamed the school for all of society's ills and laid that blame to inefficiency:

> The people have changed but not the system; it has grown antiquated and will not meet our present needs; it has indeed become a positive detriment and is producing a type of character which is not fit to meet virtuously the temptations and exigencies of modern life. The crime which stalks almost unblushingly through the land; the want of responsibility which defames our social honor; the appalling frequency of divorce; the utter lack of self-control; the abundant use of illicit means to gain political positions; are all traceable to its one great and crying defect—inefficiency.[51]

The "Efficient" Curriculum

Taylor and his backers had claimed great things for scientific management, among them the argument that its implementation would bring about:

> . . . the substitution of peace for war; the substitution of hearty brotherly cooperation for contention and strife; of both pulling hard in the same direction instead of pulling apart; of replacing suspicious watchfulness with mutual confidence; of becoming friends instead of enemies.[52]

Leading educators spoke glowingly of the potential scientific management presented them. George Strayer of Teachers College proclaimed that it led to "in the school field, no less than in other situations, demanding organizing and administrative genius, the result of investments is being measured."[53] The curriculum was a major "investment." Superintendent Frank E. Spaulding of Newton, Massachusetts, thought it undesirable to purchase Greek instruction at the rate of 5.9 pupil recitations per dollar. "The price must go down," he announced, "or we shall invest in something else."[54] Principal William L. Felter thundered in June of 1914: "Latin, justify thy presence in a twentieth century American high school curriculum!"[55]

The leader of the field of "scientific" curriculum was John Franklin Bobbitt. He deplored the waste that he asserted was widespread in schooling. Bobbitt felt, among other things, that the school plant should be used more. This was especially so since not only were the valuable plants lying idle on Saturday and Sunday but also the "street and alley time" of the weekends was undoing the "good work of the schools."[56]

There was no question in Bobbitt's mind about what the school curriculum needed. He proclaimed that the factory metaphor should be applied to how curriculum should be constructed:

> Work up the raw material into that finished product for which it is best adapted. Applied to education this means: Educate the individual according to his capabilities. This requires that the materials of the curriculum be sufficiently various to meet the needs of every class of individuals in the community; and that the course of training and study be sufficiently flexible that the individual can be given just the things he needs.[57]

This curriculum construction was possible because there were certain principles of management that had "universal applicability."[58] It was the manager's duty to set specific, measurable standards before the work commenced. Curriculum planning could, therefore, be reduced to a series of steps.[59] If a teacher could not meet these specific, pre-planned, scientifically derived objectives, then she or he was inefficient.[60] Bobbitt argued that the "intellectualists" were in support of vague, undefined objectives and were opposed to the field of scientific curriculum.[61] Those responsible for overseeing the process, thereby ensuring its scientific nature, were laymen from the field of business joined with school administrators; it was a task beyond the teachers' capability.[62]

Bobbitt had a host of allies. One of these, David Snedden, attempted to differentiate the curriculum so that the right objectives, scientifically predetermined, would be applied to the correct "case groups."[63] Snedden held that sociologists could "within reasonable probability" determine the "vocational destination of the learner."[64] Sociology was thus empowered to measure and predict the most appropriate slot for each child; thus, educators could determine the most efficient curriculum for students, one "with considerable precision" and "expert judgment as to what the next generation of workers" in various fields should study.[65] All done scientifically, of course.

Enter the Testing Expert

According to Geraldine Joncich (Clifford), Edward L. Thorndike "epitomized the scientific impulse in education."[66] His work was to provide the "scientific" basis for differentiating curriculum for students. Thorndike joined the faculty of Teachers College in 1899 and remained there until the 1930s.[67] He separated psychology from philosophy and held that the sciences, especially psychology, should benefit education.[68] Thus aided, schools would run efficiently. This would be true in two ways: 1) the methods employed in school would be in accordance with the child's nature; and 2) results, or tests, would determine the efficacy of the teaching method used.[69] Thorndike argued that the aims of schools should be stated in quantitative terms so they could be measured.[70] Teaching, indeed all of education, would be scientific if these tenets were followed.

Thorndike subscribed to social views that fit snugly into the context of the first several decades of the twentieth-century United States. Because his claim was made in the name of science, he gave credibility to positions that heretofore had lacked that status. For instance, he believed that environment was most likely of little import in determining a person's intelligence or character: "it is unsafe to assume that the differences found amongst individuals in intellect, character and skill are due chiefly to the different opportunities which the individuals have enjoyed."[71]

For Thorndike, superior intelligence was a scientific sign of other qualities as well. Intelligence was related to morality: "To him that hath a superior intellect is given also on the average a superior character."[72] Late in life he re-emphasized that position:

> It is the great good fortune of mankind that there is a substantial positive correlation between intelligence and morality, including good will towards one's fellows. Consequently our superiors in ability are on the average our benefactors, and it is often safer to trust our interests to them than to ourselves. No group of men can be expected to act one hundred per cent in the interest of mankind, but this group of the ablest men will come nearest to that ideal.[73]

Who were this group of "ablest men"? They were the Carnegies, the Rockefellers, and other corporate leaders. Thorndike opposed criticism of these men. He maintained that the rich had amassed their fortunes not by greed, by political favor or by the ruthless use of power, but by their superior intelligence.[74] Thus, a man such as Carnegie, whose income was estimated at ten million dollars annually from 1894 through 1899, was both a person of superior intelligence and someone upon whom people could depend due to his excellent character.[75]

Thorndike's intelligence tests were widely used. They were employed by many industries and by the U.S. Army in World War I as well as in schools.[76] Educators regarded them as the scientific assessors of the student's intelligence. Individuals differed in intelligence, according to Thorndike, due to their original nature, "as in stature or eye color."[77] Since his tests discerned this native intelligence level scientifically, they provided school people an infallible measure of distinguishing between students' abilities. Subsequent differentiation in curricula followed. This led, as Merle Curti pointed out, to scientific curriculum differentiation for the different social classes with increased specialization of instruction.[78] Little wonder, then, that his research was welcomed with a fond embrace by the followers of Taylor, Bobbitt, and Snedden.

Thorndike was no friend of the African American or the southern or eastern European immigrant. He maintained that the differences between African American and white students in high schools in a large city in the north central area of the United States showed the whites to be far superior in basic intelligence.[79] As for the immigrants, Thorndike lent his voice to the chorus of those who sought sterilization of the inadequate, the restriction of immigration from southern and eastern Europe, and the placing of immigrant children in the lower tracks of the curriculum where they were scientifically destined to be.[80] Thorndike apparently gave little credence to the view that fluency with the language used in the tests would affect how children scored on them.

Thorndike disagreed with the social ameliorists of the day, such as Lester Frank Ward. In a review of Ward's *Applied Sociology* he wrote: "The benefits of knowledge might need universal and equal distribution, but the knowledge itself be handed on but to a few." These few, he argued, can do more for the world's knowledge than would the attempt to equalize educational opportunity, which he termed "intellectual communism."[81] He opposed compulsory school attendance supported by public taxation, since the practice forced the distribution of schooling to those least able to benefit from it, children "who have neither the ability nor the interest to profit thereby."[82]

What would uplift the social condition of Americans for Thorndike? Not universal schooling, but the "beneficence of Mr. Carnegie and Mr. Rockefeller and others" would improve humankind's lot.[83] Even their generosity was but a temporary respite. In 1940, Thorndike felt that selective breeding and sterilization would be necessary if the human race were to improve its social situation permanently:

> By selective breeding supported by a suitable environment we can have a world in which all men will equal the top ten per cent of present men. One sure service of the able and good is to beget and rear offspring. One sure service (about the only one) which the inferior and vicious can perform is to prevent their genes from survival.[84]

Thorndike's educational theories offered the scientific base to education that administrative and curricular leaders had sought. Unfortunately, along with the service Thorndike gave to psychology and education, his social views, based on his intelligence testing, were regarded as equally scientific. Millions of children were tested, evaluated, and channeled according to his, and others', work in testing. This resulted in massive discrimination, as Clarence Karier observed, because children who were immigrants themselves or the children of immigrants often had a very inadequate understanding of the language in which the tests were given.[85] For, after all, modeled on the successful man, Thorndike insisted his tests could be used to scientifically determine intelligence, morality, and even endurance.[86] As Boyd Bode has remarked, Thorndike's work on individual differences was used to support undemocratic theories of education.[87] In his glorification of the successful man, he overlooked the inequalities that existed in American society, especially in urban areas.[88] Perhaps this was inevitable, given his emphasis on heredity over environment. While he may not have intentionally fostered a rigidly stratified society, at least his testing movement offered no opposition to that phenomenon.[89]

It is difficult to overestimate Thorndike's influence on education, particularly given the hunger for scientific, efficient operation so prevalent in his time. One of the most enlightening proofs to the extent of that influence was the special issue of the respected educational journal, *Teachers College Record*, which was dedicated to him in 1926. Entitled "In Honor of Edward L. Thorndike," it paid tribute to his contributions to Animal Psychology, Heredity, Laws of Learning, Child Psychology, Individual Differences, Psychology of Intelligence, Educational Administration, Statistics, Elementary School Subjects, General Education, Educational Measurement, and Current Investigation.[90] Perhaps the remarks made by George W. Strayer, a leading educational administrator who had accepted the scientific management ideas of Frederick W. Taylor, testify best of all to the impact Thorndike had on education. Among Thorndike's accomplishments, according to Strayer were:

> The homogeneous grouping of children, the provision of special classes for the handicapped and for the more able pupils, the differentiated courses of study in the junior and senior high schools, together with the organization which makes possible these adjustments, are based upon the scientifically determined facts that individuals vary in ability.[91]

Strayer continued his plaudits with the statement that "Those of us fortunate enough to be students in his classes" were "indebted to him primarily for guidance in our attempts to apply the scientific method."[92] Strayer wrote that before Thorndike:

> It was not possible to attack scientifically the problem of classification of pupils, the admission of young men and women to college and university, or to diagnose adequately the particular difficulties under which pupils labored until these more accurate instruments of measurement were available. The administrator in public or private schools and in colleges and universities has become a scientific worker because of the technique developed by Professor Thorndike in the measurement of intelligence and in the derivation of tests.[93]

Conclusion

Social efficiency was the dominant force in early twentieth century urban American schooling. Abetted by industrial growth and dislike for and fear of the many recent immigrants, coupled with the near-worship of the "scientific" techniques of corporate America, and sealed with the "objective" data presented by scientific testing, the movement gained widespread support. Curti contended that, with but few exceptions, educational leaders accepted the ideas and practices of corporate business, supported them by scientific data obtained through testing, and applied the results to the administration and curriculum of schools.[94] Even many liberals, who thought the scientific means of social control were needed to control the masses and shape the nation's destiny, accepted its beliefs and measures.[95] They believed, apparently, along with the movement's more zealous proponents, that scientific intelligence, if properly harnessed, could be utilized to wipe out war and all forms of social disorder.[96] Thus constituted, social efficiency, with all of its bed-fellows, is yet another cure-all in the annals of American education.

Notes

1. Quoted in Edward A. Krug, *The Shaping of the American High School 1880–1920*. Madison: The University of Wisconsin Press, 1964, p. 249.
2. R. Freeman Butts and Lawrence A. Cremin, *A History of Education in American Culture*. New York: Holt, Rinehart and Winston, 1953, p. 308.
3. Ellwood P. Cubberley, *Public Education in the United States*. Boston: Houghton Mifflin Company, 1919, p. 370.
4. S. Alexander Rippa, *Education in a Free Society: An American History*. New York: David McKay Company, 1971, p. 158.
5. Ibid., p. 159.
6. Quoted in William F. Round, "Immigration and Crime," *The Forum* VIII (December 1889): 428.
7. John Higham, *Strangers in the Land: Patterns of American Nativism 1860–1920*. New York: Atheneum, 1970, p. 103.
8. David B. Tyack, ed., *Turning Points in American Educational History*. New York: Blaisdell Publishing Company, 1967, p. 233.
9. Quoted in Carl N. Degler, *Out of Our Past: The Forces That Shaped Modern America*. New York: Harper and Row, 1970, pp. 300–301.
10. Edward A. Ross, *Foundations of Sociology*. New York: The Macmillan Company, 1905, pp. 302–303.
11. The United States Immigration Commission, "Abstract of the Report on the Children of Immigrants in Schools," *Senate Documents,* 61st Congress, 3rd Session, XIII. Washington, DC: U.S. Government Printing Office, 1911, pp. 18–19.
12. The United States Immigration Commission, *The Children of Immigrants in Schools*. I. Washington, DC: U.S. Government Printing Office, 1911, p. 97.
13. Tyack, ed., *Turning Points in American Educational History,* p. 231.
14. E. A. Steere, "The High School as a Factor in Mass Education," *National Education Association: Journal of Proceedings and Addresses 1890.* Topeka, KA: Clifford C. Baker, 1890, p. 646.
15. Charles R. Skinner, Presidential Address, "The Best Education for the Masses," *National Education Association: Journal of Proceedings and Addresses 1897.* Chicago: The University of Chicago Press, 1897, p. 530.
16. "Editorial," *Education* XI (May 1891): 573.
17. Cubberley, *Public Education in the United States,* p. 338.
18. Granville Stanley Hall, *Adolescence*. Vol. II. New York: D. Appleton and Company, 1905, p. 510.
19. Lewis M. Terman, "The Conservation of Talent," *School and Society* XIX (March 29, 1924): 363.
20. "Editorial," *Education* XXVI (October 1905): 116.
21. Fred Clayton Butler, "State Americanization: The Part of the State in the Education and Assimila-

tion of the Immigrant," *United States Bureau of Education, Bulletin No. 77*. Washington, DC: U.S. Government Printing Office, 1920, p. 11.

22. Edward A. Ross, *Social Control*. New York: The Macmillan Company, 1912, p. 168.
23. Ibid., pp. 174–176.
24. Ellwood P. Cubberley, *Changing Conceptions of Education*. Boston: Houghton Mifflin Company, 1909, p. 15.
25. Richard Pratte, *The Public School Movement*. New York: David McKay Company, Inc., 1973, p. 57.
26. David Snedden, "Educational Tendencies in America," *Educational Review* XXXIX (January 1910): 24.
27. Lawrence A. Cremin, *The Transformation of the School: Progressivism in American Education, 1876–1957*. New York: Vintage Books, 1961, p. 71.
28. Cited in Tyack, ed., *Turning Points in American Educational History*, p. 230.
29. Jane Addams, "The Public School and the Immigrant Child," *National Education Association: Journal of Proceedings and Addresses 1909*. Winona, MN: The Association, 1909, pp. 99–102.
30. Jane Addams, *Twenty Years at Hull House with Autobiographical Notes*. New York: The Macmillan Company, 1915, p. 236.
31. Pratte, *The Public School Movement*, p. 51.
32. Ross, *Foundations of Sociology*, p. 365.
33. "Report of the Committee on Resolutions," *National Education Association: Journal of Proceedings and Addresses 1894*. St. Paul: Pioneer Press, 1895, pp. 34–35.
34. William T. Harris, "City School Supervision," *Report of the Commissioner of Education for the Year 1895–1896*. Vol. I. Washington, DC: U.S. Government Printing Office, 1897, pp. xxii–xxiii.
35. Oscar T. Corson, "President's Address," *National Education Association: Journal of Proceedings and Addresses 1900*. St. Paul: The Association, 1900, pp. 58–59.
36. Ibid., p. 58.
37. Quoted in Raymond E., Callahan, *Education and the Cult of Efficiency: A Study of the Social Forces That Have Shaped the Administration of the Public Schools*. Chicago: The University of Chicago Press, 1962, p. 6.
38. Quoted in Callahan, ibid., pp. 6–7.
39. Ibid., p. 7.
40. Leonard P. Ayres, *Laggards in Our Schools: A Study of Retardation and Elimination in City School Systems*. New York: Charities Publication Committee, 1909, pp. 3–5.
41. Ibid., p. 95.
42. J. M. Rice, *Scientific Management in Education*. New York: Arno Press and The New York Times, 1969, p. vii.
43. Callahan, *Education and the Cult of Efficiency*, pp. 46–47.
44. Cited in ibid., pp. 47–48.
45. Ibid., p. 48.
46. Ibid.
47. Ibid., p. 49.
48. Ibid., p. 50.
49. Ibid., pp. 50–51.
50. Ibid., p. 51.
51. Quoted in ibid., p. 52.
52. Quoted in Herbert M. Kliebard, *The Struggle for the American Curriculum, 1893–1958*. Boston: Routledge and Kegan Paul, 1986, p. 96.
53. Quoted in Krug, *The Shaping of the American High School*, p. 304.

54. Quoted in ibid.

55. Quoted in ibid.

56. Quoted in Callahan, *Education and the Cult of Efficiency,* pp. 132–133.

57. Quoted in Kliebard, *The Struggle for the American Curriculum,* p. 98.

58. Callahan, *Education and the Cult of Efficiency,* p. 80.

59. Kliebard, *The Struggle for the American Curriculum,* p. 116.

60. Callahan, *Education and the Cult of Efficiency,* p. 82.

61. Ibid., p. 86.

62. Ibid., pp. 90–92.

63. Herbert M. Kliebard, "Bureaucracy and Curriculum Theory" in Vernon F. Haubrich, ed., *Freedom, Bureaucracy, and Schooling.* Washington, DC: Association for Supervision and Curriculum Development, NEA, 1971, p. 86.

64. David Snedden, *Sociological Determination of Objectives in Education.* Philadelphia: J. B. Lippincott Co., 1921, p. 34.

65. Ibid., p. 33.

66. Geraldine M. Joncich (Clifford), ed., *Psychology and the Science of Education: Selected Writings of Edward L. Thorndike.* New York: Teachers College Press, 1962, p. 1.

67. Ibid., p. 2.

68. Ibid., pp. 2–3.

69. Ibid., p. 6.

70. Ibid., pp. 6–7.

71. Edward L.Thorndike, "The Relation between Initial Ability and Improvement in a Substitution Test," *School and Society* I (March 20, 1915): 431.

72. Edward L. Thorndike, "Intelligence and Its Uses," *Harper's Monthly Magazine,* CXL, January, 1920, p. 233.

73. Edward L.Thorndike, "How May We Improve the Selection, Training, and Life-Work of Leaders?" in I. L. Kandel and Leta S. Hollingsworth, eds., *How Should a Democratic People Provide for the Selection and Training of Leaders in the Various Walks of Life?* New York: Teachers College Press, 1938, p. 32.

74. Thorndike, "Intelligence and Its Uses," *Harper's Monthly Magazine,* p. 232.

75. Pratte, *The Public School Movement,* p. 51.

76. Merle F. Curti, "Edward Lee Thorndike, Scientist," *The Social Ideas of American Educators.* Totowa, NJ: Littlefield, Adams & Co., 1959, p. 486.

77. Thorndike, "Intelligence and Its Uses," *Harper's Monthly Magazine,* p. 231.

78. Curti, "Edward Lee Thorndike, Scientist," *The Social Ideas of American Educators,* p. 483.

79. Edward L. Thorndike, "Intelligence Tests of Colored Pupils in High Schools," *School and Society* XVIII (November 10, 1923): 569–570.

80. Clarence J. Karier, "Testing for Order and Control in the Corporate Liberal State," in Clarence J. Karier, Paul C. Violas, and Joel Spring, *Roots of Crisis: American Education in the Twentieth Century.* Chicago: Rand McNally and Co., 1973, p. 124.

81. Edward L. Thorndike, "Education: A Sociologist's Theory of Education," *The Bookman* XXIV (November 1906): 124.

82. Thorndike, "Aims in Education," cited in "Quotation Marks," *The New York Times,* March 20, 1932, Section 9, p. 2XX.

83. Thorndike, "How May We Improve the Selection, Training, and Life-Work of Leaders?," in Kandel and Hollingsworth, eds., *How Should A Democratic People Provide?,* p. 31.

84. Edward L. Thorndike, *Human Nature and the Social Order.* New York: The Macmillan Company, 1940, p. 957.

85. Clarence J. Karier, "Business Values and the Educational State," in Karier, Violas, and Spring, *Roots of Crisis,* p. 18.
86. Ibid., p. 38.
87. Boyd H. Bode, *Modern Educational Theories.* New York: Vintage Books, 1927, pp. 307–326.
88. Curti, "Edward Lee Thorndike, Scientist," *The Social Ideas of American Educators,* p. 486.
89. Ibid., p. 487.
90. "In Honor of Edward L. Thorndike," *Teachers College Record* XXVII (February 1926).
91. George W. Strayer, "Contributions to the Field of Educational Administration," in "In Honor of Edward L. Thorndike," *Teachers College Record,* XXVII (February 1926): 542.
92. Ibid., 543.
93. Ibid.
94. Curti, *The Social Ideas of American Educators,* p. 259.
95. Clarence J. Karier, "Liberal Ideology and the Quest for Orderly Change," in Karier, Violas, and Spring, *Roots of Crisis,* p. 87.
96. Ibid., pp. 87–88.

CHAPTER SIX

The Era of Social Efficiency

Part II. Vocational Education

In the "Introduction" to their documentary history on *American Education and Vocationalism,* Marvin Lazerson and W. Norton Grubb write that:

> In the four decades surrounding 1900, America's schools were thoroughly transformed. . . . Challenged to run their schools more efficiently and economically, schoolmen adopted business models of administration. . . . No development was more crucial to this reconstruction than vocational education. . . . In all this, vocationalism led to a reassessment of the meaning of democracy in education.[1]

No longer was the common school model, advocated by Horace Mann in the first half of the nineteenth century, accepted as a sufficient illustration of democracy in education; curriculum differentiation, as embodied in the vocational movement took its place and has remained there as of this writing. Joel Spring observed that "Vocational education made the development of human capital through training an important part of the educational system"; it was paired with vocational guidance, which "became the institutional mechanism for matching students and educational programs with the needs of the labor market."[2] Together, vocational education and vocational guidance became the "silver bullets," a panacea of the second section of the era of social efficiency. This chapter will address the vocational movement in general in that context, with some specific attention directed toward young women and African Americans.

Origins of the Vocational Movement

The Russian exhibit at the Philadelphia Centennial in 1876 stimulated American interest in vocational education. This interest was spurred by the pioneering work in manual training by Calvin M. Woodward of Washington University in St. Louis and by John D. Runkle, president of the Massachusetts Institute of Technology.[3] "Industrial education," which Arthur Wirth says has its roots in the 1880s but was marked with a "fuzzy" interpretation,[4] was utilized for "neglected children" (ranging in ages from two to six in industrial schools), and was aimed at making the children of the poor reliable, law-abiding citizens at the end of their training.[5]

Apart from these "reform" schools, the first school to offer specific trade training was started in New York City in 1881 by Colonel Richard T. Auchmuty. His school was designed to protect native white American boys from being shut out of the trades by competition from immigrants and the "dysfunctional' apprentice system.[6] There was sentiment for industrial training at the time: Edward Krug quotes an 1882 editorial in *Education* that claimed that teachers were "hungering and thirsting for the practical."[7] The desire to found trade schools was far from unanimous, however; unions, in particular, feared both the end of the apprentice system that had helped their cause and the influence of industrialists in these fledgling schools.[8]

The Movement Gains Momentum

As the turn of the century grew closer, American life changed more and more. Industrialism was a major force in creating these changes in American society, in which the schools played a major role.[9] Frank Parsons became a principal figure in the increased activity of the school in the nation's economic affairs at this juncture. Parsons, the man who has been acclaimed as the founder of the vocational guidance movement, a social engineer, who also was the founder of the Boston Vocation Bureau in 1908, penned in 1895 that "Life can be molded into any conceivable form. Draw up your specifications for man . . . and if you will give me control of the environment and time enough, I will clothe your dreams in flesh and blood."[10] His approach was consistent. A year before he had written that we could learn much of worth from the training of animals in educating a child:

> . . . the training of a race-horse, and the care of sheep and chickens have been carried to the highest degree of perfection that intelligent planning can attain. But the education of a child, the choice of his employment, are left very largely to the ancient haphazard plan—the struggle for existence, and the survival of the fittest.[11]

In the North, the inhabitants of the industrial schools were to be the children of the poor, including those who were recent arrivals in the nation. Union hostility to trade schools intensified with the founding of the National Association of Manufacturers (NAM) in 1896, an organization that became deeply intertwined with industrial education. The scene was different in the South. There industrial (but not trade) education (as noted in Chapter Four), of a most limited nature, was primarily and overwhelmingly directed at African Americans. In 1899, J. P. Morgan's southern manager, William H. Baldwin, held that schooling opportunities for southern African Americans should be directly related to the type of work they would perform after graduation:

> In the negro is the opportunity in the South. Time has proven that he is best fitted to perform the heavy labor in the Southern states. . . . The South needs him; but the South needs him educated to be a suitable citizen. He will willingly fill the more menial positions, and do the heavy work, at less wages, than the American white man or any foreign race which has yet come to our shores. This will permit the Southern white laborer to perform the more expert labor, and to leave the fields, the mines, and the simpler trades for the negro.[12]

The President of the Georgia Institute of Technology developed this theme, contending that African Americans should be prepared for "the fields, the mines, and the simpler trades," as Baldwin had said:

> When the colored race all become bricklayers, somebody will have to carry the mortar. When they all become plumbers, who are going to be the helpers, the men who carry the tools? When they become scientific farmers, who are going to be laborers? Are Southerners, we Southern whites? No. We have settled that question long ago, but unless we have trade and industrial schools [for whites exclusively], our boys will have to carry the mortar for somebody, even if they have to emigrate to do it.[13]

The Twentieth Century

The curriculum differentiation opportunities presented by vocational education grew with the beginning of the twentieth century. Vocational guidance activities and the growth of vocational education generated activities that were presented not only as necessary but also as infallibly correct. Frank Parsons, writing in 1900, addressed the efficient match between schools and industry:

> Superior efficiency flows from natural fitness—education, special and general, physical, intellectual and moral—and the influence of feelings which produce enthusiastic and painstaking labor. A sensible industrial system will therefore seek to make these feelings factors in every piece of work, to put men, as well as timber, stone, and iron, in the places for which their natures fit them—and to polish and prepare them for efficient service with at least as much care as is bestowed upon clocks, electric dynamos, or locomotives.[14]

The vocational movement, especially in its narrower sense of industrial education, which led to the creation of junior high schools and comprehensive high schools, was the beneficiary of a coordinated effort to obtain federal support beginning in 1900, support which would be forthcoming in the Smith-Hughes Act of 1917.[15] Demographics contributed to this movement; in 1900, 32.9 percent of the nation's population lived in cities of more than 8,000 compared to 22.65 percent in 1880.[16] The expanding dominance of the NAM in the trade schools led union personnel to attempt to influence these schools and their curriculum. The movement tended to intensify the integration of the school and the economy and served as a justification for the utilitarian diversification of the pupils based on their expected careers.[17] As Martin Lazerson and W. Norton Grubb observed, the result was a "redefinition of the idea of educational opportunity and a rejection of the common school ideal."[18] It is crucial for our thesis to note that this educational program was advanced with claims that it would combat "social unrest, moral decay, and increasing alienation from work" and would reverse these tendencies by "eradicating urban poverty and restoring pride and dignity to manual workers."[19] Presented as a potion for reforming criminals, educators "embraced vocational education as the best way of rehabilitating society as a whole."[20]

This reform crusade led to a shift in the nature of the moral values schools were to inculcate. Those related to industrial work were accentuated: "punctuality, discipline, submission to those in authority, recognition of the rights of others and acceptance of one's place in the industrial process."[21] It was the goal of educators to "adapt the individual to the new industrial system so as to make him happy with his work and proud of his position in society."[22] The movement's potential for American society was so huge that federal aid was viewed as the salvific means to give birth to this utopia. The National Society for the Promotion of Industrial Education (NSPIE), an alliance of business leaders and educators, lobbied for this aid; the group's members were most noticeable in the Commission on National Aid to Vocational Education that Congress created in 1914.[23] It is interesting to note the shift from the traditional doctrines about the democratic opportunities common schools offered everyone to an espousal of the European model, in which the state would assign children at an early age to training schools that would prepare them for specific jobs that would then disqualify them from all other economic opportunities.[24]

New York City was one place where the trade schools were implemented. The plan of William Maxwell, superintendent of schools in 1900 represents a concrete instance of implementation. Maxwell proposed that "trade schools take the place of the last two years of work in the elementary schools . . . in tenement-house neighborhoods."[25] Maxwell's plan was endorsed the next year by Charles A. Richards of Teachers College. In an address before the NEA, Richards called for the identification of the "army of trade workers" who would be recruited by the public

schools from those children too poor to attend high school.[26] This social sentiment had been iterated by Leslie Lewis, a district superintendent in the Chicago
public schools, when he complained in 1900 that the schools had motivated too
many pupils to seek the "genteel occupations" when American society needed me-
chanics and artisans. More industrial training in schools, he averred, would prepare students for their station in life rather than lift them out of it.[27]

Vocational Education Programs for Girls

Industrial training for girls in these years centered on household arts, especially
sewing and cooking. Some years before, John D. Philbrick had opined that "No
girl can be considered properly educated who cannot sew."[28] Paul Violas has
pointed out that by 1900 nearly 75 percent of Chicago's seventh- and eighth-
grade girls were enrolled in household arts courses.[29] Immigrant girls were
thought to be particularly needy, Violas noted. They should receive an education that would fit them for life, not "definite knowledge about trade winds and
syntax."[30] Mary E. Williams, New York's director of cooking, announced in 1909
that training in the domestic arts would enable every girl to follow her "natural
vocation," to respond to the "God-given call of her mate" so that she would
abandon all other callings and assume the "position of the highest responsibility
and holiest duties of human life, those of homemaking and motherhood; upon
which the progress of civilization and of human society depend."[31] The superintendent of New York City's schools declared in 1910 that all girls in high school
and in the upper four grades of elementary school must receive domestic instruction.[32] His policy was endorsed by Mrs. W. N. Hutt at the NEA convention
that year when she stated that regardless of the vocation she chose to follow, "she
will, with it all, wake up some fine morning and find herself in some man's
kitchen, and woe be unto her if she has not the knowledge with which to cook
his breakfast."[33]

Domestic training had a more lofty goal: the uplift of the working-class urban
family. "Domestic science," a Chicago principal announced, "may become the
unsuspected, and yet not the least efficient, enemy of the saloon." It could make
the "evening meal of the factory hand . . . more tempting than the lunch counter,
and the clothing of the family, as well as the arrangement and tidiness of living
room at the home may be attractive as the gilded home of vice."[34]

This sentiment was shared. For instance, the New York City superintendent
looked to domestic arts to ally with "municipal reform in all its branches," with
special emphasis on reaching the "tenement dwellers" through homemaking
courses. He concluded his tribute to the ameliorating work of the domestic arts as
follows:

This work has been called the panacea for all evils, laying, as it does, the foundation for the support and betterment of the home. We have been a factor during the past years in helping to solve the economic questions of the nation. Not only has it been a question of careful marketing, and the saving of foods in the kitchen, but the girl's taste in being trained in the proper selection of furniture, and of inexpensive but artistic fittings and furnishings. The woman is the buyer. She uses the wage of the American citizen and expends it wisely and well, or is ignorant and foolish in such expenditure. Therefore, it goes without saying, the home, for which a large portion of the nation's money is expended, is closely connected with the public question of city reform and the nation's need. As is the home so is the nation.[35]

Household arts were to enable the urban housewife and mother to manage the home on the meager salary of the worker, contributing to the acceptance by the worker's family of the gross inequalities of wealth between the corporate leaders and the blue-collar laborers, thus achieving social peace in the industrial nation.[36]

To enable these young women to fulfill their proper roles in the family and thus in society, the curriculum of the schools needed to be appropriately arranged. The aims of mathematics, English and chemistry, for example, were related to practical household work. The programs of Boston and Cleveland were noteworthy in this regard. The description of the Cleveland Technical High School's curriculum revealed that "all technical subjects involving homemaking are taken as the basis of the course for girls, and the rest of the studies are grouped around these."[37] When she did work outside the home, after marriage, it was to be, as in Boston, in "*distinctly feminine occupations*," those occupations that were "most closely allied with the home."[38] Thus, sewing for the garment industry and general office work were common in the school training of working-class city girls.[39]

The city of Pittsburgh provides a fitting example of the efficient service for which lower-class girls were utilized. A group of upper-class women who called themselves the Pittsburgh Domestic Arts Association founded the Pittsburgh School of Domestic Arts in 1900. The school's graduates would find, the society women advertised, "excellent positions awaiting them in the homes of the members of the association."[40]

Violas reported that girls who were students in trade high schools in New York City had little academic preparation when compared with that of those fitted for higher positions in the industrial order. Indeed, many of these young women did not have the opportunity to get academic training even in the elementary schools.[41]

On occasion, special industrial programs were provided for girls. One writer complained in 1908 that educational curricula should be constructed for the special needs of girls:

When one sees the increasing demand for girls in all lines and when one hears the constant complaint of employers that girls are incompetent, unreliable, and disinterested in

their work, one is led to feel that it portends nothing but evil for the future of both the industry and the women.[42]

Separate trade schools were established to provide industrial education for girls.
Among these, founded in 1909 or 1910, were "The Girls' Trade School" in Boston,
which proposed a program of instruction "to fit girls to become skilled work-
women"; "The Milwaukee School of Trades for Girls"; and "The School of Domestic Science" in Rochester, New York, which trained girls for "home or for vocations." To enter this last school, girls were required to have completed the sixth
grade and be fourteen years old, "or nearly so."[43]

Latin was to be weighed against cooking, solid geometry against dressmaking,
and algebra against household duties in the schooling of girls, one superintendent
advised in 1907.[44] Addressing the NEA Department of Secondary Education in
1910, the Principal of Washington Irving High School for Girls in New York City
remarked that his girls wanted "to study the social amenities that make life more
pleasant and friendship more enjoyable" and wanted something in 1910 that they
could use in 1911, not be bound to the "restrictions of an unproven curriculum."[45]
But academic education for girls could be worse than wasteful and frivolous; it
could be dangerous! This principal declared that Latin was a "horrible nightmare"
for his girls[46]; the superintendent of Los Angeles schools, J. H. Francis, was said to
have stated at the NEA meeting in 1914 that the study of algebra had caused many
a girl to lose her soul.[47]

Some, believing that industrial education had a positive effect on the social
bearing of women, wanted to make that kind of training compulsory for all girls
in schools. Ida M. Tarbell, associate editor of *American Magazine,* represents that
group in her contention that:

> There is nothing in this scheme of training all girls in the domestic industries which need
> interfere with training for special shop, factory, or office work. Such training would do
> much to develop the faculties which are required in all industries—the hand sense—the
> attention and appreciation of material things—the correlation of hand and brain—all
> things in which the average girl is deficient now. She would be better able to take the
> training for some special industry because of the domestic training, and when she left that
> industry to marry, as she is almost certain to do, she will not go to her difficult business as
> an unskilled laborer. She, her family, and we, society, would be spared the economic, the
> moral, and the social consequences of her lack of knowledge and skill.[48]

Intensified Pressure for Industrial Education

The NAM was to claim an influential role in American education in particular and American society in general in the first decade of the twentieth century; its
membership swelled from 500,000 in 1897 to nearly two million in 1903. The

American Federation of Labor (AFL) doubled its numbers between 1898 and 1900, and then trebled them between 1900 and 1904.[49] Labor unrest rose. To a considerable extent, employers saw expanded union activity as a threat to their rights of ownership. David M. Parry, in his presidential address to the NAM in 1903, forcefully expressed the executive's position: "Either a man has the right to run his business or he has not. If he has not . . . it means that individual liberty is destroyed and we must bargain with such liberties as we may be allowed to possess." Organized labor, he maintained, "knows but one law, and that is the law of physical force—the law of the Hun and of the Vandals, the law of the savage. All its purposes are accomplished either by actual force or by the threat of force."[50] A majority of the conference supported his militaristic stance and approved a resolution that included the position that "no limitation should be placed upon the opportunities of any person to learn any trade to which he or she may be adapted."[51]

The formation of the Committee on Industrial Education resulted. The committee's first report, issued in 1905, held that "To authorize and found and organize trade schools in which the youth of our land may be taught the practical and technical knowledge of a trade is the most important issue before the American people today."[52] The committee's chair, Anthony Ittner, called for copying and then improving the German method of education, in which trade schools were free from the handicap of union meddling and corporations or private industrialists were the leaders.[53] It was the German method of industrial education, American industrialists believed, that had propelled Germany to the forefront in world business. Speaking to the NEA convention in 1905, Frank A. Vanderliep, vicepresident of the National City Bank of New York, expressed that conviction when he said that he was "firmly convinced that the explanation of that progress can be encompassed in a single word—schoolmaster. He is the great corner-stone of Germany's remarkable and industrial success."[54] Two years later, the superintendent of schools in Menomonie, Wisconsin, reiterated that idea to the NEA when he claimed that "Manufacturers and men of affairs . . . are *demanding* a modification of our educational system on similar lines."[55] Referring to the "outrageous opposition of organized labor" to trade education, an NAM committee concluded that "trade schools properly protected from the domination and withering blight of organized labor are the one and only remedy for the present intolerable situation" that enveloped American industrial education.[56]

The excoriation of labor's "interference" continued unabated from the side of management. The report of the Committee on Industrial Education of the NAM in 1905 argued that the right to a trade school education was a right that "Even the youth of the Empire of the Czar are free to learn"; it was denied only in this country. It was the "best thought of the Nation," the committee argued, that in addition to a common school education the "youth of our industrial centers should learn a trade or master some craftsmanship." Trade education "aids enormously in the development of manhood . . . which all are now conceding," so that the student is "better fitted physically and mentally for the battle of life," the committee claimed.[57]

The year 1906 witnessed two signal events in the panacea that trade and industrial education was fast becoming on the national scene: the report of the Douglas Commission in Massachusetts and the formation of the National Society for the Promotion of Industrial Education (NSPIE) which was to become an effective pressure group on behalf of that form of education at all levels.

Called into existence by the Massachusetts legislature in 1906, the Douglas Commission immediately held public hearings on the status of industrial education in that state. One of its subcommittees employed a special investigator, Susan M. Kingsbury, whose task it was to conduct a special inquiry on the relation of children to industries and schools.[58] The commission took the position that students should learn about productive industry in elementary school and that science courses should focus on applications of science to industry in high school (with a particular emphasis on local industries) so that students could see that science could be "utilized for the purposes of practical life." In a controversial major recommendation, the commission called for the creation of "independent industrial schools" in local communities.[59] The public schools, the commission reported, were inadequate to "meet fully the need of modern industrial and social conditions." The "broader-minded" students of education, leading citizens, saw that the new form of schooling was broad "training," which is used in the "education of the feeble-minded, in the reformation of wayward and vicious children at reform and truant schools, and that it is being used to elevate the colored race in the south."[60] The trend to leave school after the seventh grade meant that any "scheme of education which is to increase the child's productive efficiency must consider the child of fourteen."[61] (Hence the founding of the junior high school, described in the next chapter, as the effective vehicle for curriculum differentiation.) Traditional education must be reformed; the public schools as constituted were outdated and inefficient and contributed to the country's decline among the nations of the world. To benefit the individual and, more important, the nation, a complete overhaul of education was necessary. Industrial education, applied differentially, would be the solution. James E. Russell, a professor at Columbia's Teachers College, put it this way:

> How can a nation endure that deliberately seeks to rouse ambitions and aspirations in the oncoming generations which in the nature of events cannot possibly be fulfilled? If the chief objective of government be to promote civil order and social stability how can we justify our practice in schooling the masses in precisely the same manner as we do those who are to be our leaders? Is human nature so constituted that those who fail will readily acquiesce in the success of their rivals, especially if that success be the result of "cuteness," rather than honest effort? Is it any wonder that we are beset with labor troubles?[62]

Susan Kingsbury, as noted above, was a special investigator assigned to study the relation of children to industries and schools. Miss Kingsbury reported that there were 25,000 children in Massachusetts who were fourteen and fifteen years of age who were not in school, five-sixths of whom had not graduated from the grammar schools and one-half of whom had not gone beyond the seventh grade. Many of these were at work in jobs with little future.[63] Whose fault was this? The vast majority believed that is was not parents or industry but the schools that were at fault. Miss Kingsbury had consulted thirty-five to forty superintendents and all except three felt the fault resided with "the system, which fails to offer the child of fourteen continued schooling of a practical character."[64] Poverty, she contended, was an insignificant factor in their nonattendance at school. Kingsbury's interpretations were accepted as empirical facts and became the conventional wisdom for those supporting industrial training in the curriculum.[65]

Violas observed that by 1906 approximately twenty percent of the overall public high school population was enrolled in a vocational curriculum; the percentage was higher in cities.[66] This percentage reflects the switch that had taken place from manual training programs, which were regarded by vocational educators as "frilly," to specific vocational programs.[67]

The city of Chicago presents a case study of sorts for the aims of industrial education in 1906. Sponsored by the city's Commercial Club, Edwin Cooley was sent to Europe to study European systems of vocational education. One goal of the club was to completely reorganize the schools as a means of increasing the supply of workers. Cooley was impressed with what he saw in Europe. In his essay "Public School Education in Morals," he said that vocational education built morality. Vocational education was necessary, he maintained, because working-class students were not interested in academic subjects. His position took on a racial tone when he said:

> In dealing with the moral, intellectual, and social conditions of the inferior races, the statesman of to-day tries to approach them from a practical point of view and to induce them or to compel them to form habits of industry. . . . Slavery was wrong, but whatever else it did or did not do, it compelled the acquisition of habits of industry in the slave and marked a step in advance over the previous condition of slavery.[68]

Cooley argued that teaching punctuality was more important than spelling, and that the insistence of schools "on this virtue is doing much to suppress a certain kind of selfishness and waste that seems to be inseparable from the man or woman who refuses to conform to time regulations."[69] The so-called "Cooley Plan," recommended by business leaders in Chicago, was an apt illustration of dualism in schooling. The Cooley Plan, which would have placed vocational schools under the control of private, separate, corporate-run boards, was defeated.[70]

Industrial training, the U.S. Commissioner reported in 1906, was "offered in most of the negro schools, reform schools, and schools for defectives."[71] Some leaders saw this kind of training as a means to suppress the demands of African Americans for equal educational opportunity. President Taft, it was reported, indicated his support for this kind of training to Booker T. Washington in 1909, because he felt that too many of the students at Black liberal arts colleges were agitating for political rights for their people. Implicit in this belief was that industrial training graduates would be content to work with their hands and avoid such agitation.[72]

The NAM-supported movement welcomed the help of the President of the United States, Theodore Roosevelt, in 1907. Writing to the NSPIE, the president praised the public schools but called attention to what he believed was one fundamental fault—they failed "to give the industrial training which fits a man for the shop and the farm . . . we have done almost nothing to equip the private soldiers of the industrial army—the mechanic, the metal worker, the carpenter." An education was needed that would develop "industrial intelligence," for the benefit of the worker as well as for the national welfare.[73] Educators upheld the right of the civil state to engage in funneling one segment of its population into the industrial classes. For instance, L. D. Harvey, superintendent of schools in Menomonie, Wisconsin, maintained that "the state has the right to do whatever is necessary for its well-being and perpetuity," and that schools that properly prepare their workers "may be legitimately supported by public funds."[74] Harvey contended that the 25,000 children who had left school early in the Kingsbury report would have stayed in school had industrial education been available to them.[75]

Although the focus of industrial education was on city youth and industrial education, children in rural schools did not escape the attention of the panacea's devotees. Acknowledging that there was considerable opposition to teaching "practical farm work" in schools, the director of the U.S. Office of Experimental Stations claimed that influential groups were supportive of the movement, but that below the surface there was "a vast mass of stagnant or recurrent water." "Agitation" was needed, he stated, "deeper, as well as wider," until it permeated "all the mass of our rural population."[76]

David Snedden was without a doubt one of the most avid proponents of vocational education, curriculum differentiation, and social efficiency in the early twentieth century. In his view, "Vocational education means efficiency" and "efficiency means specialization." Even the study of history "must serve as instrumental to some kind of personal or social efficiency."[77] He described the "new education" as the "fountain of inspiration" for improving the life of the community. The "new education" would have a curriculum that would fit the child in his/her place in society, unlike the old curriculum that drove children from school.[78] The public schools, following his plan of social engineering, should take control of the total education of children.[79] Scientifically qualified social engineers, whose dictates the schools would follow, would achieve the good society.[80] Educators needed to be practical and recognize that economic and social factors determined aptitude as well as inherited ability.[81] Snedden felt that reform schools offered apt models to follow.[82] So did European education, which practiced "extensive differentiation at (age) twelve or earlier."[83]

In 1908, Charles W. Eliot, president of Harvard, addressed the NSPIE under the heading of "Industrial Education as an Essential Factor in our National Prosperity." Putting forth the idea of separate trade schools, that were to produce "actual journeymen for the trades," not "foremen or managers," Eliot proclaimed that "We must get rid of the notion that some of us were brought up on, that a Yankee can turn his hand to anything. . . . There is no such thing among men as equality of natural gifts, of capacity for training, or of intellectual power." [84] It was the responsibility of the "teachers of the elementary schools   to sort the pupils and sort them by their evident or probable destinies."[85] (Two years later, in 1910, Eliot reversed his position and suggested in a speech to the NEA that career choice and training should begin at age sixteen or later.[86])

The theme of differentiation in the later years of the elementary school, which led to the establishment of the junior high school, was espoused by Superintendent Maxwell of New York City. In 1908, he called on elementary school personnel to advise students to take the proper high school course, the one to which they were fitted by "natural talent," thus avoiding the costly "misdirected effort" by the students and their parents.[87] Vocational guidance was necessary if schools were to become instruments of "industrial determination" and students were to realize "their proper station of efficiency and happiness." As Edward Elliott maintained, proper course selection would "precede and underlie the maintenance of the educational equilibrium of democracy."[88]

Some educators believed, as the twentieth century entered its second decade, that the European system was preferable to the American system when it came to implementing vocational education programs. The NEA put it this way:

> The European systems of education, which have not been burdened to such an extent as our own with the ideals of a democracy have found it easy to engraft vocational instruction upon an elementary system intended only for those destined by birth to some form of industry.[89]

Horace Mann and his colleagues would have turned in their graves had they heard or read that our ideals of a democracy were a burden! That same NEA committee, gazing out at the legions of children in the nation's urban centers, recommended that differentiation begin in the seventh grade because a "large number of children have by this time demonstrated their unfitness for what may be called a professional career." Traditional studies, for them, were held to be "not profitable."[90]

The Cleveland public schools were in line with this kind of social thinking. In 1910, the district announced the beginning of dual programs in grades five through eight, with the following justification of their policy:

> The needs of children destined to terminate their school education with the elementary school are very different from children so situated that they may continue their schooling in higher institutions . . . in a district where the streets are well paved and clean, where the homes are spacious and surrounded by lawns and trees, where the language of the child's playfellows is pure, and where life in general is permeated with the spirit and ideals of America.[91]

Schools in New York City followed the same line of reasoning; thus, students in the industrial courses destined for lower types of occupations did not, in some instances, even require completion of elementary school work. Consequently, working class children did not have academic training in elementary schools.[92] Violas pointed out that this policy was consistent with the policy in working class neighborhoods in many cities; after all, those "destined for subservient roles should not be trained for autonomy."[93] One principal, J. Stanley Brown from Illinois, congratulated his audience on the progress they had made since the era and thought of Horace Mann:

> In the early days of secondary education when schools were somewhat small and poorly equipped and when funds were more difficult to obtain than at present, we had the same set of studies provided for all, regardless of sex, previous condition, or future employment, and we considered that we were rendering the best service to all, and it is now reported that there are some remote regions east of the Alleghenies even now where such an opinion is making a struggle to survive.[94]

David Snedden agreed: traditional academic fare was "barren and purposeless" for this group of students.[95]

The NAM persisted in its criticisms of school waste, finding the schools "utterly deficient" in meeting the needs of manufacturers.[96] Pressure mounted to establish trade schools apart from the public school structure. Wisconsin created separate state and local boards to administer industrial education.[97] The NAM strongly favored the reduction of elementary schooling to six years, after which students would be divided into three tracks: cultural, commercial, and industrial.[98] This system would need people to implement it. This is the foundation of vocational guidance.

Vocational Guidance

Charles A. Prosser, the executive secretary of the NSPIE, became a leader in advocating vocational guidance. Prosser, who was to urge the founding of the National

Vocational Guidance Association in 1913,[99] addressed the NEA on the importance of strategic necessity of vocational guidance in 1912:

> More and more, in our theory of the American public school system, we are swinging around to the idea that it is to be the mission of the schools of the future to select by testing and training—to adjust boys and girls for life by having them undergo varied experiences in order to uncover their varied tastes and aptitudes and to direct and to train them in the avenues for which they display the most capacity. Such a program would require a differentiation in the course of study for pupils between twelve and fourteen years of age.[100]

Guidance bureaus and counselors were called into being to eliminate guesswork, and to interpret and then apply the array of instruments that appeared to "scientifically" test intelligence, aptitudes, abilities, and interests. Sometimes students were exposed to a variety of occupations and began training in a specific one before the age of choice, as happened in New York City.[101]

Vocational guidance's task was to sort the "hand-minded" children, as they were referred to, into appropriate programs, keeping them in school, hence developing the "human capital" of the nation, estimated at $250 billion, which was undeveloped at the time.[102] Channeled into the right "slots," these youngsters would realize the joy that comes from "efficiency in work," and the nation would be able to keep up with its foreign competition, which we trailed by twenty-five years due to a seriously flawed system of schooling.[103] Prosser identified the "problem":

> Misfits in all vocations confront us everywhere. Many workers are inefficient because they are not adapted to the work they are doing and some because they have not been properly prepared for it. This lack of efficiency constitutes a permanent handicap not only to the worker but to the calling which he follows. It means lessened wage, uncertain employment, failure of promotion, economic struggle, waste in the use of material, poor workmanship, reduced output, and the lowering of standards of skill and workmanship of American industries.

He then prescribed the remedy: the schools should "*direct* and *train* all the children of all the people *for useful service* through vocational guidance."[104] The "cultural" high school, while fitting for the "abstract-minded and imaginative" children, was not the place for the "hand-minded"; it was time to cast aside the "medieval high school" and educate for the twentieth, not the twelfth century, according to an article in the *Saturday Evening Post*.[105]

Vocational guidance channeled students into courses of study based on their expected occupations in life and encouraged students to internalize goals and ideals that had previously been selected for them by experts.[106] Schoolmen pressed the theory that students of twelve years of age were "prepared to elect their future course of instruction and presumably their future life work."[107] Prosser affirmed that vocational guidance and vocational education were the "handmaidens" of the other, each "indispensable" to the success of the other.[108] Wirth observes that Prosser et al. had raised serious questions, such as "Which training programs should be offered? By whom? For whom? At what levels and for which groups?"[109] John Dewey, Ella Flagg Young, and the AFL all agreed that training programs were deficient because of their narrowness of scope; they turned schools into agencies that provided industry with a supply of docile workers who had adapted to the existing industrial regime.[110]

Extravagant claims were made on behalf of vocational education as the drive to implement it in schools steadily gained momentum. For instance, the NEA Report in 1914 alleged that "Widespread vocational training will democratize the education of the country"; "Vocational education will reduce to a minimum the waste of labor power, the most destructive form of extravagance of which a people can be guilty"; and that "Vocational Training Is Needed to Democratize the Education of the Country: By recognizing different tastes and abilities and by giving an equal opportunity to all to prepare for their life work"; and by providing "practical education," the absence of which was "one of the primary causes of social and industrial discontent."[111]

Vocational guidance remained a paramount matter in education as the second decade of the twentieth century progressed. The superintendent of schools of Ironwood, Michigan, alleged that "the demand for economic efficiency has made vocational guidance one of the leading educational questions of the hour."[112] Educators such as Meyer Bloomfield of the Boston Vocation Bureau described adolescence as the period when the "history of many an individual is finally written."[113] Such an assessment was supported by the renowned psychologist Edward L. Thorndike. When he was asked about the permanency of interests of a ten to fourteen year old, he answered that such an interest exhibited at this age remained stable throughout life:

> The importance of these facts for the whole field of practice with respect to early diagnosis, vocational guidance, the work of social secretaries, deans, advisers, and others who direct students' choices of schools, studies, and careers, is obvious.[114]

Understandably enough, the AFL was concerned. It felt that commercial interests could soon control education to the extent that the opportunities for the children of workers to get a good general education would be constricted, a turn of events that would "tend to make the workers more submissive and less independent." The labor organization wrote:

> Ever since the establishment of our public school system, there has been a constant and persistent attempt by large commercial interests to control our public system of education, and to do it for their own selfish purpose. These interests have tried time and again to control the courses of preparation and of training our children solely for the purpose of

using them in turning out a maximum of articles of exchange and commerce at the lowest possible cost to themselves . . . the future of our public schools and the character of teaching our boys and girls, depend largely upon the attitude and exercise of the forces of labor. It is for labor to say whether their children shall receive a real education in our public schools, or whether they are to be turned out as machine made products, fitted only to work and to become part and parcel of a machine instead of human beings with a life of their own, and a right to live that life under rightful living conditions.[115]

The AFL had an influential educational ally in John Dewey. Dewey, to Snedden's surprise and discouragement, criticized the mechanistic "identification of education with the acquisition of specialized skill in the management of machines at the expense of an industrial intelligence based on science and a knowledge of social problems and conditions."[116] Addressing the relationship between education and employment, Dewey penned:

> The only adequate training *for* occupations is training *through* occupations. The principle . . . that the educative process is its own end, and that the only sufficient preparation for later responsibilities comes by making the most of immediately present life, applied in full force to the vocational phases of education. The dominant vocation of all human beings at all times is living—intellectual and moral growth. In childhood and youth, with their relative freedom from economic stress, this fact is naked and unconcealed. To predetermine some future occupation for which education is to be a strict preparation is to injure the possibilities of present development.[117]

Dewey's ideas were not in the majority in the educational world. For instance, Frank E. Spaulding, at the time superintendent of schools in Minneapolis, proposed that the interests of the schools be subordinate to those of vocationalism.[118] To operationalize the position advanced by Spaulding and others, tacticians needed to reorganize the traditional curricula, develop new courses to teach about vocations, and bring about close articulation of industrial training and prevocational classes with the actual conditions of corporate industry.[119] The story of how this was accomplished is beyond the scope of this project. That it existed, however, is beyond question. One illustration of the conflicts engendered by the attempt is borne out by the warning given vocational adherents by J. Stanley Brown on the floor of the 1915 NEA convention. Brown said that the battle lines had already been drawn; students and parents were aligned against the "manufacturer, the business man, and the industrialist." Parents had support, he ventured, from "social, ethical, and religious organizations" who sought for the student "the right to develop his own life in the way which seemed best to his parent and himself and that his duties as a citizen demanded." Brown claimed that "the manufacturers, the commercialists, or the industrialists" were not at all concerned with values such as "human character, right living, and good citizenship" or with making the student to be "the best citizen, the most honest and careful man" but focused only on making "every individual employee subordinate to the production of his particular institution."[120]

Conclusion

The long-standing goal of the NSPIE, federal aid for vocational education, came to fruition with the passage of the Smith-Hughes act in the early months of 1917. The successful conclusion to the lobbying for federal funds had been aided by the exhortation of President Woodrow Wilson that the bill was necessary for the defense of the country (the United States would enter World War I in a few short months). Wirth commented that Prosser's ideas about vocational education and how its programs were to be administered were reflected in the bill.[121] The law represents a triumph for the belief that the:

> . . . primary goal of schooling was to prepare youth for the job market, in the redefinition of equality of educational opportunity that accompanied the differentiated curriculum, and in growth of vocational guidance, educational testing, and the junior high school to select students more effectively for educational programs.[122]

Further, by 1917, as Kliebard noted, many existing subjects, particularly at the secondary level, were becoming infused with criteria taken from vocational education, e.g., business English and business mathematics.[123]

Vocational education emerged as a success because, as Kliebard maintained, "certain ways of interpreting social change made the infusion of vocational education into the public school curriculum the most plausible and politically expedient."[124] The movement contributed to a widespread bias against academic work in schools, but more importantly, it assumed that "all children of the working classes were alike and that all could be helped economically through industrial education, particularly through hand work."[125]

Many educators accepted the revised idea of democracy in schooling that vocational education embodied. It became for them the magic potion that would correct the ills that beset American society in a time of social change and upheaval. Violas has reminded us that this does not mean that educators were simply "lackeys for corporate industry or that they knowingly sold out the future of their students to the interests of big business." As he stated, they heard the cries emanating from the poor in the cities; they saw the growing power of the large corporations and "accepted the modern social order as reality for the foreseeable future." Believing that it was in the best interests of many students to "share this industrial consciousness, the resultant programs emerged from an honest commitment."[126] Honest commitment it may have been, but it was also their panacea, one shared by more than a few Americans at the time.

Notes

1. Marvin Lazerson and W. Norton Grubb, "Introduction," in Lazerson and Grubb, eds., *American Education and Vocationalism: A Documentary History, 1880–1970*. New York: Teachers College Press, 1974, pp. 1–2.

2. Joel Spring, *The American School, 1642–1985*. New York: Longman, 1986, p. 107.

3. Lazerson and Grubb, "Introduction," p. 4.

4. Arthur G. Wirth, *Education in the Technological Society*. Scranton, PA: Intext, 1972, p. 2.

5. Robert L. Church and Michael W. Sedlak, *Education in the United States: An Intrepretive History*. New York: Free Press, 1976, p. 201.

6. Wirth, *Education in the Technological Society*, p. 17.

7. Edward A. Krug, *The Shaping of the American High School 1880–1920*. Madison: The University of Wisconsin Press, 1964, p. 15.

8. Lawrence A. Cremin, *The Transformation of the School: Progressivism in American Education 1876–1957*. New York: Vintage Books, 1961, p. 36.

9. Lazerson and Grubb, "Introduction," p. 8.

10. Quoted in Church and Sedlak, *Education in the United States*, p. 307.

11. Quoted in ibid., p. 308.

12. Quoted in David Nasaw, *Schooled to Order: A Social History of Public Schooling in the United States*. New York: Oxford University Press, 1979, p. 141.

13. Quoted in ibid.

14. Parsons, quoted in Clarence J. Karier, Paul Violas, and Joel Spring, *Roots of Crisis: American Education in the Twentieth Century*. Chicago: Rand McNally, 1973, p. 20.

15. Wirth, *Education in the Technological Society*, p. 2.

16. Lazerson and Grubb, "Introduction," p. 14.

17. Ibid., pp. 23–24.

18. Ibid., p. 24.

19. Ibid., p. 26.

20. Ibid.

21. Ibid., p. 27.

22. Ibid.

23. Ibid., p. 28.

24. Church and Sedlak, *Education in the United States*, p. 306.

25. Paul C. Violas, *The Training of the Urban Working Class: A History of Twentieth Century American Education*. Chicago: Rand McNally, 1978, p. 140.

26. Ibid.

27. Ibid., p. 142.

28. Quoted in ibid., p. 178.

29. Ibid.

30. Ibid., p. 55.

31. Quoted in ibid.

32. Ibid.

33. Ibid.

34. Quoted in ibid., p. 179.

35. Quoted in ibid.

36. Ibid., pp. 179–180.

37. Quoted in ibid., p. 180.

38. Ibid., p. 181.

39. Ibid., pp. 181–182.
40. Quoted in ibid., p. 182.
41. Ibid., p. 183.
42. Quoted in Melvin L. Barlow, *History of Industrial Education in the United States*. Peoria, IL: Bennett, 1967, p. 341.
43. Ibid., p. 349.
44. Krug, *The Shaping of the American High School*, p. 279.
45. Quoted in ibid., p. 279.
46. Nasaw, *Schooled to Order*, p. 142.
47. Krug, *The Shaping of the American High School*, p. 347.
48. Quoted in Barlow, *History of Industrial Education in the United States*, p. 344.
49. Wirth, *Education in the Technological Society*, p. 27.
50. Quoted in ibid., p. 28.
51. Quoted in ibid.
52. Quoted in ibid., p. 29.
53. Ibid.
54. Quoted in Raymond E. Callahan, *Education and the Cult of Efficiency*. Chicago: The University of Chicago Press, 1964, p. 12.
55. Quoted in ibid., pp. 12–13.
56. Quoted in Lawrence A. Cremin, *The Transformation of the School*. New York: Vintage Books, 1961, p. 38.
57. Quoted in Lazerson and Grubb, eds., *American Education and Vocationalism*, pp. 89, 91.
58. Krug, *The Shaping of the American High School*, pp. 218–219.
59. Quoted in ibid., pp. 220–221.
60. Quoted in Lazerson and Grubb, eds., *American Education and Vocationalism*, pp. 70–71.
61. Quoted in ibid., p. 73.
62. Quoted in Violas, *The Training of the Urban Working Class*, p. 138.
63. Krug, *The Shaping of the American High School*, p. 221.
64. Ibid., p. 222.
65. Violas, *The Training of the Urban Working Class*, pp. 138–139.
66. Ibid., p. 15.
67. Ibid., pp. 137–138.
68. Quoted in Spring, *The American School*, p. 263.
69. Ibid., pp. 263–264.
70. Wayne J. Urban and Jennings L. Wagoner, Jr., *American Education: A History*. 2nd edition. New York: McGraw-Hill, 1999, p. 212.
71. Quoted in Violas, *The Training of the Urban Working Class*, p. 137.
72. Ibid., pp. 137–138.
73. Quoted in Wirth, *Education in the Technological Society*, pp. 26–27.
74. Quoted in Violas, *The Training of the Urban Working Class*, p. 139.
75. Krug, *The Shaping the American High School*, p. 224.
76. Quoted in Krug, ibid., pp. 247–248.
77. Quoted in Walter H. Drost, *David Snedden and Education for Social Efficiency*. Madison: The University of Wisconsin Press, 1967, pp. 93, 83.
78. Quoted in Wirth, *Education in the Technological Society*, p. 149.
79. Ibid., p. 152.
80. Ibid., p. 151.
81. Ibid., p. 155.

82. Ibid., p. 152.
83. Quoted in Nasaw, *Schooled to Order*, p. 132.
84. Quoted in Wirth, *Education in the Technological Society*, pp. 99–100.
85. Quoted in ibid., p. 100.
86. Ibid., p. 101.
87. Violas, *The Training of the Urban Working Class*, p. 208.
88. Edward C. Elliott (1908), "Equality of Educational Opportunity," in Lazerson and Grubb, eds., *American Education and Vocationalism*, p. 140.
89. National Education Association, "Report of the Committee on the Place of Industries in Public Education" (1910), in Lazerson and Grubb, eds., *American Education and Vocationalism*, p. 85.
90. Ibid., p. 87.
91. Quoted in Krug, *The Shaping of the American High School*, p. 238.
92. Violas, *The Training of the Urban Working Class*, p. 183.
93. Ibid., p. 184.
94. Quoted in Nasaw, *Schooled to Order*, p. 133.
95. Drost, *David Snedden and Education for Social Efficiency*, p. 113.
96. Wirth, *Education in the Technological Society*, p. 33.
97. Ibid., p. 38.
98. Ibid., p. 39.
99. Krug, *The Shaping of the American High School*, p. 242.
100. Quoted in Wirth, *Education in the Technological Society*, p. 102.
101. Violas, *The Training of the Urban Working Class*, p. 210.
102. National Association of Manufacturers, "Report of the Committee on Industrial Education" (1912), in Lazerson and Grubb, eds., *American Education and Vocationalism*, pp. 92–93, 98.
103. Ibid., pp. 94–96.
104. Quoted in Wirth, *Education in the Technological Society*, p. 136.
105. Nasaw, *Schooled to Order*, p. 127.
106. Violas, *The Training of the Urban Working Class*, p. 216.
107. Quoted in Krug, *The Shaping of the American High School*, pp. 240–241.
108. Prosser, "Practical Arts and Vocational Guidance" (1913), in Lazerson and Grubb, eds., *American Education and Vocationalism*, p. 134.
109. Wirth, *Education in the Technological Society*, p. 219.
110. Ibid., pp. 36–37.
111. Commission on National Aid to Vocation, "Report" (1914), in Lazerson and Grubb, eds. *American Education and Vocationalism*, pp. 116–132.
112. Quoted in Violas, *The Training of the Urban Working Class*, p. 220.
113. Quoted in Spring, *Education and the Rise of the Corporate State*, p. 100.
114. Quoted in ibid.
115. American Federation of Labor, "Report of the Committee on Industrial Relations" (1915), in Lazerson and Grubb, eds., *American Education and Vocationalism*, pp. 111–113.
116. Herbert M. Kliebard, *The Struggle for the American Curriculum: 1893–1958*. Boston: Routledge and Kegan Paul, 1986, p. 147.
117. Quoted in ibid., p. 148.
118. Violas, *The Training of the Urban Working Class*, pp. 210–211.
119. Ibid., p. 211.
120. Nasaw, *Schooled to Order*, pp. 149–150.
121. Wirth, *Education in the Technological Society*, p. 219.

122. Lazerson and Grubb, "Introduction," in Lazerson and Grubb, eds., *American Education and Vocationalism,* p. 32.
123. Kliebard, *The Struggle for the American Curriculum,* p. 129.
124. Ibid., p. 152.
125. Krug, *The Shaping of the American High School,* pp. 243–244.
126. Violas, *The Training of the Urban Working Class,* pp. 230–231.

CHAPTER SEVEN

The Era of Social Efficiency

Part III. Secondary Education

~~

The third, and last, section on social efficiency will be devoted to secondary education. Specifically, it will focus on the rise of the junior high school and the implementation of the comprehensive high school.

The Junior High School

Edward A. Krug described the junior high or intermediate school as the "newest and fondest hope for the future" in the early twentieth century.[1] Krug was uncertain of its origins. Joel Spring felt that the "wedding of vocational guidance and socialization" in the school "provided the complete educational program for the new corporate system."[2] He argued that the reference to the junior high school as an "experiment in democracy" meant that the school attempted to develop individual abilities and interests through guidance, social activities, and a differentiated curriculum, which educational writers of the time called "meeting the needs of the individual."[3]

Advocates of curriculum differentiation, such as E. V. Robinson of the University of Minnesota, were ardent backers of the junior high school and its potential benefits. In 1913, Robinson maintained that children differentiate themselves: "We do not put them on the scrap-heap; they put themselves there."[4] In California, as Arthur Wirth observed, the Berkeley junior high school was regarded as early as 1910 as the "introductory high school," established, as Superintendent Frank Bunker contended, as a terminal school, to combat the waste of early dropouts.[5]

Krug wrote that the term junior high school gained rapidly in popularity after 1910; it received major support from the 1915 meeting of the NEA's Department of

Superintendence, which passed a resolution favoring "the increasing tendency to establish, beginning with the seventh grade, differentiated courses of study aimed more effectively to prepare the child for his probable future activities."[6] The movement grew; by 1922, 456 cities reported a total of 733 such schools.[7]

The junior high school proved to be an apt vehicle for the goals of social and economic efficiency. By the early teens the schoolmen did not favor separate or special schools, even those called intermediate schools.[8] Such schools were now virtual preparatory schools that served as institutions of differentiation. Krug reported that opposition to the new institution brought swift and sometimes furious retorts, as evidenced by the statement of Charles H. Judd that whoever opposed the junior high school would have to answer for it to society.[9] As the movement gained momentum in the second decade of the twentieth century, its advocates held that despite the fact that they cost more than the conventional seventh and eighth grades, they were "well worth the difference."[10]

Krug remarked that the major attraction of the new institution was its use in the campaign against tradition.[11] Charles Hughes Johnston perhaps best epitomized this attack on the old mounted by the junior high school:

> It is the name we have come to associate with new ideas of promotion, new methods of preventing elimination, new devices for moving selected groups thru subject-matter at different rates, higher compulsory school age, new and thorough analyses (social, economic, psychological) of pupil populations, enriched courses, varied and partially different curricular offerings, scientifically directed study practice (and) new schemes for all sorts of educational guidance.[12]

Johnson added that the junior high school was associated with a "new school year, a new school day, new kinds of class exercises, new kinds of laboratory and library equipment, and new kinds of intimate community service."[13] E. R. Breslich of the University of Chicago lauded this break with tradition and aristocracy and claimed that the school was "an Americanizing movement."[14] Thomas Warrington Gosling of the Wisconsin State Department of Education chimed in with the assertion that elementary and senior high schools were "so completely enmeshed in traditionalism" that they were "almost incapable of organizing and responding to the demands."[15] Judd put it this way: "The Junior High School has grown up in democratic America as the last chapter in the history of the struggle against the medieval system."[16] What enlightened person could oppose or stand idly by in the face of such a force for good?

There were other benefits. As noted above, the junior high school provided early curriculum differentiation, thus eliminating the waste incurred by the failure of many students to progress through those years of school.[17] It provided "common studies" and a "common social life" for the students[18]; fostered the "democratic principle of equality" (which the traditional institution did not do)[19]; and served as a much smoother transition to the high school.[20] Indeed, David Snedden felt that the beneficial process of differentiation of curriculum had just begun, writing that it was a period where the "differences of abilities, of extra-school conditions and of prospects will acutely manifest themselves, forcing us to differentiate curricula in more ways, probably, than are as yet expected."[21]

In his well-known work on the junior high school, Calvin Davis maintained that its most important function, one that justified the reorganization of the schools on a new basis, was its ability to "aid pupils in discovering their own capacities and limitations, interests and distastes, powers and weaknesses."[22] Even in the face of increased costs, and in the era of social efficiency, the junior high school was worth the additional expense.[23]

What, precisely, was the junior high school? In 1918 the North Central Association defined it as follows:

> *Resolved,* That the term Junior High School, as used by this association, shall be understood to apply only to schools including the ninth grade combined with the eighth grade, or with the eighth and seventh grades, in an organization distinct from the grades above and the grades below.[24]

Calvin Davis opined that some definitions, described a "vision and not a reality."[25] A. P. Jones, writing in 1918, argued that it was defined by its name:

> It is an end in itself; it sounds better to the boy and girl; it lends itself better to the formation of athletic teams, literary societies, and other school activities; it is easier to develop a feeling of pride and responsibility in a junior high school than in an intermediate school. In a word, it fulfills in itself better the purpose of the organization—that of meeting individual needs.[26]

As noted earlier, the traditionalists were opposed to this new "magic elixir" of an institution. Davis counted senior high school people and colleges among the ranks of its opponents,[27] despite the facts that its cornerstone was "justice for the individual"[28] and that it provided vast opportunities for its students.[29] Cyrus Mead of the University of California was particularly apprehensive about the baleful impact the high school could have on this fledgling institution. Writing in 1920, he stated that "It will be a sad day if this mossback element of the secondary field succeeds in dominating the policies of the new 'intermediate' school and makes of it a 'Junior' academy." It would not fulfill its true mission unless it became "an institution standing upon its own feet."[30] A contemporary of his, D. E. Phillips of the University of Denver, required more: namely, that the regular high school "must be adjusted to this new shrine of the golden age, and not vice versa."[31]

The mission of this "new shrine" remained elusive. Perhaps it would be appropriate to conclude this section of the chapter with the words of Principal S. O.

Rorem of the East Junior High School of Sioux City, Iowa. "The Junior High School," he penned in 1919, "cannot easily be defined; it is doubtful if there is a real one in existence except as someone has supposed that someone else has that one." The true essence of the junior high school, he said, was simply "Opportunity and Growth," which meant that "principals and teachers may now stir themselves to find what the school shall be to the pupils of the seventh, eighth and ninth years."[32] Rorem went on to predict a bright future for the institution, which he said no one could define:

> Two thousand schools are on the trail where ten thousand more schools may someday follow. At the head of the long line there are a few dozen sane, cautious, pioneers who bravely confront all the difficulties they encounter, while the hundreds who follow are overjoyed to have the trail made smooth and easy to traverse. These pioneers expect nothing without struggle. They ask no quarter, and give none in confronting knotty problems.[33]

Krug noted that Rorem himself attempted a definition but a year later:

> The Junior High School is the living presence of a visioned idea which had been so dearly cherished that it had been relegated to the rare rendezvous with school folk only in the quiet hour of "Best Moments."[34]

With a definition such as this, is it any wonder that the Junior High School qualifies as yet another panacea in the annals of American education?

The Comprehensive High School

High schools experienced a phenomenal growth in the early decades of the twentieth century. David Tyack noted that from 1890 to 1918 (the date of the Report of the Commission on the Reorganization of Secondary Education, more popularly known as the Cardinal Principles Report [CPR]), there was on the average more than one new high school built for every day of the year.[35] Attendance at high school rose during those years from 202,963 to 1,645,171, an increase of 711 percent, while the overall population in the nation grew by only 68 percent.[36]

Concomitant with this enrollment spurt were the challenges posed by specialization, curriculum differentiation, and American democracy. How could the nation meet these challenges concurrently? The generally accepted answer was found in the comprehensive high school. The basic principle of this institution was the maintenance of a differentiated, specialized program within one institution, for which extracurricular activities created the unity.[37]

There was, and had been, considerable discussion about the form that secondary education should take. David Snedden, for instance, recommended in 1907 that the comprehensive high school be based on the reform school model.[38] Charles A. Ellwood, a sociologist at the University of Missouri, saw it in eugenic terms; he would require each young American to serve a "sentence" in public schools until she or he passed an examination for citizenship or until she or he was sent to an institution for the feebleminded, where she or he could not marry or reproduce.[39] As I will point out in Chapter Eight, there were those who called for specialized secondary schools based on the post-high school destination of the students. The matter became a central item of discussion for the National Education Association (NEA) which had become a forum for debate over educational issues, and which included college and university personnel as well as public educators.

The CPR emerged out of the social and educational context of the early twentieth century. Its immediate source was the NEA Committee on Articulation of High School and College, which was absorbed into the CPR at the summer meeting of the NEA in 1913.[40] Clarence Kingsley, a follower of Snedden's, a former theology student who had taught mathematics in New York City high schools and at Colgate University, was its chair. Kingsley had been a social worker before becoming high school inspector for the state of Massachusetts.[41]

The Committee was not to issue its final report until 1918. In the interval, there were a number of events which merit consideration. In a preliminary draft, dated 1916, one of the seven objectives—the only one that dealt with traditional academics—"command of the fundamental processes," was missing. Edward Krug reported that it is uncertain when this aim, which appears in the final product, was added.[42]

The focus on the extracurricular, deemed so crucial by many schoolmen for developing good citizenship, is illuminating. Student government was one such item. The school was to become a democracy, which in turn would revolutionize American political life and rout ingloriously the city bosses and ward-heelers. But were the students to practice real democracy or merely learn the process and go through the motions? One writer, who defined student government as "the government of pupils by pupils under the invisible direction of teachers," wondered if this form of school governance failed "because the teachers are not skillful enough to keep their direction of affairs invisible."[43]

The school newspaper was another extracurricular activity that came in for its share of attention. One writer penned that it "meets an important demand. It is a unifying organization, and is therefore a wholesome factor if properly directed. Its purpose is to edit a school paper through which a school spirit may be awakened and nourished."[44] Another commented that "The school paper . . . will create school patriotism and an increased interest in all the activities of the school, educational, athletic, and social."[45]

Clubs took on a new function. In existence in nineteenth century high schools, they now became instruments to teach students to cooperate.[46] Athletics could produce a dual benefit: they would make the boys stronger and healthier and at the same time teach teamwork, so essential to a democratic society. A Seattle principal told the NEA in 1915 that for boys, "football is not only an aggregation of individuals organized to play, but a social instrument with common needs, working along common lines, and embodying a common purpose."[47]

Assemblies were even more critical to instilling good citizenship. The 1913 yearbook of the Francis W. Parker School in Chicago referred to the assemblies as "the family altar of the school to which each brings his offerings—the fruits of his observations and studies." The assembly balanced the practice of separating the students into separate grades and classes; that same yearbook stated that "The morning exercise is one means of impressing upon the children the unity of the whole school and of counteracting some of the undesirable effects of the separation into grades."[48]

The educational world received the CPR in 1918. The recommendations of the report spring not only from the temper of the times in which they were written and from the ideology of its leaders but also from the tasks given the group. The committee perceived its charge to be the formulation of a comprehensive program of reorganization of secondary school education and the adoption of this program in all the secondary schools of the nation.[49] To achieve this goal, it set forth seven objectives, toward which all efforts in secondary education were encouraged to be directed and by which the subjects would henceforth be evaluated. These were said to be: 1) health, 2) command of fundamental processes, 3) worthy home membership, 4) vocation, 5) citizenship, 6) worthy use of leisure, and 7) ethical character.[50] These aims were stated in terms of the effect schooling had on students rather than as processes by which students could master subject matter content. The committee apparently believed that the present needs of society determined what secondary education should be. It asserted that substantial changes had occurred in American society that necessitated a different form of high school education than had existed previously.[51] The school, the committee felt, had to be more concerned with social change and its effects because other agencies, for example the church, were doing less in the field than hitherto.[52]

The Cardinal Principles committee had sixteen "subject" committees. Many of these were new, and had not even been considered by the Committee of Ten on Secondary School Studies in 1893. Among the new fields were agriculture, art education, articulation of high school and college, business education, household arts, industrial arts, music, organization and administration of secondary education, physical education, and vocational guidance.[53] These new areas reflected the belief of the committee that the needs of society should determine curriculum content and the changes in American society, and hence the high school, that had occurred in recent years.

The main report of the Cardinal Principles Report did not consider the academic subjects except to mention them in brief fashion. The subcommittees did, however, and the way they did is important to our thesis. In the Preliminary Report, Latin had to show that it was "practical" in order to survive in a school in a democracy.[54] English was to be taught for "training for efficiency."[55] The overriding aim of social studies was "good citizenship." This subcommittee believed its field had "peculiar opportunities" to contribute to the goal of training the individual to be a worthwhile member of society. Regardless of the subjects' value to the individual, the subcommittee held that "Unless they contribute directly to the cultivation of social efficiency on the part of the pupil they fail in this most important function."[56] Civics would be rejuvenated, becoming a "study of manner of social efforts to improve mankind."[57] History was called upon to give an account of its stewardship, for it "must answer the test of good citizenship."[58]

The CPR was concerned with the goals of education in a democracy. The seven main objectives would determine constants in the curriculum; variables would be according to vocational goals of students. All subjects were to be "practical," the criterion of importance. The committee believed that the nation's form of democratic government would be endangered unless the high schools sought the development "in each individual of the knowledge, interests, ideals, habits, and powers whereby he will find his place and use that place to shape both himself and society toward even nobler ends."[59] The committee decreed that this was to be done in a democratic society, whose purpose "is to organize society that each member may develop his personality primarily through activities designed for the well-being of his fellow members and of society as a whole." As for the individual person, the committee referred to her or his dignity and "potential and perchance unique" worth.[60]

As noted earlier, assemblies were held in new-found high esteem, based on the unifying, democratic role they were to play in the high school and subsequently in society. It was "through school assemblies," the report held, that students "acquire common ideas."[61]

The report, while it did not arouse "limitless desire for discussions," was generally well received in the educational community.[62] In February 1919, the National Association of Secondary School Principals (NASSP) "heartily" endorsed the seven objectives.[63] Its Curriculum Committee asked "Can each subject in the present curriculum be justified on the ground that it contributes definitely and vitally to some or all of these seven ends? If it does not, is the proper remedy reform from within or elimination?"[64] Latin, as currently taught, could not be justified, but the committee hoped it could be reformed and thereby "justify itself."[65] Principal F. R. Willard of the high school in Watertown, Massachusetts, enthusiastically supported the report. He averred that "It will be seen at a glance that these seven main objectives take care of the whole man, body, soul, and mind."[66] Relating the objectives to the major social questions of the day, Willard penned:

> If democracy is to prevail over bolshevism and all other forms of revolution it must chiefly be by means of a system of education inculcating in the minds of youth the cardinal principles governing various kinds of controls—bodily, mental, social, economic, political, esthetic and moral.[67]

Willard's thinking involved implications of the report for social classes. The "classes," he declared, had always understood morality and power to think to be educational objectives (or at least thought they did), but the "masses" never did: "The seven objectives under discussion are of the sort that the masses can comprehend, because they deal with the stuff life is made up of."[68]

The report has been assessed as a form of moderate social efficiency. One of its most vocal critics was David Snedden, who complained that it "almost completely" missed the significance of vocational education and was too academic. He felt that secondary education should be organized into specialized, not comprehensive high schools.[69]

The citizenship thrust that both characterized the report and made it a panacea received considerable praise from the schoolmen. For instance, an associate superintendent in Pittsburgh commented in 1925 on the crucial role of the school assembly:

> Students are divided into classes according to their curricula. . . . Blocking the pathway to unity is an almost infinite variety of individual differences. The assembly is the one agency at hand capable of checking these tendencies.[70]

In support of positions such as this, the authors of a book on *Assemblies for Junior and Senior High Schools,* published in 1929, stated at the outset that:

> Junior and senior high schools daily accept the challenge to prepare students for life in a democracy. . . . Specialized organization and complex activities necessitate unification through athletics, the school newspaper, and the assembly. Because of its frequency and provision for universal participation, the assembly may be considered the foremost integrating factor.[71]

The assembly and other extra-curricular practices, designed to produce the well-rounded American citizen, were lauded by one rather well-known education writer, Thomas Briggs. He declared in 1922 that extra-curricular activities should be included in the regular high school curriculum because such an elevation would "raise these activities to the place of dignity and respect that they deserve as an educational feature of the school in the eyes of pupils, teachers, and community."[72]

Conclusion

The comprehensive high school was intended to be just that: comprehensive. For instance, in 1928, the National Congress of Parents and Teachers (PTA) adopted the seven objectives for their national platform. They called them "The Sevenfold Program of Home and School."[73] In this document the PTA spoke of educating the "whole child," as did the Cardinal Principles Report. There was a notable difference between the two, however. The report conceived of the educational program as taking place solely in the public high school, whereas the PTA envisioned a joint enterprise between home and school. The CPR reflects the position of Herbert Spencer that the school should prepare its students for "complete living." It may be seen as an attempt to educate the whole person, mind and body. The high school, in this philosophy, takes on a comprehensive and consequently more important function in the life of its students. Given the crucial position of the high school, and given the social realities of this age of social efficiency, this expanded role of secondary schooling should not be unexpected. In the second decade of the twentieth century American society faced perplexing and threatening events. Large groups of immigrants retained their native languages and customs. These people were not as yet satisfactorily assimilated into the American mainstream, according to the dominant native white view. This was especially critical after 1917 because of the global war, and the nation was not sure of the loyalties of some of its recent arrivals. Also, the country was beset by the problems resulting from rapid industrialization and urbanization. In light of this, the country looked to its schools for assistance. For the high schools, this entailed a new and different kind of program—one of fostering unity, of making good Americans, of assuming, if it could, a solitary role in shaping that segment of America's youth that needed to undergo Americanization. The Cardinal Principles Report was born in this period of national emergency and social upheaval. With it, the American public high school attempted to reorganize itself and its program, in the process becoming yet one more panacea on the educational landscape.

Notes

1. Edward A. Krug, *The Shaping of the American High School 1880–1920*. Madison: The University of Wisconsin Press, 1964, p. 327.
2. Joel H. Spring, *Education and the Rise of the Corporate State*. Boston: Beacon Press, 1972, p. 103.
3. Ibid., p. 107.
4. Quoted in Krug, *The Shaping of the American High School*, p. 239.
5. Arthur G. Wirth, *Education in the Technological Society*. Scranton, PA: Intext, 1972, p. 132.
6. Krug, *The Shaping of the American High School*, p. 240.
7. Wirth, *Education in the Technological Society*, p. 132.
8. Krug, *The Shaping of the American High School*, p. 240.

9. Ibid., p. 330.
10. Ibid., p. 328.
11. Ibid., p. 333.
12. Quoted in ibid.
13. Ibid.
14. Ibid.
15. Ibid.
16. Quoted in Calvin O. Davis, *Junior High School Education*. New York: World Book Company, 1924, p. 64.
17. Herbert M. Kliebard, *The Struggle for the American Curriculum 1893–1958*. Boston: Routledge and Kegan Paul, 1986, p. 125; Davis, *Junior High School Education*, p. 60.
18. Krug, *The Shaping of the American High School*, p. 332.
19. Davis, *Junior High School Education*, p. 69.
20. Krug, *The Shaping of the American High School*, p. 332.
21. Quoted in Kliebard, *The Struggle for the American Curriculum*, p. 112.
22. Davis, *Junior High School Education*, p. 99.
23. Ibid., p. 351.
24. Quoted in ibid., p. 1.
25. Ibid., p. 7.
26. Quoted in ibid., p. 11.
27. Ibid., p. 334.
28. Ibid., p. 359.
29. Ibid., pp. 415–416.
30. Quoted in Krug, The *Shaping of the American High School*, p. 334.
31. Quoted in ibid.
32. Quoted in ibid., pp. 334–335.
33. Quoted in ibid., p. 335.
34. Quoted in ibid.
35. David B. Tyack, *The One Best System: A History of American Urban Education*. Cambridge, MA: Harvard University Press, 1974, p. 183.
36. Ibid.
37. Spring, *Education and the Rise of the Corporate State*, p. 108.
38. Robert L. Church and Michael W. Sedlak, *Education in the United States: An Interpretive History*. New York: Free Press, 1976, p. 312.
39. Ibid., pp. 311–312.
40. Krug, *The Shaping of the American High School*, p. 300.
41. Ibid., pp. 265, 300–301.
42. Ibid., p. 385.
43. Quoted in Spring, *Education and the Rise of the Corporate State*, pp. 118–119.
44. Quoted in ibid., p. 120.
45. Ibid., pp. 120–121.
46. Ibid., p. 121.
47. Quoted in ibid., p. 122.
48. Quoted in ibid., p. 123.
49. National Education Association, *Cardinal Principles of Secondary Education*. Washington, DC: Government Printing Office, 1918, p. 8.
50. Ibid., pp. 10–11.
51. Ibid., p. 7.

52. Ibid., pp. 7–8.

53. Ibid., p. 6.

54. Walter E. Foster, "Statement of Chairman of the Committee on Ancient Languages," in *Preliminary Statements by Chairmen of Committees of the Commission of the National Education Association on the Reorganization of Secondary Education. U.S. Bureau of Education, Bulletin No. 41.* Washington, DC: Government Printing Office, 1913, pp. 31–33.

55. Commission for the Reorganization of Secondary Education, *Reorganization of English in Secondary Schools. U.S. Bureau of Education, Bulletin No. 2.* Washington, DC: Government Printing Office, 1917, p. 26.

56. Commission for the Reorganization of Secondary Education, *The Social Studies in Secondary Education. U.S. Bureau of Education, Bulletin No. 28.* Washington, DC: Government Printing Office, 1916, pp. 1–2.

57. Thomas Jesse Jones, "Statement of Chairman of the Committee on Social Studies," *Preliminary Statements by Chairmen,* pp. 16–17.

58. Ibid., pp. 17–18.

59. National Education Association, *Cardinal Principles,* p. 9.

60. Ibid.

61. Quoted in Spring, *Education and the Rise of the Corporate State,* p. 113.

62. Krug, *The Shaping of the American High School,* p. 394.

63. Ibid.

64. Ibid.

65. Ibid.

66. Quoted in ibid., p. 395.

67. Quoted in ibid.

68. Quoted in ibid.

69. David Snedden, "Cardinal Principles of Secondary Education." *School and Society* 9 (May 3, 1919): 522–523.

70. Quoted in Spring, *Education and the Rise of the Corporate State,* p. 123.

71. Quoted in ibid., p. 124.

72. Quoted in ibid., p. 112.

73. National Congress of Parents and Teachers, *Jubilee History: 50th Anniversary 1897–1947.* Chicago: The Congress, 1947, pp. 95–96.

CHAPTER EIGHT

Life Adjustment Education and Its Critics

In the "Preface" to his popular and defining 1950 work, *Education for Life Adjustment,* editor Harl Douglass wrote of the slow progress that had been made in secondary school reform since the Cardinal Principles Report of 1918. Student enrollment had vastly increased, and the "conditions of life" and the "needs imposed by these conditions have clearly indicated the increasing necessity for revamping secondary education," he told his readers. Douglass then addressed the promise life adjustment education held in carrying out this much-needed reform:

> Various movements, reports, statements, commission activities, and investigations such as the eight-year study of the thirty schools by the Progressive Education Association have come and gone, with no great effect upon the practice of the great mass of secondary schools. Only in the past few years has there seemed to be a real possibility of thoroughly reviewing the educational program of our high schools with a view to developing markedly improved opportunities for becoming adjusted to, and developing a capacity for adjusting to, life as we find it today. In the education for Life Adjustment movement there is a great probability that the spark fanned by the general education movement and the Education for All American Youth project can set off an educational prairie fire that will reach all sections of the country.[1]

This chapter will examine the movement that was life adjustment from the aspect of being a panacea; it will then deal with its pre- and post-Sputnik critics.

Life Adjustment Education

As is the case with all other movements in education, life adjustment education had its historical spawning ground. Robert Church and Michael Sedlak trace its recent origins to the Educational Policies Commission's (EPC) 1938 "The Purposes of Education in American Democracy," which boiled the proper social role of the school down to self-realization, human relations, civic efficiency, and economic competence; schools that produced students with these qualities were fulfilling their custodial function.[2] Diane Ravitch called attention to the work of Professor B. L. Dodds of Purdue's *That All May Learn,* which the NASSP published in 1939, in which she argued that the academic high school student "could with far more justification be considered abnormal." What students wanted to know, Dodds argued, was how to dress attractively, how to make friends with the opposite sex, and how to get a job.[3] Certainly the social efficiency movement, vocational education, and the Cardinal Principles Report may be seen as at least part of the ideological heritage of life adjustment. The "ten imperative needs" of youth, as delineated by the EPC in 1944, undoubtedly qualify as precursors to life adjustment education,[4] needs that served as the basis for defining the "common studies" of secondary education, subsequently to be referred to as "common learnings" courses.[5]

In 1944 the vocational education division of the U.S. Office of Education undertook a study of "Vocational Education in the Years Ahead," which led to a conference in Washington, D.C. in May–June of 1945.[6] It was at that conference, as it neared its end, that Charles A. Prosser, that long-time advocate of vocational education, was asked to summarize what had transpired at the meeting. Prosser responded with his soon-to-be famous resolution, which read:

> It is the belief of this conference that with the aid of this report in final form, the vocational school of a community will be able better to prepare 20 percent of its youth of secondary-school age for entrance upon desirable skilled occupations; and that the high school will continue to prepare 20 percent of its students for entrance to college. We do not believe that the remaining 60 percent of our youth of secondary-school age will receive the life adjustment training they need and to which they are entitled as American citizens—unless and until the administrators of public education with the assistance of the vocational education leaders formulate a comparable program for this group.[7]

The resolution went on to ask the Commissioner to call a series of regional conferences of general and vocational educators,[8] and life adjustment education was born.

The U.S. Office of Education gave life adjustment education its ringing endorsement, including support from its official organ, *School Life.*[9] As Ravitch noted, the "Prosser Resolution," as it was known, was reworded to eliminate any reference to a specific percentage, and it came to apply to *all* American youth.[10] While there was some uncertainty about its meaning, it was understood that it "represented a call to implement the profession's persistent demands for 'functional' education."[11]

Five regional conferences were held between April and November of 1946 to discuss this "new" and promising movement, which brought together professional educators from almost all precincts of the profession—except arts and science professors.[12] Five propositions were recommended to be brought before a national conference the following year, propositions that concluded that secondary schools were "failing to provide adequately and properly for the life adjustment of perhaps a major fraction" of students; that "functional experiences in the areas of practical arts, home and family life, health and physical fitness, and civic competence" were fundamental to meeting the needs of youth; that most youngsters needed a supervised work experience; that teacher educators required a "broadened viewpoint and a genuine desire to serve all youth"; and that sufficient public interest could be mobilized to support a nationwide program of life adjustment education.[13]

The national conference met as planned in May of 1947. They were greeted by co-chairman Dr. Galen Jones, who spoke of the challenge the participants faced:

> We are convened here to consider a problem which is of central importance to education and which, we will all agree I am sure, is central to the perpetuation and improvement of the American way of life. That approximately one hundred persons in key positions of leadership in American education have arranged to give these several days to planning a program of action attests to the value and possibilities of this conference.[14]

Following the reports and resolutions, Prosser euphorically concluded the conference:

> Never in all the history of education has there been such a meeting as this one. . . . Never was there such a meeting where people were so sincere in their belief that this was the golden opportunity to do something that would give to all American youth their educational heritage so long denied. What you have planned is worth fighting for—is worth dying for. . . . Because of what you have done, we are on the eve of a system of education which looks after all American youth—those who go to college and those who do not; those who enter skilled occupations and those who do not. . . . I am proud to have lived long enough to see my fellow schoolmen design a plan which will aid in achieving for every youth an education truly adjusted to life. . . . Yes, it is a dream—man's big dream. If we go all the way back to primitive man and follow him down through the ages, he has always had this grand dream, dimly seen, before him. That you will bring its realization in the bright light of today and tomorrow I have no doubt. God bless you all![15]

The conference, convoked by U.S. Commissioner of Education John W. Studebaker, a life adjustment supporter, recommended the creation of a Commission on Life Adjustment Education of Youth. Studebaker, who was quoted in *Newsweek* as saying that under life adjustment, "old standbys like Milton's 'Il Penseroso' and George Eliot's 'Silas Marner' would probably disappear from the schools,"[16] concurred, and appointed Superintendent Benjamin Willis of Yonkers, New York to serve as its chair.[17] Acknowledging that the need was to translate "theory into school practice,"[18] the commission defined the goal of life adjustment education as "designed to equip all American youth to live democratically with satisfaction to themselves and profit to society as home members, workers, and citizens."[19] The commission went on to stress the importance of personal satisfaction and the need for learning experiences appropriate to the capacities of the students.[20]

Imprecision about the meaning of life adjustment education was to plague the movement throughout its brief period of dominance in the curricular world. Commissioner McGrath, an enthusiastic backer, commented that "Terms such as 'flapdoodle' have been ruinous to certain educational projects, but I am confident that no incident of name calling can similarly endanger Life Adjustment Education. It is too well established in the public confidence."[21] The NASSP proved to be an unflinching backer of life adjustment. At its 1949 meeting, Vernon L. Nickell, state superintendent of Illinois, addressed the question "How Can We Develop an Effective Program of Education for Life Adjustment?" Relying on the the Illinois Secondary-School Curriculum Program as his model, Nickell contended that "the test of the school is in the effectiveness with which its graduates live in all of life's activities."[22] We will know our schools are good, Nickell averred, if our graduates turn out to be good citizens, family members, workers, employers, and consumers and "wholesome users of leisure time."[23] For Nickell, that was "simply another way of saying that no public secondary school can be said to be a good school unless it plans its program around the problems of living which its pupils are currently confronting and those which they will certainly encounter in the foreseeable future."[24]

Life adjustment educators claimed that their curriculum was built around real-life problems; students, they felt, saw little value in the traditional high school curriculum. As Daniel and Laura Tanner have noted, only one out of two students who entered high school in the postwar era graduated.[25] Nickell refers to a follow-up study conducted in Illinois (prepared by Harold C. Hand of the College of Education at the University of Illinois, a bitter adversary of Arthur Bestor, one of life adjustment's harshest critics), which was built around the "Basic Needs of High School Youth." The major categories were "Earning a Living," "Developing an Effective Personality," "Living Healthfully and Safely," "Managing Personal Finances Wisely," "Spending Leisure Time Wholesomely and Enjoyably," "Taking an Effective Part in Civic Affairs," "Preparing for Marriage, Home-making, and Parenthood," and "Making Effective Use of Educational Opportunities."[26]

These real-life problems were to be in accord with the "guiding principles" of life adjustment education that were developed and approved in the 1948 conference in Washington, D.C. Life adjustment education would achieve the following goals:

1. Respect the worth and personality of individuals, which was described as the "supreme test of life adjustment."
2. Enroll and retain all youth.
3. Offer required courses and course content that addressed problems of living.
4. Emphasize direct experience.
5. Use democratic principles in the planning, organization, operation, and administration of schools.
6. Use records and data constructively.
7. Evaluate in order to bring about desired changes in pupil behavior.[27]

Douglass maintained that "Few educators would disagree with the statement that the purpose of education is to foster, promote, and develop democracy as a way of life." Consequently, "education for democratic living should lead to development of democratic attitudes, habits, skills, appreciations, interests, ideals, and ways of thinking as well as acquiring information."[28] One could deduce two important implications from such a view of education:

1. That a curriculum based upon life adjustment of every youth should be based upon current and future personal, social, civic, and economic problems.
2. That the purpose of problem solving is to help youth to *develop, change,* and *fortify their behavior, i.e., their attitudes, habits, skills, ideals, interests, appreciations and ways of thinking. In other words, learning and behavior development are synonymous.*[29]

Two commissions spearheaded the movement in the late 1940s and early 1950s. The first weighed in in 1951 with *Vitalizing Secondary Education*. The report included what came to be known as the "Definition of Life Adjustment Education":

> Life adjustment education is designed to equip all American youth to live democratically with satisfaction to themselves and profit to society as home members, workers, and citizens. It is concerned especially with a sizable proportion of youth of high-school age (both in school and out) whose objectives are less well served by our schools than the objectives of preparation for either a skilled occupation or higher education. Some leaders have for years been at work in secondary schools developing a guiding philosophy and bringing about program reorganization in the direction of life adjustment education for every youth. Under such leadership, many high schools have made considerable progress in building programs of study and providing educational services basically useful to each participating pupil.
>
> Many high schools, however, continue to be dominated by traditional curriculum patterns that emphasize verbal and abstract learning or place undue emphasis on specialized courses useful to a relatively small number of pupils. As a result, many pupils unable to benefit from either of these types of instruction are left to flounder or to leave the schools as soon as the compulsory education laws will permit.[30]

The commission went on to contend that "American high schools are too se-lective to be effective instruments for furthering democratic ideals" and that there "seems to be a widespread realization that our Nation has assumed responsibility for world leadership that can be met only if citizens enjoy the benefits of an ex-tended and improved common school,"[31] something that life adjustment educa-tion alone would provide, no doubt.

The first commission existed to promote action and was a joint effort of voca-tional and general educators; it covered the first three years of activity on behalf of life adjustment education.[32] The second commission, which served from 1950 until 1953, enlarged the work of the first; each member was asked to accept re-sponsibility for "developing and encouraging life adjustment education ideas in his own geographical area and in the professional association which he repre-sented."[33] The membership of the second commission was expanded to include the American Association of Colleges for Teacher Education, the National Con-gress of Parents and Teachers, and the American School Boards Association, in ad-dition to the nine professional associations that comprised the first commission.[34]

In his excellent work on the history of curriculum, Herbert Kliebard wrote of a number of schools where life adjustment education was implemented, including Catholic schools.[35] In Billings, Montana, these included use of "activity points" (loss of points was incurred for breaking school rules) and a "Scholarship Plan" that affected graduation, and involved parents as well as students.[36] Kliebard also cited a state department educator from Connecticut, who described the "real-life problems" as "preparation for post-secondary education, preparation for work, doing an effective day's work in school, getting along well with other boys and girls, understanding parents, driving a motor car, using the English language, en-gaging in recreational activities."[37] A major point of life adjustment, one that sub-jected it to scathing criticism, and which qualified it as yet another magic elixir, was its "emphasis on the indefinite expansion of the scope of the curriculum."[38] It had no bounds.

Pre-Sputnik Criticism

Criticism of life adjustment education had been brewing long before the launching of Sputnik in 1957. Indeed, some of the critics lumped attacks on life adjustment education with attacks on progressive education, in some cases not even distin-guishing between the two. As Lawrence Cremin noted, the attack on life adjust-ment education was not an "isolated phenomenon"; it was a continuation of the storm that had been brewing since at least the early 1940s.[39] Books by Bernard Id-dings Bell and Mortimer Smith serve as illustrations of this round of criticism. Smith, in *And Madly Teach,* criticized modern educational theorists. Accusing them of fuzzy thinking, he cited an article by a leading educator on "administration," in which the educator identified "three primary functions, eight elements, nine basic principles, and five relationships" in school leadership.[40] The American ideal of "education for all" was false, he argued, because it currently meant that "everyone will be trained to *do* something and only by chance will a few be educated to *become* something."[41] Smith, who had been a school board member in Connecticut,[42] included the preparation and certification of teachers in his critique:

> . . . in most of the states in this country no new teacher can be certified who has not been exposed to "education," or method, in courses that consume about one year's time above his regular academic training. . . . Don't think the educational hierarchy doesn't rigidly enforce this system. Socrates himself would find it extremely difficult to be certified.[43]

Smith continued his onslaught against the education profession:

> . . . if anyone will take the trouble to investigate, it will be found that those who make up the staffs of the schools and colleges of education, and the administrators and teachers whom they train to run the system, have a truly amazing uniformity of opinion regarding the aims, the content, and the methods of education. They constitute a cohesive body of believers with a clearly formulated set of dogmas and doctrines, and they are perpetuating the faith by seeing to it, through state laws and the rules of state departments of education, that only those teachers and administrators are certified who have been trained in correct dogma.[44]

The popular press, no stranger to engaging in critiques of public education, joined in the censuring. This time it was *Time,* which called life adjustment education the "latest gimmick among U.S. educators" and a "school of thought which seemed to believe that the teacher's job was not so much to teach history or algebra, as to prepare students to live happily ever after."[45] The sheer volume of the critical articles, which rose from seven in 1948 to forty-nine in 1952, in such publications as *Life, Reader's Digest, Atlantic Monthly, Saturday Review of Literature,* and *McCall's* among others, attracted national attention.[46]

The schools were seen as espousing anti–intellectualism, a theme enunciated by Henry J. Fuller, a professor of botany at the University of Illinois, at the annual banquet of the Phi Beta Kappa society. Fuller included professors of education in his scathing remarks, which centered on four basic themes:

I. The falsity of the basic assumptions from which education professors commonly proceed in their anti–intellectual activities

II. The deterioration in the contemporary training of students, particularly in the high schools

III. The substitution of "socially significant" subjects for sound education in the humanities, the arts, and the sciences

IV. The confusions and inconsistencies that dominate the thinking (perhaps my use of this word is inexcusably charitable), the utterances, and the activities of many education professors.[47]

In 1953, Albert Lynd added his voice to the chorus of censure of the educationists:

> Professors of Education do all the significant thinking, so to speak, for your local schools because they have copper-riveted one of the neatest bureaucratic machines ever created by any professional group in any country anywhere since the priesthood of ancient Egypt. In nearly every state today a teacher or principal cannot go to work in a public school without a certificate or license, which can be obtained only by taking courses under a Faculty of education. When the new teacher gets his first job, he has only begun his vassalage to these superprofessionals. In a great many communities salary schedules are so rigged that he must go back again, summer after summer, for more Educational revelation if he expects to get maximum salary raises.[48]

Ravitch noted that Lynd raised some serious questions in his flaying of the educational establishment, viz., To whom do the public schools belong? Who has the right to select the social aims of education, the community or the educators?[49]

Arthur Bestor, a history professor at the University of Illinois, the chief and most effective excoriator of progressive education and life adjustment education, took center stage in the early 1950s. Taking aim at what he believed was the diversion of schools from their central function—the development of the intellect—Bestor ridiculed the ten "Imperative Needs of Youth" that had been part of life adjustment's *Education for All American Youth,* which had become the semi-official dogma of the NASSP.[50] It was *not* the task of the school to meet "the common and the specific individual needs of youth," Bestor wrote. He took educators to task for attempting to have the school "take responsibility for things that the family today is supposedly failing to do," under the guise of the label of "home and family living."[51] Writing in *The New Republic,* Bestor assailed the sixty percent figure contained in the "Prosser Resolution." He argued that this definition was anti-democratic because it assumed that a majority of students "are incapable of being benefited by intellectual training." Such a breakdown of the school population, Bestor held, "enthrones once again the ancient doctrine that the majority of people are destined from birth to be hewers of wood and drawers of water to a select few, who, by right of superior fitness, are to occupy the privileged places in society."[52]

Bestor, unlike some of the other contemporary assailants, was reluctant to associate life adjustment education with progressive education because the latter was so "vague and ambiguous." Bestor himself had studied at the Lincoln School of Teachers College, one of the most progressive schools in the country.[53] A fervent believer in the supremacy of the intellectual in schooling, Bestor did not hesitate to identify examples of anti–intellectualism in the life adjustment literature. Kliebard reports that one of his favorites was an article that appeared in the *NASSP Bulletin:*

When we come to the realization that not every child has to read, figure, write and spell
. . . that many of them either cannot or will not master these chores . . . then we shall be
on the road to improving the junior high school curriculum.

Between this day and that a lot of selling must take place. But it's coming. We shall
some day accept the thought that it is just as illogical to assume that every boy must be able
to read as it is that each one must be able to perform on a violin, that it is no more reasonable
to require that each girl shall spell well than it is that each one shall bake a good cherry pie.

When adults finally realize that fact, everyone will be happier . . . and schools will be
nicer places in which to live.[54]

It was in his book, *Educational Wastelands,* which was published in 1953, that his
attacks reached a higher crescendo. Enlarging on a charge he had flung earlier against
the sixty percent figure in the "Prosser Resolution," Bestor declared that if that were
true, it "declares invalid most of the assumptions that have underlain American democracy."[55] Strongly assailing the elimination of the study of history, political science, and economics, which provided disciplined, analytical, critical thinking, in
favor of a "common learnings" course, the educationists sailed on to "other problems
that seem to be of equal importance in their eyes—the problem of acquiring the ability to select and enjoy good motion pictures," or "the problem of acquiring the social
skills of dancing, playing party games, doing parlor stunts, etc."[56] High-sounding
objectives, such as teaching children to "help solve economic, social and political
problems," were offered as the "preambles to educational proposals of the utmost
vagueness," he contended, and that vagueness was "one of the principal dangers."[57]
No position of life adjustment suggested that intellectual training could answer
"real-life" problems, he maintained; if a student could see no practical point in "history, geography, arithmetic, and grammar, is he going to rush back to school filled
with a burning desire for sensitivity and world citizenship?" he asked.[58]

He followed *Wastelands* two years later with *The Restoration of Learning.* One
of his major points of contention in this book was that the educationists had la-
belled intellectual training an "aristocratic school." He thought that in America,
by providing educational opportunities that were enjoyed only by nobles in an
aristocratic society, we were *building* a democratic society, not *undermining* it.
The school, he argued, did not create:

. . . a democratic structure of intellectual life merely by gathering all the nation's children
within its walls. It becomes an agency of true democratization only if it sends them forth
with knowledge, cultural appreciation, and disciplined intellectual power—with the
qualities, in other words, that have always distinguished educated men from uneducated
ones. . . .

Universal public education can be defended only on the assumption . . . that needs
which require satisfaction by intellectual means are common to all men and are so important that society ought to provide the amplest possible training in the intellectual processes involved. To deny this assumption is to deny the only real argument for universal
public education.[59]

Bestor then turned his attention to the "functional" argument advanced by the educationists. He held that the nature of our government required that the "functions of an aristocracy become the functions of citizens at large." In a democracy, "the school must transmit to the public at large, not merely to its own students, a respect for knowledge and cultural achievement. . . . the school must uphold for all men this ideal of disciplined intellectual effort." For Bestor, the social order the nation needed, one that would make intellectual freedom unassailable, was obtainable through the school. That was its "great task in a democracy."[60]

Bestor had a program for school reform. First, the control of education should be removed from the hands of the educationists and given over to a coalition of parents and arts and sciences professors; second, pedagogy should be de-emphasized and academic training should be strengthened; and third, teacher training should be returned to the control of the larger university.[61] In a sense, Bestor and his allies had presented their own panaceas in their scathing critiques of life adjustment and progressive education.

Bestor's opinions reached a wider audience than academia. For instance, in 1956, he had an "Interview" published with *U.S. News & World Report,* in which he outlined when and why American schools had deteriorated, and why, in the depths of the Cold War, their Soviet counterparts far outstripped them.[62] Bestor, life adjustment's chief pre-Sputnik critic, was guilty of hyperbole and passion, which hampered his arguments.[63] But his target, life adjustment education, was an easy one to hit.

Sputnik and Its Aftermath

The launching of Sputnik by the Soviet Union on October 4, 1957 served to accelerate and intensify the criticism of American education, particularly life adjustment and progressive education that had been extant for several years. Why, the question was posed, if our schools are so strong have the Soviets beaten us into space? The dearth of American scientists was singled out as a cause of the failure, and the schools, in particular the public high schools, were held accountable for that deficiency. Tensions about how to address the situation were exacerbated.[64]

The popular press took up the issue. Cast in the context of the Cold War, the March 1958 issue of *Life* began a five part series, what it called an "urgent series," which it entitled "Crisis in Education."[65] The first issue featured an article by Sloan Wilson, entitled "It's Time to Close Our Carnival." In it Wilson pointed out that "Ten million Russians are studying English, but only 8,000 Americans are studying Russian."[66] Wilson hurled further accusations at the mediocrity the schools were fostering: one junior high principal in New York City publicly admitted "great pangs of pedagogical conscience" when he signed diplomas of students who have "completed the course of study with a satisfactory record" who cannot read above the fifth grade level or master fourth-grade arithmetic fundamentals; Secretary of Health, Education, and Welfare Marion B. Folsom was quoted as demanding fewer "so-called popular or easy courses" and "less chrome, less country-clubbing."[67] Wilson quoted Admiral Hyman Rickover, whose views we will hear more of later, about courses on love and marriage that "You can learn how to make love outside of school in the good old-fashioned ways."[68] Under the sub-heading of "Doing almost nothing well," Wilson wrote:

> The schools are becoming increasingly vulnerable to the charge that in trying to do every-thing for everyone, they are succeeding in doing almost nothing well.
>
>   The upshot is that many a brilliant youngster finds that his school has assumed the aspects of a carnival. In one room pretty girls practice twirling batons. The sound of cheers is heard from the football field. The safe-driving class circles the block in new au-tomobiles lent by an enterprising dealer. Upstairs funny Mr. Smith sits wearily on a stool in the chemistry lab trying to explain to a few boys that science can be fun, but who pays any attention to him?
>
>   It is hard to deny that America's schools, which were supposed to reflect one of history's noblest dreams and to cultivate the nation's youthful minds, have degenerated into a system for coddling and entertaining the mediocre. It is one thing to establish courses of varying purpose and of varying degrees of difficulty to fit the talents of various individuals, but it is quite another to run schools in which most of the students avoid the tough courses—and get away with it. . . .
>
>   Democracy was never supposed to substitute license for discipline. Instead, it was meant to substitute self-discipline for oppression.[69]

"An eager student," Wilson surmised, "is branded a queer duck" in American schools.[70]

Congress became involved on September 2, 1958 with the passage of The National Defense Education Act (NDEA). The keynote of the act is revealed in its language. "The security of the Nation" and the "present emergency" required financial assistance from the government to teach students science, mathematics, modern languages, and technology.[71] The NDEA upheld the belief that a good education and strong defense are closely related.[72] Federal funds augmented the academic counter-revolution that had begun in 1950 with the establishment of the National Science Foundation (NSF), which was manifest in the restructuring of physics in 1956 prior to Sputnik. (Developments in mathematics, chemistry, and biology occurred after Sputnik.)[73] Professional educators had been dominant in life adjustment; now the leaders hailed from academic departments, not schools or colleges of education, further evidence of the loss of confidence in education-ists and their subsequent loss of influence.[74]

As was the case with pre-Sputnik criticism of life adjustment, there were leaders of post-Sputnik criticism of life adjustment who castigated the movement and its responsibility for the dire state of American secondary education in particular. Arthur Bestor remained on the scene; he was joined by a number of other commentators, including the former president of Harvard, James Bryant Conant, and Admiral Hyman Rickover.

In a 1958 interview with *U.S. News & World Report,* Bestor contended that "The basic trouble is that the persons running our public-school system lost sight of the main purpose of education—namely, intellectual training." Holding that as far back as 1952 he had called attention to the danger of "anti–intellectualism" in the schools, Bestor said that professional educators tended to "pooh-pooh" the idea of mental discipline and to say that "life adjustment" should be the aim of public education "instead of thorough training in fundamental fields like science, mathematics, foreign languages, history and English." In the "light of Sputnik, 'life-adjustment education' turns out to have been something perilously close to 'death adjustment' for our nation and our children." We have wasted, he maintained, "an appalling part of the time of our young people in trivialities. The Russians have had sense enough not to do so. That's why the first satellite bears the label 'Made in Russia.'"[75]

Bestor renewed his criticism of "life adjustment" educationists, who he said, "hardly bother to hide their contempt for the teacher who knows his subject and is fired up." Teachers like that were regarded as the greatest "barrier" to education because "they have no desire to switch from French to a course in human relations, or from trigonometry to consumer education."[76] Life adjustment educators, through the Educational Policies Commission (EPC) that was appointed by the NEA and the American Association of School Administrators (AASA), were responsible for the anti–intellectual character of public-school philosophy and hence of the shortage of quality teachers. Bright young people, "repelled by most courses in education," had turned to other fields.[77] Life adjustment educators constituted a threat to the revived emphasis that Sputnik had helped bring to the schools because they had not had a "change of heart." The recent retreat by these educationists, aware that their program very likely would be "decently buried soon," possibly would result in "band-wagon jumping." Warning that the educationists had not changed their minds, Bestor commented:

> We neglected all the basic subjects because our educational-policy makers didn't think them important. They wanted the schools to deal only with so-called "practical" things, things in front of their noses—cooking, automobile driving, "better boy-girl relationships," "life adjustment" and the like. Now many of them are ready to concede that Sputnik has made science and mathematics "practical," and they are ready to plump for these two subjects. They have not really repudiated their anti–intellectual attitude toward education. They have simply taken up another fad.
>
> If educationists of this stamp control the new programs that the present crisis may bring forth, then we won't get good teaching even of science and mathematics. They will

be taught a series of specialized tricks, not as a fundamental way of thinking. And there
will be a hacking away at humanistic disciplines like history, English literature and foreign
languages, because the educationists will still brand them "impractical."[78]

Bestor's solution was for Congress to appoint a national advisory commission
on public educational policy, composed of "absolutely top-level physicists, chem-
ists, mathematicians, historians, foreign-language specialists, professors of English
literature, economists and representatives of other disciplines, fundamental to a
sound school program." The quality of teaching in our schools could only be improved by a combination of a proper educational philosophy, one that scholars had,
with knowledge of the subject taught.[79] Slogans advocated by the educationists,
such as "We don't teach the subject, we teach the child," needed to be discarded.[80]

James Bryant Conant had been a moderate in this debate ever since he
played a leading role in the publication of Harvard's *General Education in a Free
Society* in 1945. He was to continue that role in his famous *The American High
School Today,* a book made possible by a grant from the Carnegie Commission of
New York through the Educational Testing Service.[81] The book bore out
Conant's reputation as the "friendly critic" of American public education: he
called for the preservation of the comprehensive high school, ability grouping in
all subjects outside of a required senior-level social studies course, a course-study
record as a supplement to the diploma, and elimination of class rank on the basis
of an average grade based on all subjects, among other things.[82]

It was Admiral Hyman Rickover, however, who chastised the life adjustment
movement most harshly, and who advocated a rigorous intellectual training of
youth necessitated on the grounds of national defense. For him, Sputnik revealed
the costs of the American system of education that wasted its manpower by neglect-
ing intellectual training.[83] The so-called father of the nuclear American navy, Rickover believed a strong America depended on its educational system. The nation was
in jeopardy because of the policies of life adjustment education. The educationists
had erred by refusing to recognize the essentials of education, trying to make it fun:

> The educational process for all children must be one of collecting factual knowledge to
> the limit of their absorptive capacity. Recreation, manual or clerical training, etiquette,
> and similar know-how have little effect on the mind itself and it is with the mind that the
> school must solely concern itself. The poorer a child's natural endowments, the more does
> he need to have his mind trained. . . . To acquire such knowledge, fact upon fact, takes
> time and effort. Nothing can really make it "fun."[84]

Expanding on this position, Rickover stated, in an interview with Edward R.
Murrow, that scientific education was absolutely indispensable in this age. It:

> . . . is even more important than atomic power in the navy, for if our people are not
> properly educated in accordance with the terrific requirements of this rapidly spiraling

scientific and industrial civilization, we are bound to go down. The Russians have apparently recognized this.[85]

The Admiral was called on to speak on the state of education before many audiences, including the Congress of the United States. The greater part of his best-known book, *Education and Freedom,* is based on those addresses. Schools, he argued, must return to their traditional tasks in formal education in Western civilization, the "transmission of the nation's cultural heritage, and preparation for life through rigorous training of young minds to think clearly, logically, and independently."[86] The nation's waste of its talented youth was a "serious indictment of our schools." The "chronic shortage of good scientists, engineers, and other professionals which plagues us is largely the result of inadequate preprofessional education,"[87] which was due to the theories and practices of the life adjustment educators. It was their "seemingly democratic" philosophy, while espousing equality of education literally that abolished it in fact.[88] Under the influence of life adjustment theories, we had shown "an extraordinary lack of faith in the abilities of average American children"; we trailed "advanced industrial countries," due in large part to the "progressivist educationist theories and practices."[89]

The media provided yet another forum for Rickover to press his points. He appeared with Lawrence Spivak on the television program *Meet the Press* on January 24, 1960. Responding to an inquiry about a statement he had made previously, in which he had said that "Sputnik may well do for education what Pearl Harbor had done for industry and the military," Rickover replied that it had not.[90] His objection was to the "total system" of education, which has the students "waste time on many subjects which have nothing to do with education whatever." This system made "jobs for guidance counselors, athletic coaches, school administrators and so on," but it did not educate.[91] Teachers had no voice; indeed, they were fearful for their jobs in systems where so many "public school principals are ex-athletic coaches," people who should not be running our schools, but are.[92] Organized sports, conducted for the "entertainment of the parents" and to "make jobs for various people" had no place in school.[93] Education, for Rickover, was "more important" than military defense, it was of "far greater importance than anything there is in this country, any problem we have."[94] Rickover argued that the nation should revise its view of the comprehensive high school and create a multiple system of educational institutions in keeping with students' academic abilities.[95]

Conclusion

That one-time champion of educational reform, life adjustment education, was in total disarray by the mid-1950s and had all but disappeared from the landscape following Sputnik. With the movement went the ascension of the professors of education and the "interlocking directorate" with federal, state, and local educational agencies. In a time of national concern over security, life adjustment education was held accountable in some quarters for the dismal state of our schools and the poor scientific and mathematical performance of our students in particular. While the theme that the *school's concern is with the intellect alone,*" as advanced by Rickover,[96] and generally supported by Bestor and some of their contemporaries was perhaps an exaggeration, there is no question that the panacea of life adjustment had been ingloriously routed. Perhaps it is best to conclude this chapter with words of historian Richard Hofstadter, himself a severe critic of the life adjustment theory: "Life-adjustment educators would do anything in the name of science except encourage children to study it."[97]

Notes

1. Harl R. Douglass, "Preface," in Harl R. Douglass, ed., *Education for Life Adjustment: Its Meaning and Implementation.* New York: Ronald Press, 1950, pp. v–vi.
2. Robert L. Church and Michael W. Sedlak, *Education in the United States: An Interpretive History.* New York: The Free Press, 1976, p. 403.
3. Diane Ravitch, *The Troubled Crusade: American Education, 1945–1980.* New York: Basic Books, 1983, pp. 61–62.
4. Educational Policies Commission, " On Meeting the Needs of Youth" (1944), in Sol Cohen, ed., *Education in the United States: A Documentary History.* Vol. 4. New York: Random House, 1974, pp. 2622–2623.
5. Educational Policies Commission, "On Education for All American Youth" (1944), in Cohen, ed., ibid., pp. 2623–2625.
6. Lawrence A. Cremin, *The Transformation of the School: Progressivism in American Education 1876–1957.* New York: Vintage Books, 1963, pp. 333–334.
7. Quoted in Edward A. Krug, ed., *Salient Dates in American Education: 1635–1964.* New York: Harper and Row, 1966, p. 131.
8. Ibid., pp. 131–132.
9. Herbert M. Kliebard, *The Struggle for the American Curriculum 1893–1958.* Boston: Routledge and Kegan Paul, 1986, p. 249.
10. Ravitch, *The Troubled Crusade,* p. 65.
11. Ibid.
12. Cremin, *The Transformation of the School,* p. 335.
13. Ibid.
14. Quoted in Sol Cohen, ed., *Education in the United States: A Documentary History,* 4, p. 2631.
15. Quoted in ibid., p. 2632.
16. Quoted in Kliebard, "Growing Antagonism in High School-College Relations," *Journal of Curriculum Supervision* 3 (1987): 67–68.
17. Cremin, *The Transformation of the School,* p. 335.
18. Ibid., p. 336.
19. Krug, ed., *Salient Dates in American Education,* pp. 132–133.
20. Ibid., p. 133.

21. Quoted in Kliebard, *The Struggle for the American Curriculum,* p. 252.
22. Vernon L. Nickell, "How Can We Develop An Effective Program of Education for Life Adjustment?," *Bulletin of the National Association of Secondary School Principals* 33 (April 1949): 153–154.
23. Ibid., 154.
24. Ibid.
25. Daniel Tanner and Laurel Tanner, *History of the School Curriculum.* New York: Macmillan, 1990, p. 249.
26. Nickell, "How can We Develop An Effective Program of Education for Life Adjustment?," p. 154.
27. J. Dan Hull, "Development of the Current Life Adjustment Movement," in Harl R. Douglass, ed., *Education for Life Adjustment.* New York: Ronald Press, 1950, pp. 12–13.
28. Douglass, "Breaking with the Past," in Douglass., ed., ibid., p. 39.
29. Ibid.
30. Commission on Life Adjustment Education, *Vitalizing Secondary Education. U.S. Office of Education, Bulletin No. 3.* Washington, DC: United States Office of Education, 1951, p. 1.
31. Ibid., p. 44.
32. Second Commission on Life Adjustment Education for Youth, *A Look Ahead in Secondary Education. U.S. Office of Education, Bulletin No. 4.* Washington, DC: United States Office of Education, 1954, pp. 1–2.
33. Ibid., p. 3.
34. Ibid., pp. 2–3.
35. Kliebard, *The Struggle for the American Curriculum,* pp. 253–254.
36. Ibid., p. 256.
37. Ibid., p. 253.
38. Ibid.
39. Cremin, *The Transformation of the School,* p. 338.
40. Mortimer Smith, *And Madly Teach: A Layman Looks at Public School Education.* Chicago: Henry Regnery, 1949, p. 5.
41. Ibid., pp. 11–12.
42. Ravitch, *The Troubled Crusade,* p. 72.
43. Smith, *And Madly Teach,* p. 62.
44. Quoted in Cremin, *The Transformation of the School,* p. 340.
45. Quoted in Ravitch, *The Troubled Crusade,* p. 72.
46. Ibid., p. 73.
47. Quoted in Kliebard, *The Struggle for the American Curriculum,* p. 259.
48. Albert Lynd, *Quackery in the Public Schools.* Boston: Little, Brown and Company, 1953, p. 36.
49. Ravitch, *The Troubled Crusade,* p. 75.
50. Kliebard, *The Struggle for the American Curriculum,* p. 260.
51. Quoted in ibid.
52. Quoted in ibid., p. 261.
53. Ibid.
54. Quoted in ibid., pp. 261–262.
55. Arthur E. Bestor, *Educational Wastelands: The Retreat from Learning in Our Public Schools.* 2nd edition. Chicago and Urbana: University of Illinois Press, 1985, p. 82.
56. Ibid., p. 90.
57. Ibid.
58. Ibid., p. 92.
59. Arthur R. Bestor, *The Restoration of Learning: A Program for Redeeming the Unfulfilled Promise of American Education.* New York: Alfred A. Knopf, 1955, pp. 86–88.

60. Ibid., pp. 94–96.

61. Cremin, *The Transformation of the School,* pp. 345–346.

62. "Interview with Professor Arthur Bestor," *U.S. News & World Report,* November 30, 1956, p. 68.

63. Kliebard, *The Struggle for the American Curriculum,* p. 262.

64. Daniel Calhoun, ed., *The Educating of Americans: A Documentary History.* New York: Houghton Mifflin, 1969, p. 542.

65. *Life,* March 24, 1958. pp. 25, 27.

66. Ibid., p. 36.

67. Ibid.

68. Ibid.

69. Ibid., p. 37.

70. Ibid.

71. Quoted in Krug, ed., *Salient Dates in American Education,* p. 140.

72. Church and Sedlak, *Education in the United States,* p. 414.

73. Kliebard, *The Struggle for the American Curriculum,* p. 267.

74. Ibid., p. 268. For one illustration of this "changing of the guard," see Albert R. Kitzhaber, Robert M. Gorrell, and Paul Roberts, *Education for College: Improving the High School Curriculum.* New York: Ronald Press, 1961.

75. "What Went Wrong with U.S. Schools: An Interview with Prof. Arthur Bestor, University of Illinois," *U.S. News & World Report,* January 24, 1958, pp. 68–69.

76. Ibid., p. 70.

77. Ibid., p. 74.

78. Ibid., p. 75.

79. Ibid., pp. 75–76.

80. Ibid., p. 76.

81. James Bryant Conant, "Acknowledgment," in Conant, *The American High School Today: A First Report to Interested Citizens.* New York: McGraw-Hill, 1959, p. v.

82. Ibid., p. i.

83. Church and Sedlak, *Education in the United States,* p. 407.

84. H. G. Rickover, *Education and Freedom.* New York: E.P. Dutton and Co., 1959, p. 133.

85. Quoted in Joel Spring, *The American School 1642–1996.* New York: McGraw-Hill, 1997, p. 398.

86. Rickover, *Education and Freedom,* p. 18.

87. Ibid., p. 132.

88. Ibid., p. 135.

89. Ibid., pp. 136–137.

90. "Schools Must Foster National Survival," Interview with Admiral Hyman Rickover on *Meet the Press,* January 24, 1960, in W. Richard Stephens and William Van Til, eds., *Education in American Life.* Boston: Houghton Mifflin, 1972, p. 180.

91. Ibid., p. 181.

92. Ibid., p. 182.

93. Ibid., p. 183.

94. Ibid., pp. 184–185.

95. Gerald L. Gutek, *Education in the United States: An Historical Perspective.* Englewood Cliffs, NJ: Prentice-Hall, 1986, p. 277.

96. Rickover, *Education and Freedom,* p. 154.

97. Richard Hofstadter, *Anti–intellectualism in American Life.* New York: Alfred A. Knopf, 1970, p. 345.

CHAPTER NINE

The War on Poverty

Poverty is a dehumanizing tragedy wherever it occurs. It is especially calamitous in a land of plenty such as the United States. To combat it, to lessen it, and ultimately to eliminate it is a task of the highest magnitude and moral order. This chapter addresses one particular period, the 1960s, in the United States when officialdom declared an all-out war on poverty and called on the schools to be a, if not the, chief agent in its removal. A laudatory enterprise in itself, the rhetoric involved, the expectations themselves that the schools could accomplish this lofty goal, make up one more panacea. It should be noted at this point that non-school agencies, such as Head Start and Job Corps, which were a prominent part of the overall "war," will not be addressed in this chapter.

Introduction

It was Gunnar Myrdal's *An American Dilemma,* published in 1940, that highlighted the problem of poverty in the United States. Myrdal's work was followed by Michael Harrington's, *The Other America: Poverty in the United States,* which forcefully brought the issue before President John F. Kennedy in 1962. The "cycle of poverty," according to Harrington, worked something like this: the poor have restricted educational opportunities, a low standard of living, inadequate medical care, unhealthful diets, substandard housing, and subpar education for the next generation, which starts the cycle anew.[1] Harrington wrote eloquently that "tens of millions of Americans are, at this very moment, maimed in body and spirit, existing at all levels beneath those necessary for human decency."[2]

War Is Declared

As noted in Chapter 8, the federal government became actively involved in educational matters in the context of the Cold War. Following the *Brown* decisions of the Supreme Court in 1954 and 1955 that outlawed segregated faculties, including schools, the nation turned its attention to the issue of civil rights. In his "State of the Union" address on January 8, 1964, President Lyndon Johnson announced an "unconditional war on poverty in America," and he urged "this Congress and all Americans to join with me in that effort." His administration would not rest, Johnson proclaimed, "until that war is won."[3] "Better schools" were listed as the first of a number of agencies that would cooperatively wage the all-out war.[4] Joel Spring observed that this newly declared war, an expansion of common school reform, focused on three areas: 1) unemployed and delinquent youth; 2) disadvantaged students who did not have equal educational opportunity; and 3) the cycle, or circle, of poverty.[5]

In their "Annual Report" to the President in 1964, his economic advisors, chaired by Walter Heller, identified "persistent unemployment" as the country's "number one economic problem."[6] The advisors went on to state:

> Solution of the unemployment problem and its associated waste of potential output is essential to a successful attack on many of our social evils. But we cannot expect a reduction in unemployment alone to eliminate the poverty that afflicts 20 percent of American families. This degrading and self-perpetuating condition can be fully overcome only by programs that attack directly the many sources of impoverishment in our society.[7]

The roots of poverty needed to be attacked in order to destroy the "cruel legacy" whereby the poor remained poor.[8] "Expanding educational opportunities" was one way to address this problem: "The school must play a larger role in the development of poor youngsters if they are to have, in fact, 'equal opportunity.'"[9] A "broad range of intensive services," starting with preschool, would strengthen educational services to the children of the poor. When applied, it would be clear that there were few children who "are unable to benefit from good education."[10]

It was evident that the president agreed with his economic advisors. "*Let us, above all, open wide the exits from poverty to the children of the poor,*" he declared. The key to opening these doors included education, because "poverty and ignorance go hand in hand."[11] Johnson cited statistics that showed that only 8 percent of families headed by a high school graduate lived in poverty. But 37 percent of families headed by someone who had only completed grade school lived in poverty. The president contended that:

> We must upgrade the education of all our youth, both to advance human well-being and to speed the nation's economic growth. But, most vitally, and with federal support, we

must upgrade the education of the children of the poor, so that they need not follow their parents in poverty.[12]

The upgrading of educational opportunity was particularly compelling for non-whites, since only 40 percent of that group completed high school compared to 70 percent of whites. The nation's fight to end discrimination required government and all its citizens "to make sure—in operation as well as in principle—that all Americans have equal opportunities for education, for good health, for jobs, and for decent housing."[13]

Robert Church and Michael Sedlak have pointed out that the War on Poverty represented an "elevation of newer interests to a position of primacy in government policy."[14] It was clear that both Kennedy and Johnson saw the schools as important social instruments, interpreted equality in terms of equality of educational opportunity, and stressed the "production," rather than the "consumption" aspects of education.[15] The War on Poverty constituted an assault on an entire culture, the culture of poverty, which was linked directly to education. It focused not on the American economic system, but on the wage earner. The report of the President's economic advisors in 1964 bluntly stated: "Universal education has been perhaps the greatest single force, contributing both to social mobility and to general economic growth." As Spring observed, no data were presented to support this thesis.[16]

Focusing on the individual enabled the Johnson administration to place the onus of the problem on "individual faults" rather than address systematic social injustice, which was the "root of the problem."[17] Schools were to change the individual to fit society, rather than the opposite; reform would be provided without substantially affecting other citizens—there would be no redistribution of wealth. Further, by centering efforts on schools, reform would be deferred until the youth reached adulthood. Thus, the social structure of American society was to be left undisturbed.[18]

School people were generally eager to play the leading role in this combat. Church and Sedlak have asserted that the following factors accounted for their eagerness: 1) humanitarian reasons—solicitude for those who were suffering; 2) the threat to social stability posed by the poor; and 3) the shift of power from arts and science faculty in higher education, ascendant since Sputnik, to educationists. The focus in pre-collegiate education would shift from college preparation to "marketable skills." Pedagogy, counseling, and humanistic psychology would assume more importance on campus—schools of education would recover their lost dignity. Education personnel rushed to participate in the program.[19]

A contributing factor to the President's singling out the schools for a leadership role in the assault on poverty might well have been his experience. As a schoolteacher in Texas, Johnson had participated in the National Youth Administration during the Depression. From his perspective, working with malleable youth in school constituted the best hope of breaking the cycle of poverty.[20]

Compensatory Education

It was at this time that the term "educationally disadvantaged" appeared with regularity in the literature. It often was used interchangeably with "culturally deprived," "educationally deprived," or "culturally disadvantaged."[21] Perhaps the description of Benjamin Bloom, et al., in their "Introduction" to *Compensatory Education for the Culturally Deprived,* published in 1964, best represented the thinking on "culturally deprived" students:

> In the present educational system in the U.S. (and elsewhere) we find a substantial group of students who do not make normal progress in their school learning. . . .
>
> It is this group with which we are at present concerned. We will refer to this group as culturally disadvantaged or culturally deprived because we believe the roots of their problem may in large part be traced to their experiences in homes which do not transmit the cultural patterns necessary for the types of learning characteristic of the schools and larger society.
>
> A large proportion of these youth come from homes in which the adults have a minimal level of education. Many of them come from homes where poverty, large family size, broken homes, discrimination, and slum conditions further complicate the picture. The designation of cultural deprivation should not be equated with membership in an ethnic group, but should be defined in terms of characteristics of the individual and/or the characteristics of his environment.[22]

This blame-the-victim approach led to programs of "compensatory education." Most educators agreed that the poor viewed schooling foremost as a means of getting a job, an anti–intellectual position that was the result of their upbringing.[23] Spring argued that the approach of the War on Poverty, as exemplified through compensatory education, was that there was no basic conflict between the rich, the middle class, and the poor. Education was to provide the bridge for the poor to enter the opportunity structure of society. The major interest of the poor was to enter the middle class, not to change the economic system. Education, then, was the "hope of the poor and the method of the middle class."[24] Enter compensatory education for the poor.

Did the school have any responsibility for causing poverty? Overwhelmingly, the response was in the negative: poverty was due to characteristics of the individuals and their families. In Senate hearings on the Elementary and Secondary Education Act (ESEA) in 1965, Senator Robert Kennedy asked Commissioner of Education Francis Keppel for a definition of an "educationally deprived" child. Keppel responded by saying that the definition in use had been devised by the superintendents of fifteen of the biggest school systems, which was:

. . . children whose home backgrounds do not include the encouragement for study that is normal . . . in the sense that there are books at home, there is encouragement to learn to read as a child . . . educational deprivation for children from low-income families includes the lack in all too many cases of preschools to get them ready for the first grade.[25]

Keppel noted that the children were not necessarily from low-income families, their deprivation hailed from a "host of tragic family reasons." Keppel said that he was "sorry to say" that the "school system itself has created an educationally deprived system." Thus, a broad definition of educational deprivation would include both families and schools that did not provide adequate education.[26]

Not everyone accepted that schools should occupy the lead position in the war. Political groups of local individuals, community action agencies in some instances, disagreed with the social planning for the poor by "qualified professionals," including educators.[27] The professionals realized, Margaret Burnham has charged, that they needed to keep a firm hand on the operation lest the poor realize their potential power:

. . . once the poor get together they might realize that nobody was going to solve their problem. Once they understood that—and if they were given support and encouragement in organizing—they might demand more fundamental changes.[28]

As Lawrence Metcalf observed, the transfer of $11 billion to the nation's 9.3 million poor families (out of a total of 47 million) in 1965 would have raised their income to a minimum level of $3,000, thus eliminating poverty.[29] Metcalf noted that teachers in his education courses objected to this as a dole, on the grounds that it would destroy initiative and that the recipients would not spend the money wisely— hence the need for government to manage the program.[30] Metcalf suggested a different role for the schools in the "unconditional war"—to enable the poor to "make valid social criticisms." How else, he asked, will they be able to understand "why they are poor, and what can be done about poverty? How else can they acquire . . . constructive attitudes toward work and citizenship they are now said to lack?"[31]

There was dire poverty in rural as well as urban areas. Much of the attention centered on the situation in our large cities, where poverty was intertwined tightly with race. Addressing the issue in 1965, the distinguished educator James Bryant Conant referred to the situation as "social dynamite." Successfully addressing the issue was crucial, he urged, because "the fate of freedom hangs in the balance."[32]

Title I of the ESEA

The most important portion of the ESEA was Title I, which was designed to provide funds for "improved educational programs for children designated as educationally deprived."[33] The language of Title I specifically stated that the measure was intended to benefit the children of low-income families:

> . . . the Congress hereby declares it to be the policy of the United States to provide financial assistance . . . to expand and improve . . . educational programs by various means . . . which contribute particularly to meeting the special educational needs of educationally deprived children.[34]

Fully $1 billion of the $1.3 billion in ESEA was earmarked for Title I.[35] To qualify for aid, a family's annual income could not exceed $2,000.[36]

The congressional hearings on ESEA removed any doubt that Title I was the major component of the War on Poverty. Secretary of Health, Education, and Welfare Anthony J. Celebrezze explained the rationale for special educational assistance to the educationally deprived in his opening statement to the committee. Quoting the President, Celebrezze proclaimed:

> Just as ignorance breeds poverty, poverty all too often breeds ignorance in the next generation. . . . The President's program . . . is designed to break this cycle which has been running on from generation to generation in this most affluent period of our history.[37]

But could the schools, armed with the tools of compensatory education, accomplish this immense social challenge and win this war? Mario Fantini, subsequent to sketching what compensatory education involved, responded in the negative:

> *Compensatory education.* The most widely employed alternative—compensatory education, which attempts to overcome shortcomings in the learner—only deals with symptoms. It is built on a theory that fixes the locus of the problem of school failure primarily with the learner—in his physical, economic, cultural, or environmental deficits. It prescribes additives to the standard educational process. Title I of the Elementary and Secondary Education Act of 1965 is the major thrust of the compensatory movement with its fund of more than a billion dollars applied to remedial efforts for the poor. While succeeding in focusing attention on the problem, Title I has not paid off as anticipated.
>
> Compensatory measures, having little significant effect on the achievement of disadvantaged children, are viewed with increasing distrust by the parents of academic failures, who are rejecting the premise that the fault lies in their children. Rather, they are saying that the system is failing, that it is in need of fundamental rehabilitation. Ghetto parents feel that the school's obligation is to know the child and respond to him—to diagnose the learner's needs, concerns, and cognitive and affective learning style, and adjust its program accordingly.[38]

Speaking in 1966, President Lyndon Johnson had an entirely different assessment of the effectiveness of Title I, the chief arm of compensatory education. Johnson said that its "value has already been demonstrated." What was needed was to make it universal: "We cannot rest until every boy and girl who needs special help in school receives it in the most effective, imaginative form that American ingenuity can devise."[39] The president was joined in this spirit by his vice-president, Hubert H. Humphrey, who stated that what the nation required was:

> . . . an educational system that will train, rather than chain, the human mind; that will uplift, rather than depress, the human spirit; that will illuminate, rather than obscure, the path to wisdom; that will help *every* member of society to the full use of his natural talents.[40]

Title I was beset with a plethora of difficulties in its first year of implementation. Its effects were termed "impressionistic," and they did not lend themselves to evaluation. Congressional appropriations did not coordinate with the calendar of the school year, resulting in funds not being available until after the schoolyear started, thwarting school planning. This lack of timing contributed to the problem of locating and employing specialized staff, which was particularly acute in large school districts.[41] Senator Ralph Yarborough of Texas, commenting on reports from the field before the Senate Subcommittee on Education, reported that superintendents complained of the immense amount of paper work required by the program:

> . . . forms they are required to fill out under Title I are the longest and most difficult they have ever seen, and so complicated in fact that in their opinion these forms act to the detriment of the act. . . . [a] pretty serious question with a lot of districts. They say they bog down in red-tape.[42]

Superintendents also complained of the extra financial burden Title I placed on them through planning and indirect costs. Over one-half of local educators perceived ESEA as a threat of a federal takeover of schooling; the districts with the lowest income had the greatest fear.[43]

Other conflicts occurred in the communities where Title I was to do its beneficial work. Community Action Agencies (CAAs) clashed with Title I administrators over planning, in part due to ambiguity of language (some CAAs thought they had veto power over Title I projects).[44] The federal-local contention was highlighted by political differences. For instance, Representative Gerald Ford, House minority leader, speaking for the House Republicans in his State of the Union remarks on January 19, 1967, stated:

> Republicans trust local school boards to formulate policy and set priorities far more than we trust bureaucrats in Washington.
>
> Congress should take the federal handcuffs off our local educators. The best way to do this is by tax sharing and tax credits. If the Democrats, who control Congress, refuse to consider tax sharing legislation, Republicans will seek to substitute block education grants, without Federal ear-marking or controls.[45]

The National Conference on Education of the Disadvantaged, held in 1966, was the scene of discord between schools and community groups. Community action groups, including civil rights leaders, pressed for "dramatic changes in the structure of schools," citing evidence that they said demonstrated "gross failure" on the part of the schools that called for making "gross change . . . mandatory."[46] The conference, which was marked by free exchange from groups with vastly different viewpoints, asked questions such as "How Much Can Schools Really Do?," and differed widely in the responses.[47] Concerns were expressed that the school personnel were acting like "amateur sociologists"; that they were functioning as "jack-of-all-trades" (though a counter view was that schooling and social services could not be separated); that they should begin with the parents, not the children, that "Most of the things we have done are wrong. What we have is cholera. The only thing is, some people survive it."[48]

Teachers and teacher education came in for their share of criticism at this conference. Teacher education needed to be overhauled; current teachers needed to be retrained and reoriented, some felt. Certification boards needed to be overhauled so that teacher aides, who don't "extend teacher incompetence," could be freed from legalistic constraints.[49] Educational personnel, and government bureaucrats, had to change their attitudes and recognize that the poor had resources, they had "answers to problems," to which educators should listen.[50]

Vice-President Humphrey delivered one of the major addresses at the conference, titled "Education—The Ideal and the Real." Humphrey proclaimed that ESEA was the "climax" of anti-poverty programs; that through Title I:

> . . . this Nation has begun to clarify and define the true role of education in America . . . that education must lead rather than lag; that it is an instrument of creation rather than a mirror only, of the American dream.
>
> It offers to the schools the opportunity to strike at the roots of poverty by bringing intellectual awakening to millions of children who have in the past found only frustration and rejection in the classroom.[51]

Concluding, the vice-president quoted Thomas Wolfe: "our goal is nothing less than the fulfillment of the American dream." His final words to the conference, which equated Title I with the "promise of America" were:

> To every man his chance, to every man, regardless of his birth, his shining, golden opportunity. To every man the right to live, to work, to be himself, and to become whatever thing his manhood and his vision can combine to make him. This is the promise of America.[52]

President Johnson added his rhetoric to that of the vice-president. Opening with the words that he brought a "special message," President Johnson addressed the magnitude of the conference's work, saying that "No group anywhere in the Nation is charged with a problem more urgent than yours." Working on a "lonely frontier," the educators were "exposed, and in some ways, as hazardous as the soldiers' outpost in Vietnam."[53]

How large was the field of the educators' endeavors? Commissioner Harold Howe II identified 20 percent of the nation's five to seventeen year olds as the reason for Title I. It was "because of them that you and I are here in Washington tonight to share our ideas on how to make better use of the magnificent opportunity this act gives us as educators." Howe opined that James S. Coleman's *Equality of Educational Opportunity* study, commissioned by Congress in 1964, involving 60,000 teachers and 645,000 pupils in 4,000 schools, "belongs not to the Office of Education. . . . It belongs to the Nation" and would provide guidance on how the nation should proceed.[54]

Conclusion

As the 1960s came to a close, the compensatory education tide had subsided. "Law and order" was the watchword of the day. Some argued that liberals had "overpromised" to win political support, which contributed to subsequent disillusionment with the power of schooling to ameliorate, if not eradicate, poverty.[55] Compensatory programs had not stopped the urban riots; the income of African Americans had dropped and unemployment had risen during a time of high national prosperity.[56] A countermovement that emphasized heritability, headlined by Arthur Jensen and Richard Herrnstein, had arisen. This movement attributed the plight of the poor to their genes, rather than to the social environment.[57]

Christopher Jencks has argued that the wrong approach had been tried. He wrote in 1972 that:

> A successful campaign for reducing economic inequality probably requires two things. First, those with low incomes must cease to accept their condition as inevitable and just. Instead of assuming, like unsuccessful gamblers, that their numbers will eventually come up or that their children's numbers will, they must demand changes in the rules of the game. Second, some of those with high incomes, and especially the children of those with high incomes, must begin to feel ashamed of economic inequality. If these things were to happen, significant institutional changes in the machinery of income distribution would become politically feasible.[58]

These changes did not occur; "blaming the victim" remained in full sway. As Kenneth Clark, the Harvard psychologist, has observed, "The bloom was beginning to fade from the rose of compensatory education."[59] People did not accept the position that poverty would be eliminated and income more equitably distributed after the current children, fortified with compensatory education programs, grew up.[60]

Samuel Bowles and Herbert Gintis, in their provocative work, *Schooling in Capitalist America,* argued that the failure of the War on Poverty reflects the "fact that inequality under capitalism is rooted not in individual deficiencies, but in the structure of production and property relations."[61] While Bowles and Gintis' thesis was not accepted by everyone, there is no doubt but that education had not solved the problem of "equal results" by 1970. This failure, as Church and Sedlak noted, led to "a mounting frustration and defeatism within the educational establishment . . . to complement the increasing disappointment, anger and disinterest in the schools among parents and taxpayers."[62] The War on Poverty, accompanied by excessive rhetoric on the part of politicians and educators about what the schools could do, although it had some successes, was not the panacea its zealous advocates had forecasted it would be.

The New York Times reported on August 8, 1971, that the number of those on welfare rolls had doubled from 1964 to 1971; Richard Pious declared that that figure demonstrated that what was necessary was not the "paltry handouts of the Great Society but rather a fundamental commitment to spend the funds necessary to provide real opportunity for social mobility in the inner cities and depressed rural areas."[63]

That commitment had not been made, nor was it forthcoming. Instead, the schools were asked, through compensatory education programs, to be the lead institution in eradicating the vestiges of poverty from the land. The metaphor of war, used by Presidents Kennedy and Johnson, soon-to-be Economic Opportunity Director Shriver, and the House Committee on Education and Labor, connoted strife until victory was won.[64] By their very nature the schools were not able to win this war. Another worthwhile endeavor had succumbed to the American desire to use the schools to seek a panacea; in this instance, a most laudable one.

Notes

1. Michael Harrington, *The Other America: Poverty in the United States.* Baltimore: Penguin Books, 1963.
2. Ibid., p. 9.
3. Lyndon B. Johnson, "The State of the Union Message to Congress," January 8, 1964, in Johnson, *A Time for Action: A Selection from the Speeches and Writings of Lyndon B. Johnson, 1953–1964.* New York: Atheneum, 1964, p. 168.
4. Ibid., p. 169.
5. Joel Spring, *The American School 1642–1996.* New York: McGraw-Hill, 1997, p. 351.
6. *The Annual Report of the Council of Economic Advisors,* together with *Economic Report of the President.* Transmitted to Congress January 1964. Washington, DC: Government Printing Office, 1964, p. 29.
7. Ibid.

8. Ibid., pp. 69–70.
9. Ibid., p. 75.
10. Ibid., p. 76.
11. Johnson, *Economic Report of the President*. Washington, DC: Government Printing Office, 1964, p. 15.
12. Ibid., pp. 15–16.
13. Ibid., p. 16.
14. Robert L. Church and Michael W. Sedlak, *Education in the United States: An Interpretive History*. New York: The Free Press, 1976, p. 431.
15. Edgar B. Gumbert and Joel H. Spring, *The Superschool and the Superstate: American Education in the Twentieth Century, 1918–1970*. New York: John Wiley and Sons, 1974, p. 45.
16. Joel Spring, *The Sorting Machine: National Educational Policy since 1945*. New York: David McKay, 1976, p. 196.
17. Church and Sedlak, *Education in the United States*, p. 434.
18. Ibid.
19. Ibid., p. 436.
20. Spring, *The Sorting Machine*, pp. 197–198.
21. Ibid., p. 212.
22. Benjamin S. Bloom, Allison Davis, and Robert Hess, *Compensatory Education for Cultural Deprivation*. Chicago: Department of Education, University of Chicago, 1964, p. 3.
23. Spring, *The Sorting Machine*, p. 220; Frank Riessman, *The Culturally Deprived Child*. New York: Harper & Row, 1962, pp. 1–16.
24. Spring, *The Sorting Machine*, p. 229.
25. Quoted in ibid., pp. 216–217.
26. Ibid., p. 217.
27. See, for instance, Richard M. Pious, "The Phony War on Poverty in the Great Society," *Current History* 61 (November 1971): 266.
28. Margaret Burnham, "The Great Society Didn't Fail," *The Nation*, 24, July 24/ 31, 1989, p. 122.
29. Lawrence E. Metcalf, "Poverty, Government, and the Schools," *Educational Leadership* 22 (May 1965): 543.
30. Ibid.
31. Ibid., p. 546.
32. James B. Conant, "Social Dynamite in Our Large Cities: Unemployed, Out-of-School Youth," in August Kerber and Barbara Bommarito, eds., *The Schools and the Urban Crisis*. New York: Holt, Rinehart and Winston, 1965, pp. 170–171.
33. Spring, *The American School*, p. 353.
34. Public Law 89–10, 89th Congress, H. R. 2362, April 11, 1965. Appendix A in Stephen K. Bailey and Edith K. Mosher, *ESEA: Office of Education Administers a Law*. Syracuse, NY: Syracuse University Press, 1968, p. 235.
35. Ibid.
36. Ibid., p. 237.
37. U.S. Congress, House Committee on Education and Labor, *Aid to Elementary and Secondary Education: Hearings before the General Subcommittee on Education of the Committee of Education and Labor*. 89th Congress, 1st Session, 1965. Washington, DC: U.S. Government Printing Office, 1965, pp. 63–82.
38. Mario D. Fantini, "Community Control and Quality Education in Urban School Systems," in Henry M. Levin, ed., *Community Control of Schools*. New York: Simon and Schuster, 1970, p. 41.

39. Lyndon B. Johnson, "Statement by the President," May 24, 1966, in Office of Education, *National Conference on Education of the Disadvantaged. Report of a National Conference Held in Washington, DC, July 18–20, 1966.* Washington, DC: U.S. Department of Health, Education, and Welfare, 1966, p. iii.

40. Hubert H. Humphrey, in ibid., p. 1.

41. Bailey and Mosher, *ESEA: Office of Administration Administers a Law,* pp. 165–166, 190.

42. Ibid., p. 193.

43. Ibid., p. 197; Appendix C, Question 18A, pp. 300–301.

44. Ibid., p. 198.

45. Quoted in ibid., p. 213.

46. "Introduction," *National Conference on Education of the Disadvantaged,* p. 1.

47. Ibid., p. 14.

48. Ibid., pp. 14, 11, 15, 30.

49. Ibid., pp. 18, 20, 22.

50. Ibid., p. 29.

51. Ibid., pp. 55–56.

52. Ibid., p. 59.

53. Ibid., p. 65.

54. Ibid., pp. 66–67.

55. David Tyack and Elisabeth Hansot, *Managers of Virtue: Public School Leadership in America, 1820–1980.* New York: Basic Books, 1982, p. 217.

56. Ibid., pp. 230–231.

57. See Arthur R. Jensen, "How Much Can We Boost IQ and Scholastic Achievement?," *Harvard Educational Review* 39, 1 (Winter 1969) for an early illustration of the position. Both Jensen and Richard Herrnstein followed up on their arguments with books in the early 1970s.

58. Christopher Jencks, et al., *Inequality: A Reassessment of the Effect of Family and Schooling in America.* New York: Basic Books, 1972, p. 265.

59. Kenneth Clark, "Introduction," Mario Fantini, Marilyn Gittell, and Richard Magat, *Community Control and the Urban School.* New York: Praeger, 1970, p. xiv.

60. Church and Sedlak, *Education in the United States,* p. 433.

61. Samuel Bowles and Herbert Gintis, *Schooling in Capitalist America: Educational Reform and the Contradictions of Economic Life.* New York: Basic Books, 1976, p. 123.

62. Church and Sedlak, *Education in the United States,* pp. 438–439.

63. Pious, "The Phony War on Poverty in the Great Society": 272.

64. Harold and Pamela Silver, "Introduction," in *An Educational War on Poverty: American and British Policy-Making, 1960–1980.* Cambridge: Cambridge University Press, 1991, p. 7.

CHAPTER TEN

Open Education

Two anecdotes will serve as the preface to this chapter. I recall participating on a panel discussing open education at the 1977 conference of the American Educational Studies Association (AESA) in Philadelphia. One of the panelists dogmatized that if you did not embrace open education you could not be a humanistic educator. The second episode happened about the same time. I was made aware of a high school principal who, on Friday afternoon, left a message in the mailbox of each faculty member that as of the coming Monday, the school was going to be open (not just for business, but to follow the tenets of open education).

Introduction

Open education, as it came to be called, burst upon the American educational scene in the late 1960s. Actually, the forces that led to its appearance had been brewing just beneath the surface for some years. They had been brought into the open as a response to the essentialist approach of the pre- and post-Sputnik eras discussed in Chapter 8, and in consequence of some of the concerns expressed in the War on Poverty.[1] They were also a result of the turbulent decade of the 1960s, during which many institutions in American society were held up for criticism. The movement was led by so-called romantic critics, and is also known as informal education or the open classroom movement.

The ideological origins of the movement may be found in philosophers such as Rousseau, in educators such as Pestalozzi, and certainly in the theories of child-centered progressive education in the twentieth century; in that sense, it was not new. More immediately, one can locate a source of its creation in authors such as Paul Goodman. Writing in 1956, Goodman identified what he felt were the major problems of the time:

> We live increasingly, then, in a system in which little direct attention is paid to the object, the function, the task, the need; but immense attention to the role, procedure, prestige and profit. We don't get the shelter and education because not enough mind is paid to *those* things. Naturally the system is inefficient; the overhead is high; the task is rarely done with love, style, and excitement, for such beauties emerge only from absorption in real objects; sometimes the task is not done at all; and those who could do it best become either cynical or resigned.[2]

Then, in the early 1960s, the educational world was treated to A. S. Neill's *Summerhill: A Radical Approach to Child-Rearing*. Referring to how children should and should not be reared, in terms of the social purposes of learning, Neill wrote:

> You cannot *make* children learn music or anything else without to some degree converting them into will-less adults. You fashion them into accepters of the *status quo*—a good thing for a society that needs obedient sitters at dreary desks, standers in shops, mechanical catchers of the 8:30 suburban train—a society, in short, that is carried on the shabby shoulders of the scared little man—the scared-to-death conformist.[3]

In 1964, Paul Goodman wrote *Compulsory Mis-Education and the Community of Scholars*. In this book Goodman declared that there was "too much formal schooling" and that the nation must "find alternative ways of educating."[4] That was followed by a series of three articles in *The New Republic* by Joseph Featherstone, a contributing editor of that journal. Featherstone's triad was based on his observations of British primary schools, a major contributing source to the movement in several parts of England. The British "integrated day" appealed to progressive-oriented educators, and open education was "christened," as Ravitch puts it, thereafter.[5]

Open Education Defined/Described

No less a writer than Herbert Kohl, one of the leaders of the so-called romantic critics and of open education, has remarked that it is "difficult to say exactly what the open classroom is. One almost has to have been in one and feel what it is."[6] One luminary, Charles Silberman, saying that it was "not a model, still less a set of techniques," identified it thus:

> It is, rather, an approach to teaching and learning—a set of shared attitudes and convictions about the nature and purposes of teaching and learning about the nature of childhood and adolescence and ultimately about the nature of man.[7]

Silberman addressed the values that characterize open education. They included the agreement that the purpose of education "should be to educate educators,

which is to say, to turn out men and women who are able to educate themselves
... men and women who have the desire and the capacity to take responsibility
for their own education, and who are likely, therefore, to be life-long, self-directed
learners." It might, quoting Professor David Hawkins of the University of Colorado, be described as a "leading exponent of informal education," meaning "no
longer needing a teacher."[8]

Several years later Nat Hentoff, another important figure in the movement,
writing about an intermediate school in New York that had embraced the concept, quoted a teacher, Carol Lotz, on its operation in the secondary school
system of New York City:

> Open Classroom simply means that each subject is taught by presenting a variety of activ-
> ities and experiences that the student can choose from according to his abilities and inter-
> ests. The teacher is "open" to the needs of each student, helping them to discover what
> skills they need to develop and providing different ways for them to learn. Each student is
> "graded" according to his progress and effort and competes only with himself. Detailed
> records are kept on the work they have completed, and conferences between the student
> and the teachers help them to understand what skills they need to develop and their indi-
> vidual goals for learning. Parents are fully informed of the student's progress and needs at
> conferences and with detailed quarterly reports.[9]

The problem with the schools, John Holt explained, was that as compulsory
institutions they "are not and *never were meant to be* humane institutions, and
most of their fundamental purposes, tasks, missions, are not humane."[10] Perhaps
Holt best expressed the promise open education held out to American society in
response to this question from the editors of *Education News:* "If America's
schools were to take one giant step forward this year toward a better tomorrow,
what should it be?" Holt responded:

> It would be to let every child be the planner, director, and assessor of his own education,
> to allow and encourage him, with the inspiration and guidance of more experienced and
> expert people, and as much help as he asked for, to decide what he is to learn, when he is
> to learn it, how he is to learn it, and how well he is learning it. It would be to make our
> schools, instead of what they are, which is jails for children, into a resource for free and in-
> dependent learning, which everyone in the community, of whatever age, could use as
> much or as little as he wanted.[11]

Holt's depiction of current American schools as "jails," and of open education as
the liberating force, characterize the nature of this movement.

Vito Perrone, who implemented the theories of open education at the University of North Dakota, has written that open education:

> ... unlike the curriculum reform effort of the past decade, is raising questions about the
> nature of childhood, learning, and the quality of personal relationships among teachers
> and children. ... that learning is a personal matter that varies for different children,

proceeds at many different rates, develops best when children are actively engaged in their own learning, takes place in a variety of settings in and out of school, and gains intensity in an environment where children—and childhood—are taken seriously.[12]

As for curriculum, Perrone contended that open education advocates emphasized the "more integrative qualities of knowledge, skills, appreciation, and understanding," rather than the "division of knowledge and skills into various kinds of subject matter."[13] Another writer, addressing the theoretical underpinnings of open education, wrote that the movement:

> . . . primarily directs itself towards assisting the child to learn how to learn, rather than learning specific, predetermined items. It seeks to help the student develop an attitude toward learning, an attitude self-sustaining throughout life. Open education focuses on children's needs and interests, and in that sense is child-centered. It contends that the child possesses within himself potential to learn (grow), that the school (teacher) exists to assist, not direct, that process. Theorists of open education also maintain that all learning needs to be integrated, not compartmentalized or fragmented. Open education seeks to promote joy, happiness, and self-fulfillment in its pupils. It wants schools to become happy places for children.[14]

Ravitch has argued that the advocates of open education defined it by what it was not, which tended to dissociate it from the "old" ways of teaching.[15] Silberman offered the following negative means of identifying open education:

- Creating large open spaces does not, by itself, constitute open education.
- Replacing desks and chairs with "interest areas" does not, by itself, constitute open education.
- Filling the interest areas with concrete materials that children can manipulate and use does not, by itself, constitute open education.
- Individualizing instruction, does not, by itself, constitute open education.
- Placing children in multiage groups does not, by itself, constitute open education.[16]

What, precisely, does constitute open education? Lillian Weber, a New York City educator, who on return from England in 1968 established the "Open Corridor" model of open education, held that the rationale for open education centered on the child. "What does he need? What is he *interested* in? What is he *ready* for? What are his *purposes?* How does *he* follow them? What are *his* questions? What is he *playing?*"[17] In his classic *Crisis in the Classroom,* Silberman challenged the thesis advanced by Robert M. Hutchins that the purpose of education is "learning to use the mind."[18] Rather, Silberman averred, emphasis on feeling needs to be present in schooling.[19] Open education ideology demanded that teachers care for children as precious in their own right, not as proto-adults.[20] Open education would shift the emphasis from academic attainment to the schools' "impact on how children feel about themselves, about school, and about learning."[21] Herbert Kohl added that it was "difficult to say exactly what an open classroom is."[22] But he advised that "in an open classroom a pupil functions according to his sense of himself rather than what he is expected to be."[23]

The elusive character of open education was acknowledged by its most prominent proponents. Two examples of this tendency are Roland S. Barth, an urban principal and well-known writer on the subject, and Charles H. Rathbone. In his book, *Open Education and the American School*, Barth enumerated twenty-nine assumptions shared by open educators about children and learning.[24] From these assumptions, such as "children are innately curious and will explore without adult intervention," "objective measures of performance may have a negative effect on learning," and "there is no minimum body of knowledge which is essential for everyone to know,"[25] Barth concluded:

> . . . open education has no curriculum. . . . In a real sense, children's own experiences are the subject matter—the content—of their learning. These experiences are good and bad, productive and nonproductive, pleasant and unpleasant. Open educators worry less about whether a child has had a particular experience than about the quality and meaning for him of the experiences he has had. It is for time and future experience to assess the significance of a student's experience, not for the adult to judge.[26]

Charles Rathbone, writing a year before Barth, attempted to examine the underlying philosophy of open education, the end it sought, and the beliefs on which it was based.[27] Rathbone contended that "there is one basic idea that recurs in all the literature. . . . the idea that in a very fundamental way each child is his own agent—a self-reliant, independent, self-actualizing individual who is capable, on his own, of forming concepts and of learning."[28] Schools thus became social institutions "designed to facilitate the learning of individual children through the presentation of a number of situations. . . . School represents the larger world. . . . Its function is to offer and suggest . . . to help children. . . . learning to accept and to build on their own resources, learning, in fact, to become *responsible agents*."[29]

What was the situation of American schools at the time in the view of open educators? Why did they view open education as indispensable in the development of children and thus urge its adoption by all American schools? Listen to Silberman, writing in the "Foreword" to his popular *Crisis in the Classroom,* as he depicted the utmost urgency of the situation:

> Ours is an age of crisis. . . . The crisis in the classroom . . . is both a reflection of and a contributor to the larger crisis of American society. It cannot be solved unless all who have a stake in the remaking of American education—teachers and students, school board members and taxpayers, public officials and civic leaders, newspaper and magazine editors and readers, television directors and viewers, parents and children—are alerted to what is wrong and what needs to be done.[30]

After indicting the media, academicians and others, Silberman reserved his harshest criticism for the "failures of the public schools," particularly for being "grim, joyless places":

> . . . how oppressive and petty are the rules by which they are governed, how intellectually sterile and esthetically barren the atmosphere, what an appalling lack of civility obtains on the part of teachers and principals, what contempt they unconsciously display for children as children.[31]

As bad as this was, the main problem with public schools was not "venality or stupidity, but mindlessness," the "failure or refusal to think seriously about educational purpose, the reluctance to question established practice." This quality permeated not only the "entire educational system" but "indeed the entire society." Silberman's solution to the problem was "infusing the various educational institutions with purpose."[32] The most important characteristic schools share, Silberman charged, was "a preoccupation with order and control."[33] He concluded his remarks on the failures of educational reform with identifying what he considered "Our most pressing educational problem," which was "not how to increase the efficiency of the schools; it is how to create and maintain a humane society. A society whose schools are inhumane is not likely to be humane itself."[34]

Unlike some of the prior advocates of open education, Ravitch observed, Silberman universalized open education. It became, in his program, an "ideology about children, learning, and schooling that was intended to revive society and the quality of life in America." It was the "answer to the alienation, anomie, and other social ills that Silberman so eloquently described."[35]

American education was devoid of trust, open educators told us. Open education would instill such trust, Beatrice and Ronald Gross maintained:

> Teachers must trust children's imagination, feelings, curiosity, and natural desire to explore and understand their world. They must also learn to trust themselves—to be willing to gamble that they can retain the children's interest and respect once they relinquish the external means of control: testing, threats, demerits, petty rules, and rituals. School administrators, in turn, must trust teachers enough to permit them to run a classroom that is not rigidly organized and controlled but, rather, is bustling, messy, flexible, and impulsive. Parents must trust school people to do well by their children, without the assurance provided by a classroom atmosphere recognizable from their own childhoods and validated, however emptily, by standardized tests.[36]

John Holt, corroborating the Grosses' decrying of the absence of trust in American schooling, penned that while observing how the British primary schools "really worked," he and his fellow observers became aware of "how deep was our own distrust of children."[37] Open education would restore that trust, so sadly missing and so badly needed.

The lack of trust contributed to a dismal atmosphere in America's classrooms, marking those classrooms with the "grim, joyless, and destructive" qualities that characterize New York City classrooms and "almost everywhere else."[38] John Holt agreed. Writing in *Freedom and Beyond,* he noted that teachers didn't like to hear that they are in the "jail business" and objected to that description. Holt was willing to use a synonym, one that sounded better: they were "corrals" for children, because people *"don't want them anywhere else."*[39]

In his monumental work on the progressive education movement, Lawrence Cremin discussed the crucial, pivotal, and difficult role the teacher played in carrying out the demands of progressive education. He aptly phrased it:

> In the hands of first-rate instructors, the innovations worked wonders; in the hands of too many average teachers, however, they led to chaos . . . progressive education done well was very good indeed; done badly it was abominable—worse, perhaps, than the formation it had sought to supplant. Unfortunately, there were, then, too many "average" teachers, too many people, who, though willing enough, were unable, through lack of training, ability, or time to master PEA's innovations.[40]

Teachers played an equally critical role in implementing the tenets of open education. In his *Open Classroom Reader,* Silberman referred to teachers as advisers, supporters, learners, senior partners, and facilitators of learning.[41] He advised them about how to manage their time, how to use materials, and how to make the change from traditional education.[42] He acknowledged that open education "made a number of demands on teachers that the conventional classroom does not"[43] but insisted that teachers' expectations could and would affect student performance.[44] The teacher who was imbued with the ideology of open education, could make the students recognize that "school is fun."[45] As Featherstone remarked after observing the British primary schools, it was the teacher's belief "that in a rich environment young children can learn a great deal by themselves and that most often their own choices reflect their needs" that brought success to the children and hence to the program.[46] Or, as Herbert Kohl put it: "An open classroom develops through the actions of the teacher and not because of his words."[47]

Open education confronted a number of problems, problems that ultimately led to its demise, a goodly number of which were not of a pedagogical, but rather of a social, nature. One major problem was the presence of "faddism," although Silberman writes that some faddism was helpful when it served as a "useful lubricant for the wheels of change."[48] He was aware of the danger of the "pendulum of informality and child-centeredness swinging too far," resulting in the "flabbiness and anti–intellectualism" that characterized many of the progressive schools earlier in the century.[49] Another theoretician of open education, Vito Perrone, warned against "rapid, uninformed adoption of a serious educational orientation stripped of its substance and made into a slick package—the latest fad."[50] Educational innovations require sufficient time to develop, to be studied and researched, to be

modified for the best results. Open education, due to "fad" or "bandwagon" tendencies, was not afforded this luxury.

Other factors contributed to open education's decline, and ultimate disap-
pearance from the educational landscape. First, consider the teachers. Open education placed considerable demands on them. Most teachers were not prepared to
work in open settings; at times they had no input into school management's decision to adopt the approach and little training once the decision had been made.
Leonard Sealey quoted a teacher who experienced the open classroom as saying:
"The concept is beautiful, but I'm miles from it. I almost think it takes a year or
two of traditional teaching. . . . An inexperienced teacher would not survive."[51] In
the same article, Sealey wrote that "they [the teachers] considered the cyclic approach of play, structure and practice to be essential yet few of them were able to
arrange for it to become the prevailing mode."[52]

Vito Perrone concurred. Teaching in an open setting, he said, "is an exhaust-
ing endeavor for the teacher. Almost everyone I know who is working in an open
classroom setting speaks about the physical and psychological drain."[53] James
Norman, in his study seeking to identify reasons advanced by school districts in
Virginia for abandoning open approaches, supported this point with the following comments by school division representatives:

> If you take the concept of open education seriously, it is exhausting. I have seen some
> really good people give up after a few years. . . . A teacher internship program would be a
> valuable asset. . . . Teacher training was provided but somewhere it was not adequate in
> terms of individualizing and class control.[54]

These comments reveal that a dedicated teacher, with specialized training,
was required if open education was to succeed. But dedicated teachers with appropriate training were not sufficient to bring about success. Roland Barth described
an effort to open classrooms in inner-city schools. Six young teachers, all of whom
had been prepared to teach in open classrooms by their teacher education programs were asked to help open classrooms that were peopled by predominately
African American students. Their experiences were devastating. Many factors
contributed to their failure, among them teachers' misconceptions about their
students. Teachers learned "quite contrary to open educators' assumptions about
children, that trust in children's capacity to make choices is unwarranted and will
be abused."[55] Other factors played at least as great a role, and are more significant
to our situation. Barth reported that some of the most powerful pressures to end
the open education experiment came from the community at large. The almost
unanimous parental attitude was one that wanted the school to give their children
the skills necessary to make it in a white world. Forget the "whole child," they
said. "We [the parents] can take care of that."[56]

Then there was the changed social climate. The mood of the country had swung from liberal to conservative as the 1970s progressed, and the popularity of open education declined accordingly. For instance, Ravitch observed that the number of articles on open education in professional journals peaked between 1972 and 1974, then dwindled rapidly, a sign that the movement had run its course.[57] There is considerable evidence to support this mood change. The accountability movement, a reflection of the country's growing conservative tenor, grew constantly stronger as the 1970s progressed. One of its initial signs was the publication of *Every Kid a Winner: Accountability in Education,* written by Leon Lessinger in 1970. Nearly forty states passed legislation relating to educational accountability in the decade.[58] Widespread concern over social promotion, as exemplified in the "Peter Doe" case, in which a child was promoted despite his inability to read or write, is another illustration of the nation's mood.[59] Voices in popular magazines and newspapers, as well as in professional journals, expressed concern about declining test scores, especially in reading.

School districts felt pressure from taxpayers who wanted "proof" of a return for their taxes. Some hired private firms, a practice known as performance contracting, which guaranteed that students would reach acceptable achievement levels. Performance contractors promised to forfeit their fees if student test scores did not reach acceptable levels. Public backlash, directed against higher education as a result of student activism of the late 1960s and early 1970s, was directed at K-12 schools as well. Teacher militancy contributed to the public's disfavor with the schools. For example, teacher strikes, which multiplied from two in 1963–1964 to 143 in 1973–1974, were greeted with growing hostility by the public.[60]

The 1974 Gallup Poll on education reflected the public's solicitude about the supposed failure of public education. According to that poll, lack of discipline was the most serious problem confronting public schools.[61] This finding was hardly a mandate for emphasizing student freedom and choice. The growth of competency-based education programs, which were present in both public schools and in teacher education, emphasized meeting specific, measurable goals. Creative self-expression and a spirit of inquiry sustained throughout life did not readily lend themselves to such measurement. Perrone argued that there was a lack of instruments that could adequately measure the goals of open education—"critical thinking, independence in learning, trust, ability to face new problems with confidence, commitment to reading, and positive attitudes about learning" complicate the evaluation task.[62] The public was not impressed.

The direct costs of open education constituted another concern. For instance, more than one-third of the twenty-three districts in Virginia in James Norman's study indicated that finances were a major factor in the decision to terminate.[63] The financial burden of open education becomes obvious if Ronald Lajore was correct in his assertion that for it to succeed the teacher-student ratio would have to be cut "from 1–35 to 1–10," so that the "teacher can devote more time, energy

and attention to individuals," even if aides were enlisted to accomplish the reduced ratio.[64]

The public mood was not favorable for open education as the decade progressed. The failure of the public to understand what it was about contributed to
its troubles. The 1975 Gallup Poll, for example, revealed that only 27 percent of respondents understood the term "open" school; 60 percent did not. Thirteen (of
the 27) percent favored the concept; 10 percent were in opposition.[65] That poll
showed, however, that 57 percent of the respondents would send their children to
a public school that "has strict discipline, including a dress code, and that puts
emphasis on the three Rs" if they lived in a city that offered this choice.[66]

Questions about the effectiveness of open education programs were raised as
well. The public was not willing to accept the benefits of the open movement on
faith or intuition[67]; it wanted hard data before schools embarked on its uncharted
journey. Research on British primary schools, presented the following year,
strengthened those cautions. It showed that students in formal classrooms performed as well as or better than those in a mixed or informal approach.[68]

A disturbing report by Abt Associates that dealt with the educational achievement of low-income students, concluded in 1978 (after the open movement had
lost most of its force), that:

1. Highly structured basic skills programs were much more successful than "open classroom"
    approaches in raising the achievement level of low-income children.
2. Open classrooms generally failed to raise self-esteem, even though that was a primary objec-
    tive . . .[structured programs] with a primary objective of teaching basic skills, [were] most ef-
    fective in raising self-esteem, too.[69]

Conclusion

Writing in 1969, Paul Goodman described the educational scene as "a religious crisis of the magnitude of the reformation in the fifteen hundreds."[70] The crisis, the romantic critics believed, was wider than the schools; it embraced all of society. It provided an opportunity for school people, as Ewald Nyquist and Gene Hawes wrote:

> Rarely have educators, citizens, and parents in communities across the land faced a
> large alternative choice that might fundamentally improve the whole quality of teaching
> and daily life in the schools. At present, however, such a potentially far-reaching alterna-
> tive confronts us. This is the highly sophisticated form of schooling that American edu-
> cators have generally begun to call "open education."[71]

This rare opportunity, they continued, even in its early stages, was replete with evidence of its benign effects on children:

Evidence is already in on how children regard an open classroom, once they get used to it. Put simply, they love it. It leads them to skip off eagerly from home in the morning, even to fight to go to school when they're sick. For them, an open classroom makes school exciting, fun, comfortable, and fascinating. It makes learning a joy for all kinds of children, rich or poor, bright or slow, bookish or boisterous, shy or outgoing.[72]

Beatrice and Ronald Gross wrote that in children who needed stimulation, traditional education might cause mind damage or even "atrophy."[73] For the Grosses, and for those who joined in the crusade, open education was an object of faith capable of "saving" American education (and some would add American society as well).[74] Nyquist and Hawes added that:

The choice of trying and building on this momentous alternative is ours. Ultimately, the decision seems to rest on whether we put human values at the center of the way we run our schools—with all that doing this could mean for the lives of our young people and ourselves.[75]

Within three years of this quote, open education was on a downward spiral, plummeting its way to oblivion, at least for this era. If you believed its advocates, the nation had chosen the inhumane way and rejected the offer of salvation.

Notes

1. Diane Ravitch, *The Troubled Crusade: American Education 1945–1980*. New York: Basic Books, 1983, p. 239.
2. Paul Goodman, *Growing Up Absurd: Problems of Youth in the Organized Society*. New York: Vintage Books, 1956, p. xiii.
3. A. S. Neill, *Summerhill: A Radical Approach to Child Rearing*. New York: Hart Publishing, 1960, p.12.
4. Goodman, *Compulsory Mis-education and the Community of Scholars*. New York: Vintage Books, 1964, pp. 7, 12.
5. Ravitch, *The Troubled Crusade*, p. 241.
6. Herbert Kohl, *The Open Classroom: A Practical Guide to a New Way of Teaching*. New York: Vintage Books, 1969, p. 15.
7. Charles E. Silberman, "Introduction," in Charles E. Silberman, ed., *The Open Classroom Reader*. New York: Vintage Books, 1973, p. xix.
8. Ibid.
9. Nat Hentoff, *Does Anybody Give a Damn?* New York: Alfred a. Knopf, 1977, p. 101.
10. John Holt, *Freedom and Beyond*. New York: E. P. Dutton & Co., 1972, p. 242.
11. Holt, *The Under-achieving School*. New York: Pitman, 1969, p. ix.
12. Vito Perrone, *Open Education: Promise and Problems*. Bloomington, IN: Phi Delta Kappa Foundation, 1972, p. 8.
13. Ibid.
14. Thomas C. Hunt, "Open Education: A Comparison, an Assessment, and a Prediction," *Peabody Journal of Education* 53, 2 (January 1976): 110.
15. Ravitch, *The Troubled Crusade*, p. 249.

16. Silberman, "Introduction," in Silberman, ed., *The Open Classroom Reader,* p. xxi.

17. Lillian Weber, "The Rationale of Informal Education," in Silberman, ed., ibid., pp. 36, 149.

18. Charles E. Silberman, *Crisis in the Classroom: The Remaking of American Education.* New York: Random House, 1970, p. 7.

19. Ibid., p. 8.

20. Ibid., p. 230.

21. Ibid., p. 262.

22. Herbert R. Kohl, *The Open Classroom: A Practical Guide to a New Way of Teaching.* New York: Vintage Books, 1969, p. 15.

23. Ibid., p. 20.

24. Ravitch, *The Troubled Crusade,* p. 249.

25. Ibid., pp. 249–250.

26. Roland S. Barth, *Open Education and the American School.* New York: Agathon Press, Inc., 1972, p. 50.

27. Charles H. Rathbone, "The Implicit Rationale of the Open Education Classroom," in Rathbone, ed., *Open Education: The Informal Classroom.* New York: Citation Press, 1971, p. 99.

28. Ibid., p. 104.

29. Ibid., pp. 104–105.

30. Silberman, *Crisis in the Classroom,* p. vii.

31. Ibid., p. 10.

32. Ibid., p. 11.

33. Ibid., p. 122.

34. Ibid., p. 203.

35. Ravitch, *The Troubled Crusade,* p. 247.

36. Beatrice and Ronald Gross, "A Little Bit of Chaos," in Ewald B. Nyquist and Gene R. Hawes, eds., *Open Education: A Source Book for Parents and Teachers.* Toronto: Bantam Books, 1972, p. 18.

37. Holt, "Introduction," in Rathbone, ed., *Open Education,* p. 2.

38. Silberman, "Introduction," in Silberman, ed., *The Open Classroom Reader,* p. xvii.

39. Holt, *Freedom and Beyond,* pp. 243–244.

40. Lawrence A. Cremin, *The Transformation of the School: Progressivism in American Education 1876–1957.* New York: Vintage Books, 1961, pp. 348–349.

41. Silberman, ed., *The Open Classroom Reader,* pp. 209–294.

42. Ibid., pp. 295–480.

43. Silberman, *Crisis in the Classroom,* p. 267.

44. Ibid., p. 83.

45. Ibid., p. 289.

46. Quoted in Ravitch, *The Troubled Crusade,* p. 240.

47. Kohl, *The Open Classroom,* p. 33.

48. Silberman, "Introduction," in Silberman, ed., *The Open Classroom Reader,* p. xviii.

49. Silberman, *Crisis in the Classroom,* p. 321.

50. Perrone, *Open Education,* p. 31.

51. Leonard Sealey, "Open Education: Fact or Fiction." *Teachers College Record* 77 (May 1976): 617.

52. Ibid., 623.

53. Perrone, *Open Education,* p. 21.

54. James S. Norman, "A Study of Open Education in the State of Virginia, 1971–1976." Unpublished doctoral dissertation, Virginia Polytechnic Institute and State University, 1977, p. 77.

55. Barth, "Open With Care: A Case Study," in Vincent S. Rogers and Bud Church, eds., *Open Education: Critique and Assessment*. Washington, DC: Association for Curriculum Development and Research, 1975, p. 55.

56. Ibid., pp. 47–65.

57. Ravitch, *The Troubled Crusade*, p. 255.

58. Ernest R. House, Wendell Rivers, and Daniel J. Stufflebeam, "An Assessment of the Michigan Accountability System," *Phi Delta Kappan* 55 (June 1974): 663.

59. *Peter W. v. San Francisco Unified School District et al.* 131 Cal. Rpt. 854 (Cal. Ct. App. 1976). Case previously entitled *Doe v. San Francisco Unified School District*.

60. *The National Catholic Register,* September 22, 1974, p. 1.

61. George H. Gallup, "Sixth Annual Gallup Poll of Public Attitudes toward Education," *Phi Delta Kappan* 56 (September 1974): 21.

62. Perrone, *Open Education,* p. 26.

63. Norman, "A Study of Open Education," p. 76.

64. Ronald Lajore, "More Than Teaching," *Elementary English* 52 (January 1975): 58.

65. Gallup, "Seventh Annual Gallup Poll of Public Attitudes Toward Public Education," *Phi Delta Kappan* 57 (December 1975): 235.

66. Ibid., p. 231.

67. Thomas E. Gatewood, "How Effective Are Open Classrooms?: A Review of the Research," *Childhood Education* 51 (January 1975): 176.

68. Neville Bennett, *Teaching Styles and Pupil Progress*. London: Open Books, 1976, p. 153.

69. Wesley C. Becker and Siegfried Engelmann, "The Oregon Direct Instruction Model: Comparative Results in Project Follow Through—A Summary of Nine Years of Work." Eugene, OR: University of Oregon Follow Through Project, May, 1977.

70. Quoted in Silberman, *Crisis in the Classroom*, p. 27.

71. Eugene B. Nyquist and Gene R. Hawes, "Introduction," in Nyquist and Hawes, eds., *Open Education: A Sourcebook for Parents and Teachers*, p. 1.

72. Ibid., p. 2.

73. Beatrice and Ronald Gross, "A Little Bit of Chaos," in Nyquist and Hawes, eds., *Open Education*, p. 18.

74. Ravitch, *The Troubled Crusade*, p. 245.

75. Nyquist and Hawes, "Introduction," in Nyquist and Hawes, eds., *Open Education*, pp. 5–6.

CHAPTER ELEVEN

The Age of Accountability

Hard on the heels of the outcry over the alleged systemic failure of public schools to educate minority children to their potential and the charges hurled by the romantic critics of the system's dereliction in the area of spirit and feeling came what has been termed "the age of accountability." Steeped in the language of business and government, buoyed by the certainty bred of quantitative measurement, accountability was to swiftly achieve panacea status. A search of the *Education Index* in the late 1960s reveals no entries under "Accountability" until the July 1969–June 1970 issue, and then but seventeen and listed under the category of "Education—Evaluation."[1] The following year "Accountability" merited its own title ("Accountability in education"), with sixty-five entries, a number that fluctuated little until it nosedived to thirty-three in the 1975–1976 volume.[2] Entire issues of well-known educational periodicals, or substantial parts of them, were devoted to the topic in the early 1970s. Writing in 1971, John E. Morris captured the essence of the spirit of the times when he wrote:

> If the sentiment of certain educators, government, business, and lay leaders is an indication of what this decade holds, it is certainly the dawning of the age of accountability wrapped in the self-governance package of the educational profession and bound by performance contracts.[3]

Ralph W. Tyler added that accountability became a "focus of sharp controversies" in the early 1960s but was a word that "rarely appeared in educational publications and was not mentioned on the programs of educational organizations."[4] That was about to change as accountability became the watchword of the 1970s.

One prefatory note: this chapter addresses the general notion of accountability as the new utopia in the educational world. Chapter Twelve will deal with one of its major agencies, performance contracting, as a panacea in its own right.

Early Stirrings

Don Davies told the educational world in 1972 that he had it "on good authority that accountability will soon replace relevance as the 'in' word among educators. I hope this is a reliable tip. . . . second, and more important, accountability, I hope, would be more than an 'in' word, a current fashion in semantics."[5] Davies saw a promising, yet controversial future for accountability:

> This concept of accountability calls for revamping of much of our thinking about the roles of educational personnel and educational institutions at all levels. . . . shifting primary learning responsibility from the student to the school. It also means that a lot of people are going to be shaken up.[6]

The founder, or at least midwife, of accountability was acknowledged to be Leon M. Lessinger. Roger Kaufman sketched Lessinger's leadership role as follows:

> If Lessinger is not the father of educational accountability, then he must be at least the midwife. During his tenure at the Office of Education and following, not only has he assisted in the birth of accountability, but also he has assisted in providing . . . tools for achieving a realistic accountability. These tools include (but are not limited to): Auditing, Systems Analysis, and the Systems Approach.[7]

A prolific writer on the topic, Lessinger declared in 1971 that "Accountability as a modern concept first saw the light of day in 1969." By 1971, he pontificated, it was clear that the United States had entered the "age of accountability." Accountability, he maintained, had to do with "keeping promises."[8] Calling pre-accountability education a "cottage industry," Jack Stenner, then the project director of the Council of the Great City Schools, unveiled a new educational commandment as the theme of accountability: "every child shall learn."[9]

Stenner's new commandment slogan was close to the title of Lessinger's 1970 book, *Every Kid A Winner: Accountability in Education.* It was this book that provided a major impetus for Lessinger to assume the leadership role of the accountability movement. Likening schools to airplanes and automobiles, Lessinger reasoned that "If one airplane in every four crashed between takeoff and landing, people would refuse to fly. If one automobile in every four went out of control and caused a fatal accident or permanent injury, Detroit would be closed down tomorrow." Our schools, he argued, which produced a "more important product than airplanes or automobiles—somehow fail one youngster in four . . . with serious social consequences.[10] The future, however, held great promise:

> . . . thanks to a set of recent developments, so far little noted, we can now sharply cut this waste of lives and money. In fact, American educators now have an opportunity so far reaching that, with a push from the public, *we can transform our schools within this decade.*[11]

Failure to address these age-old problems with education would demonstrate more dramatically "our dereliction as educators," because "ample proof of our failures is evident," he averred. Quoting John Gardner that "in some cases we are rather strongly motivated *not* to solve them" because to do so "would endanger old, familiar ways of doing things," Lessinger called for educators to "set a goal of basic mastery for everyone and offer whatever programs are necessary to meet that goal."[12]

The Foundations of and Need for Accountability

It was Lessinger's contention that accountability rested on three fundamental bases: student accomplishment, independent review of student accomplishment, and a public report relating dollars spent to student accomplishment.[13] While he claimed that we were entering an "age of accountability" in 1970, he also observed that the concept itself had been "rediscovered" and "elaborated to meet serious conditions in the schools especially those conditions relating to galloping costs, poor student achievement, and the erosion of public authority and confidence in schools."[14] He was far from alone in his assessment that the conditions of the time called for the schools to document that they were "delivering the goods." Writing that same month (December 1970), Aaron Wildarsky, a professor in the School of Public Affairs at Berkeley, wrote that "Consumers of governmental services are entitled to know what they are getting. Truth in packaging applies just as much to government as to private industry."[15]

It was time, Lessinger contended, to establish a counter principle to that of Dr. Peter. That principle would be that "*independent, continuous and publicly reported outside review of promised results of a bureaucracy promotes competence and responsiveness in that bureaucracy.*"[16] He chastised educators for their constant resistance to "the one and only ultimate test of professional competence: *proof of results.*"[17] Such resistance could no longer be tolerated, for as Robert Garvue, a professor of educational administration at Florida State University wrote in early 1971:

> Accountability is an important concept emerging in the context of a great dissent concerning educational policies. Much of the dissent has arisen out of inflation, increasing tax loads and the realization that crucial social issues, in the long run, can be resolved principally through quality educational programs.[18]

The demand for change existed in almost all sectors of American society, including education. One writer opined, "To anyone rationally viewing the state of the world in the year 1970 one fact appears to be as nearly constant as any: this is a time of rapid change in almost every dimension viewed."[19] In education, this change took the form of accountability. The question was "Who is Accountable for What?"[20] Some viewed the uncertainty about the response to that question with alarm, at least in part because of a lack of "adequate instruments to measure important aspects of student growth" and the inability to "specify precisely the processes which lead to growth."[21] "Cooperative accountability," rather than "unbridging competitiveness," was called for on the part of all involved in the educational process. If accountability was cooperative, emphasis would be placed on working together toward a common goal. A negative evaluation, whether of a teacher or administrator, would not be a "judgment of incompetence but feedback in areas which need improvement."[22]

Regardless of the argument over how accountability was to be implemented, the statement that "In the last two years the recognition of the need for educational accountability has literally engulfed the United States" reflected the reality that was present in the educational world.[23] Writing in the January 1971 issue of *Educational Technology,* one devoted to accountability, Medill Blair, superintendent of schools for the city of Hartford, Connecticut, presented the choice that the nation faced:

> What's all this fuss about accountability, anyway? Haven't we always had it? Are we now saying that people in education have been irresponsible wastrels all these years? Are programs of education that have been developed, and that seem to be operating successfully, to be condemned and abandoned because they haven't been measured according to some of the more precise objective standards now being advanced as desirable?[24]

The options were clear for Blair: we could continue to grope with "impressions of the past" and

> . . . apologize for our abject failures, . . . *Or,* we can begin to take a leaf from business, industry, and educational leaders such as Leon Lessinger . . . and develop and promote new educational programs and techniques, refuse to commit public funds, and refuse to employ personnel, until we first establish clear goals (what student behavior do you want?), until we develop ways to measure accomplishment of these goals, and until we set up logical techniques to employ in reaching them.

It came down to a "choice between functional debility and operational accountability." The 1970s, Blair proclaimed with a certain sense of finality, would be the "decade of accountability."[25]

Support from Officialdom

Accountability appealed to all levels of government. Public K-12 education was an immense enterprise. As Lessinger pointed out in early 1971, at the national level it accounted for 44 million students and 1.9 million teachers and spent more than $30 billion of tax funds annually.[26] Little wonder that it was the focal point for politicians and others in government.

In his "Education Message" to Congress on March 3, 1970 President Richard M. Nixon recognized and endorsed the new concept:

> From these considerations we derive another new concept: *Accountability.* School administrators and school teachers alike are responsible for their performance and it is in their interest as well as in the interest of their pupils that they be held accountable.[27]

The state government has been designated by the federal constitution as the unit of government with the basic responsibility for conducting public schooling. Thus, it should come as no surprise that representatives of that level of government responded to the calls for accountability in public schooling. Often these calls were laced with the notion that the movement presented tremendous opportunity for and demands on state government. Henry Phillips, director of State Agency Cooperation, Bureau of Elementary and Secondary Education of the U.S. Office of Education, reasoned that the "regulatory function" for states was no longer sufficient; they must assume an "advocacy" role. The question, he wrote, was not "*whether* but *how* States will respond."[28] At a meeting of the Education Commission of the States in Denver in July of 1970, it was revealed that several states, Florida and Colorado, had passed legislation dealing with accountability; others were considering similar action.[29]

Individual state leaders were of like mind. For instance, Ewald B. Nyquist, commissioner of education in New York State and president of the University of the State of New York, contended that educators and government officials should "be able to say with assurance that an increase of $20 per pupil in reading will increase reading achievement by two school months in the fourth grade."[30] Such requirements called for the upgrading of state departments of education. Blair argued that state departments needed to "Exploit to the fullest" their positions. To carry out their accountability-directed mission, he maintained that the departments have to be "tooled up, to be expanded, to be properly financed, to have priorities established for them to meet the leadership role and to eliminate certain hardships and weaknesses which are inherent in their own operational procedures."[31] If the states didn't accept this challenge, Blair warned, others would do so in their stead.[32]

One such state that was highlighted for its efforts toward accountability was Oregon. There, State Superintendent of Public Instruction Dale Purnell was developing a master plan for schools that incorporated "principles of teacher accountability and management by objectives." Teachers, the reasoning ran, have to "be required to show measurable evidence that their students are learning at a prescribed level in a prescribed amount of time."[33]

Cities jumped on the accountability bandwagon. New York City highlighted the goal of accountability in the preamble of the agreement between its Board of Education and the teachers' union; San Francisco's superintendent of schools announced in 1969 that the schools there were intent on pursuing a "zero reject" program. To do so he was:

> . . . seeking accountability contracts from publishers who will bid on learning package materials and consultant services with accountability provisions which provide that the publisher will be paid on the basis of the successful student achievement of pre-negotiated standards of performance.[34]

The superintendent of San Diego's schools announced in January of 1970 that "the school system must be accountable for . . . educational results"; and that, in the final analysis, educational programs must be "accountable to the people."[35] Similar events occurred almost simultaneously in Chicago, where the superintendent of schools released, for the first time, school-by-school results on tests of achievement in reading and math.[36] The superintendent maintained that the release was justified because "we have to be accountable for our stewardship of the children entrusted to us."[37]

One last illustration on the part of government representatives, of how the accountability bandwagon, presented as the cure-all to the nation's many educational ills, will have to suffice. Speaking to the American Association of School Administrators on February 14, 1970, James E. Allen, former U.S. commissioner of education, attributed the disillusionment and lack of confidence in public schools in large measure to "our inability to substantiate results." He called for research aimed at improving the ability to assess the effectiveness of educational programs and forthrightly proclaimed that "the strengthening of the concept of accountability . . . is imperative."[38]

Accountability's Challenge

Accountability would provide measurable results, Lessinger claimed. There would be no goals like "appreciation of reading" tolerated in the new order.[39] The movement would utilize helping fields such as "systems design and analysis, management by objectives, contract engineering (including . . . performance contracts) . . . value engineering and the like" to accomplish its ends.[40] Rapid change was on the doorstep and it had to be accommodated. Every thinking person would embrace the notion of accountability, Kennedy argued: "To anyone rationally viewing the state of the world in the year 1970 one fact appears to be as nearly consistent as any: this is a time of rapid change in almost any dimension viewed."[41] This change had to be managed; it needed to be planned for, one author wrote.[42] Output was to replace input; measurable learning was to take the place of teaching in the new age.[43] One author argued that accountability would soon become a "stark necessity" in education if public support for public schooling were to be regained.[44] Lessinger was even stronger in his position. Holding that the American public had lost its faith in the public school's system to "actually deliver on its promises," he stated that "Accountability is the coming *sine qua non* for education in the 1970's."[45]

The public was demanding "educational programs that work," Lessinger held, which would prove beneficial to the decline in spirit that had plagued educators in recent years: "overburdened educators will regain a spirit of excitement and mastery that has flagged in recent years. It can save society the long-term cost of allowing its schools to depict millions of children as 'failures.'"[46] The "fast-generating" movement promised "a long overdue redevelopment of the management of the present educational system, including an overhaul of its cottage-industry form of organization." This improved management was indispensable, he argued, because of the "massive amount of money" that had been entrusted to the schools, with such dismal results.[47] Schools could meet this formidable challenge, Lessinger believed:

> If we accept competence for all as one of the major goals of education today, then we must desire a system of accountability that relates education's vast budget to results. . . . We can change the way our educational system performs so that the desired result—a competently trained young citizenry—becomes the focus of the entire process. In the same way that planning market studies, research and development, and performance warranties industrial production and its worth to consumers, so should we be able to engineer, organize, refine, and manage the educational system to prepare students to contribute to the most complex and exciting country on earth.[48]

Emphasizing Lessinger's theme, John Porter thundered: "The challenge is clear in my mind and I hope in yours. We must start to guarantee student performance."[49] Another author wrote that to reach this goal every school system had at its disposal enough "weapons" to solve all but the "most extreme problems." (He likened the situation to the Distant Early Warning System employed by the U.S. military.) The "overwhelming amount of failure in school is due to teacher failure, curriculum failure, or a combination of both," he argued. We could address school failure, and "with luck and persistence, totally eliminate it."[50] All but unlimited benefits would accrue to students, to teachers, and to the nation if accountability were to be followed in every school, Lessinger argued. He called upon school and other government officials to expunge "outmoded myths" from the conduct of schooling, then "incomplete educational tradition will be exposed and perhaps eliminated from the schools." Lessinger wrote that educators needed to get rid of the "can't do" approach and its "built in reflection of failure." This change of attitude "may well be the major benefit of accountability"; it was a necessity in a time of "widespread doubt about educational achievements."[51]

The implementation of accountability required a major concerted effort. Henry Dyer, for example, maintained that the professional staff not only needed to be clear about the four variables involved in its application—input, output, surrounding conditions, and educational process—but they also needed to be clear about the interaction among the four that had to occur if they were to "maximize pupil output." To implement accountability properly:

> . . . all variables in the system must be measured and appropriately interrelated and combined to produce readily interpretable indices by which the staff can know how much its own efforts are producing hoped-for change in pupils, after making due allowance for those variables over which it has little or no control.[52]

To carry out this task, which was obviously no small one, Dyer called for the creation of a School Effectiveness Index (SEI), which would make it "Possible, by means of a series of regressive analyses, to compute the SEI's that form the people of each school." If the SEI were used fittingly, Dyer exclaimed, the "proposed method of computing school effectiveness indices *automatically* adjusts for the differing circumstances in which schools must operate." If "understood and accepted," the SEI would "provide a mechanism for stimulating directed professional efforts toward the continuous improvement of educational practices on many fronts in all the schools."[53] Dyer concluded his exhortation with the claim that the "output of the process" is a "finished product," an individual who is "sufficiently aware of his own incompleteness to make him want to keep on growing and learning." Precisely for this reason, he averred, the "problems included in developing objective criteria of professional accountability will always be hard problems." But they were problems that "must be tackled with all the human insight and goodwill that can be mastered if the schools of this urban society are to meet the large challenges that confront them."[54]

Lessinger maintained that "educational accountability can be implemented successfully only if the educational objectives are clearly stated before the instruction starts."[55] Felix Lopez affixed several additions to Lessinger's requirement. He wrote that accountability plans "must be characterized by simplicity, flexibility, and economy." Most plans, he declared, were "installed in organizational settings that lack the necessary background and organizational traditions to accommodate them." An "organizational philosophy and determination of accountability policies" needed to be in place before implementation was begun.[56]

Richard De Novellis and Arthur Lewis had a plan to implement accountability. They began with the assertion that the "current press for accountability has developed steadily since the mid 60's when public officials used the term in spelling out a policy position." Sufficient progress had been made that the PACT approach (Planning Accountability Team), could be implemented. In fact, "The organization of the PACT is a key to the entire operation of the accountability plan."[57] They outlined all the steps that needed to be taken to allow accountability to operate. One began by determining the people/groups to be represented— teachers, administrators, citizens and students, everyone who affects the quality of education. The next step was to obtain support from state and local governments and community leaders. Then it was necessary to develop ground rules for the group; provide necessary skills for team effectiveness; relate the PACT to national, state and local goals for accountability; identify constraints; assess needs; identify institutional goals and objectives and facilitating goals; conduct an evaluation; and prepare the Accountability Report.[58] If all of these steps were taken, De Novellis and Lewis argued, the quality of education would be improved and public confidence in schools would increase. "Fortunately," they concluded, "there is one approach to accountability that curriculum and supervisory workers can believe in and conscientiously support for it holds the promise for better education."[59]

Some Questions

Not everyone in the educational world was engulfed by the tidal wave of accountability. Questions were posed; opponents arose. Tyler took note of these situations when he wrote that accountability had become a major subject in education and a "focus of sharp controversies."[60] One reviewer of Lessinger's pump-priming book, *Every Kid A Winner,* termed it a "twenty-nine-cent idea wrapped in eight-dollar covers."[61] Comparing Lessinger's ideas with those of John Franklin Bobbitt some five decades earlier, Richard Olmsted chastised Lessinger for the "atmosphere of hucksterism" that pervaded his writing.[62]

Less critical and more questioning, reviewer Donald Shipley credited Lessinger's book with merit because of the "clear and concise manner" it presented points and "places them in a framework that defines a concrete pattern of administrative action." He was not content, though:

> The question still remains, however, as to whether this pattern is an adequate exemplar for building the kind of school system that would indeed result in improved pupil achievement and needed institutional reform.[63]

Shipley proceeded to posit two questions that, he opined, "might shed light on certain limitations of accountability."

   I. What pupil outcomes are to be assessed in formulating an accountability report?

   II. Who is to decide such things as which assessment procedures are to be utilized for measuring

pupil outcomes, and which agencies will conduct the performance contracting and independent auditing?[64]

Shipley concluded his review of Lessinger's book with the statement that it "should
be read," and with the assertion that Lessinger's ideas were too limited in scope:

> Although innovative and seemingly promising, the plan has limitations, and thus repre-
> sents at best a partial approach for overcoming complex problems having to do with pupil
> achievement and school reform. It relies too much on standardized tests and an authori-
> tarian pattern of administrative management. School reform is urgently needed, but even
> more urgent is the need for an evaluative perspective that avoids duplicating the errors of
> the recent curriculum reform movement and builds on a more comprehensive ideal of
> human development and community involvement.[65]

The elusive nature of accountability attracted the attention of Dennis Gooler.
In reply to the question: "What is Accountability?," Gooler wrote:
Accountability is doing what is supposed to be done.

> Accountability is often unknown because it is difficult to find out what is being done and
> because different people have different ideas as to what is *supposed to be* done.
>   Full accountability depends on people agreeing what the goals are and on people
> knowing the progress toward these goals. Full accountability is impossible, but a high
> level of accountability can be attained.[66]

But the question remained: What should the school be doing? Gooler asserted
that part of educational accountability involved whether the school was "doing
the things it should." He called for a delineation of goals and the clarification of
the reasons for selecting these goals.[67] Donald Robinson defined accountability
as "the condition of being accountable, liable, or responsible" and asked
whether that standard applied to being humane or to reading scores.[68] Gene
Glass concurred, asking "What is genuine accountability and what is sham?"
He observed:

> Psychometricians, learning researchers, behavioral objective backers, program planners,
> evaluators, accreditation teams, economists, systems analysts *et al.* are selling accountabil-
> ity to whoever is buying. The term drips with excess meaning. In recent months it has
> been applied vigorously to 1) the statement of instructional objectives, 2) performance
> contracting, 3) voucher systems, 4) economic input-output analysis, 5) accreditation, 6)
> community participation and so forth.[69]

The word "means so much," Robinson asserted, that it was fair to ask does it
"mean anything at all?" The uncertainty that surrounded the meaning of accountability led him to declare that it was "unreasonable, undemocratic, and increasingly unworkable to give teachers no control over the setting of standards for
which they shall be held accountable."[70]

The lack of adequate measurement instruments compounded the lack of clarity that enveloped the notion of accountability. Barak Rosenshine and Barry McGraw noted that: "we are seeking to assign responsibilities and to hold people accountable when we lack adequate instruments to measure important aspects of student growth and are unable to specify precisely the processes which lead to growth."[71] Picking up on this lack of adequate instrumentation, Gooler, quoting Donald Collins, inquired:

> What do the Accountability people think of those who desire to develop children's abilities to think independently? How do you measure, how do you "performance contract," for relevance, love and independent thinking?[72]

Gooler then called attention to another potential shortcoming of the accountability movement as it was then described:

> Accountability may force us to examine our goals, and our methods of achieving those goals. But accountability may force us to pursue goals most easily attained, or most easily stated. Accountability may force a kind of naive simplicity on a complex phenomenon.[73]

If that happened, Gooler warned, we might be forced to live with the words of the Swiss historian Jacob Burckhardt, viz., that the "essence of tyranny is the denial of complexity."[74]

C. A. Bowers, commenting on Lessinger's contention that the "public expects greater relevance in what we teach," asked "Who is this public?" Does it have a "common point of view, a value system and a set of expectations" that everyone would agree on with regard to "relevant education?" He wondered if the uniform notion of accountability would unduly politicize the educational process in diverse ethnic groups. How would one implement it in a pluralistic community?[75]

Returning to the question "Who is Accountable for What"?, Rosenshine and McGraw addressed the "underlying competitiveness" of accountability and called for a cooperative version of the notion:

> Students, teachers, and administrators evaluate one another, making judgments on one another's competence, claiming that the other is not doing an adequate job. Everyone seems to want to grade everyone else and hold him accountable.

If the process were based on cooperation, there would be ongoing processes as to how educational personnel could move together towards a common goal. A negative evaluation in this context would not be a "judgment of incompetence but feedback on areas which need improvement."[76] The competitive nature of accountability as Lessinger et al. presented it led Bowers to the declaration that such a view assumed that everyone had the right to pass judgment on people's professional competence regardless of their own expertise.[77]

Robert Bhaerman was even more critical of Lessinger and his fellow account-ability advocates. He asserted that Lessinger and "other blind advocates of ac-countability" ignored the most important questions in education: "What is the major *function* of school?," and in light of that, "What should the *results* be? What are the *kinds* of student learning which should be stressed? In short, what *should* students learn?"[78] Arguing that Lessinger et al. were good on the "training" aspects of education, but fell short in the more important educational components of schooling, Bhaerman concluded his rather harsh critique:

> The pushers, for that is what they are, of such things as performance contracts, develop-mental capital and so on, *ad nauseam* certainly have injected some "innovation" verbiage into the rump of the educational system. They are correct in some ways though. The ed-ucational system needs a good shot in the. . . . Trouble is, more often than not, the push-ers miss their mark.[79]

The long time veteran leader of teacher unionism, Albert Shanker, took note of the growing phenomenon of accountability in education. Calling atten-tion to the fear with which teachers viewed the movement because it regarded them as "hired hands," Shanker reminded his readers of the dangers associated with innovations, which Americans "have learned through years of experi-ence—and rather bitter experience—that educational innovation in the Ameri-can public schools has nothing to do with the improvement of education."[80] For Shanker, accountability was essentially a "public relations device," that brought out "ideas which force teachers and children and others to march in different directions." These "gimmicks" as he referred to them, were of no help in the long run:

> Our public schools, with all their faults, are worth keeping, and their improvement will come not from gimmicks but from the same type of slow, painful, unrestricted, free, sci-entific inquiry that brought other areas of human concern into the modern world.[81]

Don Martin, George Overholt and Wayne Urban offered what was perhaps the most trenchant critique of accountability. They alleged that to adopt the ac-countability method "wholesale" was to replace education with a variety of forms of indoctrination. Quoting Paul Feyerabend, they wrote of the movement:

> It enforces an enlightened communism . . . leads to a deterioration of intellectual capabil-ities, of the power of imagination, and speaks of deep insight; it destroys the most pre-cious gift of the young, their tremendous power of imagination.[82]

Accountability, they argued, replaced reflection with adaptive behavior on the part of students, and its pedagogy was not educational but rather was "indoctrina-tion, dictated by modern educational technology."[83]

Conclusion

In 1972, Glass spoke in a modest vein about the potential benefits of accountability: "If we do not promise more than we can deliver, if we embrace genuine accountability and not some sham, we may stand a chance of making a few modest improvements in schooling."[84] Glass's call for moderation and limited expectations left him in a decided minority position. James McComas's bid for an all-embracing, pervasive role for accountability was more common:

> Accountability must include all components: teacher education, state departments, local schools and private enterprises which are involved in the education program. Within the local school system, pupils, teachers (teaching strategies), administration, supervision and pupil-personnel services are just a few components which must be defined—and their effectiveness measured. And it is clear that we have only scratched the surface in the use of technology.[85]

Leaders in education, McComas exhorted, must "*take the initiative in developing appropriate systems*" for accountability to reach its potential and to produce benefits previously unknown to American education.[86]

William Deterline offered similar thoughts:

> Accountability imposes three directions: specified performance capability will be produced; the initial components must produce those results; and an empirical development and management process must be employed. Accountability is not a punitive method of assigning blame for failure, or a method of rewarding teachers who work harder. An overhaul of the entire instructional environment—its components and its methods—is a basic requirement. The entire operation must become results-oriented, results measured in terms of students' performance capabilities stemming from the instructional events arranged for them.[87]

Lessinger foresaw substantive changes in education if the system of accountability as McComas and Deterline envisioned it were to be employed. Teaching would shift from conveying information to directing learning; schools would be more open, more flexible, and less group-oriented; the curriculum would become more relevant; "outmoded myths and incomplete traditions" would be exposed and perhaps eliminated from schools; and student unrest and boredom, two major issues of the day, would be affected by the "can do" philosophy that accompanied accountability.[88]

In support of McComas's thesis, Stephen Bruno took note of the "unusual rapidity with which the accountability concept has been assimilated in educational circles" and hypothesized that "If the development of a system is undertaken and carried through to completion, the by-products alone may well prove to be worth the effort."[89] Kaufman lent his support to the system wide approach:

It is hoped that an integration of tools and purposes may be achieved so that education may be aided, in processes and outcomes, by a cooperative, systematic, empirical, valuable attack on current and future problems.[90]

Marlin Duncan testified to the huge impact the accountability concept had had on American education by 1971 when he stated that "In the last two years the recognition of the need for educational accountability has literally engulfed the United States."[91]

Addressing accountability's "progress" in 1971, Morris commented that "But one thing is certain—Pandora's Box has been opened and will never be the same." He wrote that accountability "may be the most interesting, challenging, disruptive, and in the end, productive issue of all."[92]

Marvin Nottingham and Louis Zeyen addressed the need for a commitment to accountability if a school or school division sought success. As they put it: "A commitment to accountability is a commitment to success. Success is rewarding. It breeds success. It restores faith, a commodity currently in short supply in many schools."[93]

In a review of *Every Kid A Winner,* Milton Schwebel took on the panacea of accountability head on. He wrote:

> There are several aspects of this book that deserve special attention. First, it promotes one of the genre of concepts that has infected our thought and action, the panacea or near-panacea that becomes a fad for a few years and then fades away after having postponed once again the turning of all our energies to substantive changes. The trouble with substantive changes is that, while they make a difference, they do not do it *dramatically* and with the lightning-swift effect promised by the fads. For some, the fad is the training of teachers of teachers; for others, it is the "open classroom." For Lessinger, it is educational engineering with the aid of private industry.[94]

Two years later, in 1973, Ornstein surveyed the educational landscape that had been flooded with accountability ideology and observed: "My views are that accountability has now reached bandwagon status, and that we should temper our enthusiasm with moderation."[95]

Descriptions of the good that accountability would achieve contributed in no small measure to the bandwagon status Ornstein sketched. Certainly foremost among those who promised near-salvific benefits from accountability was Lessinger himself. As early as December of 1970, he had written:

> In the face of this void of meaning in our time, in this sustained crisis of authority in our time, education must take on different dimensions. Accountability is the public policy declaration that speaks to those different dimensions. Engineering that policy into practical, vital programs is a matter of due urgency. Dr. Peter, bureaucrats, citizens, parents, board members, educators and fellow Americans, take heed![96]

Pondering claims such as the above in 1972, who can blame Arthur Combs for observing: "Who in his right mind can really oppose the idea of accountability? That is like being against motherhood."[97] In the early 1970s, few dared to challenge the torrential downpour of accountability; the nation had another magic elixir in schooling, but alas, once again, not for long. By the end of the decade, it had all but vanished from the scene.

Notes

1. Julia W. Ehrenreich, ed., *Education Index July 1969–June 1970*. New York: The H. W. Wilson Company, 1970, p. 244.
2. Ibid., July 1970–June 1971, p. 4; July 1975–June 1976, p. 4.
3. John E. Morris, "Accountability: Watchword for the 70's." *The Clearing House* 45, 6 (February 1971): 323.
4. Ralph W. Tyler, "Accountability in Perspective," in Leon M. Lessinger and Ralph W. Tyler, eds., *Accountability in Education*. Worthington, OH: Charles A. Jones Publishing, 1971, p. 1.
5. Don Davies, "The 'Relevance' of Accountability," in Frank J. Sciara and Richard K. Jantz, eds., *Accountability in American Education*. Boston: Allyn and Bacon, 1972, p. 34.
6. Ibid.
7. Roger A. Kaufman, "Accountability, a System Approach and the Quantitative Improvement of Education—An Attempted Integration," *Educational Technology* 11, 1 (June 1971): 21.
8. Leon M. Lessinger, "Teachers . . . in an Age of Accountability," *Instructor* LXXX, 10 (June/July 1971): 19.
9. Jack Stenner, "Accountability by Public Demand," *American Vocational Journal* 48, 2 (February 1971): 33–34.
10. Leon M. Lessinger, *Every Kid A Winner: Accountability in Education*. New York: Simon and Schuster, 1970, p. 3.
11. Ibid.
12. Ibid., pp. 15, 24–25.
13. Leon M. Lessinger, "The Powerful Notion of Accountability in Education," *Journal of Secondary Education* 45, 8 (December 1970): 339.
14. Ibid., 340.
15. Aaron Wildarsky, "A Program of Accountability for Elementary Schools," *Phi Delta Kappan* 52, 4 (December 1970): 212.
16. Leon M. Lessinger, "Robbing Dr. Peter to 'Pay Paul': Accounting for Our Stewardship of Public Education," *Educational Technology* 11, 1 (January 1971): 11.
17. Ibid., p. 13.
18. Robert J. Garvue, "Accountability: Comments and Questions," *Educational Technology* XI, 1 (January 1971): 34.
19. John H. Kennedy, "Planning for Accountability Via Management by Objectives," *Journal of Secondary Education* 45, 8 (December 1970): 348.
20. Barak Rosenshine and Barry McGraw, "Issues in Assessing Teacher Accountability in Public Education," *Phi Delta Kappan* LIII, 10 (June 1972): 642.
21. Ibid.
22. Ibid., 643.

23. Marlin G. Duncan, "An Assessment of Accountability: The State of the Art," *Educational Technology* 11, 1 (January 1971): 27.
24. Medill Blair, "Developing Accountability in Urban Schools: A Call for State Leadership," *Educational Technology* 11, 1 (January 1971): 38.
25. Ibid., pp. 38–39.
26. Lessinger, "Robbing Dr. Peter to 'Pay Paul'": 13.
27. Richard M. Nixon, quoted in Lessinger, "The Powerful Notion of Accountability in Education," *Journal of Secondary Education* 45, 8 (December 1970): 339.
28. Henry L. Phillips, "Accountability and the Emerging Leadership Role of State Educational Agencies," *Journal of Secondary Education* 45, 8 (December 1970): 378.
29. Lessinger and Tyler, eds., *Accountability in Education,* p. 15.
30. Quoted in ibid., p. 26.
31. Blair, "Developing Accountability in Urban Schools," *Educational Technology* 11, 1 (January 1971): 39.
32. Ibid., p. 40.
33. Quoted in C. A. Bowers, "Accountability from a Humanist Point of View," *Educational Forum* XXXV, 4 (May 1971): 479.
34. Quoted in Lessinger, *Every Kid A Winner,* p. 107.
35. Ibid., p. 108.
36. Ibid.
37. Ibid., pp. 108–109.
38. Quoted in ibid., p. 109.
39. Lessinger, "The Powerful Notion of Accountability": 344.
40. Ibid.
41. Kennedy, "Planning for Accountability": 348.
42. Ibid., 349–350.
43. Lessinger, "The Powerful Notion of Accountability": 340.
44. James Straubel, "Accountability in Vocational-Technical Education," *Educational Technology* 11, 1 (January 1971): 44.
45. Lessinger, "Engineering Accountability for Results in Public Education," in Lessinger and Tyler, eds., *Accountability in Education,* p. 28.
46. Quoted in ibid., p. 63.
47. Lessinger, in ibid., p. 7.
48. Lessinger, "Engineering Accountability for Results," in ibid., pp. 13–14.
49. John W. Porter, "Accountability in Education," in ibid., p. 42.
50. Robert E. Wales, "The Early Warning System and the Zero Failure School: Professional Response to Accountability," *Journal of Secondary Education* 45, 8 (December 1970): 369–371.
51. Lessinger, "Teachers . . . in an Age of Accountability": 20.
52. Henry S. Dyer, "Toward Objective Criteria of Professional Accountability in the Schools of New York City," *Phi Delta Kappan* LII, 4 (December 1970): 206–207.
53. Ibid., 209–210.
54. Ibid., 211.
55. Lessinger, quoted in Morris, "Accountability: Watchword for the 70s": 326.
56. Felix M. Lopez, "Accountability in Education," *Phi Delta Kappan* 52, 4 (December 1970): 231.
57. Richard L. De Novellis and Arthur J. Lewis, *Schools Become Accountable. A PACT Approach.* Washington, DC: Association for Supervision and Curriculum Development, 1974, pp. 1, 22.
58. Ibid., pp. 26–66.

59. Ibid., pp. 70–71.
60. Tyler, "Accountability in Perspective," p. 1.
61. Richard Olmsted, review of *Every Kid A Winner: Accountability in Education,* by Lessinger. *Harvard Educational Review* 42, 3 (August 1972): 425.
62. Ibid., 426.
63. Donald R. Shipley, review of *Every Kid A Winner: Accountability in American Education,* by Lessinger. *Journal of Educational Measurement* 8, 3 (Fall 1971): 231.
64. Ibid., 231–232.
65. Ibid., 232
66. Quoted in Daniel R. Gooler, "Some Uneasy Inquiries into Accountability," in Lessinger and Tyler, eds., *Accountability in Education,* p. 63.
67. Ibid.
68. Donald W. Robinson, "Accountability for Whom? for What?," *Phi Delta Kappan* LII, 4 (December 1970): 193.
69. Gene V. Glass, " The Many Faces of Educational Accountability," *Phi Delta Kappan* LIII, 10 (June 1972): 636.
70. Ibid.
71. Barak Rosenshine and Barry McGraw, "Issues in Assessing Teacher accountability in Public Education," *Phi Delta Kappan* LIII, 10 (June 1972): 642.
72. Gooler, "Some Uneasy Inquiries," p. 63.
73. Ibid.
74. Ibid., p. 62.
75. Bowers, "Accountability from the Humanist Point of View": 480.
76. Rosenshine and McGraw, "Issues in Assessing Teacher Accountability": 642–643.
77. Bowers, "Accountability from the Humanist Point of View": 481.
78. Robert D. Bhaerman, "Accountability: The Great Day of Judgment," *Educational Technology* 11, 1 (January 1971): 62.
79. Ibid., 62–63.
80. Albert R. Shanker, "Accountability: Possible Effects on Instructional Programs," in Lessinger and Tyler, eds., *Accountability in Education,* pp. 60–62.
81. Ibid., pp. 62, 74.
82. Don T. Martin, George E. Overholt, and Wayne J. Urban, *Accountability in American Education: A Critique.* Princeton, NJ: Princeton Book Co., 1976, p. 82.
83. Ibid., pp. 78–79.
84. Glass, "The Many Faces of Accountability": 639.
85. J. D. McComas, "Accountability: How Do We Measure Up?," *Educational Technology* 11, 1 (January 1971): 31.
86. Ibid.
87. William A. Deterline, "Applied Accountability," *Educational Technology* 11, 1 (January 1971): 20.
88. Lessinger, "The Powerful Notion of Accountability in Education": 345–346.
89. Stephen M. Bruno, "An Approach to Developing Accountability Measures for the Public Schools," *Phi Delta Kappan* LII, 4 (December 1970): 196, 205.
90. Kaufman, "Accountability, a System Approach and the Quantitative Improvement of Education—An Attempted Integration": 22.
91. Marlin G. Duncan, "An Assessment of Accountability: The State of the Art": 27.
92. Morris, "Accountability: Watchword for the 70's": 324.

93. Marvin A. Nottingham and Louis D. Zeyen, "Commitment to Accountability—A Case Study," *Journal of Secondary Education* 46, 1 (January 1971): 8.
94. Milton Schwebel, review of *Every Kid A Winner: Accountability in Education,* by Lessinger. *Educational Technology* 11, 10 (October 1971): 20.
95. Allan C. Ornstein, ed., "Preface," *Accountability for Teachers and Administrators*. Belmont, CA: Fearon Publishers, 1973, p. viii.
96. Lessinger, "The Powerful Notion of Accountability": 347.
97. Arthur W. Combs, *Educational Accountability: Beyond Behavioral Objectives*. Washington, DC: Association for Supervision and Curriculum Development, 1972, p. 1.

CHAPTER TWELVE

Performance Contracting

Accountability included a number of activities that emanated from the corporate world. Systems Analysis and Program-Planning-Budgetary Systems (PPBS) were among the leaders. None, however, approached the importance and popularity of performance contracting, which brought the full weight of business and industry to the educational world. The term "performance contracting" first appeared in *Education Index* in June 1969, where its frequency peaked in 1970–71, and had all but disappeared by 1974–75.[1] Performance contracting, and the rhetoric that accompanied it during its brief stint in education, qualifies as a panacea.

Early History

In 1970, Ronald Schwartz prophesied that "Business in the education market will be hopping this fall, if a number of school districts follow through with their plans to sign performance contracts."[2] That school districts were interested, if for no other reason than as a form of "insurance," is clear from the words of an aide to Dr. Carl Marlburger, New Jersey's education commissioner:

> I got a call from someone in another state education department who wanted to know what we were doing about performance contracting. His department didn't think it would amount to anything, but they felt they had to protect their rear end in case it did.[3]

What is performance contracting? Charles Blaschke, one of the foremost leaders of the movement, said that it was a "managerial concept designed to encourage responsible innovation while holding those in charge accountable for results."[4] Blaschke went on to describe how the process usually works. Typically, a school district enters into a contract with an outside firm or teachers' group to accelerate the skill development of a limited number of educationally deficient youth, usually in areas such as mathematics or reading. Reimbursement to the contractor is based on the actual performance of students as measured by standardized achievement, or criterion-referenced and performance-based tests. When the period of the contract ends, the contractor turns over (thus the name "turnkey") the instructional program and learning systems designed, packaged, and successfully demonstrated to the school system. The contracting firm then steps out of the picture; the school district continues the program with its own staff and management.[5] Efrem Sigel maintained that "Performance contracting is a simple way of responding to demands for accountability in education." He contended that it had three origins: 1) Ideological—business can accomplish a social good for a profit; 2) Managerial—it draws on the management science/cost benefits approach used at the defense department: and 3) Pedagogical—it leans heavily on programmed instruction.[6]

Leon Lessinger called it an "important change" in what "Americans expect from their public schools." He averred that performance contracting constituted the "coming revolution in American education" because it aimed at "quality assurance and knowledge of results." In his opinion, "serious doubts have arisen about the public school system's ability to deliver on its promises." Performance contracting guaranteed that schools would achieve specific, measurable results within a specific time period for specific costs for a specific purpose, e.g., dropout prevention.[7] Early efforts of performance contractors, beginning in late 1969, were aimed at the production of learning as output, and payments were made on the basis of evidence that had occurred. Standardized achievement tests were used to determine the quantity of "output."[8] H. M. Harmes wondered whether school boards were perhaps "losing faith in the ability of educators to select, implement and operate the best programs," and were "beginning to see product output performance as their only recourse for serving the best programs for their clients, the public."[9]

Blaschke traced the movement from a 1964–1965 study at the John F. Kennedy School of Government at Harvard, conducted while he was a student there. The study showed that there was a "great irony" in our society: we were "adept in developing science and technology, we were unable, if not unwilling, to design and develop the political and managerial innovations needed to apply such technology effectively."[10] The study recommended the application of management techniques to urban problems; it was a short intellectual leap to apply these techniques to schools. The researchers recommended that government should become involved whenever the public's or students' interest were served. Blaschke held that the programs of the 1960s, "especially busing," had failed to meet the educational needs of minority children. Accordingly, performance contracting had been called upon, and business had responded with programs that "guarantee results regardless of the location of the child, the amount of resources, or class size," all the while maintaining the integrity of the neighborhood school.[11] As the argument ran, "*If we can get men to the moon, why can't we teach kids to read?*" or "*If industry had 40 percent rejects in its system, it would revise the system, therefore schools should revise their system.*"[12]

Performance contracting, then, came into existence as a "way of helping disadvantaged children who, by conventional measures, are performing far below the national average." The movement aimed to remove one cause of social problems by bringing them up to some "acceptable measure."[13]

Early Contracts

A number of contracts were signed into effect in the early months of performance contracting. Perhaps the most highly publicized one was at Texarkana, Arkansas, where the school district and Dorsett Educational Systems, Inc., signed a contract to address that district's serious dropout problem. The contract called for the firm to advance the reading and math skills of a minimum of 200 students by one grade level in each subject within 80 hours of instruction for $80 per student—or less, if more time were required.[14] Addressing minority students from low-income families, who had a high truancy rate and an alleged poor self-image, the program's onset was advertised as an "important new approach to compensatory education will have been launched."[15] The responsibility for meeting the goals resided primarily with the contractor: "The burden of achievement has rested too long on small shoulders."[16]

The Texarkana program was greeted with expressions of hope and promise. Lessinger spoke glowingly of the promise this new movement held:

> Texarkana may hold other lessons for us, but it is only the first in what we hope will be a long series of projects. The concepts of accountability and educational engineering are catching the imagination of a broad audience, including school officials, educators in a variety of corporations and non-profit centers, and leaders at the highest levels of government. With roots deep in American tradition of enterprise, responsiveness, and flexibility, these concepts are now nurturing a movement in education that will probably affect all of us.[17]

Blaschke argued that in the last analysis (despite "clouds"), which will be treated later in this chapter), the experience was "healthy." It proved, he wrote, "that a performance contract project could be implemented despite formidable political and bureaucratic hurdles."[18] Albert Mayrhofer opined that the response by public school systems to the "Texarkana breakthrough" had been great and a "sense of immediacy has been created."[19]

Promised Benefits

The range of benefits that some attached to the use of performance contracting were enormous and bountiful. Viewed cumulatively, they certainly constituted a panacea.

Since results were guaranteed, the risks involved in investment of money and in prestige of the school system were deemed low. The benefits of basing instruction on predetermined objectives, it was argued, could not be overstated.[20] Lessinger sketched the advantages of performance contracting as:

1. It "fosters the objective evaluation of educational results and also the managerial processes by which these results were achieved."

2. It makes public schools competitive.

3. It is an experiment carried out in a "responsible manner with low costs and low political and social risks."

4. It enables schools to meet students' new "bill of rights."

5. It plays a significant role in school desegregation by removing the deficiencies of minority children in a desegregated school system.

6. It "creates dynamic tension and responsible institutional change within the public school system through competition."[21]

Reed Martin and Blaschke foresaw comprehensive benefits from applying the system: "The application of contractual principles to educational performance is going to pervade every relationship schools now have." These relationships, which would have "lasting legal implications," would be an inexorable process that would result in sovereignty for the "consumer" of education:

> The basic relationship will become one of consumer versus supplier of educational services, with the contract as a primary instrument in this educational resolution leading to consumer sovereignty. . . . [this] may seem to many to be a slow process, but once it begins, it cannot be stopped. And it began this year.[22]

As noted above, the original contracts confronted basic needs of minority children in the cities. Mecklenburger and Wilson observed that the Cherry Creek, Colorado contract demonstrated that the system could be used in suburban districts as well. The experience there revealed that "the range of alternatives opened by the performance contract concept has barely begun . . . that if creative people have the opportunity, you ain't seen nuthin' yet."[23] The revised perceptions would take time, though, because "Management reform in public schools will be time-consuming and difficult to implement." However, if achievement results are significant, then "perhaps public perceptions will change as educational myths and concepts are displaced."[24]

Some critics had termed the business approach to schooling "de-humanizing."

Dr. McAndrew, school superintendent in Gary, Indiana, where one of the first contracts was employed (in the Banneker Elementary School), disagreed. He maintained that the "most dehumanizing experience is when the vast majority of our pupils are graduated and haven't learned anything." By turning this situation around, he felt, the system was anything but de-humanizing.[25]

Some performance contracting advocates proclaimed that the system was of almost infinite value to the nation and its schools and their students. For example, Albert Mayrhofer stated that "Performance contracting holds enormous promise for the children of this nation and the institutions charged with their learning."[26] Blaschke, understandably, held that once they had seen the evidence of how the system worked, "both contracting firms and school officials will see the advantages of entering into turnkey projects immediately."[27] Performance contracting should be regarded as especially beneficial by business leaders, whose involvement in education heretofore had been characterized by "Thou shalt not," the *proscriptive*, whereas in performance contracting the firms would play a *prescriptive* role, i.e., they would be asked to do a job without being told how to do it, thus encouraging a "perpetual search for efficiency."[28] The "incentive network," as he called it, was absolutely indispensable for the munificent benefits of performance contracting to flow:

> The policy implications are clear: the effective application of the fruits of educational reward and development will not occur in our public schools until a management environment conducive to innovation and risk-taking is created in the classroom through the local level. At the heart of such a system is an incentive network that encourages the attainment of school system objectives by perpetuating phased and evolutionary creative destruction and renewal.[29]

The spirit of innovation was the sine qua non of the movement, Blaschke contended; the Office of Economic Opportunity's (OEO) critical review of eighteen performance contracts was deficient in that it failed to analyze "performance contracting as a change agent":

> We cannot underestimate the importance of the spirit of willingness to innovate that has been nurtured by performance contracting. This is just one of the reasons why the contracting concept will continue, though perhaps by a different name, in spite of the distorted reports that have been circulated about its early successes and failures.[30]

The *Washington Post* took note of the movement in a 1970 editorial headlined "Better Students, More Dollars." The editorial described performance contracting as "one of the most interesting possibilities in American education in years."[31] Mecklenburger and Wilson concurred, with one reservation. If "sophistication grows and triumphs over the hucksters and panacea hounds who also flock to innovations," then "the performance contracts of the early 1970s could well be the first ripple of a new wave in education."[32]

Mayrhofer summarized what he viewed as the advantages of performance contracting. Among them were, first, that the contract "fosters the evaluation of educational results and also the managerial processes by which these results were achieved." The second advantage he enumerated was that the system could be looked upon as a "means to foster and catalyze institutional reform within a school system." Allowing lay board members "to make rational choices when choosing new credible techniques for extension in the classroom" constituted the third advantage. The opportunity to "desegregate in the most nondescriptive, educationally effective, and politically palatable manner" was the fourth benefit he catalogued. Fifth was that by enabling taxpayers to "tie results to dollars expended," boards of education "can finally establish policy and choose among alternative instructional programs."[33]

Schwartz spoke about the movement's future. Even if it faded and died, he felt, it would have a residual effect because it established relations between school officials and local industry. Their relationship would never be the same after performance contracting. But Schwartz felt optimistic about the movement's future, noting that it "continues to grow, despite the number of education company officials waiting for it to pass."[34]

Its Operation

Frank Johnson identified factors that the performance contract ought to include: a description of the student target to be involved; specific curricular subsections that would be embraced; curricular design; the instructional process; instructional management; behavioral objectives and performance criteria; evaluation design; educational audit requirements, if any; the level and kinds of material and equipment support from the school district; the length of the experiment; arrangements for supervision and the role of the supervisor; and types of remunerative agreement.[35] Johnson also added implications for pre- and inservice teacher education programs. These should include, at the very least, the "study of curriculum foundations, curriculum design, evaluation techniques, instructional management, needs survey techniques, cognitive approaches to teaching and the relationships of the affective and psychomotor domains to learning."[36]

Lessinger looked to the "independent educational accomplishment audit" as the "device through which the public can hold its school accountable, and also through which the school can learn how to improve its programs in order to meet the demands rightly made by its constituency." For him *"independent,"* was the key word, because "Bureaucracies, in the field of education, as in other fields, tend to withhold information from the public except when required to provide it or when struggles within the bureaucracy produce a news leak."[37] Lessinger hailed public news reports, such as those found in the *Wall Street Journal,* that reported that "private industry is beginning to bid for a significant new plan in public education—far beyond anything so humdrum as supplying textbooks, films or records." He applauded what he called three precedent-setting features of performance contracting: 1) once school officials have specified the results they wanted, the contractor was free to propose his or her own methods for achieving the results; 2) compensation is linked directly to the results achieved; and 3) methods and staffing are designed so they can be turned over to school officials if the results are as good as expected.[38]

In his laudatory description of how the system operates, Blaschke proclaimed that it was "simple in concept, although complex in realization, it provides an opportunity for community involvement in the determination of performance specifications and in the operation of projects, since many contractors utilize locally trained community aides."[39] The use of aides would be controversial, as we shall shortly see. Blaschke recognized that "Most firms use paraprofessionals where available; some firms would prefer to use paraprofessionals exclusively" in order to hold down costs.[40] Adoption of performance contracting would have a substantial effect on a school's teachers, because to create instructional management capabilities within the classroom "teachers will need to be retrained in attitude, as well as technical proficiencies; and incentives, in many cases, will have to be provided for the new classroom manager to help children achieve as much as possible, given time and cost constraints."[41]

Robert Stake quoted a member of a New Jersey school board on how to set up a performance contract for successful operation. His advice was that "Objectives must be stated in simple, understandable terms. No jargon will do and no subjective goals can be tolerated. Neither can the nonsense about there being some mystique that prohibits objective measurement of the educational endeavor."[42] Put simply, Blaschke denied that performance contracting was an end in itself, rather it "provides a means by which the local school system can experiment effectively, test a new instructional program, and adopt the new program, making changes within the system to insure that the potential results can be realized."[43]

Most school board members, he argued, found it difficult to decide on matters of pedagogy and methodology, but the "concept of tying costs to guaranteed or minimum results is easily understood when common sense and quality control measures are incorporated." As he opined, it is "relatively easy to gather support for a concept that can be easily communicated."[44]

Opposition

Like any "reform" movement, performance contracting had its opposition. Foremost among its opponents were the teachers' organizations, especially the American Federation of Teachers (AFT). Others pointed to the limited range of fields tested (performance contracting focused on math and reading and did not attempt to "measure" higher thought processes or the affective domain), a tendency to "teach to the test" (as the Texarkana project was indicted for doing), and a reliance on quantitative means to measure student learning gains. We will focus our attention on the teachers.

Teachers generally, and those speaking and writing on their behalf, were highly critical of various aspects of the movement. For instance, Herb Cook, executive director of the Dallas Classroom Teachers Association (DCTA) commented on the performance contracting experience in that city, alleging that the system was set up for the benefit of the "administration, not in the best interests of the students and learning situation."[45] DCTA President Jewel Howard questioned the fairness and effectiveness of the motivation incentives the system used for students: "performance contracting experiments are free to give the students radios and green stamps, while we've never been allowed to give them a piece of bubble gum or candy." Howard wondered whether the performance contract rewards were the "right kind of motivation for children" and if the effects of that practice would be "lasting."[46]

Girard Hottleman authored a highly critical piece on performance contracting, in which he alleged that relationships between former U.S. Office of Education employees and private learning corporations besmirched the movement.[47] Hottleman began his essay by characterizing Lessinger and Blaschke, two of the movement's gurus, as engaging in "mutual backslapping." He continued his critique by contending that Dr. Neil V. Sullivan, Massachusetts education commissioner, while functioning as a paid consultant for Thiokol, a performance contracting firm, lauded the involvement of industry with education and urged its spread in the enterprise.[48] The Texarkana project came in for its share of criticism from Hottleman's pen. Noting that the evaluator had revealed that there had been direct teaching of some test items so that the test results could not be used as valid measures of achievement, he pointed out that the project's programmer, Rosella Scott, was the sister of Dorsett Educational Systems president, Lloyd G. Dorsett (who had the contract). Hottleman quoted her as saying "I did everything I could to see that the company made money on the project."[49]

Maintaining that the real question was whether the movement would benefit children, and answering with a resounding "no," Hottleman took Lessinger et al. to task over their assertion that the teaching profession refused to be accountable, asserting that this position "is nothing more than pious, pompous propaganda. It is inaccurate. It is the pandering of the new self-appointed, would-be educational mandarins."[50] These performance contracting devotees were "about to sanction the wholesale production of the polluted child. The approach is almost universally mechanistic, automated, programmed, and built on extrinsic rewards." They held that students should read, not for "pleasure," "appreciation," "leisure," "understanding," but "for profit."[51] The "politically ambitious and the special interest representatives who frequently populate school boards" favored short-term gains which were "made at the considerable sacrifice of the quality of the future lives of succeeding generations." Lessinger's accusation that one out of every four students drops out was a typical statement for the leaders of the new "industrial-education complex." Tell the parents that "teachers have cheated their children," and the community will become sufficiently angry to "beg for industry to solve their problems," he wrote.[52]

Citing problems with contracts in Hartford and the Bronx, Hottleman averred that the "industrial mind-set" (profits first, humanity second) had led to some appalling behavior that was totally unacceptable.[53] You could not have accountability unless you had power, Hottleman contended. Teachers did not have power, school boards did. He concluded his fiery defense of teachers and denunciation of industrial influence through performance contracting with the statement that:

> When the day finally arrives when school boards become accountable to their public trust by permitting the conditions necessary for any real degree of teacher accountability to exist, the problem so glibly catalogued by the critics will begin to be solved. But in the meantime, let the pandering mandarins go peddle their green stamps elsewhere.[54]

Teacher organizations were critical of the system, regarding the movement as a threat to job security and collective bargaining rights. The AFT was especially caustic. Lessinger observed in 1970 that the NEA felt the movement discredited urban public schools in the eyes of the public; the AFT denounced performance contracting as "educational gimmickry" that featured "businesses exploiting children for profit."[55] The AFT called for the "outright abolition" of performance contracting agreements, viewing them as "just another fad," the product of "fly-by-night companies" who had "learned there is money to be made," and constituted "an invasion of the responsibility of teachers and grounds for strikes," according to AFT president David Selden.[56] The union and its officials greeted with cries of "hucksterism in the schools" statements such as the following by one school board member: "Performance Contracting does what (teachers) won't do—it rises or falls on *results,* not on schedules and seniority and protected mediocrity."[57] The AFT set up "listening posts" to monitor the movement and its *Non-Coloring Book on Performance Contracting* was seen in some quarters as a "vicious piece of political cartooning."[58] Albert Shanker described the movement as "a conspiracy of the Nixon Administration to ward off demands for more money for education." The OEO experiment on performance contracting in a number of jurisdictions was "phony," he said: "This isn't viewed as an experiment, it's a juggernaut. Everyone's going around saying it will succeed. Believe me, advertising will make it succeed. . . . It's the guarantee of performance that's sheer hucksterism."[59] The AFT expressed its resolve to oppose any plan, such as performance contracting, that threatened to "dehumanize the learning process; would sow distrust among teachers through a structured incentive program" and was "predicated on the assumption that educational achievement can be improved in the vacuum of a machine-oriented classroom, without changing the wider environment of the poverty-stricken child."[60]

> The NEA was less heated and acrimonious in its position on the movement. It held steadfastly that its "local associations" had to be involved in planning the contract and that "maximum use of school personnel" was required to carry it out.[61] Dr. John Lumley, assistant executive secretary for government relations and citizenship of the NEA testified before the Senate Appropriations Subcommittee on the OEO contracting plan that the NEA "deplores the OEO performance contracting program because we believe it can weaken the structure of the public school system and can discredit the schools in the eyes of the public."[62] Lumley, however, said his association favored contracts between local school systems and teachers, the latter having the "primary responsibility for the education of our youth," which "profit-making firms" did not.[63]

The Gary Teachers Union, allegedly fearing a loss of jobs, provided an example of a local union's stance on performance contracting. The union threatened to strike before the Banneker Elementary School contract got going in Gary, opposed the use of "neighborhood women" (paraprofessionals) in the place of teachers, and it also complained about pupil-teacher ratios in the contract.[64] Trouble between educators and business people, as occurred in Gary, could be partially attributed to the rhetoric of the two groups, to the extent that two authors alleged that much of the debate over performance contracting "floundered on the language dilemma": "People who talk of management, cost-effectiveness, needs assessment, and *product* emphasis rouse hostility in people who talk of the whole child, individual differences, *my* classroom, or the learning *process*."[65]

Promises

Performance contracting attracted considerable attention from the business and education communities in its first year. Some looked to the future with unbounded optimism; others were more cautious. In 1970, Ronald Schwartz took early note of the mixed reception the movement was receiving from education companies: "Performance Contracting is getting a mixed reaction from the nation's education companies—some, especially small firms, are exploring it aggressively, while others are approaching it with caution because they suspect it may be only a passing fad."[66]

The movement did experience substantial growth in its early days, increasing from one project (Texarkana) to 170 by the fall of 1970; the number of involved companies grew from ten to forty.[67] The growth spurt caused Blaschke, the founder of Educational Turnkey, to comment that "It's already become a bandwagon."[68] Even the cloud that accompanied the alleged "teaching to the tests" misstep in Texarkana could not put an end to it, as that district's superintendent, Edward D. Price, prophesied, "We haven't heard the end of performance contracting and accountability by a long shot."[69] Mayrhofer's declaration a few short months later substantiated Price's faith: "Performance Contracting holds enormous promise for the children of this nation and the institutions charged with their learning."[70]

Supportive statements were not limited to the simple declarative. Mecklenburger and Wilson waxed eloquent with their depiction as a result of the Gary experience: "Performance contracting in schools, like a crystal dropped into a stream of light, acts as a prism, displaying a colorful spectrum of fundamental educational issues and requiring they be examined anew."[71] Also addressing the Gary project, a veteran teacher, who became a "learning director," observed that "The kids seem to be enjoying school for the first time." Donald Kendrick, the "center manager," attributed the change to letting the "system teach—the teacher should manage. . . . She can't do that if she has to teach her class the old way." And it had an effect on the students, according to a retired music teacher who was the grandmother of a Banneker student: "He's the happiest he's been since he started school . . . he wants to be a teacher."[72]

In the fall of 1971, Schwartz noted that the movement continued to grow, despite the fact that a number of education company officials were waiting for it to pass.[73] According to Blaschke, the steady progress was due to the reality that "both contracting firms and school officials" would quickly see the "advantages of entering into turnkey projects immediately." What they saw, according to him, was management control and program flexibility:

> The policy implications are clear: the effective application of the fruits of educational research and development will not occur in our public schools until a management environment conducive to innovations and risk taking is created in the classroom through the local level. At the heart of such a system is an incentive network that encourages the attainment of school system objectives by perpetuating phased and evolutionary creative destruction and renewal.[74]

Limitations/Restrictions/Questions

While performance contracting was greeted with a warm embrace in some quarters, in others it received a skeptical reception. Fear of its transitory nature seemed to be one such concern, according to one school official who said in 1970 that "I wouldn't be surprised if by next year the whole idea of performance contracting will have passed into the history books."[75] The snafu in Texarkana led Lloyd G. Dorsett, president of Dorsett Educational Systems, Inc., the firm that had the contract, to write to the school superintendent that:

> I fervently hope that the misguided efforts of a harried and pressured head programmer which affected a relatively small amount of material in the last 60 days of school will not be allowed to invalidate our work of the last 14 years or the principle of educational accountability.[76]

Gary Saretsky raised a different kind of problem. He pointed out that "Performance contracts could serve as new ways to hassle the teacher, new methods for retribution," because the system was based on rewards for performance, students were handed power over teachers and contracting firms.[77]

Evaluation was a crucial ingredient for the operation of the system. Testing problems thus constituted a major hazard, should they exist. Robert Stake wrote that they did, even to the extent of constituting a "booby trap":

> Among the articles analyzing performance contracting, current leaders in the accountability sweepstakes, some are pinpointing weaknesses in the theory and booby traps in the operation. This one offers a useful examination of statistical weaknesses and test limitations.[78]

Stake observed that performance contracting arose because of dissatisfaction over the quality of the education students were getting; he argued that standardized tests could not be relied upon to report accurately outcomes of the process: "Implicit in the contracts is the expectation that available tests can measure the newly promised learning. The standardized test alone cannot measure the specific outcomes of an individual student with sufficient precision."[79]

Stake was not alone in his concern about the problem of measuring students' gains. One trio identified the movement's "real pitfalls" as using "test gains as measures of real gains in student learning." This practice resulted, they wrote, in making the process susceptible to "both practice effects and the effects of extrinsic rewards."[80] The question of evaluation was also cited as a weakness. One author commented that the movement focused "enormous attention on results, while virtually ignoring the question of how results are to be understood."[81]

Considerable attention was devoted to the opposition of teachers in a section above. Donald Rumsfield, OEO director during the Nixon administration zeroed in on the activities of those persons who were limiting the effectiveness of the movement: "A major effort has been mounted by a handful of self-appointed educational spokesmen to halt any inquiry into the possibility of educational reform."[82]

Sigel detected two jumps in the reasoning process when contract results were assessed. He asked for evidence that the prevention of dropouts depended on agreed-upon advancement in reading and math scores and for evidence that appropriate improvement in these scores helped those students obtain gainful employment.[83] Thus, gains in scores might be produced under terms of the contract, but disillusionment was possible. Sigel also wondered what the results signified and asked if the system could be set up so that "equally worthwhile, but less quantifiable, educational goals" could be achieved and measured?[84]

Perception was another limitation, according to Mecklenburger and Wilson. They contended that a stereotype of performance contracting existed that not only limited but severely hampered the movement:

> Performance contracting occurs in inner-city and depressed areas; they bring knowledge-industry businesses, with the profit motive at their heels, to salvage disadvantaged children; advocates of contracting believe schools and teachers are mossbacked, hamstrung, ineffective, and in need of salvation by contract; critics condemn contracts as the Devil's own instrument.[85]

Robert Campbell directed attention to the absence of student accountability in performance contracting. Noting that not one word in sixteen articles in the January 1971 issue of *Educational Technology* dealt with student accountability, he opined that an "accountability arrangement in education without the learner is not only inadvisable—it is impossible." Clearly, he claimed, *everyone who is a party to the process must be accountable.* Incomplete accountability, such as existed in performance contracting, "clouds the truth . . . postpones inevitable reckoning."[86]

One of performance contracting's acknowledged leading spokesmen, Charles Blaschke, cited organizational problems as an obstacle to the movement's success. Efficiency in instruction was difficult to realize, he wrote, because of internal and external opposition. Administrators and board members, he maintained, will need:

> . . . costs and other information in a format which can be used for management rather than administrative purposes *and* for educating the taxpayer, if not for countervailing the public relations of national teachers' groups. Management reform in public schools will be time-consuming and difficult to implement. If the achievement results of new alternatives such as performance contracting are significant, then perhaps public perceptions will change as educational myths and concepts are displaced.[87]

Ellis Page's account of what happened at Texarkana will serve to bring down the curtain to this section. He contended that the participants' hopes for the success of the reform movement were based on beliefs that were built on sand, making the failure of the experiment inevitable:

> Given these warning signs, *why* did the contractors, schools and the OEO sign the contracts and move so happily toward their fates? The answer is inescapable: They *really believed* that the lagging pupils were disadvantaged only in their prior experience; that the public schools were terribly ineffective teachers; and that the application of the usual psychological principles would cause extraordinary leaps in achievement.
>
> When the results were finally released, the shock was severe. The pupils fell far short of the year's gain required by contract; the contractors were immediately in deep financial danger. And the OEO was in deep embarrassment. It had achieved a rare kind of research rigor, yet the testing results were shattering. It was apparent that the hopes for PC which led to the contracts had been wildly optimistic.[88]

Conclusion

In March of 1971, Stanley Elam remarked that for the "past six months or so I have been collecting all the information I can get hold of on performance contracting." Based on that information, his assessment of the status of the movement was as follows: "One of the great dangers in any new development is that too much will be expected of it too soon. Another is that inadequate planning, misapplication, and poor management will discredit the whole concept."[89] Elam's concerns were borne out in the phenomenon called performance contracting. Sigel wrote similar thoughts that same year: "Educational fads destroy reputations as relentlessly as they build them; there's no reason to think performance contracting will do otherwise by the time it has run its course."[90]

John Wilson, director of the oft-cited OEO study on the performance contracting experiments, testified to the proclivity educators had to espouse fads, fears that evoked the OEO study: "We were afraid educators would jump on this thing without knowing what they were doing."[91] George Stern, president of Behavioral Research Laboratories, expressed similar feelings:

> My feeling is that it will be turned into a gimmick. It really could be a vehicle for changing school systems, but that depends a great deal on what the educational-industrial complex does. If they decide they're going to get on this horse and ride it till it dies, it'll die very early.[92]

Gary Saretsky, observing the publicity generated around the movement, spoke about the extravagant expectations that had been generated by performance contracting: "One shot, short-term experiments in major educational change cannot be expected to yield immediate unqualified success."[93] Mecklenburger and Wilson attested to its fragile future as they assayed the world of 1973: "One of the newest, most controversial, and perhaps least understood phrases in the contemporary lexicon of education is 'performance contracting' . . . *paying according to how much children learn.*"[94] There was hope, though, for the innovation: "If the sophistication grows and triumphs over the hucksters and panacea hounds who also flock to innovations, the performance contracts of the early 1970s could well be the first ripple of a new wave in education."[95]

Mecklenburger's and Wilson's words were published in 1973, when performance contracting had begun its plummet towards earth. Within two years it would disappear from the world of education, suffering a similar fate as the educational panaceas that had preceded it and would follow it. Along with the accountability movement that had spawned it, however, it left a residual effect. Corporate America remains influential in educational affairs to this day.

Notes

1. Julia W. Ehrenreich, ed., *Education Index July 1969–June 1970*. New York: The H. W. Wilson Company, 1970, p.794; ibid, July 1970–June 1971, pp. 618–619; ibid, July 1972–June 1973, p. 655; and Marylouise Hewitt, ed., ibid., July 1974–June 1975, p. 660.

2. Ronald Schwartz, "Performance Contracts Catch On," *Nation's Schools* 86, 2 (August 1970): 31.

3. Efrem Sigel with Myra Sobel, *Accountability and the Controversial Role of the Performance Contractors*. White Plains, NY: Knowledge Industry Publications, Inc., 1971, p. 41.

4. Charles Blaschke, *Performance Contracting: Who Profits Most?* Bloomington, IN: Phi Delta Kappa Educational Foundation, 1972, p. 7.

5. Ibid.

6. Sigel, *Accountability and the Controversial Role,* pp. i–ii.

7. Leon Lessinger, "Engineering Accountability for Results in Public Education," *Phi Delta Kappan* LII, 4 (December 1970): 217.

8. H. M. Harmes, "Specifying Objectives for Performance Contracts," *Educational Technology* 11, 1 (January 1971): 52–53.

9. Ibid., 56.

10. Blaschke, *Performance Contracting: Who Profits Most?*, pp. 9–10.

11. Ibid., p. 45.

12. James A. Mecklenburger and John A. Wilson, "Learning C.O.D.: Can the Schools Buy Success?," in Allan C. Ornstein, ed., *Accountability for Teachers and School Administrators*. Belmont, CA: Fearon Publishers, 1973, p. 80.

13. Sigel, *Accountability and the Controversial Role,* p. 63.

14. Marilyn M. Grayboff, "Tools for Building Accountability: The Performance Contract," *Journal of Secondary Education* 45, 8 (December 1970): 355.

15. Ibid., 356.

16. Ibid., 368.

17. Lessinger, *Every Kid a Winner: Accountability in Education*. New York: Simon and Schuster, 1970, p. 103.

18. Blaschke, *Performance Contracting: Who Profits Most?*, p. 17.

19. Albert V. Mayrhofer, "Performance Contracting for Instruction," in Frank J. Sciara and Richard K. Jantz, eds., *Accountability in American Education*. Boston: Allyn and Bacon, Inc., 1972, p. 239.

20. Grayboff, "Tools for Building Accountability": 356.

21. Lessinger, "Engineering Accountability for Results in Public Education": 219–220.

22. Reed Martin and Charles Blaschke, "Contracting for Educational Reform," *Phi Delta Kappan* LII, 7 (March 1971): 403, 405.

23. James A. Mecklenburger and John A. Wilson, "Performance Contracting in Cherry Creek?," *Phi Delta Kappan* LIII, 1 (September 1971): 51–54.

24. Charles Blaschke, "Performance Contracting Costs, Management Reform, and John Q. Citizen," *Phi Delta Kappan* LIII, 4 (December 1971): 247.

25. Jack Starr, "We'll Educate Your Kids—Or Your Money Back," *Look,* 35, 12, June 15, 1971, p. 64.

26. Albert Mayrhofer, "Factors to Consider in Preparing Performance Contracts for Instruction," *Educational Technology* 11, 1 (January 1971): 51.

27. Blaschke, *Performance Contracting: Who Profits Most?,* p. 39.

28. Ibid., p. 45.

29. Ibid., p. 46.

30. Ibid., p. 47.

31. "Better Students, More Dollars," *The Washington Post,* August 22, 1970, p. A-14.

32. Mecklenburger and Wilson, "Learning C.O.D.," p. 88.

33. Mayrhofer, "Performance Contracting for Instruction," pp. 237–239.

34. Ronald Schwartz, "PERFORMANCE CONTRACTING: Industry's Response," *Nation's Schools* 86, 3 (September 1971): 55.

35. Frank W. Johnson, "Performance Contracting with Existing Staff," *Educational Technology* 11, 1 (January 1971): 61.

36. Ibid.

37. Lessinger, *Every Kid A Winner: Accountability in Education,* pp. 79–80.

38. Ibid., pp. 97, 100.

39. Blaschke, *Performance Contracting: Who Profits Most?,* p. 22.

40. Ibid., p. 24.

41. George H. Voegel, "A Suggested Schema for Faculty Commission Pay in Performance Contracting," *Educational Technology* 11, 1 (January 1971): 57.

42. Quoted in Robert E. Stake, "Testing Hypotheses in Performance Contracting," *Phi Delta Kappan* LII, 10 (June 1971): 583.

43. Blaschke, *Performance Contracting: Who Profits Most?,* p. 8.

44. Ibid., p. 9.

45. "Outlook for Teacher Incentives," *Nation's Schools* 86, 5 (November 1970): 53.

46. Quoted in ibid., 53.

47. Girard D. Hottleman, " Performance Contracting Is a Hoax," in Sciara and Jantz, eds., *Accountability in American Education,* pp. 258–269.

48. Ibid., p. 262.

49. Ibid., pp. 262–263.

50. Ibid., p. 264.

51. Ibid., p. 265.

52. Ibid., p. 266.

53. Ibid., pp. 266–267.

54. Ibid., p. 268.

55. Lessinger, "Engineering Accountability for Results in Education": 225.

56. "How Education Groups View Contracting," *Nation's Schools* 86, 4 (October 1970): 86.

57. Quoted in Mecklenburger and Wilson, "Learning C.O.D.," p. 79.

58. Ibid., p. 81.

59. Quoted in Sigel, *Accountability and the Controversial Role of the Performance Contractor,* p. 42.

60. Quoted in "How Education Groups View Contracting": 87.

61. Sigel, Accountability and the Controversial Role of the Performance Contractor, p. 42.

62. Quoted in "How Education Groups View Contracting": 87.

63. Quoted in ibid., 87.

64. Star, "We'll Educate Your Kids—Or Your Money Back," p. 64.

65. Mecklenburger and Wilson, "Learning C.O.D.," p. 80.

66. Ronald Schwartz, "Performance Contracts: What Industry Thinks": 53.

67. Ibid.

68. Ibid.

69. "Performance Contracting—Clouds and Controversy over Texarkana," *Nation's Schools* 86, 4 (October 1970): 88.

70. Mayrhofer, "Factors to Consider in Preparing Performance Contracts for Instruction": 51.

71. Mecklenburger and Wilson, "The Performance Contract in Gary," *Phi Delta Kappan* LII, 7 (March 1971): 409.

72. Star, "We'll Educate Your Kids—Or Your Money Back," p. 61.

73. Schwartz, "PERFORMANCE CONTRACTING: Industry's Response": 55.

74. Blaschke, *Performance Contracting: Who Profits Most?,* p. 46.

75. Schwartz, "Performance Contracting: What Industry Thinks": 53.

76. "Performance Contracting: Clouds and Controversy over Texarkana": 86.

77. Gary Saretsky, "Every Kid a Hustler," *Phi Delta Kappan* LII, 10 (June 1971): 595.

78. Robert E. Stake, "Testing Hazards in Performance Contracts," *Phi Delta Kappan* LII, 10 (June 1971): 583.

79. Ibid., 588.

80. Roger Farr, J. Jaap Tuinman, and B. Elgit Blantum, "How to Make a Pile in Performance Contracting," *Phi Delta Kappan* LIII, 6 (February 1972): 369.

81. Sigel, *Accountability and the Controversial Role of the Performance Contractor,* p. 3.

82. Quoted in ibid., p. 43.

83. Ibid., p. 64.

84. Ibid., p. 66.

85. Mecklenburger and Wilson, "Performance Contracting in Cherry Creek?": 51.

86. Robert E. Campbell, "Accountability and Stone Soup," *Phi Delta Kappan* LIII, 3 (November 1971): 177–178.

87. Blaschke, "Performance Contracting Costs, Management Reform, and John Q. Citizen": 247.

88. Ellis B. Page, "How We All Failed at Performance Contracting," *Phi Delta Kappan* LIV, 2 (October 1972): 116.

89. Stan Elam, "The Chameleon's Dish," *Phi Delta Kappan* LII, 7 (March 1971): 402.

90. Sigel, *Accountability and the Controversial Role of the Performance Contractor,* p. 12.

91. Quoted in ibid., p. 13.

92. Quoted in ibid., p. 67.

93. Gary Saretsky, "The OEO P. C. Experiment and the John Henry Effect," *Phi Delta Kappan* LIII, 9 (May 1972): 581.

94. Mecklenburger and Wilson, "Learning C.O.D.: Can the Schools Buy Success?," p. 79.

95. Ibid., p. 88.

CHAPTER THIRTEEN

Behavioral Objectives

According to the guru of behavioral objectives W. James Popham (described by Michael Scriven as "the licensed midwife to the birth of behavioral objectives"[1]), the 1950s work of Ralph W. Tyler and Benjamin Bloom "provoked only a mild pattern of interest among educators."[2] Popham described the apathy toward objectives among teachers as follows:

> The vast majority of American teachers still wrote their largely meaningless statements of educational objectives, if at all, as part of an annual pre-school ritual under orders from the school principal. The objectives were dutifully tucked in the teacher's desk drawer, never to emerge (except, perhaps, on Parents' Back-to-School Night) and certainly never to influence the teacher's essential decisions.[3]

A New Era

This "wretched and inexcusable situation," Popham declared, thankfully was changing. Indeed:

> We are at the brink of a new era regarding the explication of instructional goals, an era which promises to yield fantastic improvements in the quality of instruction. One can only sympathize with the thousands of learners who had to obtain an education from an instructional system built on a muddle-minded conception of educational goals.[4]

What accounted for this dawn of a glorious new day in education? It was the result of the appearance of Robert Mager's "classic little book," *Preparing Instructional Objectives*.[5] Consequently, the educational community had to "come to grips with both the flexibility of using behavioral objectives and the value of such objectives to teaching and learning."[6] The upshot of this movement was to provide direction to students' learning, to distinguish between relevant and incidental material, and provide organization to subject matter.[7]

In the "Preface" to his book, Mager wrote that he assumed the reader was interested in communicating with students in "such a way that your students will be able to demonstrate their achievement of *your* instructional objectives."[8] In a parenthetical statement he advised the reader that "If you are not interested in demonstrating achievement of your objectives, you have just finished this book."[9] Student performance was to be assessed in terms of the goals set, Mager maintained. He quoted Dr. Paul Whitmore for support of this position:

> The statement of objectives of a training program must denote *measurable* attributes *observable* in the graduate of the program, or otherwise it is impossible to determine whether or not the program is meeting the objectives.[10]

Behavioral objectives also rested on the foundation of behaviorist psychology, behaviorist learning theory, as epitomized by the writings of the famous B. F. Skinner. In an article published in 1954, Skinner zeroed in on what needed to be done for teaching to result in learning:

> There is a simple job to be done. The task can be stated in concrete terms. The necessary techniques are known. The equipment needs can easily be provided. Nothing stands in the way but cultural inertia. But what is more characteristic of America than an unwillingness to accept the traditional as inevitable? We are on the threshold of an exciting and revolutionary period, in which the scientific study of man will be put into work in man's best interests. Education must play its part. It must accept the fact that a sweeping revision of educational practices is possible and inevitable. When it has done this, we may look forward with confidence to a school system which is aware of the nature of its tasks, secure in its methods, and generously supported by the informed and effective citizens whom education itself will create.[11]

The connection between behavioral objectives and the accountability movement was recognized by Popham. He responded to the question "What do educators do about the demand they produce results?" with the affirmation that *"we produce results and we become accountable."*[12] Educators achieve this goal when they increase their skills in "producing evidence that their instruction yields worthwhile results for learners."[13] Popham outlined how teachers would meet the demands of accountability by means of behavioral objectives by sketching an instructional mini-lesson. First, a teacher is given explicit instructional objectives along with a sample measurement item showing how the objective's achievement will be measured. Second, the teacher is given time to plan a lesson designed to achieve the objective. Third, the teacher instructs a group of learners for a specified period of time. Finally, the learners are measured with a post-test based on the objective but unseen previously by the teacher. A judgment of a teacher's instructional proficiency would be based on these four criteria.[14]

David Miles and Roger Robinson addressed the task of defining behavioral objectives. They wrote: "A behavioral objective is a statement which describes

what a student should be able to do after completing some unit of instruction."
It had three components: 1) a description of a class of stimuli to which the student is to respond (condition); 2) a statement containing an action or behavioral
verb which connotes or denotes the behavior the student is to perform (behavior); and 3) a description of the success criteria by which the student's behavior is
to be judged acceptable or unacceptable (criteria).[15] These authors also attested
to the controversy that enveloped behavioral objectives as the decade of the
1970s began:

> To many people associated with education, the term "behavioral objectives" evokes a
> classroom image of a free, open and humane environment with confident, self-directed
> and anxiety-free students joyfully acquiring complex intellectual and social capabilities.
> To others this very same term conjures up images of a factory-like room full of cubicles
> with dehumanized automations repetitiously memorizing useless facts. What is it about
> this concept that spawns such divergent impressions in people?[16]

Arthur W. Combs was one of the movement's most outspoken opponents.
Observing the rapid advance of behavioral objectives in the educational world, he
wrote: "The madness has even spread to some teachers colleges, where teachers
currently in training are expected to check themselves out against thousands of
teacher 'competencies,' another name for behavioral objectives."[17] Combs was far
from being finished. In his view, the virus of behavioral objectives had created an
epidemic that had the potential to create catastrophes for public schools and their
students:

> Many legislators, national funding organizations, state and local school boards, ad-
> ministrators and supervisors today are caught up in the belief that behavioral objectives
> will make a businesslike operation out of our public schools and surely save us all. . . .
> Unthinking advocacy of behavioral objectives, no matter how well intended, which
> ends only into harassing teachers into further immobility and demoralization will de-
> feat itself. Worse still, such advocacy will, in this writer's opinion, do great harm to a
> whole generation of students. . . . A system of accountability completely dependent
> upon prior definition of behavioral outcomes would produce not intelligent persons
> but automatons.[18]

In the view of Popham and other supporters of behavioral objectives, the trend
presented unlimited opportunities to the educational world. According to Combs
and others who shared his views, the movement spelled doom for education.

The Need for Behavioral Objectives

The cause of behavioral objectives was spurred on by the need for specific goals
that facilitated measurable outcomes. As Popham observed several decades after

the height of the movement, objectives such as "The student will learn to relish literature" precipitated attempts to specify objectives in behavioral terms.[19] It is to Popham we turn for the arguments that called forth behavioral objectives.

In 1969, Popham contended that modifying the "learner's behavior" was the "only sensible reason" for the educator to engage in instruction. Consequently, the "intended changes" must be described in "terms of measurable learner behavior." These statements of behavior, he felt, could be "sharply contrasted with the kinds of objectives that teachers have stated through the centuries."[20] The imprecise objectives were found, to his dismay, to be especially prevalent in the field of language arts. Instructional adequacy could only be ascertained through the meeting of instructional goals. In order to determine whether this had occurred, "the instructor must clearly specify his objectives in terms of measurable learner behavior."[21] Sharply defined goals enabled the teacher to know what the learner is supposed to become at the completion of instruction, which made it "infinitely easier to avoid activities which are really irrelevant." With "loosely defined goals," the instructor might view these activities as "somehow germane." By couching his objectives in "*unambiguous terms* the instructor can promote more relevant study behavior on the part of his students." Clarity was thus the watchword: to the extent that the instructor was somehow unclear regarding the nature of intended terminal behaviors, "the advantage of their use loses potency."[22]

The constant use of behavioral objectives also enabled a distinction to be made in the quality of instruction offered. Popham argued that teachers must be trained to "acquire the skills necessary to efficiently achieve such behavior changes." Indeed, he believed that if "teacher education institutions cannot demonstrate that they can markedly increase the teacher's ability to bring about such behavior changes in learners, they either should modify their teacher preparation programs or close up shop."[23] No friend of traditional educators, Popham commented that "most educators have been inordinately successful" in avoiding "precise objectives," in spite of the "cogent arguments" in their favor.[24]

Popham acknowledged the presence of opponents, characterizing them as a "small collection of dissident educators" who had arisen in "spite of the very favorable overall reaction to explicit objectives during the past five to ten years." Nonetheless, he averred, the risks of subscribing to behavioral goals in instruction were "minuscule in contrast with our current state of confusion regarding instructional intentions." Whether "Threatening or not," Popham said educators had no choice but to "abandon their customary practices of goal-stating and turn to a framework of precision."[25]

Popham acknowledged that the opposition to behavioral objectives had "some merit," but held that none of the reasons advanced "should be considered strong enough to deter educators from specifying all of their instructional goals in the precise forms advocated by the 'good guys' in the argument."[26] Moreover, the opponents to behavioral objectives were guilty of shoddy educational practices:

> I am committed to the point of view that those who discourage educators from pre-cisely explicating their instructional objectives are often permitting, if not promoting, the same kind of unclear thinking that has led in part to the generally abysmal quality of in-struction in this country.[27]

Popham was far from being alone in his advocacy. While noting that behav-ioral objectives could be used for "noble or destructive, human or inhuman ends," Miles and Robinson concluded that since the "basic purpose of such objectives is to clarify and expose what students learn in school," they seemed to offer a "unique potential for discovering what human characteristics are most valuable, and to *facilitate their acquisition*."[28] Johnson referred to the "educational revolu-tion" that had taken place by the coupling of accountability with behavioral ob-jectives in the past decade: "Teachers at many levels are demonstrating a willing-ness to hold themselves accountable for this instructional effectiveness. They make the assumption that teachers *cause* learning, and that if the learner fails, it is the teaching that has failed."[29] This was nowhere more apparent than in schools where teachers "specify their instructional objectives in measurable terms," dis-carding objectives from the past such as the goal of creating an "interesting intel-lectual exercise."[30]

Julie Vargas also combined the movement with accountability. "Clearly stated objectives," she wrote, "improve communication not only to the student but also to parents, educators and the general public." They present a quantifiable answer to the frequently asked question: "What am I getting for my tax dollar?"[31] When "Equipped with his behavioral objectives," Vargas penned, the "teacher knows ex-actly what he wants of his students. He can then concentrate on what, after all, is the most rewarding part of being a teacher—helping students learn."[32]

Growth and Popularity

In 1970, Popham held that the "quality of any instructional sequence must be evaluated primarily in terms of its ability to promote desired changes in the in-tended learner." It was his contention that the "increasingly widespread agree-ment with the conception of instructional effectiveness is new."[33] This growing popularity had led him to establish the Instructional Objectives Exchange, which included 35 collections covering a wide range of subjects in K-12 schooling. Most of these focused on cognitive outcomes; only two dealt with those in the affec-tive realm. He reported that the response to this Exchange was "encouraging"; in the first eighteen months more than 20,000 collections of objectives had been ordered.[34]

A year before, Popham had attested to his fear that teachers could not be trusted to participate in the behavioral objectives movement, and would require considerable prodding to do so, saying that he was:

> . . . frankly afraid that teachers, already overburdened with responsibilities far in excess of what can be accomplished in the time available, would gleefully welcome theoretical positions which endorsed the inclusion of inaccessible educational goals. . . . I suppose I am anxious to induce feelings of guilt whenever teachers are unable to explicate the measurable kinds of student behavior which would ensue from their instructional activities. I want to make them feel so guilty that they will actually set about specifying as many of their intended learner behavior changes as they can. I am afraid that, strategically, an endorsement of a position which permits, if not promotes, inaccessible objectives would allow too many teachers to absolve themselves of the responsibility of describing more of their objectives operationally.[35]

Indeed, he averred that he was not inclined to let teachers "off the hook"; rather, he would take the "hard line" and permit only "operationalized objectives" as legitimate for use in instruction.[36]

By 1972 Robert Gagne could proclaim that few people who were involved with education in the nation could be "unacquainted with 'behavioral objectives.'"[37] Gagne felt this state of affairs was proper because not only were terms such as "knowledge" and "appreciation ambiguous and unreliable" but also that it was "natural" that a person should attempt to identify the outcome of learning as "something the student is able to do following instruction which he was unable to do before instruction." Frankly, he stated: "It is somewhat surprising that parents have stood still for 'grades' for such a long period of time, considering the deplorably small amount of information they convey."[38]

J. Myron Atkin, a critic of the movement, acknowledged its strength as early as 1968. He wrote of bumper stickers at the University of Illinois and other institutions of higher education that read "STAMP OUT NONBEHAVIORAL OBJECTIVES." Behavioral objectives, he observed, had replaced academicians and general curriculum theorists, representing a "powerful tide today."[39] No matter how frequent or ardent the protests, the invasion of behavioral objectives had changed the landscape in schools and colleges of education alike.

Some Strengths and Some Claims

Even a critic such as Robert Ebel attested to the potential benefit of behavioral objectives in certain situations as "educationally useful and laudable."[40] Ralph Ojemann argued that meaningful behavioral objectives were the "best way . . .

now available" so that "teacher, supervisor, test maker, taxpayer—can communicate with one another."[41]

Responding to criticisms of Charles Silberman that behavioral objectives constituted training, but not education, Perry Rosove objected that there was:

> . . . no inherent conflict between specifying objectives in behavioral terms for specific types of curricula and the creation of humane persons and a humane society . . . in the performance of any task it is salutary to have a good idea of what one's goals or objectives are.[42]

After stating precise, measurable objectives in advance to an introductory anthropology course that he had taught for years, Rosove contended that he was "convinced now, having acquired practical experience in the use of behavioral objectives in training programs," that his instruction was more "successful" than it had been. Rosove particularly opposed Silberman's claim that the use of behavioral objectives "requires distinctions between training and education." That distinction, he maintained, was "arbitrary" and inaccurate, because there could be "no education without training and that training is more successful when it is designed on a foundation of identified behavioral objectives."[43] Because they helped instructors distinguish between "relevant and incidental material," behavioral objectives gave direction to student learning and organization to subject matter.[44] As Philip Smith put it, one of the "great strengths" of behavioral objectives was that they pushed "teachers toward greater clarity of objectives in a specific situation."[45]

The advantages of behavioral objectives were all but limitless in the eyes of some of their advocates. Popham called the "risks" involved in moving to behavioral goals "minuscule in contrast with our current state of confusion regarding instructional intentions." Even if threatening, he believed, instructors had no choice but to "abandon their customary practices of goal-stating and turn to a framework of precision."[46] Several years later he commented that "many zealots viewed behavioral objectives as the first steps on a stairway to educational paradise."[47] Louise Tyler joined in the critique of the espousal of teachers' traditional approach to objectives: "Any of the objections given by teachers to instructional objectives seem to be predicated upon inadequate conceptions of education, curriculum, or instruction."[48] Gagne added that in the present era, "grades will have to go." They would be replaced by "behavioral objectives," to which there was "no alternative" in conducting the "essential functions of communication."[49]

Opposition: Some Problems and Some Limitations

Referring to the advent of this new educational movement, Vargas noted that "New ideas always seem to generate a certain resistance."[50] As we shall see, her analysis was certainly borne out in the case of behavioral objectives. Robert Ebel, for instance, identified some general problems and limitations. These included questions about the meaning of the concept and whether behavior was the real objective of instruction. Some claimed that behavioral objectives served as a means to an end and doubted their validity. These queries moved Ebel to write that "Too much of the current reverence for behavioral objectives is a consequence of not looking closely enough at their limitations."[51]

Combs was a leader of those who argued that the movement was contrary to, or at least not congruent with, the very nature of education. Contending that it relied on stimulus-response psychology, he held that "*no information of whatever variety will affect behavior until the individual has discovered its personal meaning for him.*"[52] This adage applied to all education, he believed. For him, "behavioral objectives provide too narrow a basis for proper assessment of educational outcomes."[53] George Kneller joined Combs in holding that behavioral objectives fell short of achieving true educational status:

> For, properly conceived, education is a dialogue between persons in the community of the school, a dialogue in which the teacher encourages the student to enter into acts of learning that fulfill him personally. This is education at its finest, and the program of behavioral objectives has very little place in it.[54]

Herbert Simons maintained that underlying the belief that behavioral objectives improved education was the conviction that "by their emphasis on observable behavior, [they] are more scientific and therefore better than traditional goals of education." Somehow, they would "elevate" instruction to a level comparable to that of "behavioral and physical sciences." The fatal flaw in all of this, Simon believed, was that with their emphasis on "operational definition and observable behavior," they ignored the "crucial distinction between knowledge and behavior," with the result that the goals of instruction became "totally changing behavior rather than imparting knowledge."[55] Accepting their usefulness, to the extent that they assisted teachers and others to "think more carefully and in more specific terms about instruction," Simons concluded that this "minor benefit" hardly "justifies the important role that many would assign to behavioral objectives." Why? Because their advocates were "oblivious" to the knowledge-behavior relationship and had diverted attention away from the "real problems of developing theories of the relationship between knowledge and behavior." Consequently they provided "no real improvement over these traditional techniques" (such as teacher-made tests, rating scales, standardized tests, and the like), and it would behoove "researchers and those responsible for the allocation of educational resources " to recognize that "behavioral objectives, attractive as they may seem at first, offer a false hope for improving instruction."[56]

Atkin had a different concern. Viewing the prior positing of behavioral objectives and the reliance on meeting these pre-specified, narrow, but measurable goals, he worried about the effect they would have on outcomes that were not anticipated before instruction began. These outcomes, which he held occurred whenever you deal with "real people," would disappear or atrophy if behavioral objectives began to rule. Additionally, they would have to hamper innovations, due to the process of their very formulation.[57]

Harold Schoen acknowledged that "Behavioral objectives may be useful in planning to teach very basic skills to students" but saw "very little use for them as an aid in planning instruction of other, more complicated types." Indeed, he wrote that if they were "considered necessary and sufficient for all students" they were not "just useless, they are damaging."[58] Gene Glass thought that although "behavioral objectives were susceptible to sandbagging," schools would choose to implement them because of the easily attainable goals that would make a program a success when they were met. He felt the critical questions were "Where do we get our objectives?" and How do we determine "which objectives are of most worth?"[59]

The accusation that behavioral objectives amounted to a "closed system" received frequent mention. Combs alleged that the ends were prescribed in advance, which led teachers to manipulate students to meet predetermined goals. With ends specified in advance, innovation was discouraged, creativity stifled, and the classroom became a "dull, conforming place where people are learning right answers to problems they do not yet have." The goals of education were systematically "twisted" to concentrate on "behavior we know how to measure."[60] For him, "A system of accountability completely dependent upon prior definition of behavioral objectives would produce not intelligent persons but automatons."[61]

Ebel, while also recognizing the usefulness of behavioral objectives in certain situations, early on challenged their use as "definitions of the ultimate purposes of education," that changed the "pupil's behavior in the direction of certain classified patterns of desirable behavior."[62] John Muchmore worried that they would not only control the behavior of an individual but would also control the behavior of society in the wake of their "fit" within Skinnerian Behaviorism:

> Current literature is replete with articles concerning the introduction of behavioral objectives to virtually every discipline. The implication of every such article is that successful manipulation of behavior is a primary aim of education. Unfortunately, this implication is magnified to the level of spectre by many individuals. Such a reaction is easily explained, for the Orwellian spectacle of a totally controlled populace long has struck fear in the hearts of man.[63]

Muchmore was concerned that less attention was directed toward primary questions, such as "Is it ethical to manipulate another person's behavior?"[64] D. Woodruff

Asahel and Philip Kapfer voiced parallel solicitude, musing that behavioral objectives might transform education into a "mechanistic program devoid of real human value."[65]

As early as 1967, Elliot Eisner called attention to the strength of the drive to implement behavioral objectives when he asserted that they had been "elevated—or lowered—to almost slogan status in curriculum circles."[66] He noted that the outcomes of instruction were "far more numerous and complex for educational objectives to encompass" and that it was impossible for these outcomes to be "specified in behavioral and content terms in advance." They were particularly fallible in aesthetics, where "what is most educationally valuable is the development of that mode of curiosity, inventiveness and insight that is capable of being described only in metaphors or poetic terms."[67] Ebel likewise opined that artistic merit involved imprecise measures, noting that all objectives started with subjective impressions.[68]

Kneller addressed the link between behavioral objectives and American culture, which set a "high value on efficiency and productivity." Such a culture, he claimed, sought to "measure accomplishments by standardized units." Behavioral objectives presented "predicted, measurable outcomes and with little or no measurable 'waste'."[69] They rested on approaches to human behavior that were "reductionist, deterministic and psychicalist," and regarded learning as a "series of measurable responses to carefully prearranged stimuli."[70]

Ebel continued his critique by examining the ultimate purposes of education. He challenged the use of behavioral objectives as "definitions of the ultimate purposes of education," asking if they could determine how a person "should live," and more fundamentally, do they have the "right to do so."[71] Combs, acknowledging the movement's strength, commented that he was "deeply disturbed at what is happening to education as a consequence of our current preoccupation with the behavioral objectives approach."[72] He flailed against the defeatism that surrounded the abandonment of "complex goals and procedures" because they "cannot be simply stated."[73] He recognized the attractiveness of behavioral objectives and what he believed were the false, seductive promises they offered American education:

> The behavioral objectives approach is not wrong. It would be easier to deal with if it were. The danger lies in that it is partly right, for in the realm of human affairs, nothing is more dangerous than a partly right idea. Partly right ideas provide partial solutions and so encourage us to continue our efforts to solve the problems along the same paths we have begun in the vain hope that if we can only do this more often, more intensely, or more universally, surely we must finally arrive at perfect solutions. . . . Unfortunately, behavioral objectives also have such a logical, tangible quality that they are likely to create illusions of accuracy and efficiency far beyond the assistance they can actually deliver.[74]

Evidence of opposition to the movement existed in other quarters. The National Council of Teachers of English, for instance, rejected the use of behavioral objectives "almost in toto" at their 1970 meeting.[75] Book reviews were another source of criticism. Reviewing Popham and Baker's *Establishing Instructional Goals,* Steven Selden argued that the book was but a continuance of the "industrial means-end productivity" of Franklin Bobbitt of a half-century before. It constituted a mere attempt to "polish" Bobbitt's definition of life and the "performance of specified activities."[76]

Conclusion

Considerable emotional intensity was generated in the conflict over behavioral objectives. Schoen recognized this with his summary statement that "Most emotional arguments against behavioral objectives are matched in their irrationality by the pedantic positions of many behaviorists."[77] Atkin also referred to the inflammatory nature of the debate: "Too much of the debate related to the use of behavioral objectives has been conducted in an argumentative style that characterizes discussions of fundamental religious views among adherents who are poorly informed."[78]

Embodying this sentiment were proponents such as Popham, who saw no viable alternative to the use of behavioral objectives:

> Any risks we run by moving to behavioral goals are minuscule in contrast with our current state of confusion regarding instructional intentions. . . . To secure a dramatic increase in instructional effectiveness, we must abandon our customary practice of goal stating and turn to a framework of precision.[79]

Arguing that he could recognize the dangers of "subscribing exclusively to such goals," Popham wrote there was really no reasonable alternative if schools were to be improved:

> The advantages of explicitly stated goals outweigh their disadvantage by so much as to preclude serious objection to their widespread use. I admit a rational and visceral commitment to the proposition that operationalized instructional goals represent a key means of improving our schools.[80]

As we have seen, Popham was far from alone in his crusade for behavioral objectives. Rosove pointed out the necessity of preparing "tomorrow's educators" for the time "when they will be required to identify the behavioral objectives for curricula." Failure to do this, he averred, would be to leave "education exactly where Silberman found it—in a state of 'mindlessness'."[81]

Popham's zeal was matched by that of his opponents. Ebel complained that "Too much of the current reverence for behavioral objectives is a consequence of not looking closely enough at their limitations."[82] Combs pointed to what he called "an unfortunate and dangerous distortion" of education that had been brought about by the "current preoccupation with behavioristic and industrial approaches to educational problems."[83] Arthur Wirth spoke to the widespread appeal of this "impoverished" approach when he penned that "Education becomes simple, less controversial and more impoverished as we reduce it to imparting particles of knowledge as machine scored 'right' answers."[84]

Behavioral objectives enjoyed an immense popularity in the 1960s through the mid-1970s, despite the opposition identified above. They were embraced so intensely and devotedly by some as to constitute a panacea. They, too, however, were destined to plunge into near obscurity. The words of Popham shall constitute their epitaph. Admitting that they had helped him, Popham testified to his belief that they would help others as well. He describes his romance with behavioral objectives as follows:

> Then, I did everything I could to teach educators how to state their objectives in behavioral terms. I wrote journal articles. I gave speeches. I developed film-strip programs about objectives. I taught regular classes and short institutes in which the use of behavioral objectives was euphorized. I even had bumper stickers printed, and distributed to my UCLA classes which read: "Help Stamp Out Nonbehavioral Objectives."[85]

In a government-sponsored trip to Ethiopia to visit Peace Corps volunteers, Popham encountered one of his former students. The student, experiencing difficulty in remembering his name, eventually choked out "Doctor . . . *objectives!*" The ensuing discussion revealed that the student had remembered what he had been taught at UCLA about objectives: "cognitive, affective, psychomotor, the whole bit!" When Popham asked him if the objectives approach had been useful in his work, the former student snapped "Hell, no . . . I'm too damned busy teaching!"[86]

A far cry from the "first steps on a stairway to educational paradise."[87]

Notes

1. Quoted in W. James Popham, *Educational Evaluation*. 2nd edition. Englewood Cliffs, NJ: Prentice-Hall, 1988, p. 63.
2. W. James Popham, "Objectives and Instruction," in Popham, Elliot W. Eisner, Howard J. Sullivan, and Louise L. Tyler, eds., *Instructional Objectives*. Chicago: Rand-McNally and Co., 1969, p. 33.
3. Ibid.
4. Ibid.
5. Philippe C. Duchastel and Paul F. Merrill, "The Effects of Behavioral Objectives on Learning," *Review of Educational Research* 43, 1 (Winter 1973): 53.
6. Popham, quoted in ibid.

7. Duchastel and Merrill, "The Effects of Behavioral Objectives on Learning": 63.
8. Robert F. Mager, *Preparing Instructional Objectives*. Palo Alto, CA: Ferron Publishers, 1962, p. viii.
9. Ibid.
10. Quoted in ibid., pp. 3–4.
11. B. F. Skinner, "The Science of Learning and the Art of Teaching," *Harvard Educational Review* XXIV, 2 (Spring 1954): 86.
12. Popham, "The New World of Accountability: In the Classroom," in Julia De Carlo and Constant A. Mason, eds., *Innovations in Education for the Seventies: Selected Readings*. New York: Behavioral Publications, 1973, p. 42.
13. Ibid., p. 43.
14. Ibid., pp. 45–46.
15. David T. Miles and Roger E. Robinson, "Behavioral Objectives: An Even Closer Look," *Educational Technology* 11, 6 (June 1971): 39.
16. Ibid.
17. Arthur W. Combs, *Educational Accountability: Beyond Behavioral Objectives*. Washington, DC: Association for Supervision and Curriculum Development, 1972, p. 11.
18. Ibid., pp. 11–12.
19. Popham, *Educational Evaluation*, p. 55.
20. Popham, "Objectives and Instruction," in Popham, et al., eds., *Instructional Objectives*, p. 35.
21. Ibid., p. 39.
22. Ibid., p. 43.
23. Ibid., pp. 44–45.
24. Ibid., p. 46.
25. Ibid., p. 51.
26. W. James Popham, "Probing the Validity of Arguments Against Behavioral Goals," in Robert C. Anderson, Gerald W. Faust, Marianne C. Roderick, Donald J. Cunningham, and Thomas Andre, eds., *Current Research on Instruction*. Englewood Cliffs, NJ: Prentice-Hall, 1972, p. 66.
27. Ibid.
28. Miles and Robinson, "Behavioral Objectives: An Even Closer Look," *Educational Technology* 11, 6 (June 1971): 44.
29. Rita B. Johnson, "Objectives-Based Accountability Procedures for Classroom Use," *Educational Technology* 11, 6 (June 1971): 49.
30. Ibid.
31. Julie S. Vargas, *Writing Worthwhile Behavioral Objectives*. New York: Harper and Row, 1972, p. 5.
32. Ibid., p. 10.
33. W. James Popham. "The Instructional Objectives Exchange: New Support for Criterion-Referenced Instruction," *Phi Delta Kappan* LII, 3 (November 1970): 174.
34. Ibid., 175.
35. Popham, "Epilogue," in Popham, et al., eds., *Instructional Objectives*, p. 134.
36. Ibid., p. 135.
37. Robert M. Gagne, "Behavioral Objectives? Yes!," *Educational Leadership* 29, 5 (February 1972): 394.
38. Ibid., 395–396.
39. J. Myron Atkin, "Behavioral Objectives in Curricular Design: A Cautionary Note," *Science Teacher* 35, 5 (May 1968): 27.
40. Robert L. Ebel, "Some Comments," *The School Review* 75, 3 (Autumn 1967): 263.
41. Ralph H. Ojemann, "Should Educational Objectives Be Stated in Behavioral Terms?," Part II, *Elementary School Journal* 69, 5 (February 1969): 234.

42. Perry E. Rosove, "To Teach by Behavioral Objectives or Not?," *Educational Technology* 11, 6 (June 1971): 36–37.

43. Ibid., 37–38.

44. Duchastel and Merrill, "The Effects of Behavioral Objectives on Learning," *Review of Educational Research* 43, 1 (Winter 1973): 63.

45. Philip G. Smith, "On the Logic of Behavioral Objectives," *Phi Delta Kappan* LIII, 7 (March 1972): 430.

46. Popham, "Objectives and Instruction," p. 51.

47. Popham, "Objectives '72," *Phi Delta Kappan* LIII, 7 (March 1972): 432.

48. Louise L. Tyler, "A Case History: Formulation of Objectives from a Psychoanalytic Framework," in Popham, et al., eds., *Instructional Objectives,* p. 102.

49. Gagne, "Behavioral Objectives? Yes!": 391.

50. Vargas, *Writing Worthwhile Behavioral Objectives,* p. 12.

51. Ebel, "Behavioral Objectives: A Close Look," *Phi Delta Kappan* LII, 3 (November 1970): 172.

52. Combs, *Educational Accountability: Beyond Behavioral Objectives,* p. 21.

53. Ibid., p. 26.

54. George F. Kneller, "Behavioral Objectives? No!," *Educational Leadership* 29, 5 (February 1972): 400.

55. Herbert D. Simons, "Behavioral Objectives: A False Hope for Education," *Elementary School Journal* LXXII (January 1973): 173–174.

56. Ibid., pp. 180–181.

57. Atkin, "Behavioral Objectives in Curriculum Design: A Cautionary Note": 28–29.

58. Harold L. Schoen, " Behavioral Objectives: Some Uses and Misuses," p. 271.

59. Gene V. Glass, "The Many Faces of Educational Accountability," *Phi Delta Kappan* LIII, 10 (June 1972): 638.

60. Combs, *Educational Accountability: Beyond Behavioral Objectives,* pp. 5, 8–9.

61. Ibid., p. 12.

62. Ebel, "Some Comments," *The School Review* 75, 3 (August 1967): 263.

63. John M. Muchmore, "Behavior Control: The Matter of Ethics," *Educational Technology* 11, 6 (June 1971): 45.

64. Ibid.

65. D. Woodruff Asahel and Philip G. Kapfer, "Behavioral Objectives and Humanism in Education: A Question of Specificity," *Educational Technology* 12, 1 (January 1972): 53.

66. Elliot W. Eisner, "Educational Objectives: Help or Hindrance?," *The School Review* 75, 3 (Autumn 1967): 251.

67. Ibid., pp. 254, 257.

68. Ebel, "Some Comments": 264.

69. Kneller, "Behavioral Objectives? No!": 397.

70. Ibid., p. 398.

71. Ebel, "Some Comments": 263.

72. Combs, *Educational Accountability: Beyond Behavioral Objectives,* p. 2.

73. Ibid., p. 17.

74. Ibid., pp. 1–2.

75. Popham, "Objectives '72": 433.

76. Steven Selden, Review of W. James Popham and Eva L. Baker, *Establishing Instructional Goals.* New York: Prentice-Hall, 1970, in *Phi Delta Kappan* LIII, 7 (March 1972): 449.

77. Schoen, "Behavioral Objectives: Some Uses and Misuses," p. 272.

78. Atkin, "Behavioral Objectives in Curriculum Design: A Cautionary Note": 30.

79. Popham, "Probing the Validity of Arguments Against Behavioral Goals," p. 72.

80. Popham, "Epilogue," p. 136.

81. Rosove, "To Teach by Behavioral Objectives or Not?": 39.

82. Ebel, "Behavioral Objectives: A Close Look": 173.

83. Ibid., 39.

84. Arthur G. Wirth, *Productive Work—In Industry and Schools: Becoming Persons Again.* Washington, DC: University Press of America, 1983, p. 129.

85. Popham, *Educational Evaluation,* p. 62.

86. Ibid., p. 63.

87. Popham, "Objectives '72": 432.

CHAPTER FOURTEEN

Career Education

The chairman of the General Subcommittee on Education in the United States House of Representatives, Roman C. Pucinski, put it rather dramatically in 1971 when he wrote under the headline "THE CASE FOR CAREER EDUCATION," with a subheading entitled "The Twilight Hour," that:

> The schools have one final chance to prove their worth to the nation, in perhaps the most challenging undertaking of their history, by dedicating themselves to preparation of students for the world of work.[1]

Pucinski identified his "vision of education for the seventies," which called for a complete overhaul of American education:

> It will mean reconstructing the existing educational environment at the elementary, secondary and community college levels and creating some new institutions, as well. It will require new teacher training to meet altered demands of instructional roles. At the top— in state departments of education, federal agencies, and the halls of state legislatures and the congress—new alternatives must also be identified, both in administrative organization patterns and depth and breadth of financial commitment to such an effort.[2]

Career education burst on the scene in an address by U.S. Commissioner of Education, Sidney P. Marland, Jr., to the National Association of Secondary School Principals (NASSP) in Houston in January of 1971. Thomas Hohenshil observed that its "support has rapidly expanded" to include not only the President of the United States (State of the Union message, 1972) but also congressmen, professional educators, and the lay public.[3] Hohenshil went on to describe the tidal wave that career education represented in American schooling in the early 1970s:

> Few educational concepts during the past century have gained the instantaneous attention and support from nearly all educational and societal levels as career education. One

has difficulty finding a current professional journal or educational reference without at least some mention of the subject.[4]

Anita Webb was even more ecstatic in her assessment of the movement's impact: "Nowhere in the history of education has a movement surfaced, spread as quickly, and had such far-reaching effects in such a short time as has career education."[5] Peter Muirhead expressed similar sentiments in his appraisal of career education's potential in 1973: "If a promising approach to education can hover for generations in the back of the classroom waiting to be discovered, career education appears to be it."[6]

Education Index did not use the term "career education" in the early 1970s; as late as 1972, readers were directed to the cross-reference "vocational education."[7] But readers could find references to nearly 400 articles about career education during the period July 1973 to June 1976.[8] As the 1970s progressed, career education garnered official support from the NEA, the National Association of Chief State School Officers, the National Advisory Council on Vocational Education, the NASSP, the American Association of Junior Colleges, the College Entrance Examination Board (CEEB), the National Institute of Education (NIE), and the U.S. Chamber of Commerce.[9] Little wonder that Webb could proclaim that "Many educators, as well as non-educators, hailed the concept as 'an approach whose time has come'."[10]

It is difficult to envision a movement, institution or pedagogical technique that could qualify as a panacea as much as career education does.

The "Need" for Career Education

According to its backers, career education was the result of:

> . . . a certain combination of events which crystallized the thinking of governmental, educational and lay leaders that something must be done to increase the relevancy of the educational system to the needs of individuals as well as contemporary society.[11]

Hohenshil argued that the educational system's failure to attend to the changing times had become "increasingly evident." This failure was manifest in a number of ways, including an "alarming increase in the rate of truancy, alienation, drug addiction, unemployability, and in too many cases, almost a total ignorance of the world of work and the individual's relationships in it and society."[12] He cited as evidence that in 1970–1971, 3.7 million young people had left formal education; nearly 2.5 million of them lacked "skills adequate to enter the labor force at a level commensurate with their ability. Many . . . with no marketable skill at all." The problem was compounded when the following statistics for that time frame were added: 850,000 students dropped out of elementary or secondary school, 750,000 graduated from high school from a general curriculum, and 850,000 left college without a degree or completing an organized occupational program.[13]

It was figures such as these, Webb maintained, that led to career education programs, with the result that career education "became the 'new kid' on the block."[14] In response to the disillusionment with the state of education and the failed reforms of the 1960s, career education, a "systematic attempt to integrate the elements into the school curriculum for *all* students at *all* levels of the public schools" was born. The "difference," according to Hohenshil, was that career education embodied the "systematic fusion of the academic, technical, vocational, political and artistic areas for all students." Further, when accurately designed, career education embodied a "systematic, longitudinal approach which not only involves all instructional and administrative personnel, but also the community in a planned manner."[15]

Writing on the historical antecedents of career education, Webb noted that the development of career education "stemmed from the desire to reform schooling." This reform was sorely needed, as had been other reform attempts in the past such as "life adjustment," which had tried to make education "more meaningful." But career education was different from its predecessors, she averred:

> . . . it is seen as a response to problems accentuated by the economically and socially disadvantaged, to mobility conditions in the world of work, to accumulated knowledge of personal development and the career component of the self-concept specifically, and to problems of schooling itself, such as the ineffectiveness of existing instructional and counseling programs.[16]

Carl McDaniels, like Hohenshil and Webb, a recognized authority on career education, offered his assessment of the societal problems career education attempted to address. These included the fact that too many people left the educational system "deficient in the skills needed to adapt to a rapidly changing society"; and too many students, both graduates and dropouts, failed to see "meaningful relationships" between what they were asked to learn in school and what they will do after leaving school.[17] McDaniels, like other career education proponents, felt that the American educational system met the needs of those—a distinct minority—who would be college graduates but was deficient in emphasis on the "noneducational needs of that vast majority of students who will never be college graduates." Further, the system had not kept pace with the rapidity of change in our "post-industrial occupational society." As a consequence, many "over-educated" and "under-educated" persons, the latter afflicted with frustration, the former with boredom, contributed to the "growing worker alienation in the total occupational society."[18] Proper career education programs would remedy the problems of the large number of persons who were leaving the secondary and collegial levels "underequipped with the vocational skills, the self-understanding and career decision-making skills, or the work attitudes" that were essential for making the successful transition from school to work. Additionally, the system lagged far behind in providing appropriate career options for girls and members of minority groups. The system was not meeting the "continuing and recurrent" educational needs of adults; insufficient attention was being paid to opportunities outside formal education; and the general public, "parents and business-industry-labor," had not played an adequate role in determining educational policies.[19]

Muirhead praised the efforts of educators to make education more relevant but those efforts had been, in the main unsuccessful. As he put it, despite "concerted, and in many respects heroic, efforts in recent years to make education more relevant . . . an unconscionably large number of young people leave formal education each year ill prepared for life as productive and self-fulfilling adults."[20] Anthony Deiluio and James Young attributed the malaise to the "upper class ideal" that was prevalent in the country that delayed America's young from thinking "about a possible occupation until after they graduate from high school." "Leading educators," though, had suggested that they needed a "more successfully guided" approach:

> Presently, eight out of every ten American students are enrolled in either a college preparation or a general education curriculum designed to prepare them for college. Only two of these eight students will ever obtain a baccalaureate degree. Consequently, eight out of ten students in this country are being prepared to do what in fact six of them will not do.[21]

The issue was pressing, these authors contended, if the United States wished to "continue a viable work force and maintain a leading status in the world scene in terms of competitive production."[22]

Some commentators wondered if career education would be just another passing fancy, becoming nothing more than a "band-aid applied to the school." As one author phrased it, "Too many good concepts have had limited days in the bright sunlight of convincing leadership and seed money, only to be eclipsed by new emphases of new leaders—or blocked out by revenue withdrawal."[23]

Kenneth Hoyt and his colleagues based the movement on majority needs:

> Finally, it is important to note that, in asking for career education, we base our requests on the needs of 83 percent of our citizens—both youth and adults, in school and out of school—who will never attain a four year college degree. It is time that education serve best this real majority of our citizens. What we need is a comprehensive program of career education covering all levels of education for all citizens.[24]

Hoyt et al. called on the educational world to get busy on the challenging and mammoth work of reform:

What more is to be said? There is a massive job ahead in reorienting teacher training institutions, in retraining the current administrative and teaching corps and training new teachers, changing certification requirements, establishing home-school-community linkages, identifying learning environments outside and linking them with the classroom, inviting new prospectuses, teaching guides and curriculum—the list is almost endless.[25]

There was no time to delay; the task of reformation would be "long and arduous," an "across the board" effort and collaboration would be needed:

> . . . requiring federal and state legislation and appropriation; USOE national leadership; state and local educational agency leadership at their levels; political pressuring from national, state and local interest groups and public officials; cooperation from employers and labor organizations; innovation and dedication from classroom teachers, counselors, and administrators; and responses from students.[26]

Sidney P. Marland, Jr.

Career education soon became closely associated with Commissioner of Education Sidney Marland; it was well known that it was his pet project.[27] That Marland envisioned it as a "revolutionary instrument" that was demanded by the times was clear from his own words.[28] His influence in the development of the movement merits attention.

In an interview published in November of 1971, Marland stated that the term "career education" meant to him "basically a point of view, a concept." This concept represented three things: 1) that it would be part of the curriculum for all students; 2) that it would encompass a student's entire academic career; and 3) that every student leaving school, whenever that occurred, would possess skills necessary to earn a livelihood "for himself and his family."[29] Marland went on to state that career education, as he interpreted it, would "*heighten* the intellectual quality of education, because school work would become more meaningful and stimulating resulting in higher motivation." It would cost less than present practices, because with the "failure and disenchantment" connected with the general education curriculum, few school divisions could "afford *not* to make the switch to career education." He then expanded on the dismal, wasteful record of general education:

> One further thing: as I indicated earlier the primary reason for the failure of the schools to serve so many young people adequately (as represented by dropouts and youngsters graduated from high school prepared neither for a job nor for further education and the extra social costs that go with that failure) can be traced to what we call general education. If we could replace that curriculum with the kind of creative and productive schooling that enables youngsters to carve out careers for themselves we would save a good deal of money that to all intents and purposes is now simply going down the drain.[30]

The combination of the deficiencies of general education and the promise of career education had attracted "considerable national interest," including business, industry and labor groups. As the labor department had pointed out, "eighty percent of the tasks required by our society can be performed by people with a high school diploma." It was time to change the current situation, which found "a good many students in college" that have "no *bona fide* purpose for being there."[31] Marland ended the interview with the observation that "the real test remains. I think most people feel it is high time to make the schools truly relevant and meaningful for every youngster, and that's what career education is all about."[32]

Marland had generated interest in the nation's educational press as early as 1971. An editorial in *Nation's Schools* theorized that "If Sidney P. Marland can make his scheme to reform U.S. schools work, a grateful nation may finally remember the name of a U.S. Commissioner of Education."[33] The editor looked favorably on Marland's program of "preventive medicine," which promised a "thorough overhaul of both elementary and secondary curriculum and procedures." Marland's vision for career education was comprehensive: "nearly a cradle-to-grave continuum, with the smallest school children starting to get a general indoctrination into the world of work—the real world, in Marland's view—even as they begin learning the Three R's."[34]

In an address to the American Vocational Association (AVA) in February of 1972, Marland noted what he termed the "trial balloon" he had launched at Houston, which in his words, "has not been deflated since," to the extent of "almost universal affirmation":

> ... people within education, and most important, the people *outside* the profession, want education in this country to produce in our children the sort of competence, of preparedness, that is implicit in career education.[35]

Specifically addressing vocational educators, he commented that many of them have "dreamed and talked of the day when your field would receive recognition as being of central importance" to the educational process rather than a "peripheral and faintly inelegant school specialty." Through "combined efforts" on behalf of career education, that day had moved a "great deal closer."[36] Career education enabled all educators to address effectively the "matter of living itself, touching on all its pragmatic, theoretical, and moral aspects." The movement would indeed succeed, if "vocational educators—the most knowledgeable and sophisticated audience of all—support it."[37] He made it clear that career education was not just a "major OE priority in name only, a paper goal; career education is *the* major objective of the Office of Education at this moment in time and will remain so for the foreseeable future." Speaking music to the ears of those assembled, Marland proclaimed: "For we are truly talking about something considerably more than a curriculum. We are talking about a substantive social process."[38]

A month later Marland continued his onslaught against the general education curriculum. Its failures were "self-evident," he maintained. It had no "real goals" beyond that of graduating its students. The U.S. Office of Education emphasized instead "purposeful education," which it found present in career education.[39] People saw career education as providing "rational direction for change," which would be all-encompassing and would close the "destructive gap" between school and job. While career education might have high start-up costs, in the long run it would be eminently frugal. Relying on statistics about dropouts and the "lost" graduates of general education curricula, Marland claimed that the cost for students who should have had opportunities for "realistic education in career development, but did not" were about $28 billion, which amounted to almost one-third of the cost of the nation's entire "educational enterprise."[40] He called for the utilization of career education as a means of achieving consensus about what the schools could do to meet the concerns and needs of young people in school:

> We can bring these concerns and all of our extra, and very often separate, efforts together in a meaningful way if we have the wisdom, the courage, and the will to find a large new consensus on what the schools might be. Career education can be that goal.[41]

Byrl R. Shoemaker, director for vocational education in Ohio and a past-president of the AVA lauded Marland for his leadership. Marland, Shoemaker said, had "denounced the laissez faire concept called general education." He had been the "first educator of major importance" who dared to censure the "so-called general education program which has served to lead only to general unemployment."[42] Shoemaker was far from alone in his unstinting recognition of Marland's leadership. For instance, David Borland and Richard Harris wrote that "In the formulation and promotion of this goal so central to the *career education* concept, Sidney P. Marland, Jr., has launched a revolution in the field of education."[43]

Marland wrote a piece he did for *American Education* in April of 1972 in which he promised to set aside a "major part" of the Office of Education's "discretionary funds" for career education. Marland also pledged that he would make such funds "available directly to the States." He proceeded to applaud career education as a bridge, one that contained unmitigated benefits for the individual and society:

> Career education would be in the most fundamental sense a bridge—a bridge between school years and work years, between educators and employers, between the life of a child and the later years of adulthood, between an empty word and a full life.[44]

Commenting on the articles and speeches of Marland, Darryl Larramore argued that "Few declarations have had as much national impact as Commissioner Marland's speeches to the educational community on career education." Indeed,

Larramore maintained, the "repercussions" of his words were actually beginning to be "felt at local levels."[45]

Career Education Defined and Described

There were other major players in career education besides Marland. One of those was Kenneth Hoyt, a professor at the University of Maryland. The lead author of a book on career education in 1972, Hoyt, et al. described career education as "a total concept which should permeate all education, giving a new mentality to the objective of successful preparation for and development of a lifelong, productive career."[46] It should be perceived, Hoyt declared, not as a "lock-step method," operating as a ladder, but rather as a "broad freeway with convenient exits and entries as interests and needs change." Major changes in the way education is conducted would be required to "achieve a truly-career oriented" education. These changes would establish the "relevance" of school by "focusing on the learner's perceptions of work and of himself as a worker." The goal of career education was to "make work possible, meaningful, and satisfactory to every individual."[47] A year earlier Hoyt had identified career education with freedom of choice that was without limits, and absolute. And the right to change, he averred, was as "sacred as the right to choose."[48]

Larry Bailey and Ronald Stadt argued that career education was not "just another concept developed in the United States Office of Education"; indeed, it was so popular that "Educators can do little else but embrace it and the support which the employer-employee community gives it." As a response to the life needs of individuals, career education centered schooling on the "occupational information, self-understanding, employment, placement, continuing education function" that accounted for its widespread following.[49]

A number of organizations posited definitions of career education. In 1973, the AVA described it as "a comprehensive education program focused on careers and an educational process where people gain knowledge, attitudes, awareness, and skills necessary for success in the world of work."[50] A year later the U.S. Office of Education presented an official definition: "Career education is the totality of experiences through which one learns about and proposes to engage in work as part of her or his way of living."[51] The ESEA of 1977 (H. R. 7, Sec. 11) provided a legislative definition:

> Career education shall mean the totality of experiences which are designed to be free of bias and stereotyping (including bias or stereotyping on account of race, sex, or handicap), through which one learns about and prepares to engage in, work as part of his or her way of living and through which he or she relates work values to other life roles and choices.[52]

That same year the Career Education Implementation Incentive Act (SB 1326, Sec. 12), was passed. It contained a more lengthy definition of the movement, one that embraced the various stages of career education in addition to including the anti-bias and stereotyping conditions:

> Career education means educational programs and statistics through which educational organizations and institutions, and individual educators, counselors, and other individuals seek to improve the awareness of students of all ages of career opportunities which are, or may in the future become, available to them, and to improve the ability of such students to take advantage of such opportunities. "Career education" includes, but is not necessarily limited to, activities which involve career awareness, exploration, planning, and decision-making, activities which are free of or are designed to eliminate bias and stereotyping (including bias or stereotyping on account of race, sex, or handicap).[53]

McDaniels addressed the "basic assumptions" of career education upon which the movement was based. It is important for career education to span an individual's entire life; a career extends from preschool years to retirement years. The concept of "work" includes unpaid as well as paid labor and work activities associated with leisure time and recreational time. "Workers" include volunteers and full-time homemakers. Career education embraces a multiplicity of work values that reflect a cosmopolitan society; knowledge of these values enables each individual to ask the important question "Why should I work?" An individual's career is best viewed in a developmental rather than a fragmented way. Career education is for everyone, including the "young and the old, the mentally handicapped and the intellectually gifted, the poor and the wealthy, males and females, students in elementary schools and in graduate colleges and universities." According to McDaniels, the movement's societal objectives are to help all individuals to 1) want to work, 2) acquire skills necessary for work, and 3) engage in work that is satisfying to the individual and beneficial to society. The individualistic goals of career education are to make work possible, meaningful, and satisfying for each individual throughout his or her lifetime. Of paramount concern to career education is the protection of the individual's freedom to choose and assistance in making and implementing career decisions. Finally, the expertise required for implementing career education exists in many facets of society and is not limited to those employed in formal education.[54]

McDaniels is also the source for a consideration of "principles to consider" in career education. He maintained that career development was a life-long process of self-development, by which work was regarded as a vehicle for self-clarification. Career development included the opportunity to examine life roles, occupations, and various life-styles. Management of one's career, the power to direct one's future, the ability to maximize control over one's life constituted a major goal. The concept of "multi-potentiality," that each person has potential for success and satisfaction in a number of occupations, freed individuals from the fear of making wrong choices and increased their options. A commitment to tentativeness was integral to a concept that was based on changing individuals in a changing society, one that recognized the importance of chance or random factors in career decisions. Finally, career development was firmly wedded to the principle of "SOS," i.e., All Students, All Occupations, All Subjects.[55]

McDaniels was but one of many who outlined the three-stage process of career education. These stages, arranged chronologically, were: the Awareness Stage—Grades K-5; the Exploration Stage—Grades 6–9; and the Preparation Stage—Grades 10–14. However, persons were to explore potential careers through leisure and utilize career guidance provided by a counselor who should be present at all stages of the process.[56]

Herr, another career education luminary, observed that the movement had grown to the extent that 60 percent of state departments of education had defined career education for themselves by 1974. One of the first to combine funding with the movement was Arizona. Herr pointed out the universality of career education in the U.S. Office of Education's 1974 definition:

> Career education combines the academic world with the world of work. It must be available at all levels of education from kindergarten through the university. A complete program of career education includes awareness of the world of work, broad exploration of occupations, in-depth exploration of selected clusters, and career preparation for all students. This calls for basic education subjects to incorporate career education as an activity throughout the curriculum.[57]

Arthur Kroll and Linda Pfister called attention to a "primary element" that seemed to be present in all career education programs, namely, a "deep concern for the individual student." This concern focuses on presenting the learner with "opportunities to acquire basic skills and knowledge essential for functioning in the world of work."[58]

Career Education's Benefits

The AVA was an early and avid supporter of career education. In January of 1972, an AVA task force reported that career education "accommodates individual differences through a continuous experience-centered evaluative process which facilitates the development of awareness, orientation, exploration, decision-making and preparation." The task force recommended that the AVA provide leadership for career education's operation, since it was clearly "concerned with career choice and preparation for employment." Additionally, the report suggested that the AVA "take the leadership in identifying and promoting legislation which will authorize

categorical funding for all segments of career education, including vocational education."[59] Vocational educators were quick to foresee the potential value that career education held for their field.

An article in the *American Vocational Journal,* but two months later, gushed
that no obstacle was too formidable "to be surmounted" by career education, as
it moved on a "rising tide of enthusiasm" and was "surrounded by an unusual
glow of contentment."[60] Small wonder, then, that Carl Wells saw such a bright
future for American education, imbued as it would be with the vitality of career
education:

> The school of tomorrow, with a commitment to career education of all, may look
> quite different from the typical college-prep/general education school of today. It will be
> an extension of the community, extending far beyond the confines of the school building
> to include business institutions and industries in that community. Meaningful career ed-
> ucation is education with a purpose. That purpose is training that fulfills the needs of stu-
> dents, employers, and the community in one exciting venture.[61]

The successes of career education led one writer to state in early 1973 that it
was "fair to say that career education is no longer just a sound idea to be tried."
The "first steps" that had been taken had demonstrated its "validity in real schools
with real students." The gains made by career education at its outset convinced
him that it was the "best step yet proposed to help students more fully develop
their talents and shape a promising future." Paraphrasing Benjamin Franklin, he
wrote that it was a "way for students to move their personal sundials out of the
shadows and into the sunlight of success."[62] These sentiments were echoed a few
months later by John Ottina, yet another devotee of the movement. This author
doubted that "Education, or industry and labor leaders, or civic and ethnic
groups, or students and their parents" would allow career education to be aban-
doned or stalled, given its early successes. After all, he reasoned:

> We are talking about a curriculum restructuring that will help every one of the 54
> million children in our elementary and secondary schools, plus another 8 million young
> people in college and other post-high school programs select and prepare for careers con-
> ceivably picked from a universe of 20,000 available occupations.[63]

McDaniels identified what he called "Learner Outcomes for Career Education," which would equip students "at any age, or at any level" when they left
school. The first of these was competency in the basic skills required for adapt-
ability in our "rapidly changing society." Students would also be equipped with
good work habits and be capable of choosing a "personally meaningful set of
work values" that would foster in them a drive to work and enable them to make
career decisions in obtaining jobs. They would have vocational personal skills at a
level that would empower them to "gain entry into and attain a degree of success

in occupational society" and would make career decisions on the "widest possible set of data." Aware of the means available to them for continuing their education after they had left formal schooling, these students would be successful in paid occupations, in further education, or in "a vocation consistent with their current career education." Finally, they would be successful in incorporating work values into their "total personal value structure" in such a way that they would be able to "choose what for them is a valuable life-style."[64] Quite a feat!

Viewing the litany of successes in the summer of 1973, Paul Halverson opined that if "we face up to certain issues, anticipate certain problems, and avoid a number of pitfalls, we may see career education become a powerful component of education for all the children of all the people." However, he warned, such a future was not guaranteed. Without needed support, career education could become:

> . . . a passing fancy for all but a few parlor liberals, a few enthusiasts for vocational education, a smaller group from the academic disciplines, a still smaller group of administrators and supervisors who should be the leaders of the school, and the smallest group of all, the parents and pupils.[65]

Curriculum Issues

In 1972, Byrl Shoemaker, who was director for vocational education in Ohio and a past president of the AVA, announced that "education in America is desperately in need of a change agent."[66] Shoemaker, who credited Commissioner Marland with the impetus for career education, claimed that the origins of the Ohio program that had developed were "rooted in vocational education and guidance."[67] Vocational educators, who were historically of the opinion that they were relegated to secondary and subordinate role status, took heart in what they saw as an opportunity to fill leadership roles in the blossoming movement.

An editorial in *Nation's Schools* pondered how administrators of schools at all levels would "equip their students for a world of work that bears little resemblance to what has traditionally been taught under the heading, 'vocational education.'"[68] Major attention had been devoted to vocational programs, because of the leadership of Marland and the "protests from industry that education is not turning out students with employable skills." The "optimism" that enveloped vocational educators was due, this editor argued, primarily to the attempt of Marland to "reshape college preparatory, general curriculum, and vocational training into a new, mutually beneficial whole which he calls career education."[69]

Arlene Cross was one of the host of vocational educators who advocated embracing career education. She suggested that AVA members prepare and distribute materials and provide data for legislation and thus become a communication link to Congress; and that the AVA itself promote a White House conference on career education "which would give visibility to the movement as well as to inform the lay public."[70] She presented AVA members with a multiple challenge: to find out all they could about career education, talk to people about it, and support funding for its programs. She urged the membership to work in career education programs as they emerged in their schools:

> Don't hold so tightly to what you now do that you cannot make a contribution, because you do have the know-how. Be proud that vocational education is emerging as the focal point around which the broader program of career education is emerging. Career education is an exciting concept, and by working together we can make it a reality.[71]

Business educators were called on to "be ready to help other educators now." Specifically, they were asked to provide K-6 career education programs that emphasized children's work with concrete objects. Marla Peterson maintained that this approach rested on "sound learning theory: *Intellectual, personal, and social development take place through a sequence of concrete experiences followed by abstractions.*"[72] It will be, she declared, up to "business educators to help establish comprehensive career-development programs that will be most beneficial to the children whose futures are involved."[73]

Hoyt, in an address titled "Vocational Educators Must Bear the Main Responsibility," told a session of vocational educators that career education was not a mere add-on to the curriculum. Rather, "we are talking about getting rid of what is presently being taught and starting over with an entirely new curriculum."[74] Career education, the assistant superintendent of Pittsburgh schools told about 200 vocational education researchers, "can be the shot-in-the-arm needed to revitalize a reeling public school system."[75]

Traditionally, most vocational programs began in the junior high school. That start was deemed too late by some, who insisted that it was "essential" that career education begin in elementary school because it "enhances a child's self-concept and lays the groundwork for directly identifying with occupations" later in school. A "major objective" of elementary education in a comprehensive career education program, then, should be "to discover the talents and interests of each child and to demonstrate their relationship to the work world."[76] Hoyt concurred on the indispensable role of elementary education career programs:

> The elementary school is a powerful force in the shaping of personal values. Today millions of elementary school children are being systematically exposed neither to work values nor to a broad understanding of our rapidly changing world of work. More importantly, they are being given little opportunity to relate work understandings to themselves as their personal value systems develop. The career education movement seeks and is enlisting the help of elementary education in turning this condition around. That is why career education in its most basic form *must*—if it is to be fully effective—begin and have a strong base in the elementary school.[77]

These authors also recognized the crucial role that the classroom teacher would have to play if career education were to succeed, because "No lasting change can or should occur in America without the active support and involvement of the classroom teacher."[78] Elementary education would have to be enlisted in the cause.

The implementation of career education concepts into the curriculum was recognized as no easy task. Things that were educational priorities at the time (for example, teachers were being asked to cover more and more content and the back-to-the basics movement was going strong) could lead to the abolition of "nonessentials"—which might include career education. Some teachers felt that career education was "inappropriate" and didn't belong in their classrooms; others were inhibited by a lack of knowledge of and expertise in career education. Each of these factors could be an obstacle to full-scale adoption of career education programs.[79] Peter Finn felt, however, that the effort would prove worthwhile:

> Educators will have an extra incentive to integrate career education as they realize so doing will not only help meet their students' occupational needs, it will also further the goals of their respective subject areas, as well. In the final analysis, it is this felicitous overlapping of career education goals with subject area goals which will provide the greatest impetus to the integration of career education into every course and at every grade level.[80]

Hohenshil presented four curricular models that he said existed in 1975. The first model, the school-based comprehensive career education model, was a lifelong program of education that began with formal schooling. It was inclusive with regard to students, programs, schools, and life stages. It was not a synonym for vocational education; rather, vocational education was an "integral and important part of a total career education system."[81] The second model, "The Employer-Based Career Education Model," was designed for "alienated and unmotivated" youth between the ages of 13 and 18. "The Home-Based Career Education Model" was the third type, whose "primary purpose" was to "provide career learning experiences for young adults, 18–25, and possibly older persons, also, who have left formal schooling." The fourth and last model was "The Rural-Residential Model," set up to assist "disadvantaged rural families" so that they can "experience lasting improvements in their economic and social conditions through an intensive program at a residential center."[82]

McDaniels, whose SOS program was presented in the previous section, also contributed to the place of career education in the curriculum. The "heart of the career education effort is in classroom-related activities," he contended. A variety of approaches should be utilized to infuse career education into the students, including career visits, career guests, modern educational media that emphasized career information, career-related reading and writing assignments, expanded opportunities for leisure activities, career shadowing, work-study opportunities, cooperative work experiences, and internships.[83]

Popularity and Calls for Support

As the early 1970s passed, career education continued to gain momentum. As one writer phrased it, the "urgency for increased action" on behalf of career education was clear if one listened to Marland.[84] The movement was aided by the "increased attention by the press and television media" to "Proposals, experiments and pilot programs pertaining to career education."[85]

The movement was also abetted by what was termed the "superb leadership" that had "emerged in many local education agencies and in many state and federal agencies." So much had been gained in governmental support by 1972 that next on the agenda was the "need to plan the steps and stages in the further growth of career education over the next decade."[86]

Generally, the business community had welcomed career education with open arms, as it had with vocational education some fifty years earlier. What of labor? Labor leaders who were surveyed in the New Orleans area strongly agreed that career exploration in the classroom was important, although only 37 percent responded to the survey of 84 labor organizations. However, they urged caution about "encouraging students to make long term decisions too early in life."[87] The labor leaders who responded strongly opposed having students go to work during the school day and wished to engage in "cooperative activities" involving course content and resource speakers. The authors of the survey recognized the low response rate, yet claimed that the "potential for increasing the voluntary involvement by labor organizations in the curriculum development process of the schools seems significant."[88]

Gene Bottoms, a longtime proponent of career education and a veteran vocational education leader, warned that support for the career education concept needed to be forthcoming from the state departments of education if the movement were to avoid being "just another fad."[89] Career education could not "emerge and thrive in a school setting," he wrote, unless it was "planted, fertilized and cultivated by someone." This "someone" needed to be the state department of education if career education was to become "more than empty rhetoric."[90]

Opposition

Career education was not without its opponents, some of whom were both severe and vocal. Hohenshil, one of the movement's advocates, referred to one group who called career education a "sell-out" to the "military industrial complex."[91] It is time to consider the critiques of those who objected, sometimes vociferously.

The first area of criticism dealt with the movement's alleged subservience to the corporate social order, as indicated in Hohenshil's observation above. American workers were being told, Robert Nash and Russell Agne reported, that they would become "obsolete" unless they learned new attitudes and work skills. American educators, these authors asserted, were being urged to accept uncritically:

> . . . a type of corporate reality principle underlying high productivity; spiraling wages; automation; increasing economic growth; accelerating rates of social change; systematic administration; complex, large-scale organizations; and a technical approach to the resolution of human problems.[92]

Further, they contended, programs were being developed in which there was no speculation about their "utopian" possibilities when a "person's worth" was dependent on his being a "productive worker who contributes throughout a lifetime to an expanding economy."[93]

W. Norton Grubb and Marvin Lazerson took issue with career educators who spoke of the "dignity" of all work, especially in a capitalistic, industrial society. Such rhetoric, they felt, took on the form of a myth, given the realities of corporate capitalism:

> The assumptions of career educators about the nature of work and the demand for labor are largely a myth. The world they posit, in which career education can make all work satisfying and all training useful, is a world we would no doubt prefer to the one we inhabit. But in constructing this Utopia, career education simply reflects the more general dilemma of schooling. Capitalism is an economic system in which capital is central. As part of the drive for profits and the accumulation of capital, managers in an economic system like ours endlessly divide, simplify, and eliminate jobs. This results in an increase in unemployment and a constant status of underemployment for most workers. The economic system values capital resources at the expense of human resources. Yet the schooling system is charged with the development of human resources, and thus its central purpose is in sad contradiction to that of the economic system it serves.[94]

They were especially critical of career educators who gave students and workers the "false hope that career education will enhance worker mobility." Also coming under their sharp disapproval was the allegation being advanced by some that "working conditions are improving or that levels of job dissatisfaction will decrease." Rather, the "fragmentation of tasks" that was occurring might be "efficient by capitalist criteria" and might increase "profit by increased control and lower labor costs," but the implications for workers were "devastating." Thus, if the truth be known, "real work" in the schools might have just the opposite effect from that intended: "feelings of alienation, anomie, and disconnectedness, or physical manifestations such as hypertension, high blood pressure, and poor mental health."[95]

Grubb and Lazerson argued that it was "foolish to make claims for the efficacy of schooling programs without acknowledging the structure of labor demand." Unemployment, they maintained, was not due to the "mismatch of workers and jobs," so it could not be eradicated by training workers for jobs that didn't exist. Unemployment was "dependent on the overall health of the economy"; claims that career education can "reduce unemployment," therefore, were "seriously inflated." Career educators, they alleged, displayed a "serious misunderstanding of the economy."[96] Joel Spring agreed, noting that there was no proof that the "manpower model in education or career education works in terms of reducing unemployment and finding people jobs."[97]

The attitude of career educators toward dropouts came in for scathing criticism as well. For some youth, Grubb and Lazerson averred, leaving school was "economically rational" because the monetary returns to additional years of secondary schooling were "low or non-existent," especially for minority and youth from lower socio-economic groups.[98] They aligned discrimination with the demand for labor, arguing that if the latter "is insufficient, discrimination is serious, and the worst jobs require little skill," then some will always be "unemployed, underemployed, and additional skill training will serve no purpose."[99] Career education would have little or no impact in this scenario.

Are all jobs elevating and dignified? Paul Halverson reported on a speech by President Nixon, given to the Republican governors in the early 1970s. He recorded that the President said that the work ethic holds that labor is good in itself, a belief that is in accord with religious teachings and American tradition, and "that is why most of us consider it immoral" to be slothful. Nixon went on to state that "scrubbing floors and emptying bedpans have just as much dignity as there is in any work to be done in this country—including my own." The governors, assembled at a "lovely hotel in Williamsburg, VA" applauded. Halverson thought, however, that "most people who scrub dirty floors or empty foul-smelling bedpans for $2 an hour are unlikely to agree with Nixon that their jobs are as dignified as the President's."[100] It is not too far-fetched to think that Halverson, and Grubb and Lazerson after him, suspected some hypocrisy, at least a little portion of dishonesty, on the part of some of career education's most steadfast zealots. Some critics, as an editorial in *Nation's Schools* pointed out, viewed career education as attempting to manipulate children,[101] hardly a humanitarian act.

After calling attention to the massive influx of government money on behalf of career education programs, Nash and Agne reflected on what was a "disturbing" element to them, the lack of any criticism of the movement's underpinnings:

> Nowhere in an exhaustive review of the literature have we discovered a single word of caution or criticism concerning the possible misuse of the career education concept. Instead, we observe that the literature accepts as an unchallenged good the continued existence of a corporate social order and a concept of human behavior which is achievement motivated.[102]

Scant heed was paid to any weakness in contemporary American schooling "other than its poor performance as a feeder of skilled workers into the occupational world."[103]

The learning theory that undergirded career education came in for rather harsh review. Nash and Agne stated that career learning theory was based on "four interrelated fallacies": specialization, which reduced education to the "functional" or "superficially utilitarian"; sequentialism, which attempted to depict occupational choice in "suffocating sequential modes" rather than by a slow, developmental process; fundamentalism, which was preoccupied with "marketable skills" and neglected feelings, questioning, and noninstrumental skills that help students think about issues and problems; and credentialism, in which, despite denials to the contrary, the performance-based career education model involves the "selection, training, and certifying workers for the state."[104] The most "useful" learning, which career education ignored, these authors maintained, was "intrinsic, spontaneous, and leisurely—subordinating technical competence to growth in personal, physical, aesthetic, social and political awareness."[105]

Nash and Agne suggested three kinds of questions career educators should ask about their programs: 1) To what extent is career education enhancing the principle of maximum possibilities in education? 2) How can career education obliterate the distinction between work and leisure? and 3) How can career education be more concerned with human services? These educators predicted dire consequences unless career education drastically changed its course of action:

> Until career educators build programs committed to maximizing each person's fully lived experiences, his sense of personal and professional competence, and his affiliative relationships, and until each person is included as a decision maker in the human service process, then the corporate state will continue to exacerbate the destruction of the earth's nonrestorable commodities and the deterioration of human hope and vitality.[106]

Other criticisms of career education, such as the unsubstantiated assertion that "too many" students were in college could be scrutinized. We will bring this section to a close with the "conclusions" reached by Grubb and Lazerson, which are nearly all-encompassing:

> Many of career education's criticisms of school and work are well-taken! Schools aren't especially pleasant places, and general education programs in particular are dumping grounds which should be abolished. The educational requirements for jobs have been artificially inflated, and access to jobs has become an increasingly rigid process. There is substantial dissatisfaction with work, though in an economic recession simply having a job becomes paramount.
>
> But career education has little to offer in resolving these problems. Despite its assertions to the contrary, it is primarily a renewal and expression of vocational education, a movement that has previously proven itself ineffective in reducing the gap between rich and poor, in enhancing school learning, in solving social and economic problems, and in improving the status of physical work. Career education's view of the moral benefits of

work is incongruent with the nature of most jobs or the logic of corporate capitalism. Its presumption of training for career ladders with substantial upward mobility is largely fraudulent, given the present job structure. Finally, its argument that unemployment, underemployment, and worker dissatisfaction are largely due to a mismatch between job requirements and worker skills and expectations blames victims for crimes committed by the economic structure.[107]

Career educators, they alleged, had a "mistaken sense of priorities." The movement ignored the substance of the social issues that erupted in the 1960s:

Accepting the economic system as just, it seeks to make people satisfied with their roles in a society that distributes social goods inequitably. It stresses the importance of increasing productivity without asking what is being produced and toward what ends. It claims that American society does not need all the "intellectual and developed capabilities of its citizens in the work force, without asking whether such a waste of capabilities makes sense."[108]

Conclusion

Surveying the educational landscape in 1972, Marland recorded his vision of the future of career education, a movement he had launched but a year earlier:

Career education is viewed as a new form for all young people in school. It can embrace within itself the special concerns and special needs of nearly all educational objectives.

We can bring these concerns and all of our extra, and very often separate, efforts together in a meaningful way if we have the wisdom, the courage, and the will to find a large new consensus on what the schools might be. Career education can be that goal.[109]

"Career education," wrote Deiluio and Young in 1973, "appears to be much more than one ephemeral school fad. It is here to stay, and the curriculum will be much more relevant because of its inclusion."[110] Burdin took notice of the trend in education to embrace enthusiastically and thoughtlessly the "new" in educational history and asked, as a consequence, if career education would be "just another passing fancy—a new label for a change in form but not in substance—that will be gone and forgotten after current advocates lose interest or power?" Recent educational history of the "rise and fall of movements generated outside the educational establishment—coupled with current declines in federal funding—suggests poor odds on the success of career education."[111] Worried that career education might suffer a similar fate to the "many good concepts" that have had "limited days in the bright sunlight" only to be "eclipsed by new emphases of new leaders," or eliminated by "resource withdrawal," Burdin called on the need to involve teachers if the movement were to be sustained: *Involve those affected by change in its creation to secure intelligent, enthusiastic implementation.*[112]

The "cradle-to grave" movement, as envisioned by Marland,[113] was enthusiastically endorsed by Elmer Clark, dean of the College of Education at Southern Illinois University at Carbondale, who saw major, almost unlimited benefits accruing to career education:

> For many years much of professional labor will be devoted to pursuing major issues in career development and career education. Convention programs, periodical literature and books will work and rework this fertile ground. Experiences for children and youth and the organizational structure of schools will become more practically oriented. Pre-service and inservice preparation of professionals will be affected by career development theory and career education practice. Finally, schools will again become *community* schools, enjoying widespread support for programs which serve the developmental needs of each of the children of all of the people respective to the several major aspects of life but especially to wholesome living.[114]

Larry Bailey and Ronald Stadt agreed, observing that a return to the "good old days" might be possible "if schools somehow knit together individuals, the American dream, and employment." It "dawns clear," they wrote, that "what has been missing in too much of the American educational enterprise is occupational information, career guidance, and occupational education."[115]

Shoemaker, assessing the state of education and what he felt was the need for change, commented "My head is full of ideas. My heart is full of zeal." Change would not be in the offing, however, unless career education was implemented in American schools.[116] Pucinski agreed, calling for consolidated legislative action "based on the central thrust of *universal, lifetime, comprehensive career education for all Americans.*" This legislation relied on our "national courage to change," which would provide "economic growth, personal security and satisfaction, the vitality of our social fabric and durability of the democratic system—all will depend on the effectiveness of a strong, successful public educational system."[117]

Hoyt et al. noted that if career education was to "spread throughout the educational system and be serviceable from 'womb to tomb,' detailed, practical suggestions must be available for every stage of the preparation and pursuit of a successful working life."[118] This successful life, Borland and Harris argued, could be achieved if the "goal of American education" was to "prepare every student to enter an occupation or advanced study successfully, when he leaves the system. . . . In the formulation and promotion of this goal as central to the *career education concept*" Marland had "launched a revolution in the field of education."[119]

Career education was fervently grasped and tightly held by vocational educators, who saw in it the fulfillment of their dreams to influence significantly, if not control, the curriculum. As we have seen, vocational educators saw it as their "time in the sun" and were in the front ranks of its advocates.

Writing in 1974, but a few years after Marland's call, Hohenshil foresaw a bright future for career education:

The career education movement has gained significant support since it was first proposed as a major educational thrust in 1971. On the basis of the observations of parents, educators, and legislators, it appears that this movement will continue to grow, and thus, have a major impact on the American educational system in the years to come.[120]

This future was not to be, for career education was to fade and then, as a movement disappear from the American educational scene (to reappear in a different version and form in "school-to-work" programs more than a decade later). Utilizing phrases such as "womb-to-tomb," and "cradle-to-grave," and standing on slogans such as "All Students—All Occupations—All Subjects" career education clearly can lay claim, if any movement, institution, or pedagogical technique can, to the title of being a panacea. And, like others before it that advanced the school as the all-powerful remedy for social ills, it, too, failed to reach the lofty heights to which it aspired.

Notes

1. Roman C. Pucinski, "Prologue," in Pucinski and Sharlene Pearlman Hirsch, eds., *The Courage to Change: New Directions for Career Education*. Englewood Cliffs, NJ: Prentice-Hall, Inc., 1971, p. 8.
2. Ibid., p. 19.
3. Thomas H. Hohenshil, "Rationale for Career Education, " in Thomas C. Hunt and James G. Silliman, Jr., eds., *The American School in Its Social Setting*. Dubuque, IA: Kendall-Hunt Publishing Co., 1975, p. 315.
4. Ibid.
5. Anita H. Webb, "Career Education: An Historical Perspective," in Thomas C. Hunt, Violet Anselmini Allain, Mary Ann Lewis, Marilyn M. Maxson, James S. Norman, and Winston M. Whitehurst, Sr., eds., *Society, Culture, and Schools: The American Approach*. Garrett Park, MD: Garrett Park Press, 1979, p. 287.
6. Peter P. Muirhead, "Career Education: The First Steps Show Promise," *Phi Delta Kappan* LIV, 8 (February 1973): 370.
7. Julia W. Ehrenreich, ed., *Education Index July 1971–June 1972*. New York: The H. W. Wilson Company, 1972, p. 141.
8. Marylouise Hewitt, ed., ibid., 1974, pp. 130–132; 1975, pp. 146–148; and 1976, pp. 110–113.
9. Webb, "Career Education: An Historical Perspective," p. 287.
10. Ibid.
11. Hohenshil. "Rationale for Career Education," p. 316.
12. Ibid., pp. 316–317.
13. Ibid., p. 317.
14. Webb, "Career Education: An Historical Perspective," p. 292.
15. Hohenshil, "Rationale for Career Education," p. 315.
16. Webb, "Career Education: An Historical Perspective," p. 293.
17. Carl McDaniels, "Career Education: Current Status," p. 294.
18. Ibid.
19. Ibid., p. 295.
20. Muirhead, "Career Education: The First Steps Show Promise": 370.

21. Anthony M. Deiluio and James M. Young, "Career Education in the Elementary School," *Phi Delta Kappan* LIV, 8 (February 1973): 378.
22. Ibid.
23. Joel L. Burdin, "Career Education: Another Illusion or Opportunity?," *Journal of Teacher Education* XXIV, 2 (Summer 1973): 82, 155.
24. Kenneth B. Hoyt, Robert N. Evans, Edward F. Mackin, and Garth L. Mangum, *Career Education: What It Is and How to Do It*. Salt Lake City, UT: Olympus Publishing Company, 1972, p. 183.
25. Ibid.
26. Ibid., p. 185.
27. Hohenshil, "Rationale for Career Education," p. 315.
28. Ibid.
29. "Sidney Marland on Career Education," *American Education* 7, 9 (November 1971): 25.
30. Ibid., 26–27.
31. Ibid., 27–28.
32. Ibid., 28.
33. "Marland's Philosophy of Preventive Medicine: Will It Work?," *Nation's Schools* 88, 6 (December 1971): 38.
34. Ibid., 39.
35. Sidney Marland, "Career Education 300 Days Later," *American Vocational Journal* 47, 2 (February 1972): 14.
36. Ibid., 15.
37. Ibid.
38. Ibid., 16–17.
39. Sidney Marland, "Career Education: Every Student Headed for a Goal," *American Vocational Journal* 47, 3 (March 1972): 34.
40. Ibid., 35–36.
41. Ibid., 62.
42. Byrl R. Shoemaker, "Career Education: A CHANCE FOR CHANGE," *American Vocational Journal* 47, 3 (March 1972): 27–28.
43. David T. Borland and Richard Harris, "Preparing Career Education Specialists," *Journal of Teacher Education* XXIV, 2 (Summer 1973): 93.
44. Sidney Marland, "The Report on the Condition of Education: The Endless Renaissance," *American Education* 8, 3 (April 1972): 8–9.
45. Darryl Larramore, "Career Education Concept Filters Down," *American Vocational Journal* 47, 6 (September 1972): 45.
46. Hoyt, et al., *Career Education: What It Is and How to Do It*, p. 3.
47. Ibid., pp. 3–4.
48. Kenneth Hoyt, "Career Education and Career Choice," *American Vocational Journal* 47, 3 (March 1972): 85.
49. Larry J. Bailey and Ronald W. Stadt, *Career Development: New Approaches to Human Development*. Bloomington, IL: McKnight Publishing Company, 1973, p. 413.
50. Quoted in Webb, "Career Education: An Historical Perspective," p. 288.
51. Quoted in ibid.
52. Quoted in ibid.
53. Quoted in ibid.
54. McDaniels, "Career Education: Current Status," pp. 295–296.
55. Ibid., pp. 297–298.

56. Ibid., pp. 301–302.

57. Ibid.

58. Arthur M. Kroll and Linda A. Pfister, "Assessing Career Skills: A New Approach," *The College Board Review* 105 (Fall 1977): 19.

59. "Task Force Report on Career Education," *American Vocational Journal* 47, 1 (January 1972): 12–14.

60. Gordon I. Swanson, "Career Education: Barriers to Implementation," *American Vocational Journal* 47, 3 (March 1972): 81–82,

61. Carl E. Wells, "Will Vocational Education Survive?," *Phi Delta Kappan* LIV, 8 (February 1973): 380.

62. Muirhead, "Career Education: The First Steps Look Promising": 372.

63. John R. Ottina, "Career Education Is Alive and Well," *Journal of Teacher Education* XXIV, 2 (Summer 1973): 84.

64. McDaniels, "Career Education: Current Status," p. 300.

65. Paul M. Halverson, "Is Career Education a Passing Fancy? Some Thoughts of a Curriculum Generalist," *Journal of Teacher Education* XXIV, 2 (Summer 1973): 112.

66. Byrl R. Shoemaker, "Career Education : A CHANCE FOR CHANGE": 27.

67. Ibid., p. 31.

68. "Career Education: Equipping Students for the World of Work," *Nation's Schools* 88, 6 (December 1971): 35.

69. Ibid., 36.

70. Arlene Cross, "AVA Role in Career Education," *American Vocational Journal* 47, 3 (March 1972): 26.

71. Ibid.

72. Marla Peterson, "OCCUPACS: Simulated Career Development Experiences for Elementary School Children," *Business Education Forum* 26, 5 (February 1972): 6.

73. Ibid., p. 7.

74. Kenneth Hoyt, "Career Education Means 'An Entirely New Curriculum'," *American Vocational Journal,* 47, 2 (February 1972): 24.

75. Jerry C. Olson, "Researchers Discuss Career Education, Performance Goals," *American Vocational Journal* 47, 2 (February 1972): 25.

76. Anthony M. Deiluio and James M. Young, "Career Education in the Elementary School," *Phi Delta Kappan* LIV, 8 (February 1973): 379.

77. Kenneth B. Hoyt, Nancy M. Pinson, Darryl Larramore, and Garth L. Mangum, *Career Education and the Elementary School Teacher.* Salt Lake City, UT: Olympus Publishing Company, 1973, p. 15.

78. Ibid., p. 185.

79. Peter Finn, "Integrating Career Education into Subject Area Classrooms," *NASSP Bulletin* 62, 417 (April 1978): 65–66.

80. Ibid., 69.

81. Hohenshil, "Rationale for Career Education," p. 318.

82. Ibid., p. 321.

83. McDaniels, "Career Education: Current Status," p. 303.

84. Milton Kriesow, "Career Education for High School Teachers," *Journal of Teacher Education* XXIV, 2 (Summer 1973): 103.

85. Ibid.

86. Swanson, "Career Education: Barriers to Implementation": 82.

87. Claude Duet and John Newfield, "Labor: An Untapped Resource in Career Education," *NASSP Bulletin* 62, 417 (April 1978): 51–53.
88. Ibid., 54–55.
89. Gene Bottoms, "State Level Management for Career Education," *American Vocational Journal* 47, 3 (March 1972): 89.
90. Ibid., 89–92.
91. Hohenshil, "Rationale for Career Education," p. 315.
92. Robert J. Nash and Russell M. Agne, "Career Education: Earning a Living or Living a Life?," *Phi Delta Kappan* LIV, 6 (February 1973): 373–374.
93. Ibid., 374.
94. W. Norton Grubb and Marvin Lazerson, "Rally 'Round the Workplace: Continuities and Fallacies in Career Education," *Harvard Educational Review* 45, 4 (November 1975): 472.
95. Ibid., 466–467.
96. Ibid., 470.
97. Joel Spring, *Educating the Worker-Citizen: The Social, Economic, and Political Foundations of Education.* New York: Longmans, 1980, p. 156.
98. Grubb and Lazerson, "Rally 'Round the Workplace": 470.
99. Ibid., 471.
100. Halverson, "Is Career Education a Passing Fancy? Some Thoughts of a Curriculum Generalist": 110.
101. "Marland's Philosophy of Preventive Medicine: Will It Work?," *Nation's Schools* 88, 6 (December 1971): 40.
102. Nash and Agne, "Career Education: Earning a Living or Living a Life?": 373.
103. Ibid.
104. Ibid., 375–377.
105. Ibid., 377.
106. Ibid.
107. Grubb and Lazerson, "Rally 'Round the Workplace": 472.
108. Ibid., 473–474.
109. Marland, "Career Education: Every Student Headed for a Goal?": 62.
110. Deiluio and Young, "Career Education in the Elementary School": 379.
111. Burdin, "Career Education: Another Illusion or Opportunity?": 82.
112. Ibid., 82, 155, 153.
113. "Marland's Philosophy of Preventive Medicine: Will It Work?": 39.
114. Quoted in Bailey and Stadt, *Career Education: New Approaches to Human Development,* p. xiii.
115. Bailey and Stadt, Ibid., p. 51.
116. Shoemaker, "Career Education: A CHANCE FOR CHANGE": 31.
117. Pucinski, "The National Reform," in Pucinski and Hirsch, eds., *The Courage to Change: New Priorities for Career Education,* pp. 193–194.
118. Hoyt, et al., *Career Education and the Elementary Teacher,* p. 5.
119. Borland and Harris, "Preparing Career Education Specialists": 93.
120. Hohenshil, "Rationale for Career Education," p. 322.

CHAPTER FIFTEEN

Year-Round Education

Year-round education never gained the publicity, support or attention that career education received. During the period 1963 to 1981, the greatest number of articles published about the topic in any given academic year was only 15 in 1972–1973. Even in that year it did not merit its own heading: readers were sent to the cross-reference, "School Year—Length."[1] The Gallup Polls on education, published annually by *Phi Delta Kappan,* tell a similar story. While the polls did not begin until 1969, aside from a question or two asked early on (1970, 1971, and 1972), it was not until 1982 that a year-round education question was asked on a fairly frequent basis.[2] It qualifies as a panacea, however, as we shall shortly see.

In researching this chapter, I was struck by the vast majority of articles that viewed the movement as "new," thereby revealing their historical position. Year-round education or year-round schooling (or flexible scheduling or one of the other names that labeled this phenomenon), was anything but new. Some trace the movement back to Bluffton, Indiana in 1904.[3] Others point to nineteenth-century programs, several of which had 48-week sessions, in cities such as Chicago, Boston, Washington, DC, Cleveland, and Detroit as the historical origins of year-round education.[4] Others identify Newark, New Jersey, which beginning in 1912 hosted the program that "had the greatest impact in educational circles." The Newark program, which was a casualty of the Depression, performed a "great service, particularly to children of foreign parentage and unfavorable home conditions," allegedly keeping these children "out of mischief in the summer."[5] A program at Nashville, Tennessee, which lasted from 1927 to 1932, was described as "less successful." Operations at Omaha, Nebraska and Aliquippa, Pennsylvania sought both "economic benefits and educational goals," harbingers of things to come.[6] Advocates of the 1970s, according to Velma Adams, who claimed that a "*real* extended school year," which "puts the emphasis on improved education, instead of on a more efficient use of facilities—has *never* been tried,"[7] must have been unaware of several of these prior programs.

The rhetoric of the late 1960s and early 1970s abounded with descriptions of the "traditional school calendar" as "obsolete,"[8] sometimes accompanied with the sage advice that "these days children don't have to bale hay anymore."[9] Paul Rice and Johannes Olsen note that the "*traditional* calendar is a Misnomer"—it was the result of a compromise between urban and rural legislators. They maintained that the "educational reasons" for the movement developed after the fact and were part of its "myths and hoaxes."[10]

In 1971, Leonard Ernst ventured that, like the "fashions of the Forties, the extended school year is an idea whose time has come once again."[11] As William Ellena had written two years before:

> Now, however, the almost universal practice of leaving school plants and personnel idle at a time in our history when using available resources is needed is carefully being reexamined and hotly debated. The change in the rate of change now requires that we abandon school calendars based on a bygone era.
>
> To the practical-minded citizen, the anxious parent, and the hardheaded businessman—all desperately wanting broader and better educational opportunities for their children—the extended school year makes good sense.[12]

Various Plans

Writing in 1975, Rice and Olsen depicted examples of the kinds of year-round calendars, comparing them with the traditional school calendar.[13]

The numbers of programs varied over the years. For instance, Ernst commented that 1971 could be a "banner year" for the movement because 600 districts were studying it, and although only a "handful actually have adopted year-round plans . . . scores may follow suit before the school year's end."[14] Ernst was not exactly a prophet: in 1973 N. S. Rifkin reported that there were 27 schools with year-round plans in action in 1971 and only 55 in 1972.[15] Morris Richmond and Jack Riegle contended that in 1974 at least one school building in approximately 76 school districts, two university laboratory schools, and one private school in twenty-five states had year-round plans in operation in the nation.[16] Thomas Balakas, an administrator in the Aurora, Colorado, schools, posited that in 1980, 236 elementary schools, 33 middle and junior high schools, and 18 senior high schools in seventeen states were functioning according to some kind of year-round school model.[17]

Year-round programs were either voluntary or mandated. Voluntary programs allowed families to choose whether or not to participate; mandated programs required participation. While recognizing that extended-year programs had to be "sold" to the public, some advocates, such as George I. Thomas, adhered strictly to the notion of mandated programs, at least if the potential economic benefits were to be realized: *It must be understood at the outset that no voluntary*

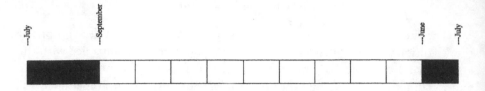

Diagram 15:1—Traditional School Year

All Students in attendance the same 180 days between September and June and all have common summer vacation between June and September.

Source: Paul D. Rice and Johannes I. Olsen, "Year-Round Education: An Overview," in Thomas C. Hunt and James G. Silliman, Jr., eds., *The American School in Its Social Setting.* Dubuque, IA: Kendall-Hunt Publishing Company, 1975, p. 303.

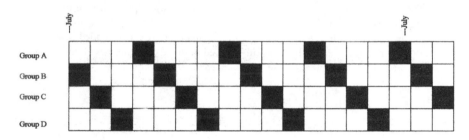

Diagram 15: 2—"45–15" School Year

Student body equally divided into 4 groups. Each block represents 15 days, therefore students attend school 45 days and then have a 15 day vacation. One-fourth of students always on vacation, if mandated.

Source: Paul D. Rice and Johannes I. Olsen, "Year-Round Education: An Overview," in Thomas C. Hunt and James G. Silliman, Jr., eds., *The American School in Its Social Setting.* Dubuque, IA: Kendall-Hunt Publishing Company, 1975, p. 304.

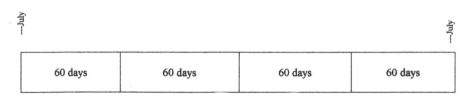

Diagram 15:3—Four Quarter School Year

Students attend school 3 of the 4 quarters. One-fourth of students always on vacation, if mandated.

Source: Paul D. Rice and Johannes I. Olsen, "Year-Round Education: An Overview," in Thomas C. Hunt and James G. Silliman, Jr., eds., *The American School in Its Social Setting.* Dubuque, IA: Kendall-Hunt Publishing Company, 1975, p. 304.

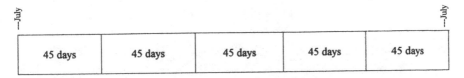

Diagram 15:4—Quinmester School Year

Students attend school 4 of the 5 time blocks. One-fifth of the students always on vacation, if mandated.

Source: Paul D. Rice and Johannes I. Olsen, "Year-Round Education: an Overview," in Thomas C. Hunt and James G. Silliman, Jr., eds., *The American School in Its Social Setting.* Dubuque, IA: Kendall-Hunt Publishing Company, 1975, p. 304.

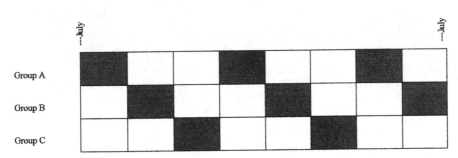

Diagram 15: 5—Concept 6

Students divided into 3 equal groups. Every block equals 43 days. One-third of students always on vacation, if mandated.

Source: Paul D. Rice and Johannes I. Olsen, "Year-Round Education: An Overview," in Thomas C. Hunt and James G. Silliman, Jr., eds., *The American School in Its Social Setting.* Dubuque, IA: Kendall-Hunt Publishing company, 1975, p. 304.

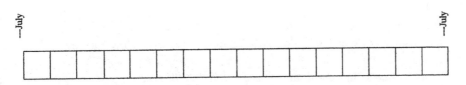

Diagram 15: 6—Multiple Access

Students attend any 12 of the 16 time blocks. Each block represents 15 days. Number of students on vacation at any one time may vary.

Source: Paul D. Rice and Johannes I. Olsen, "Year-Round Education: An Overview," in Thomas C. Hunt and James G. Silliman, Jr., eds., *The American School in Its Social Setting.* Dubuque, IA: Kendall-Hunt Publishing Company, 1975, p. 305

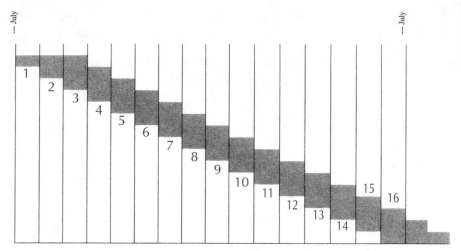

Diagram 15.7—Another variation of the Multiple Access program follows.

Students select to attend school during any 4, no overlapping time lines, e.g., selects lines 1, 4, 9, and 12. Each time line represents 45 days. Number of students on vacation at any one time may vary.

Source: Paul D. Rice and Johannes I. Olsen, "Year-Round Education: An Overview," in Thomas C. Hunt and James G. Silliman, Jr., eds., *The American School in Its Social Setting.* Dubuque, IA: Kendall-Hunt Publishing Company, 1975, p. 305.

student attendance plan will ever release enough space and dollars to realize the economy objective." [18]

Reasons Advanced

A variety of reasons were advanced for the advent of year-round education in the 1960s. Richmond and Riegle presented a comprehensive array of reasons to embrace the year-round model in their 1974 article:

1. It used plant facilities more efficiently
2. It allowed faculty and administrators to improve and reorganize the curriculum
3. It prevented students from forgetting what they had learned during the summer
4. It saved money by reducing the number of school plants needed
5. It reduced juvenile delinquency (attending school was a better use of students' summer time)
6. It saved money by delaying the cost of construction and eliminating the need for bond issues
7. It enabled faculty to provide enrichment courses in the curriculum
8. It reduced the attrition rate of students
9. It created the opportunity to conduct experiments on the effects of year-round education on the "emotional and physical well-being of students and teachers"

10. It offered a solution to crowded conditions while additional buildings were being constructed

11. It offered expanded employment opportunities to teachers that increased their salaries and professional status

12. It helped disadvantaged students do acceptable schoolwork

13. It saved money by reducing the number of pupils who had to repeat a grade

14. It made teaching more attractive to men by upping their earning capacities

15. It saved money by permitting the acceleration of bright pupils, thereby cutting out two to three years of their schooling

16. It freed the community from the obligation to provide funds for the construction of schools

17. It improved "educational achievement"

18. It met the "needs of growing enrollment" and acquired "needed classroom space."[19]

Rice and Olsen concurred with the fiscal reasons presented, and added that in a "few instances" the promise of better education for the students was held forth.[20]

Despite the fact that year-round schooling led to administrative problems (which will be addressed later in this chapter), some school administrators lauded the movement. For instance, Dr. Burton C. Tiffany, superintendent of schools in the Chula Vista (CA) Elementary School District contended that the 45–15 program not only "provides a better educational program," it also "saves money."[21] Others took refuge in criticizing the "archaic, out-moded three month vacation system"[22] or a fossil-like adherence to an "agrarian" school calendar.[23]

Rice and Olsen's identification of the "after the fact" nature of projected educational benefits was not shared by Thomas Driscoll. He wrote:

> The educational principle of "massed versus distributed learning" holds that, in general, equally distributed and spaced learning experiences will produce more and better learning. For example, thirty minutes of typing practice each day for ten days will produce greater results and more lasting results than one five-hour practice session. . . .
>
> Instead of a nine-month learning span followed by one three month major vacation period, under the 45–15 Plan, pupils will attend school four 45 day sessions (equal distribution). Each 45-day session will have at least a 15-class-day vacation (equal spacing). Truly this is an ideal arrangement to gain the benefits of distributed learning.[24]

George Jensen, chairman of the National Calendar Study Committee and former president of the Minneapolis board of education, was optimistic in 1968 about the program's future. He argued that "yesterday's school attendance pattern no longer is up to meeting today's demands on the educational program"; he was not surprised that in a space of twelve years the percentage of Americans favoring the year-round pattern had grown from ten percent to about thirty-three percent.[25]

Expected Benefits

Expected benefits, as claimed by year-round's advocates, were many and diverse. While there was indeed considerable overlap in the anticipated fruits of the movement, the approach here is to consider them by category, beginning with their overall potential.

Overall Potential

Rice and Olsen attested to the pervasive, all-reaching potential influence of the movement:

> The realization of the consequent, almost revolutionary, implications for instructional methodology and for policies and practices in areas as diverse as grading and testing, discipline, attendance, class rank, Carnegie Unit, budgeting and staff utilization can easily overwhelm faculty and administration alike, not to mention the school board and community.[26]

They cautioned that the program ought not be "sold" on its fiscal savings; that could be the "frosting on the cake!"[27] They spoke about the movement's potential for widespread good:

> Necessity surely is the mother of invention. We have encountered few problems with respect to year-round education which after someone's creative thought did not turn out to be a distinct advantage, whether in relation to the social implications for inner-city youth, jobs for students, year-round churches or summer camps. Year-round school operation can capitalize on the school's capability for individualization of instruction. In a year-round school the calendar should serve as the vehicle for a better instructional program![28]

Ronald Alvarez agreed. He contended that any school system could successfully implement year-round education if it "wins community acceptance of the plan, involves the professional staff in all aspects of the operation, and develops a model or design that does not penalize certain families."[29] Paul Miller, superintendent of schools in Cincinnati, declared forthrightly that not only was the year-round movement "inevitable," it would also bring about a "better program and far better usage of school personnel, facilities and resources."[30]

Don Glines, an ardent supporter of the movement, recognized that the movement had reached a plateau in 1978. It was originally designed to save construction costs and alleviate overcrowding; now he noted that "more are now realizing that year-round education is a viable option because of its many other advantages: choice of family life-styles, continuous year-round learning opportunities and reduction of environmental overload."[31] Robert Musca, a local superintendent of

schools near Chula Vista, California, concurred. He observed that the "economics of the plan first interested officials in his district," but after some study he had
decided that "the educational advantages are just as attractive."[32]

Financial Savings

Proponents of year-round education advanced fiscal benefits as a major selling
point. Adams, for example, listed the "chief motivations" for 600 school districts,
which she identified in "this order of urgency" as first, to save money, to make
greater use of present facilities, and to delay construction and thus "sidestep going
to taxpayers for a bond issue."[33]

Hubert Humphrey, quoted in Hermansen and Gove, focused on the waste
represented when educational facilities were allowed to lie idle:

> We must all work to make greater utilization of the educational facilities which sit idle
> for many months of the year. . . . Our educational facilities must be recognized as a valuable
> resource. We must take full advantage of their use to reap a full return on our investment.[34]

Kenneth Hermansen and James Gove saw voter dissatisfaction with the lack of efficiency and accountability in the operation of schools, which they contended had
led to bond defeats and opposition to taxation (the only opportunities for the public to voice their displeasure at schools' operation), as manifestations of the weak-
ened support of the schools by the American public. They argued that the "time
for bold, forward-looking change has truly come."[35]

George Thomas wrote in 1973 that year-round school plans "*can* be sold to
the general public by school districts." Cost analysis had demonstrated that existing school plant capacities could be increased by up to "25, 33, or 40 percent,"
which would allow school divisions to "close schools or convert existing classrooms to new and more innovative or practical learning centers."[36]

George Jensen, one of the movement's leading spokespersons, cut a wider
swath with his sweeping interpretation of the financial benefits of the development. He foresaw a "significant effect on the business and professional sector" of
the community, which would view adoption of year-round education as evidence
of a "new awareness of the necessity for local fiscal responsibility and prudence in
school operations" on the part of school officials.[37] Included in this category
would be the potential impact on personnel practices and the "load factor" in
business. Spacing vacations, he argued, would permit flexibility in family vacations and travel plans, which would make it much easier for firms to "maintain
staffing levels as well as the volume of business done or professional services rendered." Benefits would extend to all back-to-school clothing manufacturers and
sales, physicians who provided check-ups, realtors, purveyors of household goods,

those who provided moving and storage, and telephone and utilities companies, "to say nothing of the resort and travel industry." Year-round schooling would also put graduates on the labor market in a "more orderly fashion," thus "avoiding the glut of job-seekers in June."[38] Employers would have the advantage of a "constant supply of junior-grade employees," and their availability would solve many personnel problems for the daily operation of "supermarkets, gas stations, and those business and agricultural operations which need extra help during periods other than summer." Finally, Jensen argued that year-round schooling would have a major financial impact because it would result in a "markedly reduced need for educational space achieved by full-time utilization of facilities, the tax bite will be correspondingly reduced" and the "recently proven greater holding power and new relevancy" of the year-round school promised that "a much higher percentage of tomorrow's youth will be able to fend for themselves and thus reduce the taxes required to underwrite a satisfactory welfare program."[39]

Teachers

Jensen looked to the year-round model to reduce costs connected with teachers. Implementation of the program would reduce the number of teachers who must be "trained each year mostly at public expense" and lower teacher retirement costs because only those who opted to participate in year-round teaching would be offered full benefits.[40] Most writers, such as Anderson, emphasized the opportunities teachers had to work year-round if they wished. He also felt that teachers would not get "rusty" if they worked year-round.[41] Richmond added that the higher salaries teachers would enjoy by teaching in year-round programs would elevate their professional status, give them greater financial security, and "bring benefits to the community through greater teacher involvement and better student-teacher relationships."[42]

Anecdotal evidence was also presented on behalf of advantages to teachers. Elaine Yaffe quoted Judy Thompson, a fifth grade teacher in the year-round program in Colorado Springs, that Thompson was "resentful" when the program started, thinking "Why are they doing this to me?" She later stated that she "wouldn't give it up. I feel I'm successful as a teacher." The fundamental reason was "shorter vacations." According to Thompson, "without exception," teachers felt that this was the "single greatest educational advantage."[43] Thompson's opinions were supported by Luis Avila, a sixth grade teacher in the Colorado Springs system: "In a traditional school you tread water the last month. You are burned out and so are the kids. Here you don't have any times like that."[44]

According to Alvarez, teachers in Valley View, Illinois "resoundingly" supported the year-round contract available to them there.[45] Similar sentiments were expressed by a mother who visited the schools there: "All we were looking for was how to get more classrooms without building, but there are many side advantages. The discipline problem is down and the enthusiasm of the teaching staff is the highest I have ever seen it."[46] As one school principal put it, "The most exciting thing about the year-round school is what happens to some of the teachers. Their creativity and motivation are unleashed because they are not bound by school as usual."[47]

Students

Proponents of the year-round model were eloquent about the advantages that accrued to students as a consequence of adopting the year-round model. Jensen argued that multiple times for enrollment enabled a child to start school closest to her or his birthday, thereby reducing the "wide gap in intellectual development that currently exists at the early grade levels and makes for a faulty start in formal education for so many children."[48] Speaking of the benefits of the Atlanta program, Dr. E. Curtis Henson, associate superintendent of instruction there, claimed that the "attitude of the students is greatly improved. They try more subjects than before."[49]

The improved attitude of students led to academic success. Failures were "meaningless," except for sequential courses, because the student had "many options to select other courses which interest him. There are no courses by name or title which the student must take."[50] No stigma could affect a student over a course he or she "would or could not handle"; rather, they could sidestep the course and "go on to another."[51] Opportunities for acceleration and remediation became available due to the additional (fourth) term.[52] The absence of the long, three-month summer vacation helped students retain what they learned.[53] Dropouts were reduced, or at least delayed.[54] School vandalism was sharply curtailed.[55] Discipline problems were down.[56] Rice and Olsen concluded that the "Year-round school operation can capitalize on the school's capability for individualization of instruction. In a year-round school the calendar should serve as the vehicle for a better instructional program!"[57] They contended that a year-round schedule also offered opportunities to enrich the curriculum, provided greater flexibility in course offerings, and more tutoring; these things were simply not possible under the traditional calendar. It also greatly reduced tedium and boredom.[58]

Inner-city youth were singled out as illustrations of the success of year-round schooling. They did not fall prey to the temptations of the long, hot summer months in the central cities;[59] the extra term helped them catch up,[60] and teachers, encouraged by the extra money to teach in the summers, compensated for the "absence of fathers" in the inner-cities.[61] "Many juvenile authorities," Jensen claimed, said year-round schooling would lessen juvenile delinquency, which "historically occurs in the late summer months when all youth are out from under the stabilizing influence of school."[62]

The model also provided better job opportunities for students in their off-terms, the market was not "flooded," as was the case with the traditional school calendar.[63] The year-round program not only created employment opportunities for students, it also avoided the "peaks and valleys" vacation time of the conventional program.[64] As one writer put it, "100,000 students are not dumped on the street at one time."[65] Rupert Evans, a professor of vocational and technical education at the University of Illinois, debunked the value of "summer jobs and volunteer work" as not "real or meaningful for students, anyway." They "usually have bad habits and attendance" in those jobs, he contended, and in volunteer work, such as "candy-stripers," they are "introduced to the glamorous side of the job and not the nitty-gritty work."[66] Without favoring his readers with an explanation, he averred that "any type of staggered vacation schedule should lead to greater work opportunities for students and more meaningful job experience."[67]

One school principal summed up her feelings with the glowing statement that, as a result of the year-round program, "Wonderful things are happening for children. This makes all the other discomforts worthwhile."[68]

Concluding Benefits

Howard Holt offered the notion that "system shock," by which he meant the "complete restructuring of the curriculum," was perhaps the movement's "most significant characteristic." A member of the NASSP called this restructuring a disadvantage of year-round education, to which Holt replied, "A profession capable of producing such a statement has condemned itself, or at least developed a mindset that needs to be shocked."[69]

One of year-round's most vocal backers, Don Glines, the Director and Resident Consultant of the Wilson Campus School at Mankato State College in Minnesota, said year-round education possessed the quality of "humaneness." He began his treatise on the subject with the statement that "A key concept in developing a humane school is that of year-round education." Beyond the economic factors, Glines said, there was the "realization that year-round education provides opportunities for students and teachers never before available on a constant basis."[70] The most precious was the:

> . . . notion that if humaneness is to be the dominant theme of education, then schools must remain open all year round. For years we have preached concern for individual needs, interests, abilities and differences. We have claimed these cliches as basic goals, yet in school after school, year after year, all over the country, students are required to be in school from September to June and exposed to group-provided, group-paced instruction.[71]

Glines used the carpenter as an example.

In summer he must work six or seven days a week to construct buildings and earn a living for his family, because in January his work is slowed or stopped completely. But can he take a family vacation in January? Can he go swimming in February in Puerto Rico or any other place he may choose? The answer is obvious; the ritual of the public school says that the children of a family cannot swim in January and/or February. The child must be in school. He cannot miss those magic moments with the lectures, the homework, and the think-and-do books. What evidence do we have that Pete and Sally cannot learn in July or August? Why not let the family vacation in January?[72]

Glines argued that neither enriched summer school programs nor quarter systems were the answer:

> . . . the year-round environment becomes a realistic humane concept that most school districts can undertake immediately. The nuts-and-bolts details as to teacher contracts, student enrollments, staggering vacations, and all the other minutiae can be overcome by committed boards and educators.[73]

Drawing on his own experience at Wilson, Glines wrote that "Twenty-five years of research validates the notion that students learn best those things that are relevant and meaningful. Individualized instruction, independent study, and mini-courses make these factors realities." "With freedom" he claimed, "goes responsibility."[74] A clarion call for year-round education, indeed!

Disadvantages

In 1975, Rice and Olson asked "Who can responsibly ignore a plan which will increase the effective capacity of present school facilities by a third?" They pointed to documented annual savings of between 1 and 9.6 percent. They noted the disadvantages of year-round education, but quickly dismissed them as the products of poor administration and the "concerns and misconceptions" of some public and professional groups.[75]

They assembled a list, which they drew from various feasibility studies, of the "disadvantages" of year-round schooling.

1. Students may be required to do homework during the summer months.
2. The standardized testing program may need revision.
3. Truancy and delinquency may increase (pupils on vacation may influence their friends to skip school).
4. Review will be necessary in elementary schools four times a year.
5. The physical and mental health of teachers may not stand up in year-round employment.
6. It will be more trouble to repair, replace, and take inventory of institutional equipment and materials.

7. Administrative duties will increase.
8. Scheduling difficulties will occur in Grades 9–12.
9. Community agencies that provide summer programs and services will have to offer their programs year-round.
10. Maintenance problems will increase when buildings are used all but three to five weeks of the year.
11. The psychological benefits of vacation may be lost if students are forced to spend it indoors due to inclement weather.
12. There will be more starting and stopping of school programs.
13. Educational materials are currently designed for a continuous 180 day program.[76]

Rice and Olsen stated that the above list was put forth "tongue in cheek" because it "demonstrates the biases and misunderstandings" that teachers and administrators have with regard to year-round school. They also alleged that the list of drawbacks seemed to assume that the schools exist for the convenience and benefit of teachers and administrators rather than for students." They went on to assert:

> It would be ridiculous to suggest that there are *no* disadvantages to year-round school operation, but it is equally essential to point out that the disadvantages are usually the result of other decisions made by the school district, and not necessarily or automatically due to year-round school operation![77]

George I. Thomas, referred to as a "prophet" of the extended school year movement, argued that the implementation of a sophisticated curriculum that allows students to "enter and leave" a program at any time during the year "requires a completely new mind-set on the part of administrators, teachers, parents and students,—and that, as the phrase goes, is where the hang-up is."[78] Oz Johnson, the superintendent of schools of Jefferson County, Kentucky (which included Louisville), wrote as early as 1970 that the multiple tracks required in year-round schooling were "simply too difficult to administer" and that there were other problems associated with transportation of students and their use of free time.[79]

Jaffe identified several disadvantages from the perspective of administrators. "Meticulous planning" was the first one. She quoted one school administrator:

> The start of every new pattern necessitates a quantity of filing—new recommendations for educationally handicapped classes, new volunteers, revised lists of playground duty, physical education, music, new requests for materials.[80]

Her building principal added, "We really have three schools in one building," and another district administrator remarked that "In a traditional school you have two hard times, before school begins and after it ends. Year-round school is starting and ending all the time."[81] One teacher described the situation as "chaos," due to the overlap periods when the students from all three patterns were in school at the same time. Teachers were depicted as unhappy because they were doing a "lot of lugging back and forth."[82]

Richmond and Riegle also commented on the serious administrative problems brought on by year-round schools. They pointed to inadequate funding for operating extended services, scheduling conflicts between schools that operate on different (traditional and year-round) calendars, teacher opposition, community opposition, and the problems associated with the need to schedule members of the same family in the same school term.[83] Stocker concurred with a majority of these problems and added increased time in overseeing the budget, logistical difficulties when teachers needed to change rooms, more complex bus schedules, and difficulties associated with accounting for pupil attendance.[84]

Contrary to the common wisdom, some writers argued, year-round schooling did not bring about fiscal savings, and in some instances brought with it an increase, not a decrease, in operational costs. Richmond and Riegle, for instance, alleged that the program generally did not result in savings unless it avoided huge capital outlays.[85] Adams quoted the statement of William Wise of the research department of the state of Delaware that "you can shoot holes" in the savings allegations: "You may postpone building, buy time, and maybe gain a little politically. But we need about $220,000 just to go ahead with a pilot program, and every district that ever tried extended school year for economy has dropped it."[86] A New York superintendent, Edward Murphy, related how his district canceled the program. He said that it was impossible to tell if year-round schooling saves money until it had been in "operation six or seven years." And, he claimed, "today you just can't ask the community to pay more, now, without some immediate return."[87]

Opponents to year-round schooling cited adverse effects on students as a negative effect of year-round education. Some, apparently reaching a bit, even alleged that the program had a detrimental effect on students' health, because they need "direct sunlight, fresh air, and vigorous exercise" for adequate physical development. The mental and physical strain occasioned by the loss of summer vacation would prove harmful in their adult life.[88]

Opponents pointed to other reasons year-round education was detrimental to students. Some maintained that the short academic term of the 45–15 plan led to impersonal relationships between teachers and students.[89] Other stumbling blocks included articulation between elementary and secondary schooling, especially the lengthy time lags for students moving from an extended to a traditional program.[90]

Secondary schools were thought to be less fitting for year-round schooling than were elementary schools. The Carnegie unit, which "guarded the sacredness of clock hours in arriving at the definition of course credit," the "agrarian ethic" which had a "profound impact on the school calendar for reasons that are mostly anachronistic now," and interscholastic sports were given credit for this lack of fit with secondary schools.[91] James Fenwick argued that these factors accounted for the paucity of "successful attempts, or any kind of attempt, to seriously plan for implementing the 12-month school year."[92] Calvin Grinder added four problems that he deemed "critical," especially for secondary schools: 1) equalized enrollment will be "impossible to achieve and maintain," because of family vacations and employment patterns, the mobility of the population and cross-town busing: 2) it will be difficult to sequence subject matter so that beginning sections of sequential courses will be provided as necessary in each quarter; 3) it will be difficult to find qualified replacements for teachers who take the quarter off; and 4) financial savings will not be realized in the "long run" because of an increase in costs for personnel and maintenance.[93] Implementation of the year-round model would be especially difficult for "low incidence" classes of the secondary curriculum, e.g., physics,[94] and, would "play havoc" with traditional music programs, because the "continuity that is essential is disrupted."[95]

Opposition

Thomas Driscoll felt that the biggest obstacle to year-round schooling was the "break with tradition."[96] But other, more substantial, opposition soon became apparent.

Stocker opined that two things could "scuttle" the year-round plan: a non-involved community and different schedules for children of the same family.[97] B. Robert Anderson mentioned the public which "fails to grapple" with the reasons for change, and "remains solidly entrenched with ideas whose time has passed."[98] Yaffe took note of parents, some of whom had organized in opposition to year-round schooling, who asked questions such as "How can a child settle down when another vacation is just around the corner?"[99] The desultory effect on "family vacations" was frequently cited as a basis for opposition, as was the dearth of things for students to do in winter vacations.[100] Greg Stefanich thought that the essential problem originated with the lack of summer vacations ("parents' opposition became an alarming factor when children must take vacation during the winter") and consequently proposed sessions that allowed all students to take summer vacations.[101]

Opposition also flowed from professional personnel, especially teachers. Stocker observed that "teachers were uneasy" at the outset when one year-round program was instituted.[102] Anderson went farther, claiming a "natural reluctance" in the educational community to "cope with change which upsets teaching modes." Teachers recoiled at what they thought would be extra work, and statements such as "She's taught for twenty years; the first year was repeated twenty times" was an oft-heard complaint.[103] Ames voiced the view that teachers who were unable to enroll in summer school courses as they wished accounted for some of the professional opposition.[104] M. P. Heller and Max Bailey argued that there was "great doubt that the typical staff can cope with the change without extensive in-service instruction,"[105] which the teachers might not wish to commit to and the district or school might not wish to support.

Conclusion

As was the case with the other panaceas, much of the impetus for year-round schools came from forces external to education. In this instance it was "spawned from a shortage of buildings and teaching space and containing within it the need for reaction on part of the system."[106] Hermanson and Gove made it clear that great, and immediate, expectations were held for the movement: "There is no doubt that 1970–71 is the school year in which the 'great debate' over year-round education ended—the year in which action began, on a nationwide basis."[107] Yet there was concern—concern that as the movement picked up momentum and took on the appearance of a crusade, people might "jump on the bandwagon with carbon copies," and 1971 "may go down as the year of the big year-round fad."[108]

Rifkin expressed his disappointment with the "academic issue" that he felt was "getting bogged down in the infernal problem of trying to prove on paper what you feel in your bones."[109] Some school administrators were not at all reticent to express their feelings. The superintendent of the Roosevelt Elementary District in Phoenix, one of the largest and most troubled in the area, observed that "You really can't ask for more. It saves money and it helps the children." A building principal from that district noted that "It's doing everything it was expected to do," and the president of the Classroom Teachers Association stated that "It's almost shocking that nobody has anything really to gripe about. If they were unhappy they'd say so. Teachers usually do."[110]

Inevitability was a characteristic that came to mark the supporters of the year-round movement. One teacher asserted that "Year-round is the way things have to go."[111] McClain alleged that the time was now for "our society to develop a flexible, all-year school."[112] Responding to a question about why the plan hadn't been invoked before (although it had been and was discontinued), Driscoll, showing his ignorance of educational history, opined that "The answer is that individuals, groups, even school boards have wanted to try some form of year-round school plans but didn't want to be the first. Somebody has to be first."[113]

Advocates were certain that the day when the year-round program would be widely, if not universally, in use was not far off. After all, as Superintendent Jackson had said: "The things you can do with this program are unbelievable. It's a great way to live."[114] Rifkin held that the "nine-month schedule is a vanishing species—that it will be gone in ten years, possibly in five."[115] Glines was almost as optimistic; he believed that his program at Wilson would be replicated by many institutions in the future:

> We at Wilson believe that while all the many studies and plans for year-round education developed so far have much to offer, in the next ten years there will be a decided trend toward the type of program now under way at Wilson.[116]

While there were obstacles, the enthusiasm of year-round's advocates was unabated. George Jensen, president of the National Council on Year-Round Education, predicted in 1973 that 500 school districts would have year-round programs in five years. His colleague, outgoing council head Wayne White remarked that nearly all schools will be open year-round in ten years.[117]

Year-round education fluctuated in popularity throughout the late 1960s and 1970s. It would continue that fluctuation throughout the remainder of the century. For its zealots, it was indeed a panacea. But as early as 1970, M. Gene Henderson, superintendent of schools for St. Charles, Missouri, a system that had implemented the extended school year, provided a dash of realism that seems an appropriate note on which to conclude this chapter:

> If the educational advantages are outstanding, we may continue longer. For the long range, I think the voluntary four-quarter plan, like Atlanta's, has the best potential. But philosophically, I don't feel the American people will ever permit the year-round school. We are as emotional about that three-month summer vacation, as we are about apple pie, motherhood, and the flag. Maybe what we need, before people will consider the extended school year, is a Ralph Nader to uncover all the warts in education's traditional schedule.[118]

Notes

1. Julia W. Ehrenleich, ed., *Education Index: July 1972–June 1973*. New York: The H. W. Wilson Company, 1973, pp. 781–782.
2. Stanley M. Elam, ed., *A Decade of Gallup Polls toward Education 1969–1978*. Bloomington, IN: Phi Delta Kappa, 1978, and Elam, ed., *How America Views Its Schools: The PDK Gallup Polls, 1969–1994*. Bloomington, IN: Phi Delta Kappa, 1994.
3. American Association of School Administrators, *9+: The Year Round School*. Washington, DC: American Association of School Administrators, 1970, p. 9.
4. Paul D. Rice and Johannes I. Olsen, "Year-Round Education: An Overview," in Thomas C. Hunt and James G. Silliman, Jr., eds., *The American School in Its Social Setting*. Dubuque, IA: Kendall-Hunt Publishing Company, 1975, p. 203.

5. Clarence A. Schoenfeld and Neil Schmitz, *Year-Round Education: Its Problems and Prospects from Kindergarten to College*. Madison, WI: Dembar Educational Services, Inc., 1964, p. 19.

6. Ibid.

7. Velma A. Adams, "The Extended School Year: A Status Report," *School Management* 14, 6 (June 1970): 13.

8. "About the Book," Inside cover description of John D. McLain, *Year-Round Education: Economic, Educational and Sociological Factors*. Berkeley, CA: McCutchen Publishing Corporation, 1973.

9. Martin Sincoff and Tim Reid, "But in Virginia Beach, Year-Round Has Been Tried—and Scuttled," *American School Board Journal* 160, 3 (March 1973): 50.

10. Rice and Olsen, "Year-Round Education: An Overview," p. 303.

11. Leonard Ernst, "The Year-Round School: Faddish or Feasible?," *Nation's Schools* 88, 5 (November 1971): 51.

12. William J. Ellena, "Extending the School Year," *Today's Education* 58, 5 (May 1969): 48.

13. Rice and Olsen, "Year-Round Education: An Overview," pp. 303–305.

14. Ernst, "The Year-Round School: Faddish or Feasible?": 51.

15. N. S. Rifkin, "How to Make the Switch to Year-Round Schools," *American School Board Journal* 160, 2 (February 1973): 45.

16. Morris J. Richmond and Jack D. Riegle, "Current Status of the Extended School Year Movement," *Phi Delta Kappan* LV, 7 (March 1974): 494.

17. John D. Heisner, "Is the Sun Setting on Year-Round Schools?," *Instructor* 90, 4 (November 1980): 20.

18. George Isaiah Thomas, *Administrators Guide to the Year-Round School*. West Nyack, NY: Parker Publishing Company, Inc., 1973, p. 11.

19. Richmond and Riegle, "Current Status of the Extended School Year Movement": 491.

20. Rice and Olsen, "Year-Round Education: An Overview," p. 303.

21. Stephen R. Mallory, "Year-Round School: Coming, Coming, Here!," *School Management* 15, 8 (August 1971): 24–25.

22. Ingrid L. Gleason, "The Pitfalls of Our Long Summer Vacation," *Education* 92, 3 (February–March 1972): 70.

23. Howard B. Holt, "Year-Round Schools and System Shock," *Phi Delta Kappan* LIV, 5 (January 1973): 310.

24. Thomas F. Driscoll, "Schools Around the Calendar," *American Education* 7, 2 (March 1971): 23.

25. George M. Jensen, "Year-Round Calendar: The Idea, at Last, Is Beginning to Catch On," *American School Board Journal* 156, 1 (July 1968): 13.

26. Rice and Olsen, "Year-Round Education: An Overview," p. 307.

27. Ibid., p. 306.

28. Ibid., p. 307.

29. Ronald F. Alvarez, "A Look at the Year-Round School," *American Education* 9, 6 (June 1973): back cover.

30. Quoted in George M. Jensen, "Year-Round School Is Just Around the Corner," *American School Board Journal* 157, 1 (July 1969): 12.

31. Don Glines, "The Status of Year-Round Education," *Teacher* 95, 8 (April 1978): 67.

32. "Further Developments in the Year-Round Use of Schools," *School Management* 15, 8 (August 1971): 27.

33. Adams, "The Extended School Year: A Status Report": 13.

34. Quoted in Kenneth L. Hermanson and James K. Gove, *The Year-Round School: The 45–15 Breakthrough.* Hamden, CT: Linnet Books, 1971, p. 151.

35. Ibid.

36. Thomas, *Administrator's Guide to the Year-Round School,* p. 11.

37. George M. Jensen, "Year-Round Schooling Can Benefit Business," *Phi Delta Kappan* LIV, 5 (January 1973): 313.

38. Ibid.

39. Ibid.

40. George M. Jensen, "Fifteen Ways the Year-Round School Makes Sense," *American School Board Journal* 157, 1 (July 1969): 12.

41. B. Robert Anderson, "'Four Quarters' Makes a Whole Year in Atlanta," *School Management* 16, 6 (June 1972): 8.

42. Morris J. Richmond, "Effects of Extended School Year Operations," *Education* 97, 4 (Summer 1977): 393.

43. Quoted in Elaine Yaffe, "Teaching in a Year-Round School," *Teacher* 95, 8 (April 1978): 64.

44. Quoted in ibid.

45. Ronald F. Alvarez, "A Look at the Year-Round School": back cover.

46. Quoted in James Baker and Viola D. Johnson, "Another District Experiments with a 45–15 Plan," *School Management* 17, 3 (March 1973): 23.

47. Carl V. and Gretchen Patton, "A Year-Round Open School Viewed from Within," *Phi Delta Kappan* 57, 8 (April 1976): 526.

48. Jensen, "Fifteen Ways the Year-Round School Makes Sense": 12.

49. Quoted in Anderson, "'Four Quarters' Makes a Whole Year in Atlanta": 8.

50. Ibid.

51. Ibid., 10.

52. Richmond, "Effects of Extended School Year Operations": 393; Adams, "The Extended School Year": 13.

53. Richmond, ibid., 394; Adams, ibid., 13.

54. Adams, "The Extended School Year": 13.

55. Anderson, "'Four Quarters' Makes a Whole Year in Atlanta": 8; Jensen, "Fifteen Ways the Year-Round School Makes Sense": 12.

56. Anderson, ibid., p. 8; Baker and Johnson, "Another District Experiments with a 45–15 Plan": 23.

57. Rice and Olsen, "Year-Round Education: An Overview," p. 307.

58. Yaffe, "Teaching in a Year-Round School: 15; Joseph Stocker, "45–15—A Great Way to Live," *American Education* 10, 4 (May 1974): 15.

59. Patton and Patton, "A Year-Round Open School Viewed from Within": 522.

60. Adams, "The Extended School Year: A Status Report": 13.

61. Jensen, "Fifteen Ways the Year-Round School Makes Sense": 12.

62. Ibid.

63. Ibid.

64. Paul H. Howe, "Year-round School Makes Good Business Sense, Says This Boardman-Businessman," *American School Board Journal* 160, 2 (February 1973): 47.

65. Anderson, "'Four Quarters' Makes a Whole Year in Atlanta": 8.

66. Quoted in "Work Experience Should Be Year-Round, Too," *Nation's Schools* 88, 5 (November 1971): 56.

67. Ibid.

68. Patton and Patton, "A Year-Round Open School Viewed from Within": 526.

69. Holt, "Year-Round Schools and System Shock": 311.

70. Glines, "12-Month School": 70.

71. Ibid.

72. Ibid., 71–72.

73. Ibid., 73.

74. Ibid.

75. Rice and Olsen, "Year-Round Education: An Overview," p. 306.

76. Ibid.

77. Ibid.

78. Quoted in Adams, "The Extended School Year: A Status Report": 14.

79. Quoted in ibid.

80. Quoted in Yaffe, "Teaching in a Year-Round School": 66.

81. Ibid.

82. Ibid.

83. Richmond and Riegle, "Current Status of the Extended School Year Movement": 491.

84. Stocker, "45–15—A Great Way to Live": 15.

85. Richmond and Riegle, "Current Status of the Extended School Year Movement": 492.

86. Quoted in Adams, "The Extended School Year": 15.

87. Quoted in ibid., 16.

88. Richmond, "Effects of Extended School Year Operation": 394.

89. Ernst, "The Year-Round School: Faddish or Feasible?": 56.

90. Ibid.

91. James Fenwick, "The Extended School Year: Questions to Think About," *NASSP Bulletin* 59, 390 (April 1975): 1.

92. Ibid.

93. Calvin Grinder, "Year-Round Schools Raise Some Key Questions," *Nation's Schools* 90, 4 (October 1972): 18.

94. M. P. Heller and Max A. Bailey, "Year-Round School: Problems and Opportunities," *Clearing House* 49, 8 (April 1976): 363.

95. Alex B. Campbell, "The Year-Round School—Implications for the Music Program," *NASSP Bulletin* 58, 393 (October 1975): 31.

96. Driscoll, "School Around the Calendar": 23.

97. Stocker, "45–15—A Great Way to Live": 12.

98. Anderson, "'Four Quarters' Makes a Whole Year in Atlanta": 8.

99. Quoted in Yaffe, "Teaching in a Year-Round School": 66.

100. Ibid.; Robert G. Ames, "Why Our District Rejected Year-Round-Schools," *Nation's Schools* 84, 6 (December 1969): 94; and Ames, "The Rescheduled School Year," *NEA Research Bulletin* (October 1968): 68.

101. Greg P. Stefanich, "A Year-Round School Plan with Summer Vacation for Everyone," *School and Community* LVII, 6 (February 1971): 14.

102. Stocker, "45–15—A Great Way to Live": 12.

103. Anderson, "'Four Quarters' Makes a Whole Year in Atlanta": 8.

104. Ames, "Why Our District Rejected Year-Round Schools": 94.

105. Heller and Bailey, "Year-Round School: Problems and Opportunities": 364.

106. Holt, "Year-Round Schools and System Shock": 310.

107. Hermanson and Gove, *The Year-Round Schools: The 45–15 Breakthrough,* p. 147.

108. Ernst, "The Year-Round School: Faddish or Feasible?": 56.

109. Rifkin, "How to Make the Switch to Year-Round Schools": 42.

110. Quoted in Stocker, "45–15—A Great Way to Live": 11.
111. Quoted in Jaffe, "Teaching in a Year-Round School": 67.
112. McClain, *Year-Round Education: Economic, Educational and Sociological Factors,* p. 185.
113. Driscoll, "School around the Calendar": 23.
114. Quoted in Stocker, "45–15—A Great Way to Live": 15.
115. N. S. Rifkin, "A Round-Up on Year-Round Schools," *Today's Education* 63, 7 (November–December 1973): 58.
116. Don Glines, "12-Month School," *Instructor* LXXX, 1 (August–September 1970): 73.
117. "Year-Round Schools: Are the Obstacles Too Great?," *Education U.S.A.,* Washington, DC, May 21, 1973, p. 1.
118. Quoted in Adams, "The Extended School Year: A Status Report": 19.

CHAPTER SIXTEEN

School-to-Work

Part I. The Law

The functional curricula, as advanced by life adjustment and the various movements such as vocational education, accountability, performance contracting, and
especially career education, did not slumber long after the temporary demise of
career education. It was, like the phoenix, to rise from its ashes in several forms in
the 1980s and 1990s, most notably, at least for our concerns, in the form of the
School-to-Work movement. The topic is so large that I will treat it in three chapters. The first of these chapters will deal with events leading up to the passage of
the Act in May of 1994 and immediate reactions to it. School-to-work, it will be
seen, can justifiably lay claim as a *bona fide* panacea.

A Nation at Risk and Its Sequel

The nation was greeted in April of 1983 with the threatening admonition that our
schools had made us *A Nation at Risk*. David P. Gardner, the president of the University of Utah, chair of the committee that issued the report, wrote:

> . . . the educational foundations of our society are presently being eroded by a rising tide
> of mediocrity that threatens our very future as a Nation and a people. What was unimag-
> inable a generation ago has begun to occur—others are matching and surpassing our ed-
> ucational attainments.[1]

After being instructed that the world was a "global village," we were informed that
we had lost our worldwide economic supremacy to several countries. The problem was national in scope as well:

The people of the United States need to know that individuals in our society who do not possess the levels of skill, literacy, and training essential to the new era will be effectively disenfranchised, not simply from the material rewards that accompany competent performance, but also from the chance to participate fully in our national life.[2]

A Nation at Risk gave birth, at least indirectly, to a number of movements in education, one of the more noteworthy being the School-to-Work movement.

Pierre S. du Pont IV, Governor of the State of New Jersey, called attention to the plight of youth unemployment in 1985. Du Pont described "Jobs for America's Graduates," a school-to-work transition program that allegedly reduced unemployment, and predicted widespread benefits from implementing such a program:

If young people and their parents, as well as their employers, could count on a school-directed, successful transition into a job after graduation, a new era of public enthusiasm, public resources, and public commitment to education would propel the education system into a new level of prestige, influence and recognition.[3]

Maintaining that such a "program would not be difficult," du Pont cited his "Jobs for America's Graduates" plan as a model, alleging that the results were "Nothing short of startling!"[4]

The cooperation called for between schools and industry in du Pont's scheme was reinforced by James B. Campbell, a member of the board of directors of the United States Chamber of Commerce (USCC), who said in 1985 that "Business and school must work together to help solve some of the problems facing public education."[5] Campbell called attention to the substantial demographic changes that had taken place in the nation, which included a:

. . . dramatic increase in the ratio of older, retired citizens to young workers; the significant increase in minority youth enrollment in public schools, including students from non-English speaking homes, and the fact that women now exceed men in the number of new workers.[6]

He warned that unless "these factors receive immediate attention, the country could face a severe skilled worker shortage in the near future."[7]

Robert Glover and Roy Marshall, writing in 1993, argued that such cooperation was necessary because "America has the worst approach to school-to-work transition of any industrialized nation. Put simply, we have no systematic processes to assist high school graduates to move smoothly from school to employment."[8] Businesses, they maintained, hold teachers and schools accountable; they fear for the nation's international position. Businesses should set standards for schools and promise jobs to graduates who met them, especially after graduation. The federal government should get involved and "build consensus for a high-skills development strategy," with "business and labor representatives" serving as "active participants in that consensus-building strategy."[9] One writer asked "why wait?," and "play Mother, may I?" Rather, she declared:

> If educators really care about the future of *all* our young people, they can start immediately to engage in substantive discussion with their business communities about what schools and workplaces need to become in the next century.[10]

Later in 1993 the Clinton administration presented the school-to-work act to Congress. The act's findings included the statement that "the United States is the only industrialized nation that lacks a comprehensive and coherent system to help its youth acquire knowledge, skills, abilities and information about and access to the labor market necessary to make an effective transition from school to career-oriented work or to further education and training."[11] In March 1994, Robert Lerman, an economics professor at American University, proclaimed in a speech to the American Vocational Association (AVA) that "For me, the goal is to inspire you to move toward new visions of training. For you, I hope the goal is to view yourselves as empowered to build an outstanding school to career system in this country."[12] The proposed legislation, he averred, "does not simply create another program. It is much more ambitious in that it aims to change the mainstream education system that touches nearly all students." This system faced critical problems:

> **Student motivation is central to success, yet we have few incentives for students to perform well in high school.**
> **Young people are poorly informed about occupations.**
> **Schools overemphasize an academic form of learning.**
> **Major employers see youth as too immature for responsible positions.**[13]

Lerman called for the creation of a youth apprenticeship system, like systems that were prevalent in Germany, Denmark and Austria, that would improve "incentives to learn by linking education" to a "clear and achievable occupational path." Such programs would be "especially crucial" for inner-city and minority youth. He asserted that students who participate in apprenticeship programs "are enthusiastic. As they increasingly understand the relationship between their work and their learning, their grades and their skills improve."[14]

The literature in the period immediately prior to the passage of "The School-to-Work Opportunities Act" in May of 1994 contains specific examples of the kind of program Lerman recommended. One such plan was the Pennsylvania Youth Apprenticeship Program. Its director, Jan Wolfe, noted that "We want to teach students English, math and science in a way that can be applied to the workplace."[15] A similar program involved the New England Medical Center in Boston. There, Ed Doherty, president of the Boston Teachers Union, contended that if the operation of this program proved successful, the schools could prove to businesses that "with their help, we can train, educate and prepare students to fill the demand for the jobs of the future."[16]

Vocational education periodicals touted the forthcoming legislation. The AVA's Director of Communications, Paul Plauwin, announced in the March 1994 issue of *Vocational Education Journal* that readers could peruse seven "information-packed articles on School-to-Work Transition, the hot topic in vo-tech education."[17] The solution to the transition problem was across-the-board, cooperative partnerships:

> Employers, in partnership with labor, define the skill requirements for jobs, participate equally in the governance of the program, offer quality learning experiences for the students at the worksites and provide jobs for students and graduates. . . . For school-to-work programs to be successful, all partners must work together to develop curricula that will prepare students to enter and succeed in technologically complex worksites.[18]

Lynn Olson, who wrote regularly for *Education Week* on the subject, and who later would travel the country visiting school-to-work sites and write a book which highly lauded the movement, remarked in January of 1994 that the impending reform would require "a whole new infrastructure that doesn't exist now." She stated that "The real trick, however, will be to move from a handful of isolated programs that don't last to a system that helps move the majority of students from school to work." She posited that in the interim there was "little research to suggest just how well school-to-work programs succeed, whether in raising academic achievement, placing students in jobs, or moving them on to further education and training."[19]

The School-to-Work Opportunities Act and Its Immediate Aftermath

Congress passed The School-to-Work Opportunities Act (STWOA) on May 4, 1994, which President Clinton shortly signed into law. Major findings of the STWOA included that American youth were entering the workforce, especially "disadvantaged students," without necessary skills. Unemployment among this group was high; the workplace was changing due to "heightened international competition and new technologies," and the country lacked a "comprehensive and coherent system" to help its students acquire the necessary knowledge and skills to "make an effective transition from school to career-oriented work or to further education and training."[20] Students, Congress declared, learned better in context, and they would profit from the "time-honored" practice of work-based learning.[21]

The lawmakers wrote that the purposes of the act were to establish a national framework within which states could set up "systems" that would:

- be part of "comprehensive education reform"
- be integrated with the systems developed under Goals 2000 and the National Skills Standards Act of 1994
- use workplaces as "active learning environments" in the educational process by making employers joint partners with educators in providing opportunities for all students to participate in high-quality, work-based learning ventures
- use federal funds as "venture capital" to plan the systems that would be "maintained with other Federal, State, and local resources."[22]

Further, the Act was intended to "promote the formation of local partnerships" of several kinds and to "build on and advance a range of promising school-to-work activities," such as tech-prep, school-to-apprenticeship programs, and cooperative education, to name a few. Improved knowledge and skills of youth would be achieved by "integrating academic and occupational learning, integrating school-based and work-based learning, and building effective linkages between secondary and postsecondary education." Another goal of the act was to motivate all youth to stay in school, including "low-achieving youths, school dropouts, and youths with disabilities."[23] The Act would "expose students to a broad array of career opportunities, and facilitate the selection of career majors, based on individual interests, goals, strengths, and abilities"; finally, it would "increase opportunities for minorities, women, and individuals with disabilities, by enabling individuals to prepare for careers that are not traditional for their race, gender, or disability," and further the "National Education Goals set forth in Title I of the Goals 2000: Educate America Act."[24] Quite an agenda!

The Support of Vocational Educators

Vocational education advocates, who were among the staunchest backers of career education, were equally ardent in their enthusiasm for school-to-work initiatives. In 1994, only a few months after the law's passage, the AVA published a *Guide* to the STWOA. The authors straightforwardly stated their interpretation of the law and envisioned its almost unlimited prospects for reform in their "Introduction":

> The School-to-Work Opportunities Act represents the most meaningful partnership between education and industry ever envisioned by Congress. This far-reaching federal law will enable states and local communities to initiate real education reform that will increase American students' opportunities to pursue postsecondary education and high-skill wage careers.[25]

The authors were delighted to quote Secretary of Education Riley's highlighting of the restructuring of education focus of the act:

We need to reinvent the American school to find a way to catch the attention of . . . young people, to help them get a focus on life a little bit earlier. We cannot continue to sort students into either a college track or a general track that really leads to nowhere in particular.[26]

Michael Brustein and Marty Mahler reiterated Riley's call for the reinvention of America's schools, insisting that such reinvention "is really what the School-to-Work Opportunities Act is all about." Of particular concern, they wrote, was "the forgotten half," who leave American high schools each year "unprepared for further education or for work."[27] The need to create a smooth transition from school to work for all America's youth was compelling, they observed, given the high stakes of what was involved:

Numerous reports have pointed out the inadequacies of our nation's education system and workplace strategies. . . . Today we are on the brink of a major restructuring of our education system, driven by the need to protect our national economic health and our competitive position as a world power.[28]

Rep. Dale Kildee, chairman of the House Elementary, Secondary and Vocational Education Committee, set forth his vision of the goals of the act:

Programs created under this system through broad-based partnerships in states and communities will enable all students to participate in education and training programs that will better prepare them for a first job, enable them to earn portable credentials, and increase their opportunities for meaningful secondary and postsecondary education.[29]

The AVA *Guide* enumerated the three programmatic components for STWOA: a school-based learning component, a work-based learning component, and a connecting activities component, each of which had a subset of activities.[30] The *Guide*'s authors tied the act to Goals 2000 through Title IV of Goals, which required that schools identify "broad clusters of major occupations of the United States and [encourage] and [facilitate] the development of skill standards within these clusters."[31] The key elements of work-based learning were work experience, job training, workplace mentoring, instruction in workplace competencies, and instruction in all aspects of an industry, which was defined as "all characteristics of the industry or industry sector the student is preparing to enter." Workplace mentoring was singled out as especially critical, because the mentor possesses the "skills and knowledge to be mastered by the student."[32]

While school-based learning called for a significant amount of attention, the authors claimed that the "most important element of the STWOA will be the development of connecting activities which provide the common thread" between school-based learning and work-based learning. In their view, the "success or failure of any school-to-work system will hinge on the connection between the two approaches to learning."[33] They identified eight connecting activities:

1. Matching students with employers
2. Establishing liaisons between education and work
3. Providing technical assistance to schools, students, and employers
4. Helping to integrate school-based and work-based learning
5. Encouraging employers to participate
6. Providing help with job placement, continuing education, or further training
7. Collecting and analyzing post-program outcomes
8. Providing links between youth development activities and industry.[34]

Other vocational leaders added their voices to the chorus of reform. Dale Hudelson, writing in October of 1994, stated that 47 percent of high school students were headed for college, 12 percent for vocational programs, and the "remaining 41 percent are headed nowhere certain on the broad 'general education' track."[35] The STWOA "intends to change all that," he averred:

> Its goal is to give every student the opportunity to sign up for a program that provides a clear pathway to a career. The law is designed to help all states create school-to-work transition systems that replace the traditional tracks.
>
> Education reformers hope the school-to-work projects will bring about lasting change in the high schools by encouraging integration of academic and vocational coursework, teaching all aspects of an industry integrating work-based and school-based learning and promoting the formation of partnerships among elementary, middle, secondary and postsecondary schools. In the ideal school-to-work system, all students are expected to meet high academic and occupational standards.[36]

Some saw a tremendous opportunity for vocational education in the recently passed legislation. Cynthia Lyon believed that "Not since the decade after World War II" had vocational-technical education had the "opportunity to be a respected, full participant in the education of America's young people. The school-to-work movement gives us this chance."[37] She urged vocational educators to support the programs:

> As vocational-technical educators we must take advantage of this opportunity by leading all players to the table, to design quality programs that will achieve the school-to-work goals. Now is the time to act. We cannot wait to see what others are doing—we must begin work locally to mold programs appropriate for our own communities.[38]

The time was ripe for such action, Lyon averred, because American society now saw the need for a "seamless system" that moved students from high schools to "high-quality employment and/or postsecondary education." The fact that some educational reform by states exceeded federal requirements was an indication "that business and industry have taken an avid interest in education." Secondary "vocational-technical programs should act as the foundation for the work-based component" of the reforms, she recommended.[39] The key to the "successful blending" of instruction into a "sound school-to-work program is strong career guidance, beginning in elementary school, for all students." Recognizing that the "AVA was influential in the writing of the national school-to-work" legislation, Lyon called on vocational-technical educators to "use that legislation to rally all partners in the development of a truly effective school-to-work system."[40] The law, a fellow vocational writer remarked, was "nothing less than a sweeping reform of secondary education."[41]

The respected educator, W. Norton Grubb, early on posed some penetrating questions about this most recent reform. Addressing the nature of educational reforms, Grubb wrote that:

> . . . with the appeal of novelty, they have entered the lists of changes to be implemented over the next few years. The big question is whether the changes will make much difference in schools and students, or whether in ten years' time they will have vanished, swept aside by different priorities.[42]

Grubb wondered whether three tracks might emerge: a college bound track in which 20 to 25 percent of students participated; a high-quality school-to-work track in which another 20 to 25 percent were enrolled; and an "amorphous curriculum" that would account for between 50 and 60 percent of all students. (This sounds suspiciously close to the proportions advanced in the life adjustment movement.) He posed seven questions that school-to-work programs must confront: 1) How should high schools change in school-to-work programs? 2) What is the vision for the work-based component? 3) What are the "necessary connecting activities" linking the school-based and the work-based components? 4) What students will be included in school-to-work programs? "All?" 5) What is the appropriate role for nonschool programs? 6) What role should assessment play? and 7) What governance mechanism is appropriate for school-to-work programs?[43] Grubb viewed the possibilities as "enormous." But, he warned, they:

> . . . might also end up as work experience programs for a few at-risk students, or as reforms that generate allegiance only as long as federal dollars last—both implying a life expectancy of about five years. The path to true reform is infinitely more attractive—and also much more work.[44]

The Role of Government

Citing President Clinton's record as governor of Arkansas, Paul Cole, the vice-president of the American Federation of Teachers (AFT) predicted in 1993 that there would be "more of an emphasis on apprenticeships and, hopefully, more coordination of these programs on the part of the federal government and related agencies." He pointed to the government's proposal to spend $10 billion on apprenticeship programs over a four-year period in a systematic form so the programs will be "transferable and portable."[45] The assistance of the federal government would be most helpful, said Hilary Pennington, the president of "Jobs for the Future," because that would "insure maximum mobility and opportunity and regulate the standards of quality." Indeed, if the program were to be a national one, "there has to be a federal role."[46]

Clinton's interest extended beyond apprenticeships; he was concerned with "helping more young people move smoothly from education to employment."[47] With broad bipartisan support from Congress, the President's proposal was looked on as an "effective program to prepare young people for successful careers." One cautionary factor was recognized: the lack of incentives for businesses to participate in the partnerships.[48] Yet Senator Paul Simon of Illinois (D), chair of the Senate's Subcommittee on Employment and Productivity, saw easy sailing for the proposal: "We have a panoply of organizations endorsing it—labor, management, education groups—so I think we can move forward very quickly."[49] Rep. William R. Goodling of Pennsylvania (R), who co-sponsored the legislation, spoke about the grade level at which the program would begin. Noting that it focused on Grade 11 and beyond, he remarked that he wanted "to make sure that there's enough flexibility there that we can deal with middle school."[50]

And move forward very quickly they did, with support from the heads of the Departments of Education and Labor, under whose joint administration the bill was to operate. Secretary of Education Riley testified at the congressional hearings that the bill would "help millions of young people to jump-start their careers," many of whom now "just drift through schools." Secretary of Labor Robert B. Reich added that "We have to disenthrall ourselves from the premise that in order to have a good job, you have to have a four-year college degree in this country. That can't be right."[51]

After political compromise in Congress and negotiations that took place within several states, Rep. Kildee assessed the STWOA on its way to passage and a presidential signature as "a very important piece in our whole job-training network that would contribute to a 'seamless process' for training Americans."[52] Government officials were quick to praise the new act. President Clinton described it as "a whole new approach to work and learning," a "small seed" that would "give us quickly a national network of school-to-work programs."[53] Secretary of Education Riley singled out the advantages that would accrue to education; it would turn "dreary classrooms" into "places where learning is enjoyable yet challenging. . . . It offers young people college and careers—not one or the other."[54] Joan L. Wills, director of the Center for Workforce Development at the

Washington-based Institute for Educational Leadership maintained that the bill recognized the changed nature of the workplace in the industrialized nations of the world and the different way to "prepare people for it."[55]

For the bill to prove effective, the cooperation of the states was necessary. The item was a prominent part of the Council of the Chief State School Officers, who met in Columbus in the fall of 1993. These officials acknowledged the necessity for all parties to work together if the bill were to be successful. Christine Kulick, a consultant for the Work Force Policy Associates, a Washington-based firm that received planning grants on the subject from the Department of Labor, opined that "To create a state school-to-work system instead of just a new program, there needs to be an integration with the education-reform efforts of the state."[56]

Brustein and Mahler highlighted the necessity for state and local partnerships to understand the "nuances" of the state's role if they wish to avoid "navigating unchartered waters without a compass."[57] The extremely broad sweep of the STWOA is clearly and forcefully brought out by the number and kind of "Federal Programs to Be Coordinated with STWOA:

> Adult Education Act
> Carl D. Perkins Vocational and Applied Technology Act
> Elementary and Secondary Education Act
> Social Security Act (Part F of Title IV)
> Goals 2000: Educate America Act
> National Skills Standards Act
> Individuals with Disabilities Education Act
> Job Training Partnership Act
> National Apprenticeship Act
> Rehabilitation Act
> National and Community Service Act."[58]

The Doubters

Not everyone climbed aboard the school-to-work bandwagon. There were skeptics, which included some who were favorably inclined to vocational programs. For instance, Wisconsin, under the leadership of Governor Tommy G. Thompson, had developed a comprehensive program. Phil Neuenfeldt, executive director of the Wisconsin Regional Training Partnership, a labor-management group, was one of the doubters: "School-to-Work is a part of a bigger puzzle. Even though it's the sexiest thing in town, it's really not the answer to everything." He continued:

> Are there going to be enough jobs to support school-to-work efforts so there's an actual job at the end of things? I think it's good to work at the supply side, which is what this is, but we'd better start to have some discussions on the demand side soon.[59]

Daphne Muse expressed similar sentiments. While she bemoaned the "attitudes we so often demonstrate toward those who bring the food to the table, build the roads, deliver the paychecks" and supported the idea that high schools should prepare the young for the "spectrum of work sectors," she declared "BUT there must be jobs for them to prepare for."[60]

The coordinator of research for Manpower Demonstration Research Corporation also had doubts. Subsequent to describing the variations of school-to-work programs that existed across the country, Edward Pauly mused that it "remains to be seen whether schools and employers will be able to expand their school-to-work programs to serve large numbers of students with high quality programs nationwide."[61] Hudelson added several other potentially vexing problems. Recruiting businesses would be more difficult because "partnerships will be deciding how participating employers should spend their companies' money"; this would be particularly true "when organized labor is in the picture." Grant money would go to the partnerships; would this lead to union opposition? Would employers drop workers after the grant money was gone?[62]

Some identified other possible "roadblocks." For example, Olson cited the following:

> Lack of information on what others had done, employers' reluctance to provide workplace experiences, parental aversion to enrolling their children in school-to-work programs, and educators' belief that the targeting provision in some federal programs limits the use of those funds for school-to-work initiatives.[63]

Picking up on the supply side, Joan Wills of the Institute for Educational Leadership observed that "We can't talk about going to scale without addressing some of the gaps on the employer-network side." The program would not be successful if its planners and administrators had not "spent the time necessary to think through what that learning person needs to be about at the worksite." She commented that the program cannot be effective "based upon a half-time teacher just waiting for the employer to call the school. And that's basically what we found."[64] Her colleague at the Institute expressed reservations about the lack of coordination among the programs, which "tended to be little islands unto themselves even if the school had several other programs."[65]

The social context in the United States bothered Robert Glover and Alan Weisberg, who compared Europe to the United States:

> At the heart of our concern is the enormous inertia that exists in the United States to maintain educators' dominance in the offering of vocational training for American youths who do not immediately choose four-year colleges as the path to training for work. . . . If there is a single feature that distinguishes our European competitors, it is the industry-driven nature of their training for young people.[66]

Secondary schools in the United States were "plagued by the 'low status' of meeting requirements" for four-year colleges, they averred, and as a consequence the bill "provides no clear incentive for the employers whose cooperation is prerequisite to any serious reform effort." Indeed, the federal initiative might "perpetuate a system which continues to be educator-dominated."[67] These authors wholeheartedly agreed with the old adage that "education is too important to leave solely in the hands of educators," and forecast a dim future for school-to-work programs that followed that adage:

> This is doubly true when we focus on school-to-work transitions. Without the social partners at the table at all levels, state, federal, and local, the school-to-work movement will be educator-driven, market insensitive, and worst of all, not very engaging for the large proportion of young people who are bored in high school and who see very little relationship between what they do in high school and the world outside.[68]

Rather, the nation needed to adopt the European model, in which "Standards, set and recognized by industry, along with industry-wide coordinated examinations, drive education and training . . . in contrast to our 'seat time' approach to certifying young people as competent."[69]

Conclusion

As 1994 came to an end, the nation viewed an educational landscape that was heavily dotted with federal initiatives, one of the chief of which was the STWOA. States and local communities—both schools and businesses—had roles to play in this recently created federal enterprise. Hatched in an era of economic global competition, the STWOA was to become a focal point in the continuing debate over education and its place and role in American society. For some, it would provide the magic tonic that the schools and the country so desperately needed.

Notes

1. David P. Gardner, *A Nation at Risk: The Imperative for Educational Reform*. Washington, DC: United States Department of Education by The National Commission on Excellence in Education, April, 1983, p. 5.
2. Ibid., p. 7.
3. Pierre S. du Pont, IV, "School-to-Work Transition Programs—Are They Needed? What Are Their Benefits?," *NASSP Bulletin* 69, 479 (March 1985): 65.
4. Ibid., 66.
5. Quoted in "Reform at Local and State Levels," *NASSP Bulletin* 69, 479 (March 1985): 69.
6. Ibid.

7. Ibid.
8. Robert W. Glover and Ray Marshall, "Improving the School-to-Work Transition of American Education," *Teachers College Record* 94, 3 (Spring 1993): 588.
9. Ibid., 606–608.
10. Anne C. Lewis, "Why Wait to Improve the School-to-Work Transition?," *Phi Delta Kappan* 74, 7 (March 1993): 508–509.
11. Quoted in Charles H. Buzzzell, "We Can Make It Better," *Vocational Education Journal* 68, 8 (October 1993): 8.
12. Robert I. Lerman, "Reinventing Education: Why We Need the School-to-Work Initiative," *Vocational Education Journal* 69, 3 (March 1994): 20.
13. Ibid., 20–21.
14. Ibid., 21, 45.
15. Quoted in Roger S. Glass, "From School to Work," *American Teacher,* 79, February, 1993, p. 7.
16. Ibid.
17. Paul Plauwin, "Subject of the Year," *Vocational Education Journal* 69, 3 (March 1994): 6.
18. "Why Students Need More Help in Making the Transition from School-to-Work," *Vocational Education Journal* 69, 3 (March 1994): 18–19.
19. Lynn Olson, "Bridging the Gap: The Nation's Haphazard School-to-Work Link Is Getting an Overhaul," *Education Week,* 13, 18, January 26, 1994, p. 26.
20. Public Law 103–239–May 4, 1994, *United States Statutes at Large, 1994.* Part I. Washington, DC: Government Printing Office, 1995, pp. 569–570.
21. Ibid. p. 570.
22. Ibid., pp. 570–571.
23. Ibid., p. 571.
24. Ibid.
25. Michael Brustein and Marty Mahler, *AVA Guide to the School-to-Work Opportunities Act.* Alexandria, VA: American Vocational Association, 1994, p. 3.
26. Ibid., p. 14.
27. Ibid.
28. Ibid., p. 15.
29. Quoted in ibid., p. 24.
30. Ibid., p. 26.
31. Ibid., pp. 26–29.
32. Ibid., pp. 30–31.
33. Ibid., p. 30.
34. Ibid., p. 33.
35. Dale Hudelson, "Getting Off the Tracks," *Vocational Education Journal* 69, 7 (October 1994): 22.
36. Ibid.
37. Cynthia P. Lyon, "Think Globally, Act Locally," *Vocational Education Journal* 69, 7 (October 1994): 6.
38. Ibid.
39. Ibid.
40. Ibid.
41. Ann Dykman, "Let the Reforms Begin," *Vocational Education Journal* 69, 7 (October 1994): 24.
42. W. Norton Grubb, "True Reform or Tired Retread," *Education Week,* 13, 39, August 3, 1994, p. 68.

43. Ibid., pp. 68, 54.

44. Ibid., p. 54.

45. "Apprenticeships: An Advocate in the White House," *American Teacher,* 77, February, 1993, p. 7.

46. Quoted in ibid.

47. Lynn Olson, "President's School to Work Proposal Extends beyond Apprenticeship Focus," *Education Week,* 13, 1, September 8, 1993, p. 35.

48. Ibid., p. 36.

49. Quoted in Lynn Olson, "School-to-Work Proposal Gets Favorable Reception at Capitol Hill Hearings," *Education Week,* 13, 5, October 6, 1993, p. 23.

50. Quoted in ibid.

51. Quoted in ibid.

52. Quoted in Lynn Olson, "Conferees Hammer Out Agreement on School-to-Work Bill," *Education Week,* 13, 30, April 20, 1994, p. 16.

53. Quoted in Lynn Olson, "President Signs School-to-Work Transition Law," *Education Week,* 13, 33, May 11, 1994, p. 1.

54. Quoted in ibid., p. 21.

55. Quoted in ibid.

56. Quoted in Julie A. Miller, "Eyeing Reform, School-to-Work Bills, States Formulate Plans," *Education Week,* 13, 12, November 24, 1993, p. 10.

57. Brustein and Mahler, *AVA Guide to the School-to-Work Opportunities Act,* p. 38.

58. Ibid., p. 46.

59. Quoted in Lynn Olson, "Putting It All Together," *Education Week,* 13, 34, May 18, 1994, pp. 26–29.

60. Daphne Muse, "Grads Who Choose Work Get No Respect," *Vocational Education Journal* 69, 7 (October 1994): 74.

61. Edward Pauly, "Home-Grown Lessons," *Vocational Education Journal* 69, 7 (October 1994): 16, 18, 69.

62. Hudelson, "Getting Off the Tracks": 23.

63. Lynn Olson, "4 States Have School-to-Work Laws Like Clinton Proposal," *Education Week,* 13, 2, September 15, 1993, p. 27.

64. Quoted in Lynn Olson, "Employers in School-to-Work Programs Surveyed, *Education Week,* 13, 23, March 2, 1994, p. 12.

65. Ibid.

66. Robert W. Glover and Alan Weisberg, "America's School-to-Work Transition: The Case of the Missing School Partners," *Education Week,* 13, 26, March 23, 1994, p. 44.

67. Ibid., p. 44, 31.

68. Ibid. . p. 31.

69. Ibid.

CHAPTER SEVENTEEN

School-to-Work

Part II. In the Wake of STWOA

———〜———

The momentum generated by the passage of the STWOA grew in the years immediately following. Maurice Dutton, guest editor of the November/December issue of the *NASSP Bulletin* and director of research and special projects of the Center for Occupational Research and Development in Waco, Texas, put it this way:

> . . . our society expects all students to become productive, employed citizens, and that a high quality educational foundation is essential for those entering the new, high-performance work force.[1]

Two federal initiatives would be instrumental in reaching society's expectations, tech prep and school-to-work, which Dutton held were currently evolving into "Tech Prep/School-to-Work: Career Paths for All Students."[2] Rod Beaumont went further in his laudatory comments about the potential for the two, claiming that we could "look upon the advent of these two strategies as an Educational Renaissance, a rebirth of quality, standards and ability." Together they could, if:

> . . . perceived and implemented correctly by all educators, can be the model, or key to much of the crucially needed educational reform and revolution. Now is the time not for lip service to the business world, but for actions. Until the education system can achieve credibility both within its own ranks as well as outside, all educational reforms are doomed to failure.[3]

Beaumont used the words of Secretary of Education Riley as testimony to the crucial importance of these two reforms: "Our economic prosperity, our national security, and our nation's civic life have never been more linked to education that they are today as we enter the Information Age of the 21st century." Summoning his readers to the starting line, Beaumont urged his readers to action: "We're on the mark. Are you ready yet? Only then can we go!"[4]

The Good to Be Expected

W. Norton Grubb wrote that the changes that must take place, if school-to-work reform was not to "be blown away by the next cycle of revisions" rested in the "institutional structures developed in the past decade," which were potentially "more enduring ways of changing instruction." These included "large numbers of teachers and administrators," so that the changes were not "dependent on one or two." Thus, schools could "develop identities and cultures of their own," which would ensure the permanency of the reforms.[5] Grubb attested to the "enormous potential" these changes had for high schools, including replacing the "shopping mall" school.[6]

Barbara Von Villas, writing in a special issue of the *NASSP Bulletin* devoted to the topic, was ecstatic over the nigh-omnipotent power of the STWOA. She maintained that it would "inevitably change the face of public education." High school guidance counselors would assume additional power and would play a leading role in "preparing students for success in the twenty-first century."[7] Schools, she wrote, "must begin to regard their job as preparing students for life beyond graduation and measure their success as permanent employability at age 25. This will require a culture change in our nation's schools and in the communities that support them." School-to-work's sway extended well before high school, though; Von Villas opined that "career education should begin in kindergarten, and all teachers should be career educators."[8] Like the energy crisis, it had implications "across the curriculum and across society." It would "change our culture forever and move our schools toward improvements that the entire nation will at last recognize and appreciate." The "cultural changes" it would bring about would make it "unacceptable for schools to ignore the needs of business and society." A "preK-12 career education curriculum should be implemented," with particular attention focused on the "changing role of the guidance counselor, who must expand the focus from school success to a transition to the workplace."[9] Indeed, the "success or failure of the local endeavor may rest on how well counselors make the adjustment to their changing role," especially in establishing formal connection with business and industry. She warned us: "It won't come easily."[10]

Several state programs were featured in the *NASSP Bulletin* in the waning months of 1995. One such was Missouri's "A+ School Program." David May, an A+ coordinator, described it as offering "one of the most exciting opportunities to bring out the best in all of our students and teachers."[11] Called forth by the necessity of developing an "internationally competitive work force," the program was mandated to "eliminate the general education track" and put in place a curriculum that embraced the "knowledge, skills and competencies that students must demonstrate to successfully complete individual courses and a career path."[12] Russell McCampbell, Missouri's assistant commissioner for the Department of Elementary and Secondary Education's Division of Vocational and Adult Education, said the program offered the chance to "integrate vocational education with academic instruction in math, science and communication skills" and thereby make "significant progress in these and other reform activities."[13]

Oregon was another state whose reform efforts merited coverage. There the curriculum of the high school was "restructured to eliminate the general education and vocational education tracks and replace them with the tech prep/college prep curriculum and the college prep advanced diploma curriculum."[14] After lauding the benefits of the reform measures, Nancy Hargis closed with the ringing testimonial that "Multiple input has strengthened the program and gained the support of the entire community. And most important, businesses are now interested in hiring our graduates."[15]

Universal, Democratic, and Responsive to a National Need

Writing in 1995, Maurice Dutton asked "Can we be doing *both* a better and a worse job at the same time?" He answered his own question with a conditional affirmative:

> If we are improving our ability to prepare students to succeed in the disappearing industrial society and are not adequately preparing them for the emerging technological/information age, the answer to these questions is yes![16]

The purpose of public education, he theorized, was to "prepare students with the knowledge, skills, and competencies they need to be successful." There were two "driving forces" that had shaped the school-to-work reform movement: 1) the drive to "ensure that all students are provided a first-class, quality education," and 2) the drive to prepare them for "productive careers." School-to-work legislation, which rested on tech prep, had three "core elements" that enabled it to meet the changing needs of American society: 1) *School-based learning,* which integrated work and school-based learning and was founded on high academic and occupational skill standards; 2) *Work-based learning,* which consisted of work experience, structure training, and mentoring at job sites; and 3) *Connecting activities,* which

252 The Impossible Dream

built bridges between school and work, such as matching students with participating employers.[17]

Employers expected schools to "turn out young people who have essential skills," Ann Lewis remarked. The K-12 system was "*the* place to develop these skills, and thereby prepare for the legitimate economy," for the "nearly 75% of young people who never receive a four-year college degree."[18] More was at stake than businesses and the young, she averred: "In these times educators who don't believe in success at higher levels for all their students may be pushing young people toward a future that will be bleak for all of us."[19] One writer commented that the industrial world had changed; schools must prepare the young for the "wave of the future." Touting programs such as "What's Up in Factories?," he observed that:

> Recurring throughout the comments of teachers and students is recognition of the importance in the workplace of such qualities as a willingness to take responsibility, punctuality, cooperation, effective communication, and inquiry. Students were also surprised at the type of skills needed to work in manufacturing, like mathematics and computer literacy. School-to-work programs like "What's Up in Factories?" not only show students the importance of what they're learning in the classroom, but give them the opportunities to explore possible careers.[20]

The lessons learned in school-to-work ventures were not limited to traditional vocational students; rather, they applied to "all students, kindergarten through college, as well as out-of-school youth." Dutton remarked that the necessity of having "career paths for all students" was becoming widely acknowledged: many college prep students and their parents have begun to see the "value in applied academic careers and career planning, and have demanded" that college prep students also be "given these opportunities."[21]

J. D. Hoye, the director of the federal National School-to-Work office supplied explanations of how the three basic components of school-to-work programs would not only transform the school curriculum, but also were aimed to have impact "kindergarten through life."[22] School-to-work, he explained, was "clearly defined as a national investment." States and local districts needed to "invest additional capital to bring their work force preparation system up to the level of proficiency that provides access to all students." School-to-work was a "total development system." It had gone "beyond reform" and was transforming secondary schools; it represented a "fundamental shift in our educational structure."[23]

The nation was in dire needed of the kind of reform school-to-work programs provided, Hargis explained:

> As the twenty-first century nears, the role of education in the U.S. society has never been more crucial or under more pressure. Public schools are being asked to deliver much more than the traditional "three R's," and their capacities are stretched beyond their limits.[24]

In fact, she proclaimed, *"Yesterday's education will not produce the academic results we want today,"* because:

> Yesterday's education will not provide economic security tomorrow. Technology is changing the way we live and work. We bank by machine, buy groceries with credit cards, and check out library books by computer. . . . Highly paid jobs are going to people who can adapt to fast-paced technological change, solve problems, design strategies, and motivate co-workers. The foundation for such highly skilled employees is a rigorous, relevant education.[25]

It was left to James Hoerner and James Wehrley to provide the climax for the need of a relevant education, one which the current system had no hope of furnishing. It didn't take long for them to set forth their basic premises. Writing in the "Preface" to their book, *Work-Based Learning: The Key to School-to-Work Transition,* they thundered, "We begin our discussion by raising suspicions about societies that maintain education systems which nurture knowledge acquisition at the exclusion of knowledge application." The United States was obviously one of these, in their view:

> However, with many students protesting the lack of relevance in their schooling, parents questioning what they are paying for, and larger numbers of our youth not being prepared for employment, the current pattern of schooling is encountering more and more criticism.[26]

Hoerner and Wehrley had the solution: the development of:

> . . . an educational system that is career oriented and emphasizes work-based learning—*the* knowledge/learning imparted to every student from the beginning of schooling which maintains a theme or focus that people work to live and that there is a positive connectedness between the schooling process and living productive lives.[27]

They had no doubts whatsoever about what was needed: "changing the educational system for *all* students. . . . Make no mistake, we are talking about a change from kindergarten through postsecondary education."[28]

The closing pages of their book clarified their position: "It is time to get rid of the antiquated, content-based, classicist schooling process that is unconnected to the real world."[29] They expressed their perplexity at the "continuing complacency and resistance among educators to change, especially since there is a growing dissatisfaction in the educational system throughout society at large." They plaintively and rhetorically asked, "Why do most educators feel they can continue to operate our educational system unconnected to the real world!"[30] (There it is again—the clincher—the appeal to the "real world" for verification.) Moving into the field of human psychology, they lamented that "There is something about human nature that requires hitting rock bottom before change can occur. We ask: When will we believe education has hit rock bottom?"[31] Recognizing that the changes they endorsed were "no less than monumental," they concluded their tome with the following:

> So we have come full circle. . . . Societies maintaining educational systems that nurture knowledge acquisition at the exclusion of knowledge application will soon find both their ideologies and technologies eroding.[32]

A parallel message, one not laden with as much emotion, was presented by Edward Pauly, Hilary Kopp, and Joshua Haimson:

> It is now undeniably clear that many students in the United States need help making the transition from high school to postsecondary learning opportunities and to meaningful, productive, skilled work. State and federal policy makers recognize this, educators recognize it, and so does the general public.[33]

Unless schools reformed and future workers were better prepared, employers would need to "dumb down" jobs. Were this to happen, not only the individuals involved but also the nation would suffer in the "global marketplace," and the country would be unable to compete on the international scene. The situation was grim, indeed: "One does not need to read the experts' reports to realize that many young people need more and better preparation for their lives in the labor force."[34]

Finding a solution to the gap between school and work had reached crisis proportions at the national level, Donald Maxwell declared:

> Currently, those American students who fall off the "college-bound express," or never got on board in the first place, are, for the most part, left to wander unassisted across a wasteland of mediocre academic standards, ending eventually in a low-wage job. This is a national disgrace, and if it were a defense issue, we would fix it immediately. It is urgent that we find a solution to this national crisis immediately. . . . If we want to maintain our place in the world and a high standard of living, then we must make education count for *all* of our students.[35]

What was needed, Gabrielle Wacker wrote, was an all-encompassing system that included all educational personnel. For instance, she asked:

> Are all teachers serving as front-line resources so that, as questions arise in the classroom, they can provide students with accurate information on careers, employment skills, and application of curriculum to students' career needs?[36]

Principals were called on to "ensure that career development infuses the entire school curriculum." Utilization of a program such as "Career Pathways for All Students" would serve as "the most common organizer for career development through tech prep/school-to-work" because it was a "planned sequence of study beginning in elementary school and continuing through postsecondary education that prepares all students for productive career in a technological society."[37] Principals could meet their obligations relative to the STWOA of 1994 by seeing that the following challenges were met:

- All students will develop a realistic sense of self and of the world around them, including options for work.
- All students will self-determine tentative educational and occupational goals.
- All students will participate in job shadowing opportunities based on their interests and career goals.
- All students will use their goals to influence educational planning.[38]

Wacker concluded her assessment of the ways in which the STWOA should be implemented in schools with an admonition about career development through curriculum integration:

> Career development must be curriculum based so students will experience coherent learning activities that help them make informed life and work decisions that complement their career pathway. Curriculum integration should stem from common courses, units, and concepts within career pathways.[39]

The United States was hampered by the lack of a formal system that covered the transition from school-to-work. Instead, the country had a "mosaic of programs designed to make the connection between school and work."[40] Ivan Charner et al. reported that a study conducted on fourteen existing programs, although it had not located a "single path" as the "right way," nonetheless did identify ten key elements of successful programs. These were: 1) *Administrative Leadership;* 2) *Commitment of program deliverers;* 3) *Cross-sector collaboration;* 4) *Fostering self-determination in all students;* 5) *School-based learning;* 6) *Work-based learning;* 7) *Integration of career information and guidance;* 8) *Building a progressive system that starts before grade 11;* 9) *Ensuring access to postsecondary options;* and 10) *Creative financing.*[41]

Black argued that most "high schools do an outstanding job of preparing students for college, working with special needs students, and providing young people with the basics of reading, writing, and arithmetic." They fell short, however, when it came to preparing them for the world of work. Students, he proclaimed, "must understand that they will be selecting a career major when they enter high school," in order that they could "learn skills that will enable them to become productive citizens and lead a fulfilling life."[42] Charner et al. contended that high school was not early enough to begin the systematic program that was essential.

"Feeder programs," which expose young people to a range of career opportunities, such as "summer internships, job shadowing, and career exploration workshops" should begin in middle school, if they were to be effective.[43]

Partners—Government, Business, and Education

The federal government, which passed the STWOA in May of 1994, was to play a crucial role in school-to-work programs. This role was necessary, some believed, not only because of the benefit to the national economy that would follow, but also because of the nation's hope for continued international leadership. Marshall Smith and Brent Scoll, employees of the Department of Education, wrote in the spring of 1995 that "The Clinton human capital agenda focused on efforts to ensure the future strength of America's economy, as well as its democracy, by investing in education and training for the American people."[44] The joint supervision by the departments of Education and Labor would "help establish in the U.S. a system comparable to that existing in most other economically advanced countries—a challenging and vigorous curriculum option geared to preparing students for the work place."[45] They called attention to an important change in the federal role in education, witnessed earlier by the Elementary and Secondary Education Act and Goals 2000. The STWOA:

> . . . continues the federal government's efforts to protect and promote equality of educational opportunity by focusing the bulk of federal resources on the most needy students.
> . . . programs also attempt to focus on generating overall quality by promoting challenging standards of teaching and learning for all children.[46]

Olson reported that the Clinton administration had proclaimed school-to-work a "success story in progress" in 1996; Secretary of Education Riley had declared that the movement was "real, and it's on the road to success, and it's having a great impact on America."[47] Olson reported that in the twenty-eight months since the Act had been passed, students in 1,800 high schools had participated in "high intensity" activities; about 135,000 employees in ten states had taken part in 210 local partnerships; and more than 39,000 work-based learning sites and nearly 53,000 slots for students had been established.[48]

Not all of the states had cooperated, however. Five states did not turn in their applications; according to Andrew Trotter, this decision isolated them. Non-participation was seen as a consequence of the influence of conservative people who characterized school-to-work programs as "socialist" and a form of "centralized planning."[49] The federal government would spend some $304 million in grants to states and localities by the end of 1996. Some state directors said that the infusion of federal money had a limited effect because many groups did not grasp the basic school-to-work principles and thus erred in their use of the federal dollars.[50]

Congress had not been fully cooperative either. In 1995, the House of Representatives had cut support for tech prep by millions, which was just the reverse of giving "increasing attention" to this vital area, complained Eugenia Porter. She quoted Timothy J. Dwyer, executive director of the NASSP, who said that such an action showed that the "House of Representatives had gone totally mad."[51]

School-to-work backers considered partnerships between the schools, government (at the federal, state and local levels), and business (sometimes labor was included) as indispensable if they were to achieve their lofty objectives. As early as 1994, members of the leading corporate executives formed a group to involve the country's business firms in school-to-work programs. Members of the National Employment Leadership Council were ready to meet with Department of Education and Labor officials. They earned the praise of President Clinton: "The commitment these CEOs and their companies are making is a significant step toward increasing opportunities for students in every part of our nation."[52] Vocational educators were quick to extend the hand of cooperation to businesses. The "integration" model developed by the National Center for Research in Vocational Education, for instance, was created to respond to "what business expects of employees," and suggested reform in three areas:

> Schools should better align the content of student learning with what they will need to work.
> Schools should encourage more teamwork and decentralization to reflect the work environment.
> Schools should improve relationships with employers.[53]

The assistant superintendent of the St. Charles, Missouri school district, John Urkevich, expressed how the need for partnerships would become more pressing by the early twenty-first century:

> The U.S. Department of Labor predicts that by the year 2010, 20 percent of our jobs will require a four-year college education, 75 percent will require technological skills and some specialized training beyond high school, and only 5 percent will require no specialized training. We're trying to eliminate the general courses and educate our students about where the needs will exist. . . . It is imperative that schools, businesses, and the community work together more closely in preparing children for what comes after high school.[54]

Daisy Stewart took a broader view. She urged that vocational educators take the lead and "work with our education colleagues, business and industry representatives, families, and community leaders to develop state and local policies that continue this new emphasis." She singled out families as one group whose influence vocational educators needed to become more aware of.[55]

One curriculum program that was developed to reach these goals was called "Career Pathways." It was described as being "only as strong as the partnerships among the area education agency, local education agencies, students, parents, community colleges and businesses" would make it. The school-to-work curriculum was made possible by coordination among "business and industry, secondary and post-secondary schools, and business agencies."[56] Hargis reported on Oregon's comprehensive career education system that "began in kindergarten and extends through grade 12." It featured career awareness in the primary grades; career exploration, which began in seventh grade; career preparation, which started in the ninth grade, and included "materials from the workplace readiness course"; enrollment in a career cluster in the tenth grade; career preparation in the eleventh grade; and during the twelfth grade completing the "secondary course in their specialty area and conduct a career/college preview appropriate for their chosen goals."[57] She singled out for praise the Dothan City, Oregon School System and the Chamber of Commerce for their initiative in searching for national "models of schooling that focused on meeting the needs of the workplace articulated toward advanced training, and providing a degree of employability upon graduation from high school." She described the search as follows:

> A group of chamber of commerce members, public school and college administrators, and state department of education representatives gathered data, defined issues, and made specific recommendations that were accepted by the chamber of commerce, city commissions, local school board and local colleges.[58]

Work-based learning was an essential ingredient of the program, because it invigorated the "kind of student the Germans call 'school-weary.'" These students discover, Stephen and Mary Agnes Hamilton argued, that they can "learn and perform" well, and have improved "motivation," after "seeing the application" of the subject in the "real world."[59] The injection of work-based learning, possible only through the use of partners, made the transition from school-to-work achievable. The burden of accomplishing this resided mainly with the high schools:

1. High schools must make employment assistance part of the job.
2. High schools must provide time in the teacher's paid workday to do this.
3. High schools must provide some incentives for teachers to do this.
4. Teachers must build personal relationships of trust with employers, determine their needs, and design curricula and student evaluations that reflect those needs, in order to match recruits and employers and provide dependable evaluations for the employers who will hire their graduates.[60]

Stern and colleagues wrote that the transition from school-to-work "seldom means an abrupt transition from full-time schooling to full-time employment"; it usually took several years. A successful school-to-work program would enable young people to "master the process of learning while they work."[61] This was essential in a fast-changing economy, the authors felt. But a successful program would also require the collaborative work of many people and agencies.

Opposition

As could be expected, the school-to-work "reform" movement met with some queries, obstacles, and conflict. Pauly et al., after studying sixteen programs nationally, felt that the future of school-to-work would be determined by answers to the following three questions: 1) Will classrooms become a dynamic learning environment for a broad range of students?, 2) Will employers come forward in large numbers to share in the training of young people?, and 3) Will students commit themselves to becoming more engaged in school and achieving academic and occupational mastery?[62] Susan Goldberger and Richard Kazis saw a different potentially powerful block, viz., the promotion of reform by "outsiders," which had prompted some widespread, formidable resistance from within the educational community:

> Teachers of academic disciplines fear that moving toward a more applied, project-based curriculum and having students spend significant time outside the classroom will make it impossible to cover the required curriculum. Many within the vocational education community see a threat to their jobs and fear that they will be asked to add academic rigor to their courses that goes beyond their training. Some administrators are concerned about spending scarce time and resources on "boutique" programs that do not help them achieve their primary goal of creating a schoolwide environment conducive to high-quality learning.[63]

These authors also recognized that the question of balance needed to be addressed: "The central dilemma in the design of a school-to-career system in the United States is how to balance the education and employment goals of career-oriented schooling." It was, they believed, a question of achieving balance between "educational and labor-market goals."[64]

James Gregson also recommended balance. But the balance he wrote of urged espousal of democratic principles in implementing school-to-work programs. He recognized not only that consideration "*should*" but "*must*" be given to the needs of industry but also that there should be as much "concern with meeting the needs of students, parents, and communities" as with "meeting the needs of industry."[65]

Some felt that the implementation of a federal system in the United States simply would not work because of the "varied goals and circumstances of different communities and the deeply rooted traditions of local school governance."[66] Pauly, Kopp, and Haimson expressed concern that higher educational institutions might not accept school-to-work credits for admission, and advocates wanted to get assurance that "state-funded programs" did not exclude students who participated in these programs.[67] Eva West, director of the Milwaukee public schools' school-to-work program, wondered if employers might balk at hiring inner-city youth and hinder the reform effort.[68] Hargis pointed to barriers identified by a collaborative Oregon group that had determined the "need for change in the schools and the workplace," and had come up with school-to-work as the answer. These were: fragmented curricula that students were expected to integrate and somehow make fit together, high expectations for some students and low expectations for others, watered-down content in some courses to accommodate low expectations, school leaders and teachers who did not think the current system needed to be changed, and staff and students who saw no connection between school and work.[69]

Conservative groups were said to be in the forefront of opposition to school-to-work programs. Even Miss America, Shawntel Smith, became involved in the swirling controversy. Subsequent to her having chosen school-to-work as her "platform issue," secretaries Riley and Reich praised her as an "ambassador to youth."[70] But a Republican senator from her home state of Oklahoma, James M. Inhofe, asked her to stop giving the impression that she supported one of the Clinton administration's educational initiatives, school-to-work. She should "avoid cheerleading," as she travelled the nation, he said, especially for a "Hillary Clinton issue."[71]

There was other opposition to the program as well. Frank M. Keating, governor of Oklahoma, maintained that by accepting federal funds for school-to-work programs a state would be "buying into a system that emphasizes centralized economic planning." If a state were to do this, it would create "by accident, the European model where my 16-year-old son is a 'soon to be' riveter."[72] Conservatives in other states expressed their disagreement with the programs. In New Hampshire, some argued that the federal program was an invasion of the state's authority. Phyllis Schlafly, founder of the Eagle Forum, linked the program to outcomes-based education. Both, she averred, were attempts by the federal government to impose national standards on state and local governments. The result would be a "third-world education to accustom Americans to third-world wages."[73]

Dani Hansen, state chairwoman of the Idaho Citizens for Quality Education and chairwoman of Idaho's affiliate of the Eagle Forum criticized what she thought were exaggerated claims put forth on behalf of school-to-work. Under the heading of "No Wonder Johnny Can't Read," she charged that advocates of this "federal program claim that it is the remedy for all of society's ills, from poor citizenship and lazy or illiterate workers to spoiled and undisciplined children."

The much-ballyhooed success stories were really "smoke and mirrors," consisting only of:

> . . . anecdotes of short-term projects, not stories of the long-term impact such programs have had on participants' job placement and success. There is absolutely no evidence that school-to-work programs successfully prepare all schoolchildren to make significant—or even adequate—contributions to the workplace.[74]

Hansen asked, "Do we want our federal money going to an educational quick fix that has yet to be evaluated?" Assuming a negative response, she worried that the "reins of control" were "slipping away from the schools and teachers." As a consequence, teachers were "losing control" of how they spent their time in the classroom. "Most important, they are losing the creativity and authority to determine what the students need to know to progress and succeed."[75]

Gary Clabaugh took the President, Congress, and Miss America to task in a stinging attack on school-to-work as a needless rip-off of the taxpayers:

> This year it looks as though education and captains of industry will once again divvy up taxpayers' dollars to fund school-to-work initiatives. By happy coincidence, Shawntel Smith's 1996 Miss America "platform" also was school-to-work education. Despite Clinton's, Congress', and Miss America's endorsements, however, the School-to-Work Opportunities Act is a federal boondoggle of majestic proportions. Why? Because schooling is already *too* successful in preparing students for "seamless" transition to the world of work.[76]

Schooling, he held, was currently "eerily effective" in getting the young ready for whatever "the world" demands. It accustomed them to meaningless platitudes, being treated like "chattel," and "massive merger layoffs," which were far from being "aberrations" or "deviations." Workers could look forward to the following inhumane treatment at the hands of corporate America:

> After spending the best years of their lives working for a corporation, are employees astonished to find themselves on the street and out of luck so the company president can pocket $10 million extra? Not if they attended a typical school-as-factory they aren't. They have already learned (by living) that their humanity doesn't count.[77]

Gerald Bracey saw more than a little hypocrisy in claims made by school-to-work zealots. He saw the movement as a "distressing indicator of the increasing corporate control of education," which was accompanied by the surrender of legitimate authority on the part of the government "long ago." He quoted Alan Wurtzel, chairman of the board of Circuit City who said that his firm was "looking for people who are able to provide very high levels of customer service, who are honest, and who have a positive, enthusiastic, achievement-oriented work ethic."[78] Bracey noted that Wurtzel didn't say anything about the $4.25 per hour pay, which was the minimum wage, that his firm paid the warehouse staff, nor did he comment about his sales staff which was compensated solely on commission. Schools, Bracey averred, were preparing people for work in a way that "reveals a massive triumph of propaganda and conditioning that would make both Pavlov and B. F. Skinner beam." They ignored the fact that much of work is "ugly, hard, demeaning, and dangerous." Surveys, he claimed:

> . . . have repeatedly found that most jobs are dull and boring with no intrinsic meaning. Should schools collude in the preparation of students to endure the boredom of meaningless, small, repetitive, dull, unhealthy tasks?. . . The alliance between business and schools is itself an alliance made in hell.[79]

The view that employers wanted schools to make the young "critical thinkers" was both "ludicrous and hypocritical." Critical thinkers, after all, would "challenge the idiotic rules laid down by businesses." Corporations wanted the schools to condition students to be docile, to not question the reality that while "productivity is rising, wages are falling."[80] What the country needed, Bracey argued, was the kind of civic education Jefferson had recommended, one that would call for a liberal education that would prepare students to "live rich, generous lives in the hours they are free from work." They could be trained for jobs after they finished their formal schooling. Bracey aligned himself with Israel Sheffler who defined education as:

> . . . the formation of habits of judgment and the development of character, the elevation of standards, the facilitation of understanding, the development of taste and discrimination, the stimulation of curiosity and wondering, the fostering of style and a sense of beauty, the growth of a thirst for new ideas and visions of the yet unknown.[81]

School-to-work was anything but this!

Conclusion

A little more than two years after its passage, the STWOA had become a lightning rod for conflict, not only on issues such as the relative importance of economic and political affairs but also on matters that involved fundamental positions on the respective rights and roles of the various levels of government and those of parents and families in schooling. Its backers insisted that it was a cure-all, not only for the schools but also for American society. Its critics argued that its implementation would sound the death knell for what "education" really was. The tensions generated by the STWOA and its interpretations were to dominate the debate over the proposed reforms in the last years of the twentieth century.

Notes

1. Maurice Dutton, "Introduction: Preparing All Students for Careers," *NASSP Bulletin* 79, 574 (November 1995): 1–2.
2. Ibid.
3. Rod Beaumont, "Tech Prep and School to Work: Working Together to Foster Educational Reform," *The High School Journal* 79, 1 (December 1995/January 1996): 107.
4. Ibid., 112.
5. Grubb, "The New Vocationalism: What It Is, What It Could Be," *Phi Delta Kappan* 77, 8 (April 1996): 545.
6. Ibid., 546.
7. Barbara A. Von Villas, "The Changing Role of High School Guidance: Career Counseling and School-to-Work," *NASSP Bulletin* 79, 573 (October 1995): 81.
8. Ibid., 82.
9. Ibid., 83–85.
10. Ibid., 86–87.
11. Quoted in Robert A. Robison, "Missouri's A+ School Program: Providing Quality Education for All Students," *NASSP Bulletin* 79, 574 (November 1995): 26.
12. Ibid., 28, 31.
13. Quoted in ibid., 31.
14. Nancy Hargis, "Oregon's Educational Act for the Twenty-First Century: Planning for the Long Term," *NASSP Bulletin* 79, 575 (December 1995): 31.
15. Ibid., 33.
16. Maurice Dutton, "The Evolution of Tech Prep/School-to-Work: Career Paths for *All* Students," *NASSP Bulletin* 79, 574 (November 1995): 3.
17. Ibid., 4–7.
18. Anne C. Lewis, "Washington Commentary: Schools and Preparation for Work," *Phi Delta Kappan* 76, 9 (May 1995): 660.
19. Ibid., 661.
20. Robert A. Miller, "What's Up in Factories?," *Educational Leadership* 33, 8 (May 1996): 32.
21. Dutton, "The Evolution of Tech Prep/School-to-Work: Career Paths for *All* Students": 10–11.
22. "An Interview with J. D. Hoye, Director of the Federal National School-to-Work Office," *NASSP Bulletin* 79, 575 (December 1995): 18.
23. Ibid., 19–20.
24. Hargis, "Oregon's Educational Act for the Twenty-First Century: Planning for the Long Term": 21.
25. Ibid., 22.
26. James L. Hoerner and James B. Wehrley, *Work-Based Learning: The Key to School-to-Work Transition*. Westerville, OH: Glencoe/McGraw-Hill, 1995, p. xiii.
27. Ibid.
28. Ibid., p. xiv.
29. Ibid., p. 119.
30. Ibid.
31. Ibid.
32. Ibid., p. 121.
33. Edward Pauly, Hilary Kopp, and Joshua Haimson, *Homegrown Lessons: Innovative Programs Linking School and Work*. San Francisco: Jossey-Bass, 1995, p. 1.
34. Ibid., pp. xv, 2.

35. Donald Maxwell, "Lessons Campaign Can Rally the Community behind Reforms That Work," *American Teacher,* 80, April, 1996, p. 7.
36. Gabrielle Banick Wacker, "Enhancing Career Development for All Students Through Tech Prep/School-to-Work," *NASSP Bulletin* 79, 575 (December 1995): 1.
37. Ibid., 2, 4.
38. Ibid., 5.
39. Ibid., 8.
40. Ivan Charner, Bryna Shore Fraser, Susan Hubbard, Anne Rogers and Richard Horne, "Reforms of the School-to-Work Transition," *Phi Delta Kappan* 77, 1 (September 1995): 40.
41. Ibid., 58–59.
42. Karl Black, "Tech Prep/School-to-Work: Preparing Students for Life Beyond High School," *NASSP Bulletin* 79, 575 (December 1995): 11–13.
43. Charner, et al., "Reforms of the School-to-Work Transition": 59.
44. Marshall S. Smith and Brent W. Scoll, "The Clinton Human Capital Agenda," *Teachers College Record* 96, 3 (Spring 1995): 389.
45. Ibid., 400.
46. Ibid., 401.
47. Lynn Olson, "Report Declares School-to-Work Program on 'Road to Success'," *Education Week,* 16, 4 September 25, 1996, p. 28.
48. Ibid.
49. Andrew Trotter, "Practical Issues Hamper School-to-Work Applicants," *Education Week,* 16, 13, November 27, 1996, p. 16.
50. Olson, "Report Declares School-to-Work Program on 'Road to Success'," p. 28.
51. Eugenia Cooper Porter, "This Month," *NASSP Bulletin* 79, 575 (December 1995): 1.
52. Quoted in Lynn Olson, "Leading Business Executives Create Council to Promote School-to-Work Programs," *Education Week,* 14, 15, December 14, 1994, p. 19.
53. "Bridging the Gap Between School and Work," *NASSP Bulletin* 79, 574 (November 1995): 2.
54. Robison, "Missouri's A+ School Program: Providing Quality Education for All Students": 32.
55. Daisy L. Stewart, "A Reaction to Way and Rossman's Family Contributions to Adolescent Readiness for School-to-Work Transition," *Journal of Vocational Education Research* 21, 2 (1996): 49–50.
56. Dennis L. Adkisson and Steven Lane, "Tech Prep + School-to-Work = Career Pathways," *NASSP Bulletin* 79, 574 (November 1995): 34–35.
57. Hargis, "Oregon's Educational Act for the Twenty-First Century: Planning for the Long Term": 31–33.
58. Ibid., p. 28.
59. Stephen F. Hamilton and Mary Agnes Hamilton, "When Is Learning Work-Based?," *Phi Delta Kappan* 78, 9 (May 1997): 681.
60. James E. Rosenbaum and Stephanie Alter Jones, "Creating Linkages in the High School-to-Work Transition: Vocational Teachers' Networks," in Maureen T. Hallinan, ed., *Restructuring Schools: Promising Practices and Policies.* New York: Plenum Press, 1995, p. 255.
61. David Stern, Neal Finkelstein, James R. Stone III, John Latting, and Carolyn Dornsife, *School to Work: Research on Programs in the United States.* London: Falmer Press, 1995, p. 129.
62. Edward Pauly, Hilary Kopp, and Joshua Haimson, *Homegrown Lessons: Innovative Programs Linking School and Work.* San Francisco: Jossey-Bass, 1995, p. 259.
63. Susan Goldberger and Richard Kazis, "Revitalizing High Schools: What the School-to-Career Movement Can Contribute," *Phi Delta Kappan* 77, 8 (April 1996): 547.
64. Ibid., 554.

65. James A. Gregson, "The School-to-Work Movement and Youth Apprenticeship in the U.S.: Educational Reform and Democratic Renewal," *Journal of Industrial Teacher Education* 33, 3 (1995): 22.

66. Pauly, Kopp, and Haimson, *Homegrown Lessons: Innovative Programs Linking School and Work,* p. 32.

67. Ibid., pp. 247–248.

68. Peter West, "'Translators' Seen Needed to Ease Transition to Jobs," *Education Week* 15, 15, December 13, 1995, p. 3.

69. Hargis, "Oregon's Educational Act for the Twenty-First Century: Planning for the Long Term": 28–30.

70. Peter Schmidt, "Miss America Reiterates Support for Federal Program," *Education Week,* 15, 7, October 25, 1995, p. 22.

71. Peter Schmidt, "Miss America's Platform Ruffles Partisan Feathers," *Education Week,* 15, 6, October 11, 1995, p. 20.

72. Quoted in Peter West, "Okla. Officials Debate School-to Work Oversight," *Education Week,* 15, 35, May 22, 1996, p. 18.

73. Quoted in Peter West, "N.H. Critics Target Federal Voc-Ed Funds," *Education Week,* 15, 6, October 11, 1995, p. 14.

74. Quoted in "Working and Learning," *Education Week,* 15, 32, May 1, 1996, p. 34.

75. Ibid.

76. Gary K. Clabaugh, "School-to-Work: Razing Miss America's Platform," *Educational Horizons* 74, 1 (Fall 1995): 6.

77. Ibid., 7.

78. Gerald W. Bracey, "Schools Should *Not* Prepare Students for Work," *NASSP Bulletin* 80, 581 (September 1996): 109.

79. Ibid., 109–110.

80. Ibid., 110–111.

81. Israel Sheffler, quoted in ibid., 111–112.

CHAPTER EIGHTEEN

School-to-Work

Part III. 1997–1999: The Later Years

The momentum that had been generated around and by the school-to-work movement continued unabated in the last years of the twentieth century. As the force that propelled it grew stronger, though, so did the opposition. Questions became more pointed about what would happen when the federal financial support would end on October 1, 2001, or "sunset," as the educationese jargon would have it.

Its Purpose, Benefits and Need

Richard W. Riley and Alexis M. Herman, the Secretaries of the Departments of Education and Labor respectively, reported to Congress on the implementation of the STWOA in September of 1997. They characterized the law as the "cornerstone of an ambitious national initiative to encourage States and local communities to change how they educate students." The initiative was a "systemic education reform that offers students the way experts say they learn best—through application of rigorous academics," the cabinet officials declared.[1] They cited the following statistics as documentation of their assertion that the law had borne fruit. Partnerships had increased from 294 in eleven states at the end of December, 1995 to 932 in forty-one states and Puerto Rico by the end of June 1996. Between January 1, 1996, and June 30, 1996, approximately one out of every thirteen high school students had participated in a program. Twenty-three percent of elementary and secondary schools in the nation offered at least one component of STW as of June 30, 1996. Two percent of high school students participated in *comprehensive* STW activities, i.e., a career major with integrated curricula and paid or unpaid work experience linked to school. The number of business firms participating in STW initiatives had grown from 135,000 to 200,000 in that six-month period.[2] Prior to listing eight challenges that they saw lay ahead, the secretaries wrote positively to Vice-President Gore and Speaker Gingrich that their assessment of the STW program:

> . . . continues to be that the school-to-work effort shows promising signs of achieving the Congress' objective. To date, thirty-seven States and more than 1,000 communities have been funded for implementation and are putting in place the school and work-based components of school-to-work.[3]

Adria Steinberg alleged that the need for school-to work programs was pressing, because students' commitment to school was at an all-time low. School-to-work made the notion of schooling as a "passive activity" irrelevant by getting students involved, and hence interested, through connecting them with the "real world." Like many other advocates, Steinberg provided as anecdotal evidence of this success that she had witnessed a new teacher of biology who had worked hard on developing his lesson plans but was greeted by an indifferent student who had met her eyes with the expression of "as if I care."[4] School-to-work would change all this!

Barbara Hopkins, Darl Naumann, and Frederick Wenzel focused on the law's purpose in contemporary society:

> The purpose of the federal legislation that created School-to Work or School-to-Career was to meet the educational, economic, occupational, and skill-training needs of our future workforce. It was also to address the needs of employers as they face the challenge of competing in a global economy.[5]

"Today's worksites, and those of the twenty-first century, require a new kind of worker," she added, one who was flexible, one who was comfortable "competing with and working with a very diverse set of co-workers and clients."[6] Consequently, the "goal (of STW) is to prepare *all* students for postsecondary education, careers, and citizenship." The legislation was "not designed to be just another expensive job-training program," it was "about building a seamless system for developing academic and occupational skills for high-wage careers."[7]

The program was here to stay: it would not "go away" when the federal seed money was gone in 2001. Nor was it "another top-down federal program." It was not limited to the "vocational students" who would attend "technical schools." It was not more of the same, for it would require change in the schools and in the workplaces. It was about utilizing "authentic" activities for students. It looked to schools to prepare "all students for future employment and lifelong learning, matching them to the best postsecondary option for their career path."[8] Quite a program! Quite the accomplishments!

Ann Lewis spoke about the universal, egalitarian focus of school-to-work activities:

> What all these efforts are trying to do is to get more students successfully through school and into lifelong learning that includes postsecondary education options for all. Perhaps that makes those who want to preserve college as an elite privilege uneasy.[9]

Several experiences in New York State addressed the concern of businesses that too many students were graduating from high school unprepared, and that schools needed to concentrate on all of their students. For instance, in Westchester County, a New York City suburb, an education coalition surveyed eighteen businesses and reported that "local school districts were graduating students who were not adequately prepared to meet the needs and expectations of the workplace." In their view, these students displayed a:

> . . . lack of a serious work ethic; lack of understanding of the real value of having a job; poor work habits and attitudes; inadequate reading, writing, and computer skills; poor punctuality; and lack of motivation, commitment, and initiative.[10]

The group also faulted schools for "tolerating student failure and for not addressing the problem of ill-prepared students at its root." (One wonders what they thought that was.) The commercial leaders suggested that schools view themselves as businesses in the service industry that need to get to know their customers.[11]

"Underlying rapid and radical change" was given as the reason for the White Plains, New York, schools began their work-based programs. Alleging that "While no one questions that basic and lofty goal of education—the pursuit of knowledge for its own sake," this school system confessed that they were "beginning to realize that our students may not be as well prepared as they could be to function as productive workers."[12]

The "general lack of school spirit" was presented as the impetus for school-to-work reform in Hawaii. Asking the question "How could we turn these young people back on to education?" the Hawaii program focused on what "these students need to know and be able to do to become contributing members of this community." They needed to discover "what *wasn't* working."[13] No longer could they live with students who "were not excited about taking classes and sitting in rooms, day after day, with no understanding of why they had to learn these things." The remedy was to turn back to the "culture of yesteryear"—the "double-hulled canoe." Students became interested, learned, and a majority went on to post-secondary institutions.[14]

Marie Canny reported on another successful school-to-work program, this one in Fairfax City, Virginia, in the Landmark Career Academy. The school's purpose was "to combine academic learning with real-world work experience." One student expressed approval of the program with these words: "School starts at 9:00 and ends at 3:00 so you're more awake here."[15] Canny commented on parental dissatisfaction with educational institutions that leave their children bereft of any "real-world" skills:

> Clearly, too many parents are growing frustrated seeing their kids graduate from high school, and even college, without the real-world skills necessary to persuade employers to give them decent job opportunities.[16]

Little wonder, considering that "only 55 percent of Virginia students who enter college actually graduate. And those who do graduate have no guarantee of finding suitable jobs—or even any jobs at all."[17] Evidently the school-to-work movement would rectify that unacceptable situation!

West Virginia presented yet another illustration of school-to-work in action. Carol Roberts asked her sixth grade class at Long Drain Elementary School in Wetzel County "How in the world can I find out what jobs are out there?"[18] The best way to bring about the necessary change to "prepare young people for tomorrow's workplace," the author proclaimed, is to "take children out into the world of work and bring the working world to the classroom." The kind of "fundamental change" championed by the STWOA was "critical if schools are to help students compete in a rapidly changing, global, and highly technical economy. Indeed, it is every bit as essential, they say, as higher academic requirements, which have accompanied school-to-work in most places."[19]

A final method to be considered is that of the cooperative apprenticeship. Observing that workers under the age of 25 who only had a high school diploma were earning 28 percent less in 1997 than they were fifteen years earlier, Jeffrey Cantor called for the development of an "American system of apprenticeship, blending vocational and academic education in high school." The goal of this program would be to provide students with "meaningful work experience linked to continued education and training after graduation."[20] These apprenticeships should constitute a "major thrust of a school-to-work initiative," because they would also "serve as a catalyst for binding secondary and vocational schools and business to promote cooperation for worker preparation and local economic development." He alleged that "conservative estimates" were that businesses were spending between $300 and $400 million annually on appropriate training, an indication of the potential for success cooperative apprenticeships had in the construction and manufacturing industries alone.[21]

Taking note that "nearly half" of America's youth could not get "good jobs" out of high school, Charles E. M. Kolb, president of the Committee for Economic

Development, a group of 250 national leaders in business and education, observed that "This is an egregious waste of human potential that costs our society and economy dearly."[22] The answer to this social catastrophe was the "school-to-career movement," which addressed the waste by "linking the workplace more closely to the classroom."[23] The "potential impact" of the school-to-work movement was "staggering," Jane Swanson and Nadya Fouad asserted, because it could directly affect the vocational outcomes of potentially 75 percent or more of youth in the United States.[24]

But there was more to it than simply putting schools and workplaces together in a loosely constructed, unplanned fashion. Mary Agnes and Stephen Hamilton maintained that there were seven principles that undergirded successful school-to-work programs:

1. *Youths gain basic and high-level technical competence through challenging work.*
2. *Youths gain broad technical competence and understand all aspects of the industry.*
3. *Youths gain personal and social competence in the workplace.*
4. *Workplace teachers convey clear expectations to youths and assess progress toward reaching them.*
5. *Youths learn from adults with formally assigned teaching roles.*
6. *Youths achieve high academic standards.*
7. *Youths identify and follow career paths.*[25]

Once these principles were established, the following steps, most critical to success, must be put in place:

1. Willingness to participate.
2. *Form partnerships,* among "employers, employees, and their organizations; educators and school systems; legislators and government agencies; parents; youths; and community organizations."
3. *Build a school-to-work system.*
4. *Continuous research and development,* to assist in learning how to accomplish the goals of school-to-work.[26]

The above was an urgent imperative for the nation, because the growing economic imbalance threatened the American way of life:

> The growing disparity between the well-educated affluent and the inadequately educated who struggle to maintain a decent standard of living must be reduced if the United States is to remain a prosperous and secure democracy. Education cannot redress that disparity without complementary changes in the job market. But education in the form of school-to-work initiative[s] and especially work-based learning is a powerful means of improving the knowledge and skills of the American work force, which is, after all, most of our citizens. Work-based learning that adheres to the principles we have stated will contribute to but also depend on never-ending progress toward the promise of freedom and opportunity that is the American dream.[27]

And, to achieve the American dream, school-to-work programs cannot be just for the "forgotten half"; rather, they must be for all of America's young, thereby becoming:

> . . . a means of fundamentally restructuring all of American education so that there are no longer winners and losers, college bound and the "other" students, the upwardly mobile and the bored and the desperate, but rather a range of students and a range of teachers involved in a common quest to use the world of work to master the skills and attitudes needed to understand and improve the world around them.[28]

The Federal Government and the National Interest

The STWOA was a Clinton initiative that had broad bipartisan support in Congress. Upon passage, the act was to be jointly administered by the departments of Education and Labor. Some feared what they felt was an intrusion by the federal government into the legitimate rights of the states and local communities; more will be said about that later. Others, however, thought that the action of the federal government was required by the national interest.

Robert Holland, opinion editor of the *Richmond Times-Dispatch,* was one who spoke out against the enlarged federal activity, observing that there had always been competing visions for education. Now, he argued:

> . . . with its merger of education and labor policy, the national government is attempting to end the debate by fiat. Education is to be about training to meet government economic objectives. Period. Education is not to be about preparing a well-rounded, liberally educated individual to make his or her own decisions.[29]

Holland did not speak for everyone. The Committee for Economic Development, which saw the nation's vital interests at stake in the STWOA, warned of the waste to the nation brought about by squandering our "most valuable resource" and of the "widening inequity" that it sustained:

> Our nation cannot afford to waste the productive potential of its most valuable resource—its young people. Nor can we afford a society sharply divided into "haves" and "have nots" by differences in education and skills. Widening inequality threatens social cohesion and stability. . . . A coherent sequence of work experiences related to academic studies should become part of the core curriculum for high school students.[30]

In the "Preface" to his edited book, *Workforce Readiness: Competencies and Assessment,* Harold O'Neil reiterated the dangers to the nation inherent in the lack of a skilled work force:

> The need of American management for workers with greater skills who can take on greater responsibility has spawned many commissions, task forces, and studies. . . . Many high schools and college graduates lack the necessary knowledge and skills to be productive members of a workforce that focuses on high-performance, high-paying jobs. By "high performance" we mean work settings committed to excellence, product quality, and customer satisfaction. Lack of skills for such a workplace in an entry-level workforce may be a major reason for potential U.S. economic noncompetitiveness.[31]

John Krumboltz and Roger Worthington averred that the STWOA "initiated a new chapter in an old book that has tried to help young people to translate their school experience into marketable skills." Based on the human capital theory, the STWOA workers trained under this mantle would not only be qualified for skilled jobs but they would also make the nation "more competitive in the global economy." Viewed in this light, the STWOA is an "*investment* education to enhance the human capital characteristics of youth" and at the same time "will increase opportunities for youthful workers and the economic well-being of the nation."[32]

Partnerships: Business and Labor

The AVA was heavily involved in and a strong supporter of school-to-work from the outset. That support continued as the years progressed. In March of 1997, the AVA published a "School-to Work Partners Directory," which listed the 38 members and gave the reader a toll-free phone number to call for information. "The coalition of business and education leaders aims to put school-to-work transition on the agenda of every community in the U.S." proclaimed the AVA.[33]

The CEO of General Motors, John F. "Jack" Smith, was emphatic in what educators ought do. "I suggest three things for educators: Get more involved in the workplace, get more involved in the workplace, get more involved in the workplace!"[34] Stephanie Powers, the director of the National School-to-Work Office in 1998, argued that schools, to their detriment, had become "insular" over time and had "gotten away from having businesses in."[35]

Establishing partnerships between business and education was no simple matter, Richard Greenberg wrote. There existed a "culture shock" between the two; business was "results oriented," and valued "accountability, flexibility and speed," while education was "process oriented," a part of a bureaucracy that "tends to move slowly and resist change."[36] The gap must be closed, however, because only then could the technical and academic be brought together in the curriculum so the student will have an answer as to "Why do I have to learn this?"[37]

Foreign countries provided a model for the United States, Samuel Halperin alleged. Recent study missions to Europe and Israel revealed that in some places employers not only supported schools they also ran them. In those schools, he penned:

. . . we never once observed the bars, metal detectors, or graffiti so common in American high schools. On the contrary, schools were characterized by quiet corridors and students absorbed in their work.[38]

Recognizing that this form of school operation took many years to develop, he nonetheless saw a model with much potential for the future in this country:

Yet the fact that it happened is encouraging for all who believe that schools and employers can work together to produce high schools that work, future employees with impressive skills, and, most important, the kind of young people whose personal values the critics on the political left and right ought to find appealing.[39]

Partnerships also gave students the opportunity to understand the applicability of learning. Lynn Olson, an *Education Week* reporter turned author, told about what she learned on her yearlong trip to visit school-to-work programs across the country:

I heard an almost constant refrain: "Now I understand why I have to learn this. What I do at work matters because somebody else is relying on me. Suddenly there are lots of adults talking to me about my future."[40]

While she recognized that there were obstacles confronting successful school-to-work programs and partnerships between education and business, she concluded that "I believe that the forces drawing employers and educators—and work and learning—closer together are irresistible."[41]

What was it that employers looked to the schools to provide? *Techniques* reported that employers were dissatisfied with the "quality of the labor pool."[42] Of first-order importance, Richard Kazis opined, was the need to have the "active involvement of local employers," else the program would lack "authenticity." Specific goals included increased productivity of workers; better public images for the participating firms; screening of potential new hires, thereby avoiding the high cost of turnovers; and improving employee morale by working with young people.[43] Kazis instructed high school principals that they should heed the advice in the Committee for Economic Development's report, *The Employer's Role in Linking School and Work,* which suggested that principals find out what employers want and need before launching a program; accept the dual role of business as both a pressure and support for school improvement; design a school-to-career effort that advanced both academic performance and school planning; secure support and resources from the district office; and partner with local organizations that could help manage ongoing school-to-career activities.[44] If successful, the principal might experience the rapt feeling expressed by a Proctor and Gamble official who had taken part in a school-to-career program: "For me, it's hard to put into words, just seeing the kids mature, becoming part of the work force, becoming successful. I personally haven't found any of it hard, it's so interesting. It makes you feel young again."[45]

Susan Black wrote euphorically about the role of business and industry, which, in her words, were "reaping the real benefits of school-to-work partnerships." It was, she declared with a certain finality, "a merger made in heaven: graduates looking for work and businesses looking for workers."[46] There were concerns, though. Marsha Silverberg, a researcher at the Princeton, New Jersey–based Mathematica Policy Research firm, which was monitoring the effectiveness of the implementation of school-to-work programs for the Education and Labor departments, said that the support by businesses was in large part superficial:

> . . . the most prevalent type of support businesses give to schools in terms of curriculum and instruction is simply providing guest speakers who talk about their companies and the nature of their work to students in classrooms or at large assemblies.[47]

Lawrence Hardy reported similar feelings on the part of Mathematica. Alan Hershey, its project director, communicated that "tension" existed between the "broad-based, 'low intensity' programs involving many students and 'high intensity' programs (such as) internships for a few." The former was "prevailing," Hershey said, and was "Likely to continue to do so."[48] Hershey noted that the involvement of many companies in school-to-work programs followed very traditional practices and did not represent reform at all; this was a far cry from what STWOA's zealous devotees envisioned:

> . . . the most common type of employer involvement is in long-standing practices—having them speak to classes and participate in career fairs—hardly the kind of systemic involvement that many advocates of the act had envisioned.[49]

In their report to Congress in 1997, secretaries Riley and Herman listed the following business groups that had endorsed school-to-work: the National Alliance of Business, the National Association of Manufacturers, the Committee for Economic Development, the American Business Conference, the National Conference of State Legislatures, and the U.S. Conference of Mayors.[50] On the surface, at least, this was an impressive array indeed!

What about labor unions, the "lesser partner" in American industry and commerce? Some concern about the use of unpaid student labor existed in labor circles, but some labor leaders did endorse school-to-work programs. For instance, Paul Cole, secretary-treasurer of the New York State AFL-CIO, was forthright in his support of the system, holding that it:

... provides students with an awareness of the knowledge, skills, and abilities required in the workplace and a pathway to achieve them. High-quality workplace learning, coupled with contextualized school-based learning is an effective way of helping all students achieve high academic standards and career readiness.[51]

In fact, the AFT sponsored a program, "Reaching the Next Step," that recommended that students be exposed to the workplace in "ways that reinforce and show the relevance of academic learning, providing training and support for teachers in school-to-career programs and creating initiatives for students to study and achieve."[52] The union was quick to point out that it was not arguing for "narrow vocational programs that only prepare students for specific jobs." Rather, the:

... AFT's vision of school to career calls for providing students with the solid academic foundations that can enable them to go on to college if they choose, enter quality postsecondary training and degree programs, and retrain easily for other jobs should a shift in the labor market occur or an opportunity for promotion present itself.[53]

Some believed that the participation of labor was indispensable for the success of the program. Maxwell described unions as an "often overlooked, but crucial, third party" (to schools and businesses) in the process. Anne Freeman, state apprenticeship coordinator of the New Jersey department of education, argued that "If you don't give unions and employers and school districts an opportunity to work these issues out, they'll never develop a deep understanding . . . that a successful system can be built on."[54] Maxwell's plan envisioned that schools, unions, and employers would have the chance to work out any problems that arose. For example, if there were more applications than openings for apprenticeships, these groups could collectively decide who got in, who made the decision, and the criteria by which the decision was made. "Usually," Maxwell wrote, "it's easy to convince unions of the value of STC programs."[55]

Students and Teachers

Much of the "evidence" presented on behalf of student approval of school-to-work programs was anecdotal. For instance, a student in the Siemens, New York, program was quoted as saying:

I like this better [than my regular classes] because it's more hands-on. You actually get to use what you're learning. This job teaches you a lot about reality, about real life. It teaches you that everything isn't as easy as it looks, and that you have to achieve your goals. Your goals just don't happen.[56]

Several examples were given of the benefits of student-run businesses, as in the "Coffee Carts" program in Oregon that was started on school grounds. There a proud teacher commented that "The students at this expresso bar learn what it takes to earn a profit from an actual business. The skills and confidence they gain will help them become productive members of the workforce."[57] Student commitment was mixed. For example, at the Bob Howard Chevrolet firm in Oklahoma City, one student proclaimed that "We can learn a lot more out here than in school." But another student in Tulsa folded an airplane during a job interview, and others were just "sitting around."[58]

Many recognized that the implementation of school-to-work (or school-to-career) programs would require a substantial change in the role of the teacher. Teachers would "need to change, not only what they teach, but also how they teach." This would be tantamount to requiring changes in teacher preparation, certification, and standards of accountability—a tall order indeed.[59] It would also necessitate sharing decision-making with the partners and would demand funds for the hiring of a school coordinator and for support of activities beyond the regular school budget.[60]

Charlotte Coomer recalled how much opposition there was to teaching out of one's field. She wondered about "teaching out of context." Teacher training would have to undergo changes so that teachers could begin to connect learning to their "partners in meaningful ways." "Teaching the Context" would require joining study groups, learning to work together, learning from business how to analyze scenarios and situations, reading publications outside the field of education, going on field trips to businesses and other appropriate sites, taking part in seminars, engaging in teacher externships, and sharing in the assessment of school-to-work activities.[61] This vastly changed role for teachers, which would lead to their opposition in some instances, influenced the U.S. Department of Education to study "effective models of professional development for contextual teaching and learning." The results should have "high utility" for the preparation of teachers, Coomer noted:

> Educators have the challenge and responsibility of planning and delivering the kind of experience they desire for their own children and their communities. But we cannot meet the challenge without proper training—and we're obliged to pursue it.[62]

More Problems and More Opposition

Between 1997 and 1999, problems that were both internal and external to the movement arose. As the movement grew, opposition to it increased proportionately. First, let us consider the problems.

L. Sunny Hansen accused some current career development theorists of ignoring history: "They have not attended much to the historical context of what has been done to promote students' career development in the schools over the past 25 to 30 years." She alleged that it appeared that STW proponents paid little attention to "how students make career decisions, at what levels, with what kinds of help, or with what kind of socialization."[63] There were even more important questions that had not been addressed:

> Who is to decide whether students are work-based or college bound? When do students know themselves well enough to make these decisions? What are the respective roles of business and industry, school counselors, teachers, parents, universities, and students themselves?[64]

The well-known career development theorist, Edwin L. Herr, added that school-to-work theories had little to say about the "transition processes or services per se."[65]

Thomas Owens pointed out some very practical difficulties which came to light in some of the visits to Tech Prep sites:

> How to make time in school-day schedules for hands-on, contextual learning so students can apply theoretical concepts to practice. . . . How, despite high student-to-counselor ratios, to make the most of existing resources and get students to plan their educational path with future career goals in mind. . . . How to sustain fruitful collaboration between high school and community college faculty, beyond the initial links formed to create curriculum articulation. . . . How to promote students' interest in technology and its central place in careers to which they might aspire.[66]

Owens also acknowledged some pedagogical problems: "Just placing a student at an employer's site does not ensure that learning will take place."[67] Michael Ferrari, Roger Taylor, and Kurt Van Laha, while recognizing the potential benefit of work simulations as a pedagogical technique, saw "potential problems with narrow content or with sacrificing learnability for realism" as impediments with computer simulations in school-to-work programs.[68]

Mentors and the process of mentoring constituted critical elements in job-shadowing and other areas. The mentors needed to be prepared. Georgia Yeager, the technical assistance coordinator for Cambria County, Pennsylvania, stated candidly: "Many mentors simply do not understand." She urged educators to write out expectations for the job mentors.[69] Owens added that educators couldn't assume that a "willing employer automatically understands effective ways of challenging and guiding young people."[70] Matthew Dembicki advised that it was not as difficult to convince businesses to participate in school-to-work programs as some had thought. Yet providing internships did not necessarily translate to a learning experience for the students, especially if the internship was simply busy-work.[71] There was, Dembicki observed, no reliable measure that had been set up to gauge what happened at internships; indeed, some schools did not pay attention to what occurred there. He cited Jack Gravener, a partner in a school-to-work consulting firm in Apple View, California, who said that "Very few companies had jumped in wholeheartedly and participated" in the programs there.[72] One reason advanced for the hesitancy of businesses, according to J. D. Hoye, former director of the National School-to-Work Office, was that businesses were "trying to make sure this is not just another fad."[73]

Rural education presented a unique set of challenges for school-to-work programs. Craig Howley observed that "work" in rural areas, which were "colonies to cities," meant low pay, even in technologically related fields.[74] What was the real meaning of "work" in a rural context, he inquired? He found it "bothersome" to "accept job holding as the purpose of education," and he came out in favor of reconsidering what "work means." In rural areas, school-to-work was much more than an "abstract notion." Earning a living was very important, Howley acknowledged, but:

> . . . equally important to the very survival of rural places is the development of community. And if school-to-career simply prepares young people to seek high-tech, high-wage jobs the young people will continue to abandon their communities.[75]

In rural areas, an ethic that amounted to a "radical change in the concept of work" was part of school-to-work programs: leave the workplace better than one found it and work to become a thoughtful steward. Most important for educators, he felt, was to recognize that work has to do with "larger purposes and commitments that are worthy to be the true object of education."[76]

Some concluded that school-to-work programs had limited benefits; they did not extend to all children.[77] Others argued that there was little connection between school-to-work programs and other programs designed to raise standards and improve student achievement: "Until they do, that $1 billion in public and private funds earmarked for school-to-work programs looks like a better investment for business than for schools."[78]

Susan Beerman and Theodore Kowalski presented another reason for skepticism. They commented that schools do not respond well to politically imposed change. In the case of school-to-work initiatives there was little evidence that teachers and administrators embraced the philosophical underpinnings of change, plus there was the added burden the programs would be for school principals. Teachers could well resent being forced into team-teaching in interdisciplinary areas because it reduced their autonomy.[79] When added to the "skepticism that school-to-work is another passing education fad," some education researchers argued that "teachers may be reluctant to let students out of class for work experience when they're being pressured to meet new curricula standards and to improve academic proficiency."[80] David Singer, a spokesman for the school-to-work office of the state of Massachusetts admitted that "Unless we can make this an easy proposition, and prove that it helps immediately and makes [a teacher's] job easier, it is a hard sell."[81]

Grubb noted that subsequent to the publishing of A *Nation at Risk,* economic issues had surpassed political issues in schools. Now the development of "skills" was more important than the development of political and moral judgment. He maintained that the "restoration of civic education is crucial" because the present scene had led to some "truly disastrous policies, working against the majority of citizens."[82] Grubb felt that the civic learning could be restored to its rightful place in schools without harming "occupational programs" by using occupational issues to study history, social studies, economics, and other social issues.[83]

Then there were the potential obstacles of scale, quality and selectivity. Thomas Bailey, Katherine Hughes, and Tavis Barr pointed out that if 25 percent of all high school juniors and seniors took part, 1.5 million work placements would be needed annually.[84] How could that many intern placements be made with "high intensity," high quality? What would be the cost? If a lesser percentage were of high quality, although the others might well be a financial boon to the participating firms, that practice would "run the risk of promoting excessive selectivity for interns" and prohibit many students from obtaining "higher quality opportunities," which would ultimately cost school-to-work programs whatever support they had from their local communities.[85]

The most formidable challenge and the source of the fiercest opposition, as we shall soon see, were spokespersons for parents or parents themselves. Kenneth Gray, in a balanced commentary, observed that as the school-to-work programs began to operate it was "becoming clear that we may have failed to win over the most important constituent group: parents of school-age children."[86] He noted that opposition was building because of the failure to convince parents about the value of school-to-work reforms. He was optimistic about the outcomes of informing parents completely about the movement:

> Ultimately parents must decide what is best for their child, and they deserve to know the facts. Some may blame the messenger and many will not like the news, but in the end most will welcome the truth.[87]

Some writers were less charitable about parents who clashed with school-to-work advocates. Chung-Dai Vo alleged that the backlash to school-to-work programs was "fueled by small pockets of worried parents who don't understand the reform and conservatives who see it as government intrusion."[88] Jack Jennings, director of the Center on National Education Policy, advised convincing those who could be convinced with the truth and going ahead in spite of them if they were unable to grasp the truth, lest their opposition spread and foil the enterprise:

Some people believe in a lot of conspiracies. There's no way to convince them otherwise. What school people have to do is to refute what's wrong and agree with what's right. If you don't (refute the misconceptions), they'll convince the next 5 percent, then the next 5 percent.[89]

The usurpation of the rights of parents, states, and/or local communities by the federal government was put forth by some "conservatives" as the rationale for school-to-work reform. The Family Foundation, for example, saw the federal government, in collusion with industry, usurping the rights of parents and "replacing American education with a federal work-force preparation system."[90] Oregon Representative Ron Sunseri, in a publication of the National Center for Education and the Economy, saw school-to-work as the "first step to a federally managed system of labor."[91]

The Heritage Foundation spoke in a similar vein. It asked this rhetorical question: "School-to-Work: Is Government Mismanaging the Lives of Our Children?" The movement was castigated for requiring "students to participate in vocational training" and forcing them to "choose a career pathway by the 8th grade."[92] Phyllis Schlafly, director of the Eagle Forum and publisher of the *Phyllis Schlafly Report* that was distributed to parents, reported that school-to-work programs tracked "children into specific lines of work as chosen by business-school partnerships." The "Directions" for this action "come from the federal government. It's an attempt to control the curriculum."[93] Resistance such as this moved Irene Lynn, the acting director of the National School-to-Work Office in Washington, to remark in the summer of 1998 that there was a "continuing assault on school-to-work from the far right" that was "well-organized and extremely vocal."[94]

In November of 1998, Hardy recognized that school-to-work reform was "at a crossroads." The conservatives, a "small but passionate group," charged that school-to-work programs would "weaken academics and pigeonhole students into careers based, not on their own interests, but on the labor needs of local industries."[95] The federal funding would end in three years, and then it would be up to the states and local partnerships to keep the effort going. A year earlier Halperin identified the conservative threat to educational reform. He wrote that conservative critics said that the:

> . . . fledgling American school-to-work movement is a nefarious plot by Big Government, abetted by willful or unwitting industrialists, to control the academic content of learning and dictate the occupational futures of American youths. . . . Our schoolchildren are in danger of becoming pawns in a computer-driven national labor-market information system that will funnel them into whatever jobs the economy needs filled.[96]

Halperin alleged that the conservatives were not alone. They were joined in the assault on school-to-work reform by the far left, who saw a corporate plot to trample on the American working class:

Instead of regarding school-to-work efforts as key elements of genuine school reform, critics from the political right see a government-directed scheme to control the minds, the values, and ultimately the occupations and earnings of American workers—all of which will allegedly subordinate family values to the imperatives of the economy. For its part, too, the anti-capitalist political left envisages generations of human automatons and worker bees, brainwashed to serve the needs of corporate capitalism in cahoots with government bureaucracies. No longer capable of independent thought and self-realization, our young people are to become little more than cogs in the nation's industrial and economic machinery.[97]

Conclusion—And a Peek into the Future

Taking cognizance of some of the passionate objections hurled at school-to-work reform, J. D. Hoye, director of the National School-to-Work Office in 1997, penned that some people wanted classrooms to be "museums of their past."[98] But critics objected, arguing that the movement forced students to make decisions before they were ready to serve the labor needs of local businesses, diluted academic standards by inserting vocational work into the curriculum, took away students' and parents' free choice, and transferred power from elected officials to bureaucracies dominated by business interests and government, especially the federal.[99] Schlafly would agree. This conservative spokesperson referred to school-to-work as training, not education.[100] John Krumboltz and Roger Worthington took the movement to task for its "procedure that results in the matching of industry specific training with employment opportunities after formal schooling has been completed." Less concern was given, they observed, to the "degree to which youth will be satisfied with their field of employment, specific employer, or work technologies, and ultimately how participating in the world of work will lead to satisfying and enriching lives."[101]

Others criticized the movement for ignoring "working conditions and workers' rights," instead concentrating on "inculcating work attitudes and skills defined by industry." Students, they postulated, should be educated "about work" and taught to use critical thinking to ask questions about working conditions, which "is not really" something that the "school-to-work movement seems to be about."[102] Douglas Noble noticed the absence of such questions as the following in the positions of those advocating school-to-work reforms:

> Will there be a decent, secure job for me in the future? Why can't people on welfare find decent jobs? How is education related to my future work? How do I become a professional? How will I be treated at work and what are my rights? How do I handle problems that arise in my part-time job?[103]

Noble believed that "part of the problem" was that "teachers within school-to-work programs are rarely encouraged to reflect critically on their own work and the work of others, or on how work should be taught."[104] Noble also suggested a different strategy in implementing curricular programs. Rather then be dependent on businesses, he recommended that teachers collaborate with workers from labor unions, going directly to them and discussing pertinent issues; business involvement should be secondary. As Noble put it: "We must link more closely two priorities in school reform, critical thinking and preparation for work."[105]

Noble's sentiments do not appear to have affected the movements' backers, who held that "we shouldn't allow outdated biases to deprive academically gifted students of an opportunity to view the workplace as a site for continued learning."[106] Olson called for the development of "substantive connection between education and work so that young people can be better prepared for the rapidly changing world that awaits them." The young needed skills "that the schools have rarely taught—the ability to work with complex knowledge and to make decisions under conditions of conflicting or inadequate evidence."[107] But Owens detected that school-to-work ideology represented a limited view, and needed:

> . . . increased emphasis on lifelong learning; additional content, including family living and how to balance work, family, and community involvement, expansion of teachers' roles to include learning manager, coach, and mentor; and involvement of family, business, labor, and community members in the instructional process.[108]

The Mathematica Policy Research Inc. of Princeton, New Jersey, which was charged with evaluating school-to-work programs, predicted little chance of renewed federal funding after October of 2001. The overall vision of the reform "may slip into the shadows of the many other competing demands on schools and teachers," it reported.[109] To survive, it would need funding commitments for state and local partnerships and would have to be at the core of states' efforts to raise academic standards. Bill McCarthy, spokesperson for the House Education and Workplace Committee, said the report's findings appeared to justify the government's decision to discontinue funding: "We've provided the seed money, but it doesn't appear it can stand on its own and it hasn't met its objectives."[110] Hopkins et al. challenged this bleak picture of the school-to-work movement. It was not designed to be "just another expensive job-training program," they stated. Rather, "It is about building a seamless system for developing academic and occupational skills for high-wage careers." It would not disappear when the seed money was gone; school-to-work, they promised, "is not going to go away."[111] Indeed, Barbara Von Villas declared, with a certain note of finality, that:

> Change fueled by need is uncompromising; however, it crumbles the old bureaucracy as it commands attendant response. School-to-work requires that kind of cultural change. The only question is how long will it take to accomplish.[112]

Everything was at stake, Bragg opined. The academic disciplines were incapable of leading "the way to education through occupations." Reform demanded a "spirited debate over academic and vocational education." For, the "future of public education in America may well depend on it."[113] Leo Giglio and Lawrence Bauer agreed; school-to-work reform was crucial for the American future:

> The future, therefore, requires that the education community take the steps necessary to satisfy their customer, business and industry, by providing the basic education and skills identified by SCANS [Labor Secretary's Commission on Achieving Necessary Skills]. . . . The school-to-work philosophy will hopefully help schools redirect their focus to the future of our students and our country.[114]

People needed to be patient with school-to-work reform, Kazis maintained. It takes "a long time to sink roots."[115] The private sector needed to assume some responsibility for the future of programs that held such promise for the general welfare of the nation.

Backers cited more optimistic statistics, released by a report from the Public Forum Institute, a non-partisan policy and education research, which differed widely from Mathematica's statement. Considerable progress had been made: there were STW programs in 50,000 schools in all states, which involved "career-awareness activities, internships, job-shadowing and mentoring programs, and school-based enterprises."[116] By the time the law expired on October 1, 2001, the federal government would "have invested $1.8 billion in STW programs," Stephanie Powers, director of the national STW office said. Her position was clear: "It doesn't make sense" to let the program, which enjoyed such strong "customer satisfaction," to end.[117] According to the data provided in the report:

- More than 80 percent of participants said the benefits to students in STW met or exceeded their expectations;
- Ninety-seven percent of employer/labor participants agreed that STW experiences were beneficial for students who planned to attend college; and
- Ninety-seven percent of employer/labor participants agreed that STW was a "good strategy" for building a competitive workforce in the future.[118]

Powers's group also agreed that school-to-work reform had opened up an "unprecedented dialogue" among business, education, and other community partners. Ninety percent of employer and labor participants and 80 percent of other participants said they would remain in school-to-work initiatives over the next five years, and 89 percent of participants supported the development of career majors for high school students.

And yet the questions remain, including those based on the notion that STW is the latest passing fad. Perhaps even more bothersome are the alleged failings in the humanitarian realm. Hansen wrote somewhat disparagingly of this aspect, the bandwagon tendency, and the movement's cost:

> In their zeal to prepare students for the workforce, the human dimension—student development—has been forgotten. I do not think applying any of the theories of the STW movement will erase any of its basic flaws. It is the latest bandwagon, driven by business and industry, implemented largely by vocational education, costs billions of dollars, and is legislated to sunset October 1, 2001. When STW ends, career development theory and research still will have much to offer all students, apart from the STW initiative.[119]

Joe Kincheloe raised some fundamental questions about the school-to-work movement in his excellent book *Toil and Trouble: Good Work, Smart Workers, and the Integration of Academic and Vocational Education.* Much of the literature published by zealots of the movement had overlooked or ignored the issues he raised. He wrote in his "Preface":

> . . . if we possessed a vision of good work and economic democracy, what type of education would we need to prepare students for such a reality? Such an education would be called "work education" but not in the narrow sense that we commonly use the term "vocational education." Such an education would prepare students as thoughtful, knowledgeable, democratic citizens with moral awareness and civic courage, as well as preparing them to take their place in the economic life of the nation.[120]

Even more compelling are some of the points made in his concluding chapter. "There is great need," he wrote, for:

> . . . literature that explores the complexities and ambiguities of work, the conflicts between life and work and life in other domains, the moral and ethical issues that confront workers, and the joys of good work.[121]

Students should be helped to "identify and speak from the particularity of their own lived experience and social placement"; they should realize that as "aspiring workers their access to knowledge is severely limited," and they should have the opportunity to engage critical pedagogy, which includes the exposure of the "ways corporations and other wielders of power suppress information that fails to serve their interests."[122] Students should be helped to "develop the ability to invoke the values that accompany the humanities, as they analyze the workplace and their own roles as workers." "Wage differentials" could function as a "generative theme for discussions and research. Who gets what and why."[123] The "possibilities are endless," he posited, for "new curricula and methodological innovations" in programs that "critically integrate academic and vocational education."[124]

Adria Steinberg acknowledged that the goals of the school-to-work movement were "certainly utopian—an educational system in which all students are engaged and all students succeed."[125] As of this writing, in December of 2000, it is uncertain that the movement will survive the cessation of federal funding and, if it does not, perhaps it will fade away as so many reforms have done that have promised a utopia before it. If it survives, will it be the version of those who extolled its many unparalleled virtues, the school-preserving and nation-saving "reform" that brings the entire curriculum under its umbrella? And if so, what will happen to the democratic, critical-thinking, intellectual, humanistic, and aesthetic features of American education that have been obscured, if not eliminated, by the strident views of those school-to-work dogmatists who use the economic role of the school, necessary as it is, as THE ONE remedy to ALL of our schools' and some of our nation's ills and shortcomings?

Notes

1. Richard W. Riley and Alexis M. Herman, *Implementation of the School-to-Work Opportunities Act of 1994. Report to Congress.* Washington, DC: Department of Education, Department of Labor, September, 1997. ED 415 400, p. 5.
2. Ibid., p. 7.
3. Ibid., p. 4.
4. Adria Steinberg, *Real Learning, Real Work: School-to-Work as High School Reform.* New York: Routledge, 1998, pp. xiii, 2.
5. Barbara J. Hopkins, Darl Naumann, and Frederick C. Wenzel, *Building the Schools-to-Work System.* Bloomington, IN: Phi Delta Kappa Educational Foundation, Fastback # 46, 1999, p. 7.
6. Ibid., p. 9.
7. Ibid., pp. 20, 24.
8. Ibid., p. 25.
9. Anne C. Lewis, "Washington Commentary: School-to-Work, Certificates of Mastery, and Standards," *Phi Delta Kappan* 79, 8 (April 1998): 564.
10. Carol Rhoder and Joyce M. French, "School-to-Work: Making Specific Connections," *Phi Delta Kappan* 80, 7 (March 1999): 534.
11. Ibid., 534–535.
12. Ibid., p. 535.
13. Anna K. Hickcox, "The Canoe Is Their Island," *Educational Leadership* 55, 8 (May 1998): 58.
14. Ibid.
15. Marie C. Canny, "Shopping Mall 101," *The American School Board Journal* 183, 4 (April 1998): 48.
16. Ibid.
17. Ibid.
18. Quoted in Lawrence Hardy, "What Do You Want to Be?," *The American School Board Journal* 185, 11 (November 1998): 24.
19. Ibid., 25.
20. Jeffrey A. Cantor, *Cooperative Apprenticeships: A School-to-Work Handbook.* Richmond: Technomic Publishing Co., Inc., 1997, p. xi.
21. Ibid.

22. Committee for Economic Development, *Employer Roles in Linking School and Work: Lessons from Four Urban Communities.* New York: Committee for Economic Development, 1998, p. ix.

23. Ibid., p. x

24. Jane L. Swanson and Nadya A. Fouad, "Applying Theories of Person-Environment Fit to the Transition from School to Work," *The Career Occupational Quarterly* 47, 4 (June 1999): 337.

25. Mary Agnes and Stephen F. Hamilton, "When Is Work a Learning Experience?," *Phi Delta Kappan* 78, 9 (May 1997): 682–688.

26. Ibid., 688–689.

27. Ibid., 689.

28. Steinberg, *Real Learning, Real Work: School-to-Work as High School Reform,* p. vii.

29. Quoted in Lawrence Hardy, "What Do You Want To Be?,": 27.

30. Ibid., p. 26.

31. Harold F. O'Neil, Jr., "Preface," in O'Neil, ed., *Workforce Readiness: Competencies and Assessment.* Mahwah, NJ: Lawrence Erblaum Associates, Publishers, 1997, pp. vii–viii.

32. John D. Krumboltz and Roger L. Worthington, "The School-to-Work Transition from a Learning Theory Perspective," *The Career Development Quarterly* 47, 4 (June 1999): 312–313.

33. "AVA School-to-Work Partners Directory," *Techniques,*72, 3, March, 1997, pp. 46–48.

34. "Employers Want Basic and Technical Skills, Says General Motors CEO," *Techniques* 72, 5, May, 1997, p. 25.

35. "Interview with Stephanie Powers," *Techniques,* 73, 8, November/December, 1998, p. 30.

36. Richard Greenberg, "Get With the Partnership," *Techniques,* 74, 4, April, 1999, p. 15.

37. "Employers Want Basic and Technical Skills, Says General Motors CEO," p. 25.

38. Samuel Halperin, "School-to-Work, Employers, and Personal Values," *Education Week,* 16, 24, March 12, 1997, p. 38.

39. Ibid.

40. Lynn Olson, *The School-to-Work Revolution: How Employers and Educators Are Joining Forces to Prepare Tomorrow's Skilled Workforce.* Reading, MA: Addison-Wesley, 1997, p. ix.

41. Ibid., p. 257.

42. "Interview with Business and Industry: What Do Employers Want?," *Techniques,* 72, 5, May, 1997, p. 22.

43. Richard Kazis, "Minding their Business: What Employers Look for in School-to-Career Programs," *The High School Magazine,* 6, 6, April, 1999, p. 17.

44. Ibid., p. 18.

45. Quoted in ibid.

46. Susan Black, "Learning to Work," *The American School Board Journal* 185, 3 (March 1998): 36.

47. Quote in ibid., 38.

48. Quoted in Hardy, "What Do You Want To Be?": 26–27.

49. Ibid.

50. Riley and Herman, *Implementation of the School-to-Work Opportunities Act of 1994: Report to Congress,* p. 56.

51. Quoted in ibid., p. 35.

52. "Meeting High Standards through School-to-Career Programs," *American Teacher,* 81, March, 1997, p. 3.

53. Ibid.

54. Bruce Maxwell, "Labor's Role in Work-Based Learning," *Techniques,* 73, 1, January, 1998, p. 22.

55. Ibid., pp. 22, 20.

56. Quoted in Olson, "The New Basics in School-to-Work," *Educational Leadership* 55, 6 (March 1998): 53.

57. Lauren E. Lindstrom, Michael R. Benz, and Michael D. Johnson, "From School Grounds to Coffee Grounds," *Teaching Exceptional Children* 29, 3 (January/February 1997): 24.
58. Mary Ann Zehr, "Driven to Succeed," *Education Week,* 17, 23, February 18, 1998. pp. 34–35.
59. Carol Rhoder and Joyce M. French, "School-to-Work: Making Specific Connections," *Phi Delta Kappan* 80, 7 (March 1999): 542.
60. Olson, "The New Basics in School-to-Work": 52.
61. Charlotte Coomer, "Mastering the Context to Deliver the Content," *The High School Magazine,* 6, 6, April, 1999, pp. 19–20.
62. Ibid., p. 21.
63. L. Sunny Hansen, "Beyond School to Work: Continuing Contributions of Theory and Practice to Career Development of Youth," *The Career Development Quarterly* 47, 4 (June 1999): 355–356.
64. Ibid., 356.
65. Edwin L. Herr, "Theoretical Perspectives on the School-to-Work Transition: Reactions and Recommendations," *The Career Development Quarterly* 47, 4 (June 1999): 362.
66. Thomas R. Owens, "On the Way: A Journey toward Work-Relevant Education," *Journal of Vocational Education Research* 22, 2 (1997): 95–96.
67. Ibid., 96.
68. Michel Ferrari, Roger Taylor, and Kurt Van Laha, "Adapting Work Simulations for Schools," *Journal of Computing Research* 21, 1 (1999): 50.
69. Quoted in Jason Prucey, "Writing the Book on Mentoring," *Techniques,* 73, 1, January, 1998, p. 39.
70. Owens, "On the Way: A Journey through Work-Relevant Education": 98–99.
71. Matthew Dembicki, "Mid-Term Review," *Techniques,* 75, 8, November/December, 1998, p. 21.
72. Ibid.
73. Ibid.
74. Craig Howley, "Doing the Right Thing: Rural School-to-Career," *The High School Magazine,* 6, 6, April, 1999, p. 26.
75. Ibid., pp. 26–27.
76. Ibid., p. 27.
77. Chung-Dai Vo, "Not for *My* Child," *Techniques,* 71, 3, January, 1997, p. 23.
78. Susan Black, "Learning to Work," *American School Board Journal* 185, 3 (March 1998): 38.
79. Susan E. Beerman and Theodore J. Kowalski, "Program Change and Administrative Roles in Indiana's School-to-Work Pilot Site High Schools," *Contemporary Education* 69, 2 (Winter 1998): 77.
80. Matthew Dembicki, "Shipping Teachers Out to Bring Them on Board," *Techniques,* 73, 8, November/December, 1998, p. 21.
81. Quoted in ibid.
82. W. Norton Grubb, "Not There Yet: Prospects and Problems for Education through Occupations," *Journal of Vocational Education Research* 22, 2 (1997): 88.
83. Ibid.
84. Thomas Bailey, Katherine Hughes, and Tavis Barr, "Achieving Scale and Quality in School-to-Work Internships," *Educational Evaluation and Policy Analysis* 22, 1 (Spring 2000): 41.
85. Ibid., 58–59.
86. Kenneth Gray, "The Gatekeepers," *Techniques,* 71, 9, January, 1997, p. 24.
87. Ibid., pp. 24, 27.
88. Vo, "Not for *My* Child," p. 23.
89. Quoted in ibid., p. 23.

90. Quoted in Hardy, "What Do You Want To Be?": 27.
91. Quoted in ibid.
92. Quoted in Steinberg, "Teaching School-to-Work: Why Polarizing Rhetoric May Deprive Us of a Promising Pathway to Reform," *Education Week,* 17, 28, March 25, 1998, p. 56.
93. Quoted in Mary Ann Zehr, "School-to-Work Opponents Unable to Block Funding," *Education Week,* 18, 8, October 28, 1998, p. 20.
94. Quoted in ibid.
95. Hardy, "What Do You Want To Be?": 25.
96. Samuel Halperin, "School-to-Work, Employers, and Personal Values," *Education Week,* 16, 14, March 12, 1998, p. 52.
97. Ibid.
98. Quoted in Thomas Bailey and Donna Merritt, "School-to-Work for the College Bound," *Education Week,* 17, 9, October 29, 1997, p. 32.
99. Hardy, "What Do You Want To Be?": 27.
100. Phyllis Schlafly, "School-to-Work and Goals 2000," *The Phyllis Schlafly Report,* 30, 9, April 1997. Available online at http://www.eagleforum.org/psr/1997/apr97/ psrapr97.html, p. 2.
101. John D. Krumboltz and Roger L. Worthington, "The School-to-Work Transition from a Learning Theory Perspective," *The Career Development Quarterly* 47, 4 (June 1999): 317.
102. Douglas D. Noble, "Work-Based Curriculum: A Labor Approach to School-to-Work," *Education Week,* 17, 13, November 19, 1997, p. 32.
103. Ibid.
104. Ibid.
105. Ibid., p. 35.
106. Bailey and Merritt, "School-to-Work for the College Bound," p. 37.
107. Olson, *The School-to-Work Revolution,* pp. vii–viii.
108. Owens, "On the Way: A Journey through Work-Relevant Education": 103.
109. Cited in Mary Ann Zehr, "School-to-Work Movement Faces Test, Study Says," *Education Week,* 18, 14, December 2, 1998, pp. 1, 29.
110. Ibid., p. 29.
111. Hopkins, Naumann, and Wenzel, *Building the School-to-Work System,* pp. 24–25.
112. Barbara Von Villas, "The Changing Role of High School Guidance: Career Counseling and School-to-Work," *NASSP Bulletin* 79, 573 (October 1995): 87.
113. Debra Bragg, "Grubb's Case for Compromise: Can 'Education through Occupations' Be More?," *Journal of Vocational Education Research* 22, 2 (1997): 121.
114. Leo Giglio and Lawrence Bauer, "School-to-Work Programs and Partnerships," *Educational Horizons,* 76, 2, Winter, 1998, p. 68.
115. Quoted in James Hettinger, "The Buck Stops Soon," *Techniques,* 73, 8, November/December, 1998, p. 23.
116. "Story of the Day, September 19, 2000" from "What Works in Teaching and Learning," *Education Daily Online.* Available online at http:www.aspen publishers.com/pgWW.html, December 7, 2000, p. 1.
117. Ibid., p. 2.
118. Ibid., pp. 2–3.
119. Hansen, "Beyond School to Work: Continuing Contributions of Theory and Practice to Career Development of Youth," p. 357.
120. Joe L. Kincheloe, *Toil and Trouble: Good Work, Smart Workers, and the Integration of Academic and Vocational Education.* New York: Peter Lang, 1995, p. ix.

121. Ibid., p. 320.
122. Ibid., pp. 320–321.
123. Ibid., pp. 321–322.
124. Ibid., p. 323.
125. Steinberg, *Real Learning, Real Work: School-to-Work as High School Reform*, p. viii.

Index

Teachers *(continued)*
  performance contracts, 163
  and school-to-work reforms, 276
  strikes or threats of strikes, 135, 166
  training, 55, 107, 122
  year-round education, 222, 228–9
Teachers College Record, 61
Terman, Lewis M., 52
Thayer, Jesse B., 27, 29
Thomas, George I., 215–16, 221, 226
Thompson, Judy, 222
Thompson, Tommy G., 244
Thorndike, Edward, 58–60, 61
Tiffany, Burton C., 219
Total quality management (TQM), xx
Trade schools. *See* vocational schools
Trade Unions
  career education, support for, 204
  Committee on Industrial Education, 73
  labor unrest, 73
  public school curriculum, influence on, 69,
    81–2
  School-to-Work Opportunities Act, support
    for, 274
  and school-to-work reforms, 282
  and vocational schools, 67–8
Trotter, Andrew, 256
Tyack, David, xv–xvi, xvii, xviii–ix, 24, 90
Tyler, Louise, 181
Tyler, Ralph W., 140, 148, 175

U.S. Bureau of Education, 52
U.S. Chamber of Commerce, 191
U.S. Conference of Mayors, 274
U.S. National School-to-Work Office, 252, 272,
    278, 280, 281
U.S. Office of Education, 99–100, 100–1, 165,
    196
U.S. Office of Experimental Stations, 76
Unitarian church, 31–2
Universal education, 3, 117
Urban, Wayne, 151
Urban schools, 50, 55
Urkevich, John, 257

Vanderliep, Frank A., 73
Van Laha, Kurt, 277
Vargas, Julie, 179, 181
Violas, Paul, 70, 71, 75, 78

Vocational schools
  and career education, 195
  Chicago, 70, 75
  Cleveland, 78
  democratization of education, 80, 82
  enrollment statistics, 75
  for girls, 70, 72
  New York City, 69, 70–1, 78, 79
  origins, 66–7
  "Prosser Resolution," 99
  public schools, separation from, 77, 78
  universal access to, 73
  Wisconsin, 78
  See also career education
Von Villas, Barbara, 250, 282

Wacker, Gabrielle, 254, 255
Ward, Lester Frank, 60
Washington, Booker T., 44, 45, 76
Webb, Anita, 191, 192
Weber, Lillian, 130
Webster, Daniel, 1
Wehley, James, 253–4
Weisberg, Alan, 245
Wells, Carl, 200
Wenzel, Frederick, 267
West, Eva, 260
Whipple, George, 36
Whitford, William C., 25
Whitmore, Paul, 176
Wildarsky, Aaron, 142
Willard, F. R., 93–4
Williams, Mary E., 70
Wills, Joan L., 243–4, 245
Wilson, John A., 161, 162–3, 170, 171–2
Wilson, Sloan, 107–8
Wilson, Woodrow, 82
Wirth, Arthur, 67, 80, 87, 186
Wise, William, 227
Wolfe, Jan, 237
Woodward, Calvin M., 67
Work Force Policy Associates, 244
Worthington, Roger, 272, 281
Wright, H. A., 23
Wurtzel, Alan, 261–2

Yaffe, Elaine, 222, 226–7, 228
Yarborough, Ralph, 121
Yeager, Gloria, 277

History of Schools and Schooling

THIS SERIES EXPLORES THE HISTORY OF SCHOOLS AND SCHOOLING in the United States and other countries. Books in this series examine the historical development of schools and educational processes, with special emphasis on issues of educational policy, curriculum and pedagogy, as well as issues relating to race, class, gender, and ethnicity. Special emphasis will be placed on the lessons to be learned from the past for contemporary educational reform and policy. Although the series will publish books related to education in the broadest societal and cultural context, it especially seeks books on the history of specific schools and on the lives of educational leaders and school founders.

For additional information about this series or for the submission of manuscripts, please contact the general editors:

Alan R. Sadovnik   Susan F. Semel
Rutgers University-Newark   The City College of New York, CUNY
Education Dept.   138th Street and Convent Avenue
155 Conklin Hall   NAC 5/208
175 University Avenue   New York, NY 10031
Newark, NJ 07102

To order other books in this series, please contact our Customer Service Department:

800-770-LANG (within the U.S.)
212-647-7706 (outside the U.S.)
212-647-7707 FAX

Or browse online by series at:

www.peterlangusa.com